TOM CLARKE was born in
Birmingham and Warwick
industrial relations. He beca
Sociology at Trent Polytech
conducting research into ind
author of *The Workers' Coop   ...periment*
(forthcoming).

LAURIE CLEMENTS was born in Cardiff and educated at
Bristol and Warwick University in sociology, economics
and industrial relations. He is conducting research on
local labour markets and has taught extensively with
Nottingham University Department of Adult Education.
He is at present Lecturer in Industrial Sociology at Trent
Polytechnic.

T.U.U.C.   A

Edited by
Tom Clarke and Laurie Clements

Trade Unions under Capitalism

Fontana/Collins

First published in Fontana 1977
Copyright © Tom Clarke and Laurie Clements 1977

Made and printed in Great Britain by
William Collins Sons & Co. Ltd, Glasgow

Contents

6   Contents

1 Introduction
The Raison D'Etre of Trade Unionism

Tom Clarke

The trade unions remain the most maligned organizations in society. If the mass media are to be believed, then trade unions are responsible single-handedly for the disruption of industry, the decline of the economy, and the undermining of the social rights and privileges that traditionally have held together the delicate fabric of society. Implicit in such lurid descriptions is the belief that the trade union movement has attained a position of unassailable power which threatens the foundations of democracy: governments, it is sometimes even asserted, are mere playthings in the hands of the big battalions of the unions. But a common characteristic of the holders of such opinions, which are pronounced so freely, is an alarming ignorance of the real nature of contemporary union organization, activity and goals. When these are examined in detail, a different, and more complex, picture emerges.

The irony of the prevailing view that trade unions are essentially subversive organizations is that the very opposite conception may be nearer to the truth. Trade unions may have *originated* as organizations of working people dedicated to militantly representing their interests (which were otherwise ignored), and in some important cases at least, directed ultimately towards transforming capitalist society. Today, however, the unions can be seen to exert constantly a restraining influence upon the workers, and seem to have lost sight of any vision of an alternative socialist society. Thus the purpose of this book is to survey the extent to which trade unions have presented, and are still capable of presenting, an effective challenge to capitalist control of society; and in contrast to examine the degree to which unions have been so subdued by capitalism, that they have now become a component part of that very system of domination – the struggle against which was once the raison d'être of their existence. But first it would be helpful to review briefly the salient features of contemporary trade unionism.

Trade unions attained their highest peak of membership ever by the mid 1970s, and, with 12 million members, for the first time in history half the working population was organized in trade unions in Britain. The significance of this achievement is considerable: 'Trade union organization is thus immensely stronger and more extensive than when Marx wrote: in relation to the labour force, unionization has probably increased more than ten times.'[1] As Table 1 reveals, in conjunction with the *growth* in membership there has been a considerable *decline* in the number of trade unions. Now over a half of union members are organized in the ten largest trade unions, and over a quarter of union members are organized in the two largest unions, the TGWU and AUEW. In short, never before have trade unions enjoyed such a position of numerical and organizational strength.

Table 1: Union Membership and Density in UK

Year	No. of Trade Unions	Total Union Membership ('000)	Labour Force ('000)	Membership Density(%)
1892	1233	1576	14126	11·2
1901	1322	2025	16101	12·6
1913	1269	4135	17920	23·1
1920	1384	8348	18469	45·2
1933	1081	4392	19422	22·6
1945	781	7875	20400	38·6
1954	711	9566	21658	44·2
1964	598	10079	23706	42·5
1970	540	11179	23446	47·7
1974	498	11755	23689	49·6
1975	488	11950	23502	51·0

Derived from: *Department of Employment Gazette*, HMSO, Nov. 1975, Nov. 1976 and Dec. 1976; and R. Price and G. S. Bain, 'Union Growth Revisited: 1948–1974 In Perspective', *British Journal of Industrial Relations*, vol. xiv Nov. 1976.

However, the structural development of trade unions has not been planned or co-ordinated, and modern union organization bears intimately the imprint of the history of unionism: a constant struggle to recruit members and become established in the face of severe obstacles, and a dynamic tension between the orientation to extend and unify and the opposing orientation to exclude and maintain sectional privilege.[2] The consolidation of unions therefore has not been systematic, but rather, 'the structural history of British trade unions during the present century records long periods of rigidity interspersed with bursts of amalgamation'.[3] This amalgamation has removed much of the basis for the traditional distinction between craft, industrial and general unions, and though such distinctions may still influence the unions, none of the largest unions fall easily into the category of a particular union type. Thus the earliest unions were craft unions which recruited workers with a particular skill; however, many of these unions, such as the AUEW, now recruit on an industry basis. The industrial unions which recruited in basic industries such as coal, cotton and railways are declining in size and importance where they have not extended their activities into other general areas (though the NUM has recently more than made up for in militancy what strength it has lost in membership). Finally, the general unions have revealed the greatest capacity for growth in modern industrial conditions where there is a constant pressure from employers to replace established industries by newer ones and to degrade craft work into semi-skilled machine work.

The most recent phenomenon in trade union development has been the growth of the white collar unions: several white collar trade unions are now among the largest unions (NALGO, ASTMS and NUT), and also they form substantial sections of the two major unions (ACTS in the TGWU and TASS in the AUEW). They became established in the public sector in the first decades of the century, but experienced a difficult growth in private industry, in the face of entrenched employer resistance, until the late 1960s when they began to expand rapidly. The reasons for this have been accounted for by Bain, who suggests the major determinant of white collar trade union growth is not only the degree of concentration of clerical and technical workers in large offices, providing conditions similar to the shop floor; but also the willingness of employers – prompted by government encouragement – to recognize, and negotiate with, the independent organizations of white collar workers, with whom employers once had a paternalistic relationship.[4] This reveals one of the weaknesses of white collar trade unionism, that its growth has depended on the willingness of public and private employers to accept it, rather than on a determined effort on the part of the workers to secure recognition, which typified the development of manual unions. However, the militancy exhibited by some white collar trade unions, such as ASTMS, in pursuit of recognition, and more recently by others pressing claims, reveals that they can act with an aggressive independence in certain circumstances. Another complication of white collar unionism is that the extent to which it reveals an adoption of a proletarian orientation remains problematic: there are some grounds for believing that traditional trade union organization is supported by clerical and technical workers principally as a means of restoring previous status. However, where white collar workers pursue broader goals, due to their closer proximity to control structures, the potential impact of their action in industry is very considerable.

A further problem of trade union growth is that of the recruitment of women members. Although the proportion of women trade unionists has increased dramatically since 1950, women still only constituted 26·8 per cent of TUC membership in 1975, while women composed over 40 per cent of the total labour force.[5] Reasons for this are not only that women, as a corollary of their domestic subjection, are concentrated in low status, low wage occupations such as in the service industries which are difficult to organize; but also the fact that institutionalized male supremacy pervades the trade unions as extensively as in every other organization in society. The extent of the discrimination against women is seen in the gross under-representation of women in official positions which prevails in almost every union, for example, the shopworkers' union USDAW had 125 men and only 5 women as full-time officials in 1974, though 56·4 per cent of the membership was female.[6]

This leads to a final problem concerning trade union growth and membership: although half the labour force is unionized, this still means that every other worker is without the protection of a trade union. Contrary to the Conservative Party myth, the vast majority of workers who remain unorganized do so not out of choice, but because they are deprived of the opportunity to organize. These workers, composed largely of women, young and old workers, and ethnic minorities, are concentrated in poorly paid work where they are closely controlled by their employers.

The unions themselves must accept a large share of the responsibility for the predicament of the unorganized, since even the general unions' drive to organize has on occasion ebbed as they have come to recognize sectional interests: 'The most effective strategy could then appear to be the creation of a stronghold of unionism isolated from the broader labour market: excluding the alternative labour force seemed easier than organizing it.'[7]

Such organizational weaknesses inherent in contemporary unionism are related to the fundamental problem of the ambiguity of the aims of trade unionism. There has been considerable conflict since the origin of trade unions as to what their basic purpose was: whether merely to represent the sectional economic interests of particular occupational groups; or to advance the general interests of the working class in combating capitalism. The development of this conflict may be traced in the historical growth of trade unionism. Thus the earliest workers' organizations were militantly opposed to the horrors of capitalist industrialization: workers responded to social and economic deprivation, at first violently in the machine-breaking of Luddism, and later politically in the mass movement to gain political rights of Chartism. Throughout the early decades of the nineteenth century the British working class displayed an aggressive refusal to be subject to the growing power of capital: 'In no other country . . . has the war between the two classes assumed such colossal dimensions, such distinctly palpable features.'[8] Yet these early radical movements failed in the face of severe physical and legal repression, and due to their own theoretical and organizational immaturity. Chartism finally collapsed in 1848, which, incidentally, was the year that the Communist Manifesto was published: the maximum ardour and insurgency of the British proletariat in the nineteenth century therefore had occurred before a systematic socialist programme was available to define the strategy and goals of working-class organization.[9]

Insurgency gave way gradually to the accommodation of workers' organizations to capitalism with the formation of the craft unions in the second half of the nineteenth century. The distinguishing feature of these views was 'a centralized and businesslike financial administration, with firm control by executives over strikes and strike pay'.[10] The leaders of these unions, named 'The Junta' by the Webbs, had for a time almost complete control over the trade union movement though 'they were extreme only in their caution and moderation'.[11] Such leaders repeatedly warned their members against 'the dangerous practice of striking'; they argued that wages depended upon a simple law of supply and demand; they even encouraged their unemployed members to emigrate. Murphy later condemned these activities of trade union leaders:

> The whole period is full of such attempts to escape the class war. They did not aspire to become the ruling class. They repudiated the idea of a unified class organization. Each union wanted to be on its own and on good terms with the employers. Their highest aspiration for the workers was for them to be respectable citizens of capitalist society. Politics they wanted to leave to liberal gentlemen.[12]

The deference and passivity of the craft union leaders was instrumental in thawing the relations between employers and unions, and some businessmen even came to favour union organization as a means of avoiding conflict.[13]

The split between the labour aristocracy of the conservative craft unions and the mass of unorganized workers began to be overcome with the 'new unionism' of 1889 onwards. The decreasing differentiation between workers under the impact of advancing industrialism, the lifting of legal restrictions on trade unions, and a new enthusiasm for recruiting unorganized occupations sparked by the successful London dockers' strike, precipitated a great surge of organization which went beyond the confines of narrow trade unionism, gave the movement a revolutionary or socialist leadership and made the factory once again a major class battleground. As Engels commented at the time,

> these unskilled are very different men from the fossilized brothers of the old trade unions, not a trace of the old formalist spirit, of the craft exclusiveness . . . on the contrary a general cry for the organization of all trades in one fraternity and for a direct struggle against capital.[14]

However, the early militancy of the new unions subsided as they became subject to similar pressures as the craft unions: though fired by the new political doctrine of socialism they adopted collective bargaining as their major activity, and refused to recognize the political implications of their industrial action.

Yet one school of thought is emphatic about the achievements gained by unions through collective bargaining: 'Trade unions, by doggedly sticking to their immediate ends and refusing to be captured and exploited by any political party, have gradually transformed society.'[15] Thus the apologists of trade union collective bargaining maintain that this has led to a fundamental redistribution in the balance of wealth and power, indeed, that the establishment of collective bargaining is the arrival of 'industrial democracy'. But the most cursory sociological investigation belies this optimism.

Despite the efforts of trade unions over the last century, poverty and inequality – which traditionally have plagued capitalist economies – have remained acute problems to the present day. It has been estimated that the number of people living in poverty in Britain is between two and five million, consisting mainly of the aged, the unemployed, and the low paid; and yet the poverty line itself is set at a very low level, normally less than half average earnings.[16] Government incomes policies largely have neglected the low paid, and consolidated existing inequalities.[17] Poverty will never be eliminated from capitalist society, because it is an indispensable part of that society: poverty is an integral support to a competitive economic system, and is simply one pole of the great class inequalities that exist.[18]

Indeed a focus on poverty is often part of a conscious attempt to avoid the more politically sensitive area of the wider class inequalities. Evidence of the extreme inequality that still pervades capitalist society has recently been produced: Table 2 shows that the top 1 per cent of the population owns considerably more wealth than the bottom 80 per cent of the population.

The share of the personal wealth of the top 20 per cent of the population has shown a remarkable stability, 89·8 per cent in 1960 and 85·7 per cent in 1974, despite the supposed onslaught of egalitarian government policies and aggressive union pay claims. Some forms of wealth, particularly private property yielding dividends such as company shares, are more unequally distributed still – with 1 per cent of the population owning over 70 per cent of these assets.[19] Trends in the distribution of personal income also give considerable cause for concern: even after tax the top 20 per cent received six times as much income as the bottom 20 per cent in 1972, the total income of the bottom 20

Table 2: Trends in the Distribution of Personal Wealth Since 1960 in GB[1]

	1960 %	1964 %	1970 %	1974 %
Top 1%[2]	38·2	34·4	29·0	23·9
Top 5%	64·3	59·3	56·3	48·0
Top 10%	76·7	73·5	70·1	65·0
Top 20%	89·8	88·4	89·0	85·7
Bottom 80%	10·2	11·6	11·0	14·3

1. Royal Commission on the Distribution of Income and Wealth, Report No. 1, HMSO, 1975. Derived from Tables 45 and 49, pp. 102, 104. (1974 figures are a projection on the 1973 figures.)
2. Percentage of population aged 18 and over covered by Inland Revenue estimates, assuming persons not covered by the Inland Revenue have no wealth.

per cent was less than half the income of the top 5 per cent after tax.[20] Class inequalities extend beyond income and wealth into every area of social life. To take just one example: good health is undoubtedly of prime importance to everyone, yet it is found that not only do workers experience a much greater incidence of illnesses such as ulcers, heart disease and nervous disorders, which are commonly associated with the professional classes, but the working class experience also a wide range of other illnesses, diseases, and industrial accidents, which are practically non-existent in the middle class; it is the ultimate irony that even disease is 'class conscious'.[21]

The vast inequalities which prevail in modern Britain remain in purely *moral* terms totally indefensible: the fact that these inequalities have been continually defended and maintained by the rich reveals the necessity of treating material inequalities as a *political* problem, not simply an economic or moral one – thus there is a need for a focus on the unequal access to, and control over, the political and ideological resources in the society. It should be remembered that treatment of income inequality has usually been secondary in Marxian analysis, since: 'To be a proletarian is not to be poor, it is to be a commodity.'[22] So the reformist emphasis on economic growth and redistribution as the means to attain an egalitarian society is fundamentally unsound – since growth in a capitalist economic system involves a consolidation of the wealth and power of capitalists, who will voluntarily distribute this wealth only to the extent that it enhances their control over their employees. However it is rare that any conception of the oppressive nature of the employment relationship emerges; one explanation for this is that: 'The prevailing cultural assumptions . . . systematically suppress any consciousness that power and exploitation might be intrinsic to the production and distribution of wealth.'[23] Indeed it is usually assumed that people are basically independent and autonomous in their working lives, but in fact, 'people do not come together freely and spontaneously to set up work organization; the propertyless many are forced by their need for a livelihood to seek access to resources owned or controlled by the few, who derive therefrom very great power.'[24] The problem of why the quiescent labour movement has permitted a society to continue unchanged which is based on the ongoing exploitation of workers can only be resolved in terms of the distortion of workers' consciousness by the power which confronts them. The economic and political control of capitalists permits their intellectual and moral control over the rest of society – that is the creation of a dominant ideology, or hegemony: 'Hegemony refers to a set of ideas which are dominant as a consequence of a particular structure of power . . . bourgeois hegemony (is) a legitimating mask over the predatory nature of class domination.'[25] As long as this hegemony prevails there need be no resort to coercive means of control, since constraints are internalized and assimilated by workers and their organizations which remove any serious threat to capitalism.

If the goal of trade unionism *is* the socialist transformation of capitalist society, then, so far, it has certainly failed: private property and wage labour continue to define the fundamental and unchanged characteristic of capitalism which is 'a radical division between those subject to insecurity, subordination, and exploitation in the employment relationship, and those for whom labour is merely a cost of production and a resource to be manipulated'.[26] Contemporary trade union action involves coming to terms with the power of capital rather than attempting to overthrow that power: collective bargaining is a process of defensive accommodation to the existing external power structure, and involves the relief or suppression of immediate grievances rather than any attempt to tackle the underlying cause of workers' problems. Therefore the conventional role of trade unionism may be accepted as merely a protective function exercised within the constraints of capitalist domination of the employment contract: collective negotiation may secure better terms for the sale of labour power – but it does not begin to question the acceptability of wage slavery.[27] Thus workers' organizations, which were created in opposition to capitalist control, may have come to serve as an element in that control structure.

Much of the socialist promise of unionism was dissipated in the course of the organizational development of trade unionism. Unions were moulded according to the contours of capitalist industry and accepted as legitimate the sectional interests which resulted; sectionalism blurred any awareness of the common problems of workers inherent in capitalist work relations – which necessitate a class response:

> Sectionalism could only have been held in check if the unions had been capable of generating a programme of a sufficiently broad sweep as to make the differences between workers seem petty and trivial. Such a programme would of necessity have needed to be a *political* programme: trade union practice stood in the way of that too.[28]

Crucial in the historical development of these tendencies was the growth of union bureaucracy, with official leaders who institutionalized sectionalism and consolidated oligarchical control.

Michels thought the oligarchical process in the trade union movement was so pronounced that he employed it as evidence of the 'iron law of oligarchy' in democratic organizations, a theory which remains one of the most potentially damning critiques of unionism.[29] He argued that direct democracy was impractical in the conduct of large-scale union organization which required a centralized bureaucracy with specialist leadership. Officials, once created, were found to enjoy virtual permanence of office: they became personally attached to their privileged positions and strove to retain them; they developed an expertise which was thought to be indispensable; furthermore, the rank-and-file normally felt duty-bound to support the leaders. This situation permitted the leadership to impose its own policies upon the organization, even against the wishes and interests of the majority of members. However, since they are deprived of the information possessed by the leadership, the members frequently are not in a position to resist. Free of the constraints of membership control union leaders developed a superior life style and a more conservative ideological orientation, which were both strongly influenced by the middle classes with whom the union leaders now predominantly interacted. Finally (and the most significant aspect of Michels' theory), the union organization comes to be regarded as an end in itself, rather than merely a means to an end : union leaders are committed to protecting their organization's interests, rather than the working class members' interests which the organization was intended to represent.

Despite the immediate plausibility of Michels' theory, and the numerous academic studies which have supported his conclusions, significant countervailing tendencies have been noted by Hyman.[30] Firstly, if members are assumed to be subject to the informed official leadership, this implies that workers' orientation to unionism is instrumental: they regard the union as the provision of a service. Membership expectation of satisfactory economic benefits from the union, therefore, provides an important constraint to leadership autonomy: if the membership becomes dissatisfied with the benefits provided by the union then this opens up the prospect of rank-and-file revolt. Secondly, it is generally accepted that trade unions *ought* to act democratically, and this restricts the scope of the activity of union leaders. Often management is eager to reveal that leaders are unrepresentative of their employees; officials must therefore ensure the support of the members; 'public opinion' and politicians are attentive also to any split between union leaders and their membership. Furthermore, union leaders often originated as lay activists committed to democratic principles; though on assuming office they may indulge in rationalizations concerning the effectiveness of their representation of members' interests, there must be *some* substance to these, and the extremes of cynical manipulation are normally precluded. Thirdly, Michels limits his analysis to the formal, national channels of decision-making. At this level, direct membership control is obviously difficult, but this does not exclude membership participation and control at other levels. In Britain, shopfloor trade unionism has become the principal means of workers' economic struggles. Workshop organization has increased earnings in the factory, and eroded management control at the point of production. In this way the rank-and-file may exert influence over, or act independently of, the union leadership.

More general weaknesses in Michels' theory may be recognized. The constant interaction with the oligarchical organizations of capital, which is necessary for the basic trade union function of negotiation and compromise, exerts a constant influence upon union organization to become oligarchic also. It is very difficult for a democratically controlled organization to have a conciliatory working relationship with the controllers of capitalist organizations who do not accept democratic values and practices in economic life: even technically, this relationship is difficult to arrange. For example, employers and government officials often exhibit extreme impatience with union leaders who genuinely wish to consult their membership before arriving at important decisions. Thus the limited economic benefit to be gained from collective bargaining is often at the expense of democratic practice. This leads to a further conception: that capitalist organizations may make a deliberate attempt to subvert democratic principles and encourage oligarchic control in trade unions. The external influence of capitalist organizations on the membership and internal processes of trade unions may be considerable: this influence upon workers commences with socialization into anti-democratic values; proceeds with the formative experience of the uniformly oligarchical organizations and institutions of capitalist society; and finally, this influence may be intensively reinforced by use of the mass media to project anti-democratic ideas on specific issues. From this argument it follows that the only way successfully to defeat the oligarchic tendency of trade unionism, and the oligarchy which pervades wider society, is to overthrow capitalism itself.

Therefore a fundamental question must be faced: what part, if any, can trade unions play in the struggle for the revolutionary change of society? The *normal* activities of unions which necessitate established bargaining relationships with employers, conciliation and compromise, and the division of the working class along the lines of sectional interests, clearly serve to strengthen, rather than weaken, capitalist relations of production. Thus: 'Unions are naturally oriented towards furthering the interests of their own members within the framework of capitalism rather than the interests of the whole class through the abolition of capitalism.'[31] Indeed, Hinton and Hyman have argued further, that:

> In conditions of stable capitalism, to speak of revolutionary trade unionism involves a contradiction in terms: trade union action is necessarily structured by the level of consciousness general among the rank-and-file and by the potential for reform inherent in the objective situation. And even in the course of revolutionary crisis, trade unionism which becomes revolutionary thereby negates and transcends trade unionism.[32]

A major paradox inherent in trade unionism thus emerges: 'although unions are incapable of initiating revolutionary change it is only through such change that they will achieve their basic aim.'[33]

Important economic and political changes have taken place in recent years, however, which threaten imminently to disturb this stalemate. The economic growth and stability of the post-war period, which provided the means to buy off workers' immediate grievances without significant changes in the social and economic system, is now threatened by recurrent crises and permanent instability. Meanwhile monopoly capital is concentrating at the supra-national level to pursue corporate policies regardless of the interests of the working class. These policies include the intensification of capitalist 'rationalization', with widespread redundancies, greater work intensity and stricter pay controls. Confronted by these developments, instead of forging radical policies to deal with these new concentrations of irresponsible private economic power, governments have been constrained to intervene in the economy on their behalf. Thus the policies of successive governments on incomes, industrial relations and industry reveal *not* the intervention of a reforming government to alleviate problems of common concern, but rather the *interpenetration* of the state and monopoly capitalism in order to more vigorously pursue the aims of capitalist industry. The most significant aspect of the interpenetration of the state and capital has proved the attempt by governments to directly control the level of earnings of working people in order to maintain and improve corporate profitability: this is fraught with serious political consequences, not only because the attempt to control incomes has met with considerable resistance, but also because it has increased awareness on the part of the working population of state-supported inequalities and inconsistencies. As Blackburn has argued: 'The most critical field of State intervention in the advanced capitalist economy is that of incomes policies. The attempt to regulate the overall levels of profits and wages is potentially the most explosive development of all those which constitute the new form of capitalism.'[34]

The instability of the present system is compounded by the fact that workers, who have experienced a gradual raising of their expectations, are now encountering a considerable deterioration in their opportunities, pay, conditions and life style. Thus prices are rising more rapidly than ever before, whilst pay is controlled, and over a million people join the long-term unemployed. The existence of these problems lends mass appeal to basic trade union demands such as the preservation of the right to work and the defence of living standards. But these primary demands are now invested with a revolutionary potential, for the assumption of class-oriented trade union militancy to protect even basic rights of workers, in the context of the present problems of capitalism, may place upon that system an additional, and intolerable, burden.

Yet most present trade union leaders have shown immense reluctance to lead this struggle. Revolutionary workers' political organizations are therefore indispensable, not only to generalize the struggle to wider society, but within the unions to fight for militant and uncompromising representation of workers' interests. In this task it is necessary to secure leaders who are committed and reliable, and also to develop the awareness and involvement of the rank-and-file so that they are less dependent upon the leadership.[35] Any such resurgence of militancy within workers' organizations will certainly lead to renewed attempts by capital to control trade unionism by incorporation, and, where this fails, by coercion; to remove the revived threat of unionism to the survival of the capitalist order. If workers *are* to protect hard-won rights and to advance towards socialist change, they need a clear conception of the relationship between trade unionism and capitalism, and the role of unionism in the struggle for socialism: it is hoped the readings set out in this book are a step towards accomplishing that clarity.

The aim of this work is to collect within a single volume selections from the contribution of both classical socialist theorists and modern radical sociologists to the analysis of trade unionism in capitalist society. Hence the distinctive feature of this work is a critical approach not only towards trade unionism, but also the social and economic structure within which the trade unions are situated; and, in turn, this permits a more fundamental questioning of the aims and achievements of unionism than is normally attempted. In Part One of the book is presented a selection from the classical works which previously were rather inaccessible, and have been largely ignored: thus the studies of the Webbs have remained the accepted orthodoxy on the origin and development of trade unionism despite the existence of socialist thought which presented a sharply contrasting picture and, therefore, offered more radical prescriptions.[36] Part Two of the readings looks at one of the periods in the history of the British labour movement when workers' organizations explicitly assumed a revolutionary intent and explored ways of independently implementing a socialist society. Part Three includes some critical perspectives on trade unionism and capitalism developed within contemporary sociology, which challenge the pragmatism and panaceas of conventional analysis.[37] Part Four examines the relationship between the worker and his job, and how the union organization may assist or impair workers' attempts to gain autonomy and satisfaction in their work by wresting control of it from the dictation of management and market forces. In Part Five, the final readings assess the changes in the position of unions and advanced capitalism: realizing that recent economic and social changes make the maintenance of normal union activity unlikely, the possible directions of the future development of unions is investigated.

A final point is worth consideration: though all the readings are critical of the shortcomings of trade unionism and orientated towards significant social change, it is important to emphasize that the views of the editors, both in the introductions and in their papers, are their own. The other readings have been chosen, because they are interesting in themselves and also contribute to a continuing debate on the roles of trade unionism, not because they necessarily correspond with the views of the editors: indeed, in some cases they clearly do not. If this book stimulates further debate on the purposes of trade unionism, it will have served its purpose.

NOTES

1. R. HYMAN, *Industrial Relations: A Marxist Introduction*, Macmillan, 1975, p. 29.

2. ibid., p. 41.

3. H. A. CLEGG, *The System of Industrial Relations in Great Britain*, Blackwell, 1970, p. 55.

4. G. S. BAIN, *The Growth of White Collar Trade Unionism*, Oxford University Press, 1970.

5. *Studies for Trade Unionists*, vol. 1, no. 3, Sept. 1975, p. 8.

6. ibid., p. 10.

7. R. HYMAN, op. cit., p. 52.

8. MARX and ENGELS, *Marx-Engels on Britain*, Moscow Foreign Languages, 1953, p. 402.

9. PERRY ANDERSON, 'Origins of the Present Crisis', *New Left Review*, 23.

10. ALLAN FLANDERS, *Trade Unions*, Hutchinson, 1970, p. 13.

11. ibid.

12. J. T. MURPHY, *Preparing for Power*, Pluto Press, 1972, pp. 64–5.

13. E. J. HOBSBAWM, 'Trends in the British Labour Movement Since 1850', in *Labouring Men*, Weidenfeld & Nicolson, 1964.

14. MARX and ENGELS, Selected Correspondence, p. 463.

15. A. FLANDERS, 'What are Trade Unions for?' reproduced in W. McCarthy (ed.), *Trade Unions*, Penguin, 1972.

16. A. B. ATKINSON, *The Economics of Inequality*, Clarendon Press, 1975, p. 197.

17. R. HYMAN, 'Ideology, Inequality, and Industrial Relations', *BJIR*, 1974, p. 179.

18. J. C. KINCAID, *Poverty and Equality in Britain*, Penguin, 1973, p. 13. Also see, J. H. WESTERGAARD and H. RESLER, *Class in a Capitalist Society*, Penguin, 1976.

19. Royal Commission on the Distribution of Income and Wealth, Report No. 2, 'Income From Companies and Its Distribution', pp. 36–7, Table 17.

20. Royal Commission on the Distribution of Income and Wealth, Report No. 1, pp. 133, 136.

21. B. PRESTON, 'Statistics of Inequality', *Sociological Review*, vol. 22, no. 1, 1974 and P. KINNERSLY, *The Hazards of Work*, Pluto Press, 1973.

22. R. L. DAVIS and J. COUSINS, 'The New Working Class and the Old' in M. BULMER, *Working Class Images of Society*, Routledge, 1975.

23. R. HYMAN and I. BROUGH, *Social Values and Industrial Relations*, Blackwell, 1975, p. 201.

24. A. FOX, 'Industrial Relations: A Social Critique of Pluralist

Ideology', in J. CHILD (ed.), *Man and Organisation*, George Allen &
Unwin, 1973, p. 216.

25. J. FEMIA, 'Hegemony and Consciousness in the Thought of
Antonio Gramsci', *Political Studies*, March 1975, p. 47, also S. LUKES,
Power: A Radical View, Macmillan, 1974, p. 24.

26. R. HYMAN and R. FRYER, 'Trade Unions: Sociology and
Political Economy' in MCKINLAY, *Processing People: Studies of
Organizational Behaviour*, Holt, Rinehart and Winston, 1975, p. 158.

27. A detailed discussion of this question, in particular the thorny
issue of the extent to which trade unions have increased the share of
wages in the national income, is contained in A. FOX, 'Collective
Bargaining, Flanders and the Webbs', *BJIR*, vol. XIII, no. 2, 1975, p.
156.

28. T. LANE, *The Union Makes Us Strong*, Arrow, 1974, p. 268.

29. R. MICHELS, *Political Parties*, The Free Press, 1968.

30. R. HYMAN, *Marxism and the Sociology of Trade Unionism*,
Pluto Press, 1971, pp. 28–33.

31. J. HINTON and R. HYMAN, *Trade Unions and Revolution*, Pluto
Press, 1975, p. 59.

32. ibid.

33. V. L. ALLEN, *The Sociology of Industrial Relations*, Longman,
1971, p. 50.

34. R. BLACKBURN, 'The New Capitalism' in R. BLACKBURN (ed.),
Ideology in Social Science, Fontana, 1972, p. 183.

35. HINTON and HYMAN, op. cit., p. 59.

36. S. and B. WEBB, *Industrial Democracy*, vols. I and II, Longmans,
1897, and S. and B. WEBB, *The History of Trade Unionism*, Longmans,
2nd edition, 1896.

37. J. E. T. ELDRIDGE, 'Panaceas and Pragmatism in Industrial
Relations', *Industrial Relations Journal*, vol. 6, no. 1, 1975.

Part One
Classical Analysis

The nature of trade unionism, particularly its potential as an agency of revolutionary change, has always been a central focus for socialists directed towards working-class mobilization and the transformation of capitalist society. Socialist analysis has perceived how – with the structural and ideological changes within capitalism – the role of trade unions has changed over time, and different theories have been elucidated in response to this change. Thus it has been suggested that, 'There has never existed a single unambiguous marxist theory of trade unionism'.[1] Hence different socialist analyses have reflected the dialectical nature of the interaction between trade unions and capitalist society in the contradiction between what Hyman has termed the 'optimistic interpretation' which recognizes a revolutionary potential in trade union activity and the 'pessimistic interpretation' which maintains that trade union activity does not in itself promote, and indeed may inhibit, the transformation of capitalist society.[2]

Marx and Engels were active participants in the labour movement of the nineteenth century, though they subsumed their theory of the role of trade unionism under a more general consideration of the nature of the proletariat, and a political and economic critique of capitalism. Capitalist industrialization involved workers being evicted from the land and crowded into towns where they were forced to work long hours in melancholy factories and live in grinding poverty, whilst capitalists reaped great fortunes. Marx and Engels argued that the development of capitalism thus forces together workers whose common experience of exploitation leads them to form combinations; in economic terms, they argued, these could do little more than prevent employers reducing wages to the lowest possible level, since union achievements were limited by long-term economic laws. Yet unions overcome the competition of the labour market and develop workers' class consciousness and solidarity, hence, due to the limited economic achievements of unionism, the political aspect of workers' action assumes central significance and the organization necessary for the revolutionary overthrow of capitalist domination may be created:

> The essential condition for the existence, and for the sway of the bourgeois class, is the formation and augmentation of capital; the condition for capital is wage-labour. Wage-labour rests exclusively on competition between the labourers. The advance of industry, whose involuntary promoter is the bourgeoisie, replaces the isolation of the labourers, due to competition, by their revolutionary combination, due to association. The development of Modern Industry, therefore, cuts from under its feet the very foundation on which the bourgeoisie produces and appropriates products. What the bourgeoisie, therefore, produces, above all, is its own grave diggers. Its fall and the victory of the proletariat are equally inevitable.[3]

The first reading, from Engels' account of the condition of the English working class in 1844, reveals the intensity of the conflict engendered by the early development of capitalist industrialization. Several examples are cited for the 'social war' which existed between the bourgeoisie – constantly attempting to reduce wages to the lowest possible level and raise profits – and the proletariat – forced together by the attempt to resist this process and to abolish the commodity status of labour; also documented is the severe punishment meted out to those workers who dissipated the strength of the union by black-legging. Engels was confident of the revolutionary possibilities of trade unionism: 'Unions direct themselves against the vital nerve of the present social order . . . If the competition of the workers among themselves is destroyed, if all determine not to be further exploited by the bourgeoisie, the rule of property is at an end.' And yet, whilst he applauded the determination and resilience of the working class, nonetheless he was aware that 'something more is needed than Trade Unions and strikes to break the power of the ruling class'.

In the first section of the Marx reading, part of an angry polemic against the French socialist Proudhon in 1847, Marx condemned the views of economists and utopian socialists who denigrated the achievements of combinations by focusing on their economic activities and ignoring their more significant, if latent, political dimension. He insisted that although the initial aim of combination may be the protection of wages, ultimately, as workers form unions to confront the organization of the capitalists, 'the maintenance of the association becomes more necessary to them than that of wages . . . once it has reached this point, association takes on a political character'. In the ensuing struggle, association generates class consciousness among workers, changing them from a class 'in itself' to a class 'for itself', capable of revolutionary change. In the second section of the reading, written almost two decades later and delivered as part of an address to the International Working Men's Association, Marx offered a more critical prognosis of the role of trade unionism: economically, trade union activity is primarily *defensive* – preventing the permanent depression of wages below the value of labour power (otherwise a chronic tendency of early capitalism was to reduce pay below the level necessary to reproduce the next generation of wage labourers). The trade union struggle was to limit the rate of surplus value extracted from labour, whilst real wages were largely determined by market forces.[4] Any increase in the extraction of surplus value would, Marx suggested, increase the subservience of labour to capital, advance the capital intensity of industry, and increase the alienation of the worker from the product of his labour. Therefore, in their economic struggles, workers were fighting only the effects of the capitalist system, and Marx urged that they should turn their organization against the system itself.

In his article 'On Strikes', written at the end of the nineteenth century, Lenin shared much of the enthusiasm of Marx and Engels for the revolutionary promise of trade union struggles: 'Every strike brings thoughts of socialism very forcibly to the worker's mind.' However, strike activity exposed not only the role of capital, but also that of the state in the repression of the working class. Therefore, strikes alone were not sufficient, he argued; a socialist workers' party is necessary to launch a political attack upon capitalism, transforming individual strikes into a general class struggle. However, in *What Is To Be Done?* a sustained polemic against rival political tendencies in the

Russian Social-Democratic Party who uncritically endorsed the saliency of trade union activity in revolutionary organization, Lenin contended that the limitations of trade unionism such as sectionalism and economism, which Marx and Engels treated as exceptional, are, in fact, endemic to the normal activities of unions. Thus the 'spontaneous' experience of the workers, Lenin argued, was limited to the problems of their economic struggle; a wider sense of political objectives could not be derived from such experience, and workers became trapped by the ineffectual reformism of trade union politics. Lenin maintained that in isolation unions are capable of achieving only trade union consciousness which is subservient to bourgeois ideology since it merely aims at improving the workers' relative position, thereby enhancing the process of the integration of the working class into the existing social framework, whereas: 'Social Democracy leads to the struggle of the working class, not only for better terms for the sale of labour power, but for the abolition of the social system that compels the propertyless to sell themselves to the rich.'

The emphasis Lenin placed on the monopoly of revolutionary theory possessed by the party was to a great extent a product of the particular social conditions existing in Russia at the turn of the century, and provoked a keen debate with Rosa Luxemburg.[5] The central theme of Lenin's analysis though remains familiar: that trade unions, capable of achieving their limited economic objectives within capitalism, are a means of integration of the working class into the existing society.

Writing some decades later, when Europe was gripped by the profound economic and political upheaval of the 1930s, Trotsky insisted that in conditions of capitalist crisis trade unions were vulnerable to a deliberate strategy of incorporation by government and employers. The decay of capitalism, Trotsky argued, undermined the basis of reformist trade unionism; however, trade union leaders used their traditional authority both to obstruct the development of revolutionary purpose in the unions and to assist capitalists in controlling workers. With the development of monopoly capital, trade union leaders are forced by their own ideology to turn meekly to the state for assistance; and the independence of trade unions is further eroded by the reinforced demands of employers that unions should become agents of repression. Trotsky thus presented a stark alternative: 'Under these conditions trade unions can either transform themselves into revolutionary organizations or become lieutenants of capital in the intensified exploitation of the workers.' The dismal history of the trade union movement of the 1930s is painful proof of which alternative trade union leaders adopted. Moreover, the current economic difficulties of Western capitalism have invested Trotsky's theory of trade union incorporation with much contemporary significance: at the national level, trade union leaders have been persuaded to accept incomes policies which negate even their traditionally restricted role of collective bargaining in return for a dubious participation in the framing of other – essentially anti-working class – policies; secondly at the factory level there have been repeated legislative attempts of successive governments spurred on by employers, to curtail independent shop floor organization, which, despite the lack of revolutionary leadership deemed essential by Trotsky, has proved a recurring threat to the stability of capitalism.

NOTES

1. J. HINTON and R. HYMAN, *Trade Unions and Revolution*, Pluto Press, 1975, p. 58.

2. R. HYMAN, *Marxism and the Sociology of Trade Unionism*, Pluto Press, 1971.

3. MARX and ENGELS, 'Manifesto of the Communist Party', *Selected Works*, 1958, vol. 1, p. 45.

4. M. C. HOWARD and J. E. KING, *The Political Economy of Marx*, Longman, 1975, pp. 133–5. Some general definitions would be useful here.

Labour Power: Marx argued that in capitalist society the labourer did not sell himself to capital but his labour power, that is, the workers' capacity to work, or control over the workers' creative abilities. Labour power not labour is the commodity traded on labour markets.

Surplus Value: Labour power is bought by the capitalist in order to create surplus value; this is the amount of labour supplied in excess of the amount of labour required to produce the equivalent of the wage paid for it. Surplus value is equal to the amount of unpaid labour the worker provides for his employer.

Real Wages: Real Wages are determined by the expansion and contraction of labour supply and labour demand, leaving the industrial reserve army of the unemployed. The stability of real wages has been reflected in the constancy of the share of labour in the national product over the last century.

5. R. LUXEMBURG, 'Organizational Questions of Russian Social Democracy,' 1904. Published in pamphlet form as *Leninism or Marxism?*

2 Labour Movements

F. Engels

Reprinted with permission from F. Engels, 'Labour Movements', from *The Condition of the Working Class in England*, in K. Marx and F. Engels, *Collected Works*, vol. 4, Lawrence & Wishart, 1975, pp. 502–13.

... The revolt of the workers began soon after the first industrial development, and has passed through several phases. The investigation of their importance in the history of the English people I must reserve for separate treatment, limiting myself meanwhile to such bare facts as serve to characterize the condition of the English proletariat.

The earliest, crudest, and least fruitful form of this rebellion was that of crime. The working man lived in poverty and want, and saw that others were better off than he. It was not clear to his mind why he, who did more for society than the rich idler, should be the one to suffer under these conditions. Want conquered his inherited respect for the sacredness of property, and he stole. We have seen how crime increased with the extension of manufacture; how the yearly number of arrests bore a constant relation to the number of bales of cotton annually consumed.

The workers soon realized that crime did not help matters. The criminal could protest against the existing order of society only singly, as one individual; the whole might of society was brought to bear upon each criminal, and crushed him with its immense superiority. Besides, theft was the most primitive form of protest, and for this reason, if for no other, it never became the universal expression of the public opinion of the working men, however much they might approve of it in silence. As a class, they first manifested opposition to the bourgeoisie when they resisted the introduction of machinery at the very beginning of the industrial period. The first inventors, Arkwright and others, were persecuted in this way and their machines destroyed. Later, there took place a number of revolts against machinery, in which the occurrences were almost precisely the same as those of the printers' disturbances in Bohemia in 1844; factories were demolished and machinery destroyed.

This form of opposition also was isolated, restricted to certain localities, and directed against one feature only of our present social arrangements. When the momentary end was attained, the whole weight of social power fell upon the unprotected evil-doers and punished them to its heart's content, while the machinery was introduced nonetheless. A new form of opposition had to be found.

At this point help came in the shape of a law enacted by the old, unreformed, oligarchic Tory Parliament, a law which never could have passed the House of Commons later, when the Reform Bill had legally sanctioned the distinction between bourgeoisie and proletariat, and made the bourgeoisie the ruling class. This was enacted in 1824, and repealed all laws by which coalition between working men for labour purposes had hitherto been forbidden. The working men obtained a right previously restricted to the aristocracy and bourgeoisie, the right of free association. Secret coalitions had, it is true, previously existed, but could never achieve great results. In Glasgow as Symons[1] relates, a general strike of weavers had taken place in 1812, which was brought about by a secret association. It was repeated in 1822, and on this occasion vitriol was thrown into the faces of two working men who would not join the association, and were therefore regarded by the members as traitors to their class. Both the assaulted lost the use of their eyes in consequence of the injury. So, too, in 1818, the association of Scottish miners was powerful enough to carry on a general strike. These associations required their members to take an oath of fidelity and secrecy, had regular lists, treasurers, book-keepers, and local branches. But the secrecy with which everything was conducted crippled their growth. When, on the other hand, the working men received in 1824 the right of free association, these combinations were very soon spread over all England and attained great power. In all branches of industry trade unions were formed with the outspoken intention of protecting the single working man against the tyranny and neglect of the bourgeoisie. Their objects were to deal, *en masse*, as a power, with the employers; to regulate the rate of wages according to the profit of the latter, to raise it when opportunity offered, and to keep it uniform in each trade throughout the country. Hence they tried to settle with the capitalists a scale of wages to be universally adhered to, and ordered out on strike the employees of such individuals as refused to accept the scale. They aimed further to keep up the demand for labour by limiting the number of apprentices, and so to keep wages high; to counteract, as far as possible, the indirect wages reductions which the manufacturers brought about by means of new tools and machinery; and finally, to assist unemployed working men financially. This they do either directly or by means of a card to legitimate the bearer as a 'society man', and with which the working man wanders from place to place, supported by his fellow-workers, and instructed as to the best opportunity for finding employment. This is tramping, and the wanderer a tramp. To attain these ends, a President and Secretary are engaged at a salary (since it is to be expected that no manufacturer will employ such persons), and a committee collects the weekly contributions and watches over their expenditure for the purposes of the association. When it proved possible and advantageous, the various trades of single districts united in a federation and held delegate conventions at set times. The attempt has been made in single cases to unite the workers of one branch over all England in one great union; and several times (in 1830 for the first time) to form one universal trades association for the whole United Kingdom, with a separate organization for each trade. These associations, however, never held together long, and were seldom realized even for the moment, since an exceptionally universal excitement is necessary to make such a federation possible and effective.

The means usually employed by these unions for attaining their ends are the following: If one or more employers refuse to pay the wage specified by the union, a deputation is sent or a petition forwarded (the working men, you see, know how to recognize the absolute power of the lord of the factory in his little state); if this proves unavailing, the union commands the employees to stop work, and all hands go home. This strike is either partial when one or several, or general when all employers in the trade refuse to regulate wages according to the proposals of the unions. So far go the lawful means of the union, assuming the strike to take effect after the expiration of the legal notice, which is not always the case. But these lawful means are very weak when there are workers outside the union, or when members separate from it for the sake of the momentary advantage offered by the bourgeoisie. Especially in the case of partial strikes can the manufacturer readily secure recruits from these black sheep (who are known as knobsticks), and render fruitless the efforts of the united workers.

Knobsticks are usually threatened, insulted, beaten, or otherwise maltreated by the members of the union; intimidated, in short, in every way. Prosecution follows, and as the law-abiding bourgeoisie has the power in its own hands, the force of the union is broken almost every time by the first unlawful act, the first judicial procedure against its members.

The history of these unions is a long series of defeats of the working men, interrupted by a few isolated victories. All these efforts naturally cannot alter the economic law according to which wages are determined by the relation between supply and demand in the labour market. Hence the unions remain powerless against all *great* forces which influence this relation. In a commercial crisis the union itself must reduce wages or dissolve wholly; and in a time of considerable increase in the demand for labour, it cannot fix the rate of wages higher than would be reached spontaneously by the competition of the capitalists among themselves. But in dealing with minor, single influences they are powerful. If the employer had no concentrated, collective opposition to expect, he would in his own interest gradually reduce wages to a lower and lower point; indeed, the battle of competition which he has to wage against his fellow-manufacturers would force him to do so, and wages would soon reach the minimum. But this competition of the manufacturers among themselves is, *under average conditions*, somewhat restricted by the opposition of the working men.

Every manufacturer knows that the consequence of a reduction not justified by conditions to which his competitors also are subjected, would be a strike, which would most certainly injure him, because his capital would be idle as long as the strike lasted, and his machinery would be rusting, whereas it is very doubtful whether he could, in such a case, enforce his reduction. Then he has the certainty that if he should succeed, his competitors would follow him, reducing the price of the goods so produced, and thus depriving him of the benefit of his policy. Then, too, the unions often bring about a more rapid increase of wages after a crisis than would otherwise follow. For the manufacturer's interest is to delay raising wages until forced by competition, but now the working men demand an increased wage as soon as the market improves, and they can carry their point by reason of the smaller supply of workers at his command under such circumstances. But, for resistance to more considerable forces which influence the labour market, the unions are powerless. In such cases hunger gradually drives the strikers to resume work on any terms, and when once a few have begun, the force of the union is broken, because these few knobsticks, with the reserve supplies of goods in the market, enable the bourgeoisie to overcome the worst effects of the interruption of business. The funds of the union are soon exhausted by the great numbers requiring relief, the credit which the shopkeepers give at high interest is withdrawn after a time, and want compels the working man to place himself once more under the yoke of the bourgeoisie. But strikes end disastrously for the workers mostly, because the manufacturers, in their own interest (which has, be it said, become their interest only through the resistance of the workers), are obliged to avoid all useless reductions, while the workers feel in every reduction imposed by the state of trade a deterioration of their condition, against which they must defend themselves as far as in them lies.

It will be asked, 'Why, then, do the workers strike in such cases, when the uselessness of such measures is so evident?' Simply because they *must* protest against every reduction, even if dictated by necessity; because they feel bound to proclaim that they, as human beings, shall not be made to bow to social circumstances, but social conditions ought to yield to them as human beings; because silence on their part would be a recognition of these social conditions, an admission of the right of the bourgeoisie to exploit the workers in good times and let them starve in bad ones. Against this the working men must rebel so long as they have not lost all human feelings, and that they protest in this way and no other, comes of their being practical English people, who express themselves in *action*, and do not, like German theorists, go to sleep as soon as their protest is properly registered and placed *ad acta*, there to sleep as quietly as the protesters themselves. The active resistance of the English working men has its effect in holding the money-greed of the bourgeoisie within certain limits, and keeping alive the opposition of the workers to the social and political omnipotence of the bourgeoisie, while it compels the admission that something more is needed than trades unions and strikes to break the power of the ruling class. But what gives these unions and the strikes arising from them their real importance is this, that they are the first attempt of the workers to abolish competition. They imply the recognition of the fact that the supremacy of the bourgeoisie is based wholly upon the competition of the workers among themselves; i.e., upon their want of cohesion. And precisely because the unions direct themselves against the vital nerve of the present social order, however one-sidedly, in however narrow a way, are they so dangerous to this social order. The working men cannot attack the bourgeoisie, and with it the whole existing order of society, at any sorer point than this. If the competition of the workers among themselves is destroyed, if all determine not to be further exploited by the bourgeoisie, the rule of property is at an end. Wages depend upon the relation of demand to supply, upon the accidental state of the labour market, simply because the workers have hitherto been content to be treated as chattels, to be bought and sold. The moment the workers resolve to be bought and sold no longer, when, in the determination of the value of labour, they take the part of men possessed of a will as well as of working-power, at that moment the whole political economy of today is at an end.

The laws determining the rate of wages would, indeed, come into force again in the long run, if the working men did not go beyond this step of abolishing competition among themselves. But they must go beyond that unless they are prepared to recede again and to allow competition among themselves to reappear. Thus once advanced so far, necessity compels them to go further; to abolish not only one kind of competition, but competition itself altogether, and that they will do.

The workers are coming to perceive more clearly with every day how competition affects them; they see far more clearly than the bourgeois that competition of the capitalists among themselves presses upon the workers, too, by bringing on commerical crises, and that this kind of competition, too, must be abolished. They will soon learn *how* they have to go about it.

That these unions contribute greatly to nourish the bitter hatred of the workers against the property-holding class need hardly be said. From them proceed, therefore, with or without the connivance of the leading members, in times of unusual excitement, individual actions which can be explained only by hatred wrought to the pitch of despair, by a wild passion overwhelming all restraints. Of this sort are the attacks with vitriol mentioned in the foregoing pages, and a series of others, of which I shall cite several. In 1831, during a violent labour movement, young Ashton, a manufacturer in Hyde, near Manchester, was shot one evening when crossing a field, and no trace of the assassin discovered. There is no doubt that this was a deed of vengeance of the working men. Incendiarisms and attempted explosions are very common. On Friday 29 September 1843, an attempt was made to blow up the saw-works of Padgin, in Howard Street, Sheffield. A closed iron tube filled with powder was the means employed, and the damage was considerable. On the following day, a similar attempt was made in Ibbetson's knife and file works at Shales Moor, near Sheffield. Mr Ibbetson had made himself obnoxious by an active participation in bourgeois movements, by low wages, the exclusive employment of knobsticks, and the exploitation of the Poor Law for his own benefit. He had reported, during the crisis of 1842, such operatives as refused to accept reduced wages, as persons who could find work but would not take it, and were, therefore, not deserving of relief, so compelling the acceptance of a reduction. Considerable damage was inflicted by the explosion, and all the working men who came to view it regretted only 'that the whole concern was not blown into the air'. On Friday 6 October 1843, an attempt to set fire to the factory of Ainsworth and Crompton, at Bolton, did no damage; it was the third or fourth attempt in the same factory within a very short time. In the meeting of the Town Council of Sheffield, on Wednesday 10 January 1844, the Commissioner of Police exhibited a cast-iron machine, made for the express purpose of producing an explosion, and found filled with four pounds of powder, and a fuse which had been lighted but had not taken effect, in the works of Mr Kitchen, Earl Street, Sheffield. On Sunday 21 January 1844, an explosion caused by a package of powder took place in the sawmill of Bentley & White, at Bury, in Lancashire, and produced considerable damage. On Thursday 1 February 1844, the Soho Wheel Works, in Sheffield, were set on fire and burnt up.

Here are six such cases in four months, all of which have their sole origin in the embitterment of the working men against the employers. What sort of a social state it must be in which such things are possible I need hardly say. These facts are proof enough that in England, even in good business years, such as 1843, the social war is avowed and openly carried on, and still the English bourgeoisie does not stop to reflect! But the case which speaks most loudly is that of the Glasgow Thugs,[2] which came up before the Assizes from the 3rd to the 11th of January 1838. It appears from the proceedings that the Cotton-Spinners' Union, which existed here from the year 1816, possessed rare organization and power. The members were bound by an oath to adhere to the decision of the majority, and had during every turnout a secret committee which was unknown to the mass of the members, and controlled the funds of the union absolutely. This committee fixed a price upon the heads of knobsticks and obnoxious manu-facturers and upon incendiarisms in mills. A mill was thus set on fire in which female knobsticks were employed in spinning in the place of men; a Mrs McPherson, mother of one of these girls, was murdered, and both murderers sent to America at the expense of the association. As early as 1820, a knobstick named McQuarry was shot at and wounded, for which deed the doer received twenty pounds from the union, but was discovered and transported for life. Finally, in 1837, in May, disturbances occurred in consequence of a turnout in the Oatbank and Mile End factories, in which perhaps a dozen knobsticks were mal-treated. In July, of the same year, the disturbances still continued, and a certain Smith, a knobstick, was so maltreated that he died. The committee was now arrested, an investigation begun, and the leading members found guilty of participation in conspiracies, maltreatment of knobsticks, and incendiarism in the mill of James and Francis Wood, and they were transported for seven years. What do our good Germans say to this story?[3]

The property-holding class, and especially the manufacturing portion of it which comes into direct contact with the working men, declaims with the greatest violence against these unions, and is constantly trying to prove their uselessness to the working men upon grounds which are economically perfectly correct, but for that very reason partially mistaken, and for the working man's understanding totally without effect. The very zeal of the bour-geoisie shows that it is not disinterested in the matter; and apart from the direct loss involved in a turnout, the state of the case is such that whatever goes into the pockets of the manufacturers comes of necessity out of those of the worker. So that even if the working men did not know that the unions hold the emulation of their masters in the reduction of wages, at least in a measure, in check, they would still stand by the unions, simply to the injury of their enemies, the manufacturers. In war the injury of one party is the benefit of the other, and since the working men are on a war footing towards their employers, they do merely what the great potentates do when they get into a quarrel. Beyond all other bourgeois is our friend Dr Ure, the most furious enemy of the unions. He foams with indignation at the 'secret tribunals' of the cotton-spinners, the most powerful section of the workers, tribunals which boast their ability to paralyse every disobedient manufacturer,[4] 'and so bring ruin on the man who had given them profitable employment for many a year'. He speaks of a time[5] 'when the inventive head and the sustaining heart of trade were held in bondage by the unruly lower members'. A pity that the English working men will not let themselves be pacified so easily with thy fable as the Roman Plebs, thou modern Menenius Agrippa! Finally, he relates the following: At one time the coarse mule-spinners had misused their power beyond all endurance. High wages, instead of awakening thankfulness towards the manufacturers and leading to intellectual improvement (in harmless study of sciences useful to the bourgeoisie, of course), in many cases produced pride and supplied funds for supporting rebellious spirits in strikes, with which a number of manufacturers were visited one after the other in a purely arbitrary manner. During an unhappy disturbance of this sort in Hyde, Dukinfield, and the surrounding neighbourhood, the manufacturers of the district, anxious lest they should be driven from the market by the French, Belgians, and Americans, addressed themselves to the machine-works of Sharp, Roberts & Co., and requested Mr Sharp to turn his inventive mind to the construction of an automatic mule in order 'to emancipate the trade from galling slavery and impending ruin'.[6]

He produced in the course of a few months, a machine apparently instinct with the thought, feeling, and tact of the experienced workman – which even in its infancy displayed a new principle of regulation, ready in its mature state to fulfil the functions of a finished spinner. Thus, the Iron Man, as the operatives fitly call it, sprang out of the hands of our modern Prometheus at the bidding of Minerva – a creation destined to restore order among the industrious classes, and to confirm to Great Britain the empire of art. The news of this Herculean prodigy spread dismay through the Union, and even long before it left its cradle, so to speak, it strangled the Hydra of misrule.[7]

Ure proves further that the invention of the machine, with

which four and five colours are printed at once, was a result of the disturbances among the calico printers; that the refractoriness of the yarn-dressers in the power-loom weaving mills gave rise to a new and perfected machine for warp-dressing, and mentions several other such cases. A few pages earlier this same Ure gives himself a great deal of trouble to prove in detail that machinery is beneficial to the workers! But Ure is not the only one; in the Factory Report, Mr Ashworth, the manufacturer, and many another, lose no opportunity to express their wrath against the unions. These wise bourgeois, like certain governments, trace every movement which they do not understand to the influence of ill-intentioned agitators, demagogues, traitors, spouting idiots, and ill-balanced youth. They declare that the paid agents of the unions are interested in the agitation because they live upon it, as though the necessity for this payment were not forced upon them by the bourgeois, who will give such men no employment!

The incredible frequency of these strikes proves best of all to what extent the social war has broken out all over England. No week passes, scarcely a day, indeed, in which there is not a strike in some direction, now against a reduction, then against a refusal to raise the rate of wages, again by reasons of the employment of knobsticks or the continuance of abuses, sometimes against new machinery, or for a hundred other reasons. These strikes, at first skirmishes, sometimes result in weighty struggles; they decide nothing, it is true, but they are the strongest proof that the decisive battle between bourgeoisie and proletariat is approaching. They are the military school of the working men in which they prepare themselves for the great struggle which cannot be avoided; they are the *pronunciamentos* of single branches of industry that these too have joined the labour movement. And when one examines a year's file of the *Northern Star*, the only sheet which reports all the movements of the proletariat, one finds that all the proletarians of the towns and of country manufacture have united in associations, and have protested from time to time, by means of a general strike, against the supremacy of the bourgeoisie. And as schools of war, the unions are unexcelled. In them is developed the peculiar courage of the English. It is said on the Continent that the English, and especially the working men, are cowardly, that they cannot carry out a revolution because, unlike the French, they do not riot at intervals, because they apparently accept the bourgeois *régime* so quietly. This is a complete mistake. The English working men are second to none in courage; they are quite as restless as the French, but they fight differently. The French, who are by nature political, struggle against social evils with political weapons; the English, for whom politics exist only as a matter of interest, solely in the interest of bourgeois society, fight, not against the Government, but directly against the bourgeoisie; and for the time, this can be done only in a peaceful manner. Stagnation in business, and the want consequent upon it, engendered the revolt at Lyons, in 1834, in favour of the Republic: in 1842, at Manchester, a similar cause gave rise to a universal turnout for the Charter and higher wages. That courage is required for a turnout, often indeed much loftier courage, much bolder, firmer determination than for an insurrection, is self-evident. It is, in truth, no trifle for a working man who knows want from experience, to face it with wife and children, to endure hunger and wretchedness for months together, and stand firm and unshaken through it all. What is death, what the galleys which await the French revolutionist, in comparison with gradual starvation, with the daily sight of a starving family, with the certainty of future revenge on the part of the bourgeoisie, all of which the English working man chooses in preference to subjection under the yoke of the property-holding class? We shall meet later an example of this obstinate, unconquerable courage of men who surrender to force only when all resistance would be aimless and unmeaning. And precisely in this quiet perseverance, in this lasting determination which undergoes a hundred tests every day, the English working man develops that side of his character which commands most respect. People who endure so much to bend one single bourgeois will be able to break the power of the whole bourgeoisie . . .

NOTES

1. *Arts and Artisans*, p. 137, *et seq*.
2. So called from the East Indian tribe, whose only trade is the murder of all the strangers who fall into its hands.
3. 'What kind of wild justice must it be in the hearts of these men that prompts them, with cold deliberation, in conclave assembled, to doom their brother workman, as the deserter of his order and his order's cause, to die as a traitor and deserter; and have him executed, since not by any public judge and hangman, then by a private one: – like your old

Chivalry *Femgericht*, and Secret Tribunal, suddenly in this strange guise become new; suddenly rising once more on the astonished eye, dressed now not in mail-shirts, but in fustian jackets, meeting not in Westphalian forests but in the paved Gallowgate of Glasgow! . . . Such temper must be widespread, virulent among the many, when even in its worst acme, it can take such a form in a few.' Carlyle, *Chartism*, p. 40.

4. DR URE, *Philosophy of Manufactures*, p. 282.

5. ibid., p. 282.

6. ibid., p. 367.

7. ibid., p. 366, *et seq*.

3 Capital and Labour

Karl Marx

Reprinted with permission from K. Marx, 'Strikes and Combinations of Workers', *The Poverty of Philosophy*, in K. Marx and F. Engels, *Collected Works*, vol. 6, Lawrence & Wishart, 1976, pp. 206–12; and from K. Marx, 'Wages, Prices and Profit', in K. Marx and F. Engels, *Selected Works*, Lawrence & Wishart, 1968, pp. 224–9.

Every upward movement in wages can have no other effect than a rise in the price of corn, wine, etc., that is, the effect of a dearth. For what are wages? They are the cost price of corn, etc.; they are the integrant price of everything. We may go even further: wages are the proportion of the elements composing wealth and consumed reproductively every day by the mass of the workers. Now, to double wages . . . is to attribute to each one of the producers a greater share than his product, which is contradictory, and if the rise extends only to a small number of industries, it brings about a general disturbance in exchange: in a word, a *dearth* . . . It is impossible, I declare, for strikes followed by an increase in wages not to culminate in a *general rise in prices*: this is as certain as that two and two make four. (Proudhon, tome I, pp. 110 and 111.)

We deny all these assertions, except that two and two make four.

In the first place, there is no *general rise in prices*. If the price of everything doubles at the same time as wages, there is no change in price, the only change is in terms.

Then again, a general rise in wages can never produce a more or less general rise in the price of goods. Actually, if every industry employed the same number of workers in relation to fixed capital or to the instruments used, a general rise in wages would produce a general fall in profits and the current price of goods would undergo no alteration.

But as the relation of manual labour to fixed capital is not the same in different industries, all the industries which employ a relatively greater mass of fixed capital and fewer workers, will be forced sooner or later to lower the price of their goods. In the opposite case, in which the price of their goods is not lowered, their profit will rise above the general rate of profits. Machines are not wage-earners. Therefore, the general rise in wages will affect less those industries, which, compared with the others, employ more machines than workers. But as competition always tends to level the rate of profits, those profits which rise above the general rate cannot but be transitory. Thus, apart from a few fluctuations, a general rise in wages will lead, not as M. Proudhon says, to a general increase in prices, but to a partial fall, that is a fall in the current price of the goods that are made chiefly with the help of machines.

The rise and fall of profits and wages express merely the proportion in which capitalists and workers share in the product of a day's work, without influencing in most instances the price of the product. But that 'strikes followed by an increase in wages culminate in a general rise in prices, in a dearth even' – these are notions which can blossom only in the brain of a poet who has not been understood.

In England, strikes have regularly given rise to the invention and application of new machines. Machines were, it may be said, the weapon employed by the capitalists to quell the revolt of specialized labour. The *self-acting mule*, the greatest invention of modern industry, put out of action the spinners who were in revolt. If combinations and strikes had no other effect than that of making the efforts of mechanical genius react against them, they would still exercise an immense influence on the development of industry.

'I find,' continues M. Proudhon, 'in an article published by M. Léon Faucher . . . September 1845, that for some time the English workers have got out of the habit of *combination*, which is assuredly a progress for which one cannot but congratulate them: but this improvement in the morale of the workers comes chiefly from their economic education. "It is not on the manufacturers," cried a spinning-mill worker at a Bolton meeting, "that wages depend. In periods of depression the masters are, so to speak, merely the whip with which necessity arms itself, and whether they want to or not, they have to deal blows. The regulative principle is the relation of supply to demand: and the masters have not this power" . . . Well done,' cries M. Proudhon, 'these are well-trained workers, model workers,' etc., etc. 'Such poverty did not exist in England; it will not cross the Channel.' (Proudhon, tome I, pp. 261 and 262.)

Of all the towns in England, Bolton is the one in which radicalism is the most developed. The Bolton workers are known to be the most revolutionary of all. At the time of the great agitation in England for the abolition of the Corn Laws, the English manufacturers thought that they could cope with the landowners only by thrusting the workers to the fore. But as the interests of the workers were no less opposed to those of the manufacturers than the interests of the manufacturers were to those of the landowners, it was natural that the manufacturers should fare badly in the workers' meetings. What did the manufacturers do? To save appearances they organized meetings composed, to a large extent, of foremen, of the small number of workers who were devoted to them, and of the real *friends of trade*. When later on the genuine workers tried, as in Bolton and Manchester, to take part in these sham demonstrations, in order to protest against them, they were forbidden admittance on the ground that it was a *ticket meeting* – a meeting to which only persons with entrance cards were admitted. Yet the posters placarded on the walls had announced public meetings. Every time one of these meetings was held, the manufacturers' newspapers gave a pompous and detailed account of the speeches made. It goes without saying that it was the foremen who made these speeches. The London papers reproduced them word for word. M. Proudhon has the misfortune to take foremen for ordinary workers, and enjoins them not to cross the Channel.

If in 1844 and 1845 strikes drew less attention than before, it was because 1844 and 1845 were the first two years of prosperity that English industry had had since 1837. Nevertheless none of the *trades unions* had been dissolved.

Now let us listen to the foremen of Bolton. According to them manufacturers have no command over wages because they have no command over the price of products, and they have no command over the price of products because they have no command over the world market. For this reason they wish it to be understood that combinations should not be formed to extort an increase in wages from the masters. M. Proudhon, on the contrary, forbids combinations for fear they should be followed by a rise in wages which would bring with it a general dearth. We have no need to say that on one point there is an *entente cordiale* between the foremen and M. Proudhon: that a rise in wages is equivalent to a rise in the price of products.

But is the fear of a dearth the true cause of M. Proudhon's rancour? No. Quite simply he is annoyed with the Bolton foremen because they determine value by *supply and demand* and hardly take any account of *constituted value*, of value which has passed into the state of constitution, of the constitution of value, including *permanent exchangeability* and all the other *proportionalities of relations* and *relations of proportionality*, with Providence at their side.

A workers' strike is *illegal*, and it is not only the Penal Code that says so, it is the economic system, the necessity of the established order . . . That each worker individually should dispose freely over his person and his hands, this can be tolerated, but that workers should undertake by combination to do violence to monopoly, is something society cannot permit. (Tome I, pp. 334 and 335.)

M. Proudhon wants to pass off an article of the Penal Code as a necessary and general result of bourgeois relations of production.

In England combination is authorized by an Act of Parliament, and it is the economic system which has forced Parliament to grant this legal authorization. In 1825, when, under the Minister Huskisson, Parliament had to modify the law in order to bring it more and more into line with the conditions resulting from free competition, it had of necessity to abolish all laws forbidding combinations of workers. The more modern industry and competition develop, the more elements there are which call forth and strengthen combination, and as soon as combination becomes an economic fact, daily gaining in solidity, it is bound before long to become a legal fact.

Thus the article of the Penal Code proves at the most that modern industry and competition were not yet well developed under the Constituent Assembly and under the Empire.

Economists and socialists[1] are in agreement on one point: the condemnation of *combinations*. Only they have different motives for their act of condemnation.

The economists say to the workers: Do not combine. By combination you hinder the regular progress of industry, you prevent manufacturers from carrying out their orders, you disturb trade and you precipitate the invasion of machines which, by rendering your labour in part useless, force you to accept a still lower wage. Besides, whatever you do, your wages will always be determined by the relation of hands demanded to hands supplied, and it is an effort as ridiculous as it is dangerous for you to revolt against the eternal laws of political economy.

The socialists say to the workers: Do not combine, because what will you gain by it anyway? A rise in wages? The economists will prove to you quite clearly that the few ha'pence you may gain by it for a few moments if you succeed, will be followed by a permanent fall. Skilled calculators will prove to you that it would take you years merely to recover, through the increase in your wages, the expenses incurred for the organization and upkeep of the combinations. And we, as socialists, tell you that, apart from the money question, you will continue nonetheless to be workers, and the masters will still continue to be the masters, just as before. So no combination! No politics! For is not entering into combination engaging in politics?

The economists want the workers to remain in society as it is constituted and as it has been signed and sealed by them in their manuals.

The socialists want the workers to leave the old society alone, the better to be able to enter the new society which they have prepared for them with so much foresight.

In spite of both of them, in spite of manuals and utopias, combination has not ceased for an instant to go forward and grow with the development and growth of modern industry. It has now reached such a stage, that the degree to which combination has developed in any country clearly marks the rank it occupies in the hierarchy of the world market. England, whose industry has attained the highest degree of development, has the biggest and best organized combinations.

In England they have not stopped at partial combinations which have no other objective than a passing strike, and which disappear with it. Permanent combinations have been formed, *trades unions*, which serve as bulwarks for the workers in their struggles with the employers. And at the present time all these local *trades unions* find a rallying point in the *National Association of United Trades*, the central committee of which is in London, and which already numbers 80,000 members. The organization of these strikes, combinations, and *trades unions* went on simultaneously with the political struggle of the workers, who now constitute a large political party, under the name of *Chartists*.

The first attempts of workers to *associate* among themselves always take place in the form of combinations.

Large-scale industry concentrates in one place a crowd of people unknown to one another. Competition divides their interests. But the maintenance of wages, this common interest which they have against their boss, unites them in a common thought of resistance – *combination*. Thus combination always has a double aim, that of stopping competition among the workers, so that they can carry on general competition with the capitalist. If the first aim of resistance was merely the maintenance of wages, combinations, at first isolated, constitute themselves into groups as the capitalists in their turn unite for the purpose of repression, and in face of always united capital, the maintenance of the association becomes more necessary to them than that of wages. This is so true that English economists are amazed to see the workers sacrifice a good part of their wages in favour of associations, which, in the eyes of these economists, are established solely in favour of wages. In this struggle – a veritable civil war – all the elements necessary for a coming battle unite and develop. Once it has reached this point, association takes on a political character.

Economic conditions had first transformed the mass of the people of the country into workers. The domination of capital has created for this mass a common situation, common interests. This mass is thus already a class as against capital, but not yet for itself. In the struggle, of which we have pointed out only a few phases, this mass becomes united, and constitutes itself as a class for itself. The interests it defends become class interests. But the struggle of class against class is a political struggle.

In the bourgeoisie we have two phases to distinguish: that in which it constituted itself as a class under the regime of feudalism and absolute monarchy, and that in which, already constituted as a class, it overthrew feudalism and monarchy to make society into a bourgeois society. The first of these phases was the longer and necessitated the greater efforts. This too began by partial combinations against the feudal lords.

Much research has been carried out to trace the different historical phases that the bourgeoisie has passed through, from the commune up to its constitution as a class.

But when it is a question of making a precise study of strikes, combinations and other forms in which the proletarians carry out before our eyes their organization as a class, some are seized with real fear and others display a *transcendental* disdain.

An oppressed class is the vital condition for every society founded on the antagonism of classes. The emancipation of the oppressed class thus implies necessarily the creation of a new society. For the oppressed class to be able to emancipate itself it is necessary that the productive powers already acquired and the existing social relations should no longer be capable of existing side by side. Of all the instruments of production, the greatest productive power is the revolutionary class itself. The organization of revolutionary elements as a class supposes the existence of all the productive forces which could be engendered in the bosom of the old society.

Does this mean that after the fall of the old society there will be a new class domination culminating in a new political power? No.

The condition for the emancipation of the working class is the abolition of all classes, just as the condition for the emancipation of the third estate, of the bourgeois order, was the abolition of all estates[2] and all orders.

The working class, in the course of its development, will substitute for the old civil society an association which will exclude classes and their antagonism, and there will be no more political power properly so-called, since political power is precisely the official expression of antagonism in civil society.

Meanwhile the antagonism between the proletariat and the bourgeoisie is a struggle of class against class, a struggle which carried to its highest expression is a total revolution. Indeed, is it at all surprising that a society founded on the *opposition* of classes should culminate in brutal *contradiction*, the shock of body against body, as its final denouement?

Do not say that social movement excludes political movement. There is never a political movement which is not at the same time social.

It is only in an order of things in which there are no more classes and class antagonisms that *social evolutions* will cease to be *political revolutions*. Till then, on the eve of every general re-shuffling of society, the last word of social science will always be:

Le combat ou la mort; la lutte sanguinaire ou le néant. C'est ainsi que la question est invinciblement posée.

George Sand.[3]

THE STRUGGLE BETWEEN CAPITAL AND LABOUR AND ITS RESULTS

1. Having shown that the periodical resistance on the part of the working men against a reduction of wages, and their periodical attempts at getting a rise of wages, are inseparable from the wages system, and dictated by the very fact of labour being assimilated to commodities, and therefore subject to the laws regulating the general movement of prices; having, furthermore, shown that a general rise of wages would result in a fall in the general rate of profit, but not affect the average prices of com-modities, or their values, the question now ultimately arises, how far, in this incessant struggle between capital and labour, the latter is likely to prove successful.

I might answer by a generalization, and say that, as with all other commodities, so with labour, its *market price* will, in the long run, adapt itself to its *value*; that, therefore, despite all the ups and downs, and do what he may, the working man will, on an average, only receive the value of his labour, which resolves into the value of his labouring power, which is determined by the value of the necessaries required for its maintenance and re-production, which value of necessaries finally is regulated by the quantity of labour wanted to produce them.

But there are some peculiar features which distinguish the *value of the labouring power, or the value of labour*, from the values of all other commodities. The value of the labouring power is formed by two elements – the one merely physical, the other historical or social. Its *ultimate limit* is determined by the *physical* element, that is to say, to maintain and reproduce itself, to perpetuate its physical existence, the working class must receive the necessaries absolutely indispensable for living and multiplying. The *value* of those indispensable necessaries forms, therefore, the ultimate limit of the *value of labour*. On the other hand, the length of the working day is also limited by ultimate, although very elastic, boundaries. Its ultimate limit is given by the physical force of the labouring man. If the daily exhaustion of his vital forces exceeds a certain degree, it cannot be exerted anew, day by day. However, as I said, this limit is very elastic. A quick succession of unhealthy and short-lived generations will keep the labour market as well supplied as a series of vigorous and long-lived generations.

Besides this mere physical element, the value of labour, is in every country determined by a *traditional standard of life*. It is not mere physical life, but it is the satisfaction of certain wants springing from the social conditions in which people are placed and reared up. The English standard of life may be reduced to the Irish standard; the standard of life of a German peasant to that of a Livonian peasant. The important part which historical tradition and social habitude play in this respect, you may learn from Mr Thornton's work on *Over-population*, where he shows that the average wages in different agricultural districts of England still nowadays differ more or less according to the more or less favourable circumstances under which the districts have emerged from the state of serfdom.

This historical or social element, entering into the value of labour, may be expanded, or contracted, or altogether extinguished, so that nothing remains but the *physical limit*. During the time of the anti-Jacobin war, undertaken, as the incorrigible tax-eater and sinecurist, old George Rose, used to say, to save the comforts of our holy religion from the inroads of the French infidels, the honest English farmers, so tenderly handled in a former chapter of ours, depressed the wages of the agricultural labourers even beneath that *mere physical minimum*, but made up by Poor Laws the remainder necessary for the physical perpetuation of the race. This was a glorious way to convert the wages labourer into a slave, and Shakespeare's proud yeoman into a pauper.

By comparing the standard wages or values of labour in different countries, and by comparing them in different historical epochs of the same country, you will find that the *value of labour* itself is not a fixed but a variable magnitude, even supposing the values of all other commodities to remain constant.

A similar comparison would prove that not only the *market rates* of profit change, but its *average* rates.

But as to *profits*, there exists no law which determines their *minimum*. We cannot say what is the ultimate limit of their decrease. And why cannot we fix that limit? Because, although we can fix the *minimum* of wages, we cannot fix their *maximum*. We can only say that, the limits of the working day being given, the *maximum* of profit corresponds to the *physical minimum of wages*; and that wages being given, the *maximum of profit* corresponds to such a prolongation of the working day as is compatible with the physical forces of the labourer. The maximum of profits is, therefore, limited by the physical minimum of wages and the physical maximum of the working day. It is evident that between the two limits of this *maximum rate of profit* an immense scale of variations is possible. The fixation of its actual degree is only settled by the continuous struggle between capital and labour, the capitalist constantly tending to reduce wages to their physical minimum, and to extend the working day to its physical maximum, while the working man constantly presses in the opposite direction.

The matter resolves itself into a question of the respective powers of the combatants.

2. As to the *limitation of the working day* in England, as in all other countries, it has never been settled except by *legislative interference*. Without the working men's continuous pressure from without that interference would never have taken place. But at all events, the result was not to be attained by private settlement between the working men and the capitalists. This very necessity of *general political action* affords the proof that in its merely economic action capital is the stronger side.

As to the *limits* of the *value of labour*, its actual settlement always depends upon supply and demand, I mean the demand for labour on the part of capital, and the supply of labour by the working men. In colonial countries the law of supply and demand favours the working man. Hence the relatively high standard of wages in the United States. Capital may there try its utmost. It cannot prevent the labour market from being continuously emptied by the continuous conversion of wages labourers into independent, self-sustaining peasants. The position of wages labourer is for a very large part of the American people but a probational state, which they are sure to leave within a longer or shorter term. To mend this colonial state of things, the paternal British Government accepted for some time what is called the modern colonization theory, which consists in putting an artificial high price upon colonial land, in order to prevent the too quick conversion of the wages labourer into the independent peasant.

But let us now come to old civilized countries, in which capital domineers over the whole process of production. Take, for example, the rise in England of agricultural wages from 1849 to 1859. What was its consequence? The farmers could not, as our friend Weston would have advised them, raise the value of wheat, nor even its market prices. They had, on the contrary, to submit to their fall. But during these eleven years they introduced machinery of all sorts, adopted more scientific methods, converted part of arable land into pasture, increased the size of farms, and with this the scale of production, and by these and other processes diminishing the demand for labour by increasing its productive power, made the agricultural population again relatively redundant. This is the general method in which a reaction, quicker or slower, of capital against a rise of wages takes place in old, settled countries. Ricardo has justly remarked that machinery is in constant competition with labour, and can often be only introduced when the price of labour has reached a certain height, but the appliance of machinery is but one of the many methods for increasing the productive powers of labour. This very same development which makes common labour relatively redundant simplifies on the other hand skilled labour, and thus depreciates it.

The same law obtains in another form. With the development of the productive powers of labour the accumulation of capital will be accelerated, even despite a relatively high rate of wages. Hence, one might infer, as Adam Smith, in whose days modern industry was still in its infancy, did infer, that the accelerated accumulation of capital must turn the balance in favour of the working man, by securing a growing demand for his labour. From this same standpoint many contemporary writers have wondered that, English capital having grown in the last twenty years so much quicker than English population, wages should not have been more enhanced. But simultaneously with the progress of accumulation there takes place a *progressive change* in the *composition of capital*. That part of the aggregate capital which consists of fixed capital, machinery, raw materials, means of production in all possible forms, progressively increases as compared with the other part of capital, which is laid out in wages or in the purchase of labour. This law has been stated in a more or less accurate manner by Mr Barton, Ricardo, Sismondi, Professor Richard Jones, Professor Ramsay, Cherbuliez, and others.

If the proportion of these two elements of capital was originally one to one, it will, in the progress of industry, become five to one, and so forth. If of a total capital of 600, 300 is laid out in instruments, raw materials, and so forth, and 300 in wages, the total capital wants only to be doubled to create a demand for 600 working men instead of for 300. But if of a capital of 600, 500 is laid out in machinery, materials, and so forth, and 100 only in wages, the same capital must increase from 600 to 3600 in order to create a demand for 600 workmen instead of 300. In the progress of industry the demand for labour keeps, therefore, no pace with accumulation of capital. It will still increase, but increase in a constantly diminishing ratio as compared with the increase of capital.

These few hints will suffice to show that the very development of modern industry must progressively turn the scale in favour of the capitalist against the working man, and that consequently the general tendency of capitalistic production is not to raise, but to sink, the average standard of wages, or to push the *value of labour* more or less to its *minimum limit*. Such being the tendency of *things* in this system, is this saying that the working class ought to renounce their resistance against the encroachments of capital, and abandon their attempts at making the best of the occasional chances for their temporary improvement? If they did, they would be degraded to one level mass of broken wretches past salvation. I think I have shown that their struggles for the standard of wages are incidents inseparable from the whole wages system, that in 99 cases out of 100 their efforts at raising wages are only efforts at maintaining the given value of labour, and that the necessity of debating their price with the capitalist is inherent in their condition of having to sell themselves as commodities. By cowardly giving way in their everyday conflict with capital, they would certainly disqualify themselves for the initiating of any larger movement.

At the same time, and quite apart from the general servitude involved in the wages system, the working class ought not to exaggerate to themselves the ultimate working of these everyday struggles. They ought not to forget that they are fighting with effects, but not with the causes of those effects; that they are retarding the downward movement, but not changing its direction; that they are applying palliatives, not curing the malady. They ought, therefore, not to be exclusively absorbed in these unavoidable guerrilla fights incessantly springing up from the never-ceasing encroachments of capital or changes of the market. They ought to understand that, with all the miseries it imposes upon them, the present system simultaneously engenders the *material conditions* and the *social forms* necessary for an economical reconstruction of society. Instead of the *conservative* motto, '*A fair day's wage for a fair day's work!*' they ought to inscribe on their banner the *revolutionary* watchword, '*Abolition of the wages system!*'

After this very long and, I fear, tedious exposition which I was obliged to enter into to do some justice to the subject-matter, I shall conclude by proposing the following resolutions:

Firstly. A general rise in the rate of wages would result in a fall of the general rate of profit, but, broadly speaking, not affect the prices of commodities.

Secondly. The general tendency of capitalist production is not to raise, but to sink, the average standard of wages.

Thirdly. Trades unions work well as centres of resistance against the encroachments of capital. They fail partially from an injudicious use of their power. They fail generally from limiting themselves to a guerrilla war against the effects of the existing system, instead of simultaneously trying to change it, instead of using their organized forces as a lever for the final emancipation of the working class, that is to say, the ultimate abolition of the wages system.

NOTES

1. That is, the socialists of that time: the Fourierists in France, the Owenites in England. *F. E.*

2. Estates here in the historical sense of the estates of feudalism, estates with definite and limited privileges. The revolution of the bourgeoisie abolished the estates and their privileges. Bourgeois society

knows only *classes*. It was, therefore, absolutely in contradiction with history to describe the proletariat as the 'fourth estate'. *F. E.*

3. 'Combat or death, bloody struggle or extinction. Thus the question is inexorably put.' (George Sand, *Jean Ziska. Episode de la guerre des hussites*. Introduction.)

4 On Strikes

V. I. Lenin

Reprinted with permission from V. I. Lenin, *On Strikes*, in V. I. Lenin, *Collected Works*, vol. 4, Lawrence & Wishart, 1961.

In all countries the wrath of the workers first took the form of isolated revolts – the police and factory owners in Russia call them 'mutinies'. In all countries these isolated revolts gave rise to more or less peaceful strikes, on the one hand, and to the all-sided struggle of the working class for its emancipation, on the other.

What significance have strikes (or stoppages) for the struggle of the working class? To answer this question, we must first have a fuller view of strikes. The wages of a worker are determined, as we have seen, by an agreement between the employer and the worker, and if, under these circumstances, the individual worker is completely powerless, it is obvious that workers must fight jointly for their demands, they are compelled to organize strikes either to prevent the employers from reducing wages or to obtain higher wages. It is a fact that in every country with a capitalist system there are strikes of workers. Everywhere, in all the European countries and in America, the workers feel themselves powerless when they are disunited; they can only offer resistance to the employers jointly, either by striking or threatening to strike. As capitalism develops, as big factories are more rapidly opened, as the petty capitalists are more and more ousted by the big capitalists, the more urgent becomes the need for the joint resistance of the workers, because unemployment increases, competition sharpens between the capitalists who strive to produce their wares at the cheapest (to do which they have to pay the workers as little as possible), and the fluctuations of industry become more accentuated and crises[1] more acute. When industry prospers, the factory owners make big profits but do not think of sharing them with the workers; but when a crisis breaks out, the factory owners try to push the losses on to the workers. The necessity for strikes in capitalist society has been recognized to such an extent by everybody in the European countries that the law in those countries does not forbid the organization of strikes; only in Russia barbarous laws against strikes still remain in force (we shall speak on another occasion of these laws and their application).

However, strikes, which arise out of the very nature of capitalist society, signify the beginning of the working-class struggle against that system of society. When the rich capitalists are confronted by individual, propertyless workers, this signifies the utter enslavement of the workers. But when those propertyless workers unite, the situation changes. There is no wealth that can be of benefit to the capitalists if they cannot find workers willing to apply their labour-power to the instruments and materials belonging to the capitalists and produce new wealth. As long as workers have to deal with capitalists on an individual basis they remain veritable slaves who must work continuously to profit another in order to obtain a crust of bread, who must for ever remain docile and inarticulate hired servants. But when the workers state their demands jointly and refuse to submit to the money-bags, they cease to be slaves, they become human beings, they begin to demand that their labour should not only serve to enrich a handful of idlers, but should also enable those who work to live like human beings. The slaves begin to put forward the demand to become masters, not to work and live as the landlords and capitalists want them to, but as the working people themselves want to. Strikes, therefore, always instil fear into the capitalists, because they begin to undermine their supremacy. 'All wheels stand still, if your mighty arm wills it,' a German workers' song says of the working class. And so it is in reality: the factories, the landlords' land, the machines, the railways, etc., etc., are all like wheels in a giant machine – the machine that extracts various products, processes them, and delivers them to their destination. The whole of this machine is set in motion by *the worker* who tills the soil, extracts ores, makes commodities in the factories, builds houses, workshops, and railways. When the workers refuse to work, the entire machine threatens to stop. Every strike reminds the capitalists that it is the workers and not they who are the real masters – the workers who are more and more loudly proclaiming their rights. Every strike reminds the workers that their position is not hopeless, that they are not alone. See what a tremendous effect strikes have both on the strikers themselves and on the workers at neighbouring or near-by factories or at factories in the same industry. In normal, peaceful times the worker does his job without a murmur, does not contradict the employer, and does not discuss his condition. In times of strikes he states his demands in a loud voice, he reminds the employers of all their abuses, he claims his rights, he does not think of himself and his wages alone, he thinks of all his workmates who have downed tools together with him and who stand up for the workers' cause, fearing no privations. Every strike means many privations for the working people, terrible privations that can be compared only to the calamities of war – hungry families, loss of wages, often arrests, banishment from the towns where they have their homes and their employment. Despite all these sufferings, the workers despise those who desert their fellow workers and make deals with the employers. Despite all these sufferings, brought on by strikes, the workers of neighbouring factories gain renewed courage when they see that their comrades have engaged themselves in struggle. 'People who endure so much to bend one single bourgeois will be able to break the power of the whole bourgeoisie,' said one great teacher of socialism, Engels, speaking of the strikes of the English workers. It is often enough for one factory to strike, for strikes to begin immediately in a large number of factories. What a great moral influence strikes have, how they affect workers who see that their comrades have ceased to be slaves and, if only for the time being, have become people on an equal footing with the rich! Every strike brings thoughts of socialism very forcibly to the worker's mind, thoughts of the struggle of the entire working class for emancipation from the oppression of capital. It has often happened that before a big strike the workers of a certain factory or a certain branch of industry or of a certain town knew hardly anything and scarcely ever thought about socialism; but after the strike, study circles and associations become much more widespread among them and more and more workers become socialists.

A strike teaches workers to understand what the strength of the employers and what the strength of the workers consists in; it teaches them not to think of their own employer alone and not of their own immediate workmates alone but of all the employers, the whole class of capitalists and the whole class of workers. When a factory owner who has amassed millions from the toil of several generations of workers refuses to grant a modest increase in wages or even tries to reduce wages to a still lower level and, if the workers offer resistance, throws thousands of hungry families out into the street, it becomes quite clear to the workers that the capitalist class as a whole is the enemy of the whole working class and that the workers can depend only on themselves and their united action. It often happens that a factory owner does his best to deceive the workers, to pose as a benefactor, and conceal his exploitation of the workers by some petty sops or lying promises. A strike always demolishes this deception at one blow by showing the workers that their 'benefactor' is a wolf in sheep's clothing.

A strike, moreover, opens the eyes of the workers to the nature, not only of the capitalists, but of the government and the laws as well. Just as the factory owners try to pose as benefactors of the workers, the government officials and their lackeys try to assure the workers that the tsar and the tsarist government are equally solicitous of both the factory owners and the workers, as justice requires. The worker does not know the laws, he has no contact with government officials, especially with those in the higher posts, and, as a consequence, often believes all this. Then comes a strike. The public prosecutor, the factory inspector, the police, and frequently troops, appear at the factory. The workers learn that they have violated the law: the employers are permitted by law to assemble and openly discuss ways of reducing workers' wages, but workers are declared criminals if they come to a joint agreement! Workers are driven out of their homes; the police close the shops from which the workers might obtain food on credit, an effort is made to incite the soldiers against the workers even when the workers conduct themselves quietly and peacefully. Soldiers are even ordered to fire on the workers and when they kill unarmed workers by shooting the fleeing crowd in the back, the tsar himself sends the troops an expression of his gratitude (in this way the tsar thanked the troops who had killed striking workers in Yaroslavl in 1895). It becomes clear to every worker that the tsarist government is his worst enemy, since it defends the capitalists and binds the workers hand and foot. The workers begin to understand that laws are made in the interests of the rich alone; that government officials protect those interests; that the working people are gagged and not allowed to make known their needs; that the working class must win for itself the right to strike, the right to publish workers' newspapers, the right to participate

in a national assembly that enacts laws and supervises their fulfilment. The government itself knows full well that strikes open
the eyes of the workers and for this reason it has such a fear of
strikes and does everything to stop them as quickly as possible.
One German Minister of the Interior, one who was notorious for
the persistent persecution of socialists and class-conscious
workers, not without reason, stated before the people's representatives: 'Behind every strike lurks the hydra [monster] of
revolution.' Every strike strengthens and develops in the workers
the understanding that the government is their enemy and that
the working class must prepare itself to struggle against the
government for the people's rights.

Strikes, therefore, teach the workers to unite; they show them
that they can struggle against the capitalists only when they are
united; strikes teach the workers to think of the struggle of the
whole working class against the whole class of factory owners and
against the arbitrary, police government. This is the reason that
socialists call strikes 'a school of war', a school in which the
workers learn to make war on their enemies for the liberation of
the whole people, of all who labour, from the yoke of government officials and from the yoke of capital.

'A school of war' is, however, not war itself. When strikes are
widespread among the workers, some of the workers (including
some socialists) begin to believe that the working class can confine itself to strikes, strike funds, or strike associations alone;
that by strikes alone the working class can achieve a considerable
improvement in its conditions or even its emancipation. When
they see what power there is in a united working class and even
in small strikes, some think that the working class has only to
organize a general strike throughout the whole country for the
workers to get everything they want from the capitalists and the
government. This idea was also expressed by the workers of other
countries when the working-class movement was in its early
stages and the workers were still very inexperienced. *It is a
mistaken idea*. Strikes are *one* of the *ways* in which the working
class struggles for its emancipation, but they are not the only
way; and if the workers do not turn their attention to other
means of conducting the struggle, they will slow down the growth
and the successes of the working class. It is true that funds are
needed to maintain the workers during strikes, if strikes are to be
successful. Such workers' funds (usually funds of workers in

separate branches of industry, separate trades or workshops) are maintained in all countries; but here in Russia this is especially difficult, because the police keep track of them, seize the money, and arrest the workers. The workers, of course, are able to hide from the police; naturally, the organization of such funds is valuable, and we do not want to advise workers against setting them up. But it must not be supposed that workers' funds, when prohibited by law, will attract large numbers of contributors, and so long as the membership in such organizations is small, workers' funds will not prove of great use. Furthermore, even in those countries where workers' unions exist openly and have huge funds at their disposal, the working class can still not confine itself to strikes as a means of struggle. All that is necessary is a hitch in the affairs of industry (a crisis, such as the one that is approaching in Russia today) and the factory owners will even deliberately cause strikes, because it is to their advantage to cease work for a time and to deplete the workers' funds. The workers, therefore, cannot, under any circumstances, confine themselves to strike actions and strike associations. Secondly, strikes can only be successful where workers are sufficiently class-conscious, where they are able to select an opportune moment for striking, where they know how to put forward their demands, and where they have connections with socialists and are able to procure leaflets and pamphlets through them. There are still very few such workers in Russia, and every effort must be exerted to increase their number in order to make the working-class cause known to the masses of workers and to acquaint them with socialism and the working-class struggle. This is a task that the socialists and class-conscious workers must undertake jointly by organizing a socialist working-class party for this purpose. Thirdly, strikes, as we have seen, show the workers that the government is their enemy and that a struggle against the government must be carried on. Actually, it is strikes that have gradually taught the working class of all countries to struggle against the governments for workers' rights and for the rights of the people as a whole. As we have said, only a socialist workers' party can carry on this struggle by spreading among the workers a true conception of the government and of the working-class cause. On another occasion we shall discuss specifically how strikes are conducted in Russia and how class-conscious workers should avail themselves of them. Here we must point out that strikes are, as we said above, 'a school of war' and not the war itself, that strikes are only one means of struggle, only one aspect of the working-class movement. From individual strikes the workers can and must go over, as indeed they are actually doing in all countries, to a struggle of the entire working class for the emancipation of all who labour. When all class-conscious workers become socialists, i.e., when they strive for this emancipation, when they unite throughout the whole country in order to spread socialism among the workers, in order to teach the workers all the means of struggle against their enemies, when they build up a socialist workers' party that struggles for the emancipation of the people as a whole from government oppression and for the emancipation of all working people from the yoke of capital – only then will the working class become an integral part of that great movement of the workers of all countries that unites all workers and raises the red banner inscribed with the words: 'Workers of all countries, unite!'

NOTES

1. We shall deal elsewhere in greater detail with crises in industry and their significance to the workers. Here we shall merely note that during recent years in Russia industrial affairs have been going well, industry has been 'prospering', but that now (at the end of 1899) there are already clear signs that this 'prosperity' will end in a crisis: difficulties in marketing goods, bankruptcies of factory owners, the ruin of petty proprietors, and terrible calamities for the workers (unemployment, reduced wages, etc.).

5 What Is To Be Done?

V. I. Lenin

Reprinted with permission from V. I. Lenin, *What Is To Be Done?* in V. I. Lenin, *Collected Works*, vol. 5, Lawrence & Wishart, 1961, pp. 375–408.

THE SPONTANEITY OF THE MASSES AND THE CONSCIOUSNESS OF THE SOCIAL-DEMOCRATS[1]

We have said that *there could not have been* Social-Democratic consciousness among the workers. It would have to be brought to them from without. The history of all countries shows that the working class, exclusively by its own effort, is able to develop only trade union consciousness, i.e., the conviction that it is necessary to combine in unions, fight the employers, and strive to compel the government to pass necessary labour legislation, etc.[2] The theory of socialism, however, grew out of the philosophic, historical, and economic theories elaborated by educated representatives of the propertied classes, by intellectuals. By their social status, the founders of modern scientific socialism, Marx and Engels, themselves belonged to the bourgeois intelligentsia. In the very same way, in Russia, the theoretical doctrine of Social-Democracy arose altogether independently of the spontaneous growth of the working-class movement; it arose as a natural and inevitable outcome of the development of thought among the revolutionary socialist intelligentsia. In the period under discussion, the middle nineties, this doctrine not only represented the completely formulated programme of the Emancipation of Labour group, but had already won over to its side the majority of the revolutionary youth in Russia.

Hence, we had both the spontaneous awakening of the working masses, their awakening to conscious life and conscious struggle, and a revolutionary youth, armed with Social-Democratic theory and straining towards the workers. In this connection it is particularly important to state the oft-forgotten (and comparatively little known) fact that, although the *early* Social-Democrats of that period *zealously carried on economic agitation* (being guided in this activity by the truly useful indications contained in the pamphlet *On Agitation*, then still in manuscript), they did not regard this as their sole task. On the contrary, *from the very beginning* they set for Russian Social-Democracy the most far-reaching historical tasks, in general, and the task of overthrowing the autocracy, in particular. Thus, towards the end of 1895, the St Petersburg group of Social-Democrats, which founded the League of Struggle for the Emancipation of the Working Class, prepared the first issue of a newspaper called *Workers' Cause*. This issue was ready to go to press when it was seized by the gendarmes, on the night of 8 December 1895, in a raid on the house of one of the members of the group, Anatoly Alexeyevich Vaneyev,[3] so that the first edition of *Workers' Cause* was not destined to see the light of day. The leading article in this issue (which perhaps thirty years hence some Russian antiquary will unearth in the archives of the Department of Police) outlined the historical tasks of the working class in Russia and placed the achievement of political liberty at their head. The issue also contained an article entitled 'What Are Our Ministers Thinking About?'[4] which dealt with the crushing of the elementary education committees by the police. In addition, there was some correspondence from St Petersburg, and from other parts of Russia (e.g., a letter on the massacre of the workers in Yaroslavl Gubernia). This 'first effort', if we are not mistaken, of the Russian Social-Democrats of the nineties was not a purely local, or less still, 'Economic', newspaper, but one that aimed to unite the strike movement with the revolutionary movement against the autocracy, and to win over to the side of Social-Democracy all who were oppressed by the policy of reactionary obscurantism. No one in the slightest degree acquainted with the state of the movement at that period could doubt that such a paper would have met with warm response among the workers of the capital and the revolutionary intelligentsia and would have had a wide circulation. The failure of the enterprise merely showed that the Social-Democrats of that period were unable to meet the immediate requirements of the time owing to their lack of revolutionary experience and practical training. This must be said, too, with regard to the *St Petersburg Workers' Bulletin* and particularly with regard to the *Workers' Gazette* and the *Manifesto* of the Russian Social-Democratic Labour Party, founded in the spring of 1898. Of course, we would not dream of blaming the Social-Democrats of that time for this unpreparedness. But in order to profit from the experience of that movement, and to draw practical lessons from it, we must thoroughly understand the causes and significance of this or that shortcoming. It is therefore highly important to establish the fact that a part (perhaps even a majority) of the Social-Democrats, active in the period of 1895–98, justly considered it possible even then, at the very beginning of the 'spontaneous' movement, to come forward with a most extensive programme and a militant tactical line. Lack of training of the majority of the revolutionaries, an entirely natural phenomenon, could not have roused any particular fears. Once the tasks were correctly defined, once the energy existed for repeated attempts to fulfil them, temporary failures represented only part misfortune. Revolutionary experience and organizational skill are things that can be acquired, provided the desire is there to acquire them, provided the shortcomings are recognized, which in revolutionary activity is more than halfway towards their removal.

But what was only part misfortune became full misfortune when this consciousness began to grow dim (it was very much alive among the members of the groups mentioned), when there appeared people – and even Social-Democratic organs – that were prepared to regard shortcomings as virtues, that even tried to invent a *theoretical* basis for their *slavish cringing before spontaneity*. It is time to draw conclusions from this trend, the content of which is incorrectly and too narrowly characterized as 'Economism' . . .

TRADE-UNIONIST POLITICS AND SOCIAL-DEMOCRATIC POLITICS

Everyone knows that the the economic[5] struggle of the Russian workers underwent widespread development and consolidation simultaneously with the production of 'literature' exposing economic (factory and occupational) conditions. The 'leaflets' were devoted mainly to the exposure of the factory system, and very soon a veritable passion for exposures was roused among the workers. As soon as the workers realized that the Social-Democratic study circles desired to, and could, supply them with a new kind of leaflet that told the whole truth about their miserable existence, about their unbearably hard toil, and their lack of rights, they began to send in, actually flood us with, correspondence from the factories and workshops. This 'exposure literature' created a tremendous sensation, not only in the particular factory exposed in the given leaflet, but in all the factories to which news of the revealed facts spread. And since the poverty and want among the workers in the various enterprises and in the various trades are much the same, the 'truth about the life of the workers' stirred *everyone*. Even among the most backward workers, a veritable passion arose to 'get into print' – a noble passion for this rudimentary form of war against the whole of the present social system which is based upon robbery and oppression. And in the overwhelming majority of cases these 'leaflets' were in truth a declaration of war, because the exposures served greatly to agitate the workers; they evoked among them common demands for the removal of the most glaring outrages and roused in them a readiness to support the demands with strikes. Finally, the employers themselves were compelled to recognize the significance of these leaflets as a declaration of war, so much so that in a large number of cases they did not even wait for the outbreak of hostilities. As is always the case, the mere publication of these exposures made them effective, and they acquired the significance of a strong moral influence. On more than one occasion, the mere appearance of a leaflet proved sufficient to secure the satisfaction of all or part of the demands put forward. In a word, economic (factory) exposures were and remain an important lever in the economic struggle. And they will continue to retain this significance as long as there is capitalism, which makes it necessary for the workers to defend themselves. Even in the most advanced countries of Europe it can still be seen that the exposure of abuses in some backward trade, or in some forgotten branch of domestic industry, serves as a starting-point for the awakening of class-consciousness, for the beginning of a trade union struggle, and for the spread of socialism.[6]

The overwhelming majority of Russian Social-Democrats have of late been almost entirely absorbed by this work of organizing the exposure of factory conditions. Suffice it to recall *Workers' Thought* to see the extent to which they have been absorbed by it – so much so, indeed, that they have lost sight of the fact that this, *taken by itself*, is in essence still not Social-Democratic work, but merely trade union work. As a matter of fact, the exposures merely dealt with the relations between the workers *in a given trade* and their employers, and all they achieved was that the sellers of labour-power learned to sell their 'commodity' on better terms and to fight the purchasers over a purely commercial deal. These exposures could have served (if properly utilized by an organization of revolutionaries) as a beginning and a component part of Social-Democratic activity; but they could also have led (and, given a worshipful attitude towards spontaneity, were bound to lead) to a 'purely trade union' struggle and to a non-Social-Democratic working-class movement. Social-Democracy leads the struggle of the working class, not only for better terms for the sale of labour-power, but for the abolition of the social system that compels the propertyless to sell themselves to the rich. Social-Democracy represents the working class, not in its relation to a given group of employers alone, but in its relation to all classes of modern society and to the state as an organized political force. Hence, it follows that not only must Social-Democrats not confine themselves exclusively to the economic struggle, but that they must not allow the organization of economic exposures to become the predominant part of their activities. We must take up actively the political education of the working class and the development of its political consciousness. *Now* that *Dawn* and *The Spark* have made the first attack upon Economism, 'all are agreed' on this (although some agree only in words, as we shall soon see).

The question arises, what should political education consist in? Can it be confined to the propaganda of working-class hostility to the autocracy? Of course not. It is not enough *to explain* to the workers that they are politically oppressed (any more than it is *to explain* to them that their interests are antagonistic to the interests of the employers). Agitation must be conducted with regard to every concrete example of this oppression (as we have begun to carry on agitation round concrete examples of economic oppression). Inasmuch as *this* oppression affects the most diverse classes of society, inasmuch as it manifests itself in the most varied spheres of life and activity – vocational, civic, personal, family, religious, scientific, etc., etc. – is it not evident that *we shall not be fulfilling our task* of developing the political consciousness of the workers if we do not *undertake* the organization of the *political exposure* of the autocracy *in all its aspects*? In order to carry on agitation round concrete instances of oppression, these instances must be exposed (as it is necessary to expose factory abuses in order to carry on economic agitation).

One might think this to be clear enough. It turns out, however, that it is only in words that 'all' are agreed on the need to develop political consciousness, *in all its aspects*. It turns out that *Workers' Cause*, for example, far from tackling the task of organizing (or making a start in organizing) comprehensive political exposure, is even trying *to drag The Spark* which has undertaken this task, *away from it*. Listen to the following: 'The political struggle of the working class is merely [it is certainly not 'merely'] the most developed, wide, and effective form of economic struggle' (programme of *Workers' Cause*, published in issue No. 1, p. 3). 'The Social-Democrats are now confronted with the task of lending the economic struggle itself, as far as possible, a political character' (Martynov, *Workers' Cause*, No. 10, p. 42). 'The economic struggle is the most widely applicable means of drawing the masses into active political struggle' (resolution adopted by the Conference of the Union Abroad and 'amendments' thereto, *Two Conferences*, pp. 11 and 17). As the reader will observe, all these theses permeate *Workers' Cause* from its very first number to the latest 'Instructions to the Editors', and all of them evidently express a single view regarding political agitation and struggle. Let us examine this view from the standpoint of the opinion prevailing among all Economists, that political agitation must *follow* economic agitation. Is it true that, in general,[7] the economic struggle 'is the most widely applicable means' of drawing the masses into the political struggle? It is entirely untrue. *Any and every* manifestation of police tyranny and autocratic outrage, not only in connection with the economic struggle, is not one whit less 'widely applicable' as a means of 'drawing in' the masses. The rural superintendents and the flogging of peasants, the corruption of the officials and the police treatment of the 'common people' in the cities, the fight against the famine-stricken and the suppression of the popular striving towards enlightenment and knowledge, the extortion of taxes and the persecution of the religious sects, the humiliating treatment of soldiers and the barrack methods in the treatment of the students and liberal intellectuals – do all these and a thousand other similar manifestations of tyranny, though not directly connected with the 'economic' struggle, represent, in general, *less* 'widely applicable' means and occasions for political agitation and for drawing the masses into the political struggle? The very opposite is true. Of the sum total of cases in which the workers suffer (either on their own account or on account of those closely connected with them) from tyranny, violence, and the lack of rights, undoubtedly only a small minority represent cases of police tyranny in the trade union struggle as such. Why then should we, beforehand, *restrict* the scope of political agitation by declaring only *one* of the means to be 'the most widely applicable', when Social-Democrats must have, in addition, other, generally speaking, no less 'widely applicable' means?

In the dim and distant past (a full year ago! . . .) *Workers' Cause* wrote: 'The masses begin to understand immediate political demands after one strike, or at all events, after several', 'as soon as the government sets the police and gendarmerie against them' [*August* (No. 7) 1900, p. 15]. This opportunist theory of stages has now been rejected by the Union Abroad, which makes a concession to us by declaring: 'There is no need whatever to conduct political agitation right from the beginning, exclusively on an economic basis' (*Two Conferences*, p. 11). The Union's repudiation of part of its former errors will show the future historian of Russian Social-Democracy better than any number of lengthy arguments the depths to which our Economists have degraded socialism! But the Union Abroad must be very naïve indeed to imagine that the abandonment of one form of restricting politics will induce us to agree to another form. Would it not be more logical to say, in this case, too, that the economic struggle should be conducted on the widest possible basis, that it should always be utilized for political agitation, but that 'there is no need whatever' to regard the economic struggle as the *most* widely applicable means of drawing the masses into active political struggle?

The Union Abroad attaches significance to the fact that it has substituted the phrase 'most widely applicable means' for the phrase 'the best means' contained in one of the resolutions of the Fourth Congress of the Jewish Workers' Union (Bund). We confess that we find it difficult to say which of these resolutions is the better one. In our opinion they are *both worse*. Both the Union Abroad and the Bund fall into the error (partly, perhaps unconsciously under the influence of tradition) of giving an Economist, trade unionist interpretation to politics. Whether this is done by employing the word 'best' or the words 'most widely applicable' makes no essential difference whatever. Had the Union Abroad said that 'political agitation on an economic basis' is the most widely applied (not 'applicable') means, it would have been right in regard to a certain period in the development of our Social-Democratic movement. It would have been right in regard to the *Economists* and to many (if not the majority) of the practical workers of 1898–1901; for these practical Economists *applied* political agitation (to the extent that they applied it at all) *almost exclusively on an economic basis*. Political agitation on *such* lines was recognized and, as we have seen, even recommended by *Workers' Thought* and the Self-Emancipation Group. *Workers' Cause* should have *strongly condemned* the fact that the useful work of economic agitation was accompanied by the harmful restriction of the political struggle; instead, it declares the means most widely app*lied* (*by the Economists*) to be the most widely app*licable*! It is not surprising that when we call these people Economists, they can do nothing but pour every manner of abuse upon us; call us 'mystifiers', 'disrupters', 'papal nuncios', and 'slanderers'[8]; go complaining to the whole world that we have mortally offended them; and declare almost on oath that 'not a single Social-Democratic organization is now tinged with Economism'.[9] Oh, those evil, slanderous politicians! They must have deliberately invented this Economism, out of sheer hatred of mankind, in order mortally to offend other people.

What concrete, real meaning attaches to Martynov's words when he sets before Social-Democracy the task of 'lending the economic struggle itself a political character'? The economic struggle is the collective struggle of the workers against their employers for better terms *in the sale of their labour-power*, for better living and working conditions. This struggle is necessarily a trade union struggle, because working conditions differ greatly in different trades, and, consequently, the struggle *to improve* them can only be conducted on the basis of trade organizations (in the Western countries, through trade unions; in Russia, through temporary trade associations and through leaflets, etc.). Lending 'the economic struggle itself a political character' means, therefore, striving to secure satisfaction of these trade demands, the improvement of working conditions in each separate trade by means of 'legislative and administrative measures' (as Martynov puts it on the ensuing page of his article, p. 43). This is precisely what all workers' trade unions do and always have done. Read the works of the soundly scientific (and 'soundly' opportunist)

Mr and Mrs Webb and you will see that the British trade unions long ago recognized, and have long been carrying out, the task of 'lending the economic struggle itself a political character'; they have long been fighting for the right to strike, for the removal of all legal hindrances to the co-operative and trade union movements, for laws to protect women and children, for the improvement of labour conditions by means of health and factory legislation, etc.

Thus, the pompous phrase about 'lending the economic struggle *itself* a political character', which sounds so 'terrifically' profound and revolutionary, serves as a screen to conceal what is in fact the traditional striving *to degrade* Social-Democratic politics to the level of trade union politics. Under the guise of rectifying the one-sidedness of *Spark*, which, it is alleged, places 'the revolutionizing of dogma higher than the revolutionizing of life',[10] we are presented with the *struggle for economic reforms* as if it were something entirely new. In point of fact, the phrase 'lending the economic struggle itself a political character' means nothing more than the struggle for economic reforms. Martynov himself might have come to this simple conclusion, had he pondered over the significance of his own words. 'Our Party,' he says, training his heaviest guns on *The Spark*, 'could and should have presented concrete demands to the government for legislative and administrative measures against economic exploitation, unemployment, famine, etc.' (*Workers' Cause*, No. 10, pp. 42–43). Concrete demands for measures – does not this mean demands for social reforms? Again we ask the impartial reader: Are we slandering the readers of *Workers' Cause* by calling them concealed Bernsteinians when, as their point of *disagreement* with *The Spark*, they advance their thesis on the necessity of struggling for economic reforms?

Revolutionary Social-Democracy has always included the struggle for reforms as part of its activities. But it utilizes 'economic' agitation for the purpose of presenting to the government, not only demands for all sorts of measures, but also (and primarily) the demand that it cease to be an autocratic government. Moreover, it considers it its duty to present this demand to the government on the basis, *not* of the economic struggle *alone*, but of all manifestations in general of public and political life. In a word, it subordinates the struggle for reforms, as the part to the whole, to the revolutionary struggle for freedom and for socialism. Martynov, however, resuscitates the theory of stages in a new form and strives to prescribe, as it were, an exclusively economic path of development for the political struggle. By advancing at this moment, when the revolutionary movement is on the upgrade, an alleged special 'task' of struggling for reforms, he is dragging the Party backwards and is playing into the hands of both 'Economist' and liberal opportunism.

To proceed. Shamefacedly hiding the struggle for reforms behind the pompous thesis of 'lending the economic struggle itself a political character', Martynov advanced, as if it were a special point, *exclusively economic* (indeed, exclusively factory) *reforms*. As to the reason for his doing that, we do not know it. Carelessness, perhaps? Yet if he had in mind something else besides 'factory' reforms, then the whole of his thesis, which we have cited, loses all sense. Perhaps he did it because he considers it possible and probable that the government will make 'concessions' only in the economic sphere?[11] If so, then it is a strange delusion. Concessions are also possible and are made in the sphere of legislation concerning flogging, passports, land redemption payments, religious sects, the censorship, etc., etc. 'Economic' concessions (or pseudo-concessions) are, of course, the cheapest and most advantageous from the government's point of view, because by these means it hopes to win the confidence of the working masses. For this very reason, we Social-Democrats *must not* under any circumstances or in any way whatever create grounds for the belief (or the misunderstanding) that we attach greater value to economic reforms, or that we regard them as being particularly important, etc. 'Such demands,' writes Martynov, speaking of the concrete demands for legislative and administrative measures referred to above, 'would not be merely a hollow sound, because, promising certain palpable results, they might be actively supported by the working masses . . .' We are not Economists, oh no! We only cringe as slavishly before the 'palpableness' of concrete results as do the Bernsteins, the Prokopoviches, the Struves, the R.M.s, and *tutti quanti*! We only wish to make it understood (together with Nartsis Tuporylov) that all which 'does not promise palpable results' is merely a 'hollow sound'! We are only trying to argue as if the working masses were incapable (and had not already proved their capabilities, notwithstanding those who ascribe their own philistinism to them) of actively supporting *every* protest against the autocracy, even if it *promises absolutely no palpable results whatever*!

Let us take, for example, the very 'measures' for the relief of unemployment and the famine that Martynov himself advances. *Workers' Cause* is engaged, judging by what it has promised, in drawing up and elaborating a programme of 'concrete [in the form of bills?] demands for legislative and administrative measures', 'promising palpable results', while *The Spark*, which 'constantly places the revolutionizing of dogma higher than the revolutionizing of life', has tried to explain the inseparable connection between unemployment and the whole capitalist system, has given warning that 'famine is coming', has exposed the police 'fight against the famine-stricken', and the outrageous 'provisional penal servitude regulations'; and *Dawn* has published a special reprint, in the form of an agitational pamphlet, of a section of its 'Review of Home Affairs', dealing with the famine.[12] But good God! How 'one-sided' were these incorrigibly narrow and orthodox doctrinaires, how deaf to the calls of 'life itself'! Their articles contained – oh horror! – *not a single*, can you imagine it? – not a single 'concrete demand' 'promising palpable results'! Poor doctrinaires! They ought to be sent to Krichevsky and Martynov to be taught that tactics are a process of growth, of that which grows, etc., and that the Economic struggle *itself* should be given a political character!

'In addition to its immediate revolutionary significance, the economic struggle of the workers against the employers and the government ["*economic* struggle against the government"!] has also this significance: it constantly brings home to the workers the fact that they have no political rights' (Martynov, p. 44). We quote this passage, not in order to repeat for the hundredth and thousandth time what has been said above, but in order to express particular thanks to Martynov for this excellent new formula: 'the economic struggle of the workers against the employers and the government.' What a pearl! With what inimitable skill and mastery in eliminating all partial disagreements and shades of differences among Economists this clear and concise proposition expresses the *quintessence* of Economism, from summoning the workers 'to the political struggle, which they carry on in the general interest, for the improvement of the conditions of all the workers', continuing through the theory of stages, and ending in the resolution of the conference on the 'most widely applicable', etc. 'Economic struggle against the government' is precisely trade unionist politics, which is still very far from being Social-Democratic politics . . .

NOTES

1. In complete contrast to the contemporary meaning, at the turn of the century revolutionary working-class political parties were called 'social-democratic'. The social-democratic parties of the Second International established in 1889, in the first decades of this century gradually decayed into reformism and formed bourgeois coalition governments. The Communist International was then formed to coordinate the international movement, but as this became a tool of Stalin, the Fourth International was founded in 1938 to continue the revolutionary struggle. (Editors).

2. Trade unionism does not exclude 'politics' altogether, as some imagine. Trade unions have always conducted some political (but not Social-Democratic) agitation and struggle. We shall deal with the difference between trade union politics and Social-Democratic politics in the next chapter.

3. A. A. Vaneyev died in Eastern Siberia in 1899 from consumption, which he contracted during solitary confinement in prison prior to his banishment. That is why we considered it possible to publish the above information, the authenticity of which we guarantee, for it comes from persons who were closely and directly acquainted with A. A. Vaneyev.

4. See Collected Works, vol. 2, pp. 87–92.

5. To avoid misunderstanding, we must point out that here, and throughout this pamphlet, by economic struggle, we imply (in keeping with the accepted usage among us) the 'practical economic struggle', which Engels described as 'resistance to the capitalists', and which in free countries is known as the organized-labour, syndical, or trade union struggle.

6. In the present chapter we deal only with the political struggle, in its broader or narrower meaning. Therefore, we note only in passing, merely as a curiosity, Workers' Cause charge that The Spark is 'too restrained' in regard to the economic struggle (Two Conferences, p. 27, rehashed by Martynov in his pamphlet, Social-Democracy and the Working Class). If the accusers computed by the hundredweights or reams (as they are so fond of doing) any given year's discussion of the economic struggle in the industrial section of The Spark in comparison with the corresponding sections of Workers' Cause and Workers' Thought combined, they would easily see that the latter lag behind even in this respect. Apparently, the realization of this simple

truth compels them to resort to arguments that clearly reveal their confusion. *The Spark*, they write, 'willy-nilly [!] is compelled [!] to reckon
with the imperative demands of life and to publish at least [!!] correspondence about the working-class movement' (*Two Conferences*, p. 27).
Now this is really a crushing argument!

7. We say 'in general', because *Workers' Cause* speaks of general
principles and of the general tasks of the Party as a whole. Undoubtedly, cases occur in practice when politics really *must* follow economics,
but only Economists can speak of this in a resolution intended to apply
to the whole of Russia. Cases do occur when *it is possible* 'right from
the beginning' to carry on political agitation 'exclusively on an
economic basis'; yet *Workers' Cause* came in the end to the conclusion that 'there is no need for this whatever' (*Two Conferences*, p. 11).
In the following chapter, we shall show that the tactics of the 'politicians' and revolutionaries not only do not ignore the trade union
tasks of Social-Democracy, but that, on the contrary, they alone *can
secure* their consistent fulfilment.

8. These are the precise expressions used in *Two Conferences*, pp. 31,
32, 28, and 30.

9. *Two Conferences*, p. 32.

10. *Workers' Cause* No. 10, p. 60. This is the Martynov variation
of the application, which we have characterized above, of the thesis
'Every step of real movement is more important than a dozen programmes' to the present chaotic state of our movement. In fact, this is
merely a translation into Russian of the notorious Bernsteinian
sentence: 'The movement is everything, the final aim is nothing.'

11. P. 43. 'Of course, when we advise the workers to present certain
economic demands to the government, we do so because in the *economic*
sphere the autocratic government is, of necessity, prepared to make
certain concessions.'

12. See V. I. LENIN, *Collected Works*, vol. 5, pp. 253–74.

6 Marxism and Trade Unionism
L. Trotsky

Excerpts from: 'Leon Trotsky On the Trade Unions,' pp. 53-7, 59-62, 68-75, Pathfinder Press, 1969. By permission of the executor of L. Trotsky's literary estate.

THE UNIONS IN BRITAIN (1933)

The trade union question remains the most important question of proletarian policy in Great Britain, as well as in the majority of old capitalist countries. The mistakes of the Comintern in this field are innumerable. No wonder: a party's inability to establish correct relations with the class reveals itself most glaringly in the area of the trade union movement. That is why I consider it necessary to dwell on this question.

The trade unions were formed during the period of the growth and rise of capitalism. They had as their task the raising of the material and cultural level of the proletariat and the extension of its political rights. This work, which in England lasted over a century, gave the trade unions tremendous authority among the workers. The decay of British capitalism, under the conditions of decline of the world capitalist system, undermined the basis for the reformist work of the trade unions. Capitalism can continue to maintain itself only by lowering the standard of living of the working class. Under these conditions trade unions can either transform themselves into revolutionary organizations or become lieutenants of capital in the intensified exploitation of the workers. The trade union bureaucracy, which has satisfactorily solved its own social problem, took the second path. It turned all the accumulated authority of the trade unions against the socialist revolution and even against any attempts of the workers to resist the attacks of capital and reaction.

From that point on, the most important task of the revolutionary party became the liberation of the workers from the reactionary influence of the trade union bureaucracy. In this decisive field the Comintern revealed complete inadequacy. In 1926-7, especially in the period of the miners' strike and the General Strike, that is, at the time of the greatest crimes and betrayals of the General Council of the trade unions, the Comintern obsequiously toadied to the highly placed strikebreakers, cloaked them with its authority in the eyes of the masses, and helped them remain in the saddle. That is how the Minority Movement was struck a mortal blow. Frightened by the results of its own work, the Comintern bureaucracy went to the extreme of ultraradicalism. The fatal excesses of the 'third period' were due to the desire of the small Communist minority to act as though it had a majority behind it. Isolating itself more and more from the working class, the Communist Party counterposed to the trade unions, which embraced millions of workers, its own trade union organizations, highly obedient to the leadership of the Comintern but separated by an abyss from the working class. No better favour could be done for the trade union bureaucracy. Had it been within its power to award the Order of the Garter, it should have so decorated all the leaders of the Comintern and Profintern.

As was said, the trade unions now play not a progressive but a reactionary role. Nevertheless they still embrace millions of workers. One must not think that the workers are blind and do not see the change in the historic role of the trade unions. But what is to be done? The revolutionary road is seriously compromised in the eyes of the left wing of the workers by the zig-zags and adventures of official Communism. The workers say to themselves: The trade unions are bad, but without them it might be even worse. This is the psychology of being in a blind alley. Meanwhile, the trade union bureaucracy persecutes the revolutionary workers ever more boldly, ever more impudently replacing internal democracy by the arbitrary action of a clique, in essence transforming the trade unions into some sort of concentration camp for the workers during the decline of capitalism.

Under these conditions, the thought easily arises: Is it not possible to bypass the trade unions? Is it not possible to replace them by some sort of fresh, uncorrupted organization of the type of revolutionary trade unions, shop committees, soviets, and the like? The fundamental mistake of such attempts lies in that they reduce to organizational experiments the great political problem of how to free the masses from the influence of the trade union bureaucracy. It is not enough to offer the masses a new address. It is necessary to seek out the masses where they are and to lead them.

Impatient leftists sometimes say that it is absolutely impossible to win over the trade unions because the bureaucracy uses the organizations' internal régimes for preserving its own interests, resorting to the basest machinations, repressions and plain crookedness, in the spirit of the parliamentary oligarchy of the era of 'rotten boroughs'. Why then waste time and energy? This argument reduces itself in reality to giving up the actual struggle to win the masses, using the corrupt character of the trade union bureaucracy as a pretext. This argument can be developed further: Why not abandon revolutionary work altogether, considering the repressions and provocations on the part of the government bureaucracy? There exists no principled difference here, since the trade union bureaucracy has definitely become a part of the capitalist apparatus, economic and governmental. It is absurd to think that it would be possible to work against the trade union bureaucracy with its own help, or only with its consent. Insofar as it defends itself by persecutions, violence, expulsions, frequently resorting to the assistance of government authorities, we must learn to work in the trade unions *discreetly*, finding a common language with the masses but not revealing ourselves prematurely to the bureaucracy. It is precisely in the present epoch, when the reformist bureaucracy of the proletariat has transformed itself into the economic police of capital, that revolutionary work in the trade unions, performed intelligently and systematically, may yield decisive results in a comparatively short time.

We do not at all mean by this that the revolutionary party has any guarantee that the trade unions will be completely won over to the socialist revolution. The problem is not so simple. The trade union apparatus has attained for itself great independence from the masses. The bureaucracy is capable of retaining its positions a long time after the masses have turned against it. But it is precisely such a situation, where the masses are already hostile to the trade union bureaucracy but where the bureaucracy is still capable of misrepresenting the opinion of the organization and of sabotaging new elections, that is most favourable for the creation of shop committees, workers' councils, and other organizations for the immediate needs of any given moment. Even in Russia, where the trade unions did not have anything like the powerful traditions of the British trade unions, the October Revolution occurred with Mensheviks predominant in the administration of the trade unions. Having lost the masses, these administrations were still capable of sabotaging elections in the apparatus, although already powerless to sabotage the proletarian revolution.

It is absolutely necessary right now to prepare the minds of the advanced workers for the idea of creating shop committees and workers' councils at the moment of a sharp change. But it would be the greatest mistake to 'play around' in practice with the slogan of shop councils, consoling oneself, with this 'idea', for the lack of real work and real influence in the trade unions. To counterpose to the existing trade unions the abstract idea of workers' councils would mean setting against oneself not only the bureaucracy but also the masses, thus depriving oneself of the possibility of preparing the ground for the creation of workers' councils.

In this the Comintern has gained not a little experience: having created obedient, that is, purely Communist, trade unions, it counterposed its sections to the working masses in a hostile manner and thereby doomed itself to complete impotence. This is one of the most important causes of the collapse of the German Communist Party. It is true that the British Communist Party, insofar as I am informed, opposes the slogan of workers' councils under the present conditions. Superficially, this may seem like a realistic appraisal of the situation. In reality, the British Communist Party rejects only *one form* of political adventurism for *another*, more hysterical, form. The theory and practice of social-fascism and the rejection of the policy of the united front creates insurmountable obstacles to working in the trade unions, since each trade union is, by its very nature, the arena of an ongoing united front of revolutionary parties with reformist and non-party masses. To the extent that the British Communist Party proved incapable, even after the German tragedy, of learning anything and arming itself anew, to that extent can an alliance with it pull to the bottom even the ILP, which only recently has entered a period of revolutionary apprenticeship.

Pseudo-Communists will, no doubt, refer to the last congress of trade unions, which declared that there could be no united front with Communists against fascism. It would be the greatest folly to accept this piece of wisdom as the final verdict of history. The trade union bureaucrats can permit themselves such boastful formulas only because they are not immediately threatened by fascism, or by Communism. When the hammer of fascism is raised over the head of the trade unions, then, with a correct policy of the revolutionary party, the trade union masses will show an irresistible urge for an alliance with the revolutionary wing and will carry with them on to this path even a certain portion of the apparatus. Contrariwise, if Communism should become a decisive force, threatening the General Councils with the loss of positions, honours, and income, Messrs Citrine and Company would undoubtedly enter into a bloc with Mosley and Company against the Communists. Thus, in August 1917, the Russian Mensheviks and Social-Revolutionaries together with the Bolsheviks repulsed General Kornilov. Two months later, in October, they were fighting hand in hand with the Kornilovists against the Bolsheviks. And in the first months of 1917, when the reformists were still strong, they spouted, just like Citrine and Company, about the impossibility of them making an alliance with a dictatorship either of the right or left.

The revolutionary proletarian party must be welded together by a clear understanding of its historic tasks. This presupposes a scientifically based programme. At the same time, the revolutionary party must know how to establish correct relations with the class. This presupposes a policy of revolutionary realism, equally removed from opportunistic vagueness and sectarian aloofness. From the point of view of both these closely connected criteria, the ILP should review its relation to the Comintern as well as to all other organizations and tendencies within the working class. This concerns first of all the fate of the ILP itself.

TRADE UNIONS IN THE TRANSITIONAL EPOCH (1938)

In the struggle for partial and transitional demands, the workers now more than ever before need mass organizations, principally trade unions. The powerful growth of trade unionism in France and the United States is the best refutation of the preachments of those ultra-left doctrinaires who have been teaching that trade unions have 'outlived their usefulness'.

The Bolshevik-Leninist stands in the frontline trenches of all kinds of struggles, even when they involve only the most modest material interests or democratic rights of the working class. He takes active part in mass trade unions for the purpose of strengthening them and raising their spirit of militancy. He fights uncompromisingly against any attempt to subordinate the unions to the bourgeois state and bind the proletariat to 'compulsory arbitration' and every other form of police guardianship – not only fascist but also 'democratic'. Only on the basis of such work within the trade unions is successful struggle possible against the reformists, including those of the Stalinist bureaucracy. Sectarian attempts to build or preserve small 'revolutionary' unions, as a second edition of the party, signify in actuality the renouncing of the struggle for leadership of the working class. It is necessary to establish this firm rule: self-isolation of the capitulationist variety from mass trade unions, which is tantamount to a betrayal of the revolution, is incompatible with membership in the Fourth International.

At the same time, the Fourth International resolutely rejects and condemns trade union fetishism, equally characteristic of trade unionists and syndicalists.

(a) Trade unions do not offer and, in line with their task, composition, and manner of recruiting membership, cannot offer a finished revolutionary programme; in consequence, they cannot replace the *party*. The building of national revolutionary parties as sections of the Fourth International is the central task of the transitional epoch.

(b) Trade unions, even the most powerful, embrace no more than 20 to 25 per cent of the working class, and at that, predominantly the more skilled and better-paid layers. The more oppressed majority of the working class is drawn only episodically into the struggle, during a period of exceptional upsurges in the labour movement. During such moments it is necessary to create organizations *ad hoc*, embracing the whole fighting mass: strike committees, factory committees and, finally, soviets.

(c) As organizations expressive of the top layers of the proletariat, trade unions, as witnessed by all past historical experience, including the fresh experience of the anarcho-syndicalist unions in Spain, developed powerful tendencies towards compromise with the bourgeois-democratic régime. In periods of acute class struggle, the leading bodies of the trade unions aim to become masters of the mass movement in order to render it harmless. This is already occurring during the period of simple strikes, especially in the case of the mass sit-down strikes which shake the principle of bourgeois property. In time of war or revolution, when the bourgeoisie is plunged into exceptional difficulties, the trade union leaders usually become bourgeois ministers.

Therefore, the sections of the Fourth International should always strive not only to renew the top leadership of the trade unions, boldly and resolutely in critical moments advancing new militant leaders in place of routine functionaries and careerists, but also to create in all possible instances independent militant organizations corresponding more closely to the tasks of mass struggle against bourgeois society; and if necessary, not flinching even in the face of a direct break with the conservative apparatus of the trade unions. If it be criminal to turn one's back on mass organizations for the sake of fostering sectarian fictions, it is no less so to passively tolerate subordination of the revolutionary mass movement to the control of openly reactionary or disguised conservative ('progressive') bureaucratic cliques. Trade unions are not ends in themselves; they are but means along the road to proletarian revolution.

Factory Committees

During a transitional epoch, the workers' movement does not have a systematic and well-balanced, but a feverish and explosive character. Slogans as well as organizational forms should be subordinated to the indices of the movement. On guard against routine handling of a situation as against a plague, the leadership should respond sensitively to the initiative of the masses.

Sit-down strikes, the latest expression of this kind of initiative, go beyond the limits of 'normal' capitalist procedure. Independently of the demands of the strikers, the temporary seizure of factories deals a blow to the idol, capitalist property. Every sit-down strike poses in a practical manner the question of who is boss of the factory: the capitalist or the workers?

If the sit-down strike raises this question episodically, the *factory committee* gives it organized expression. Elected by all the factory employees, the factory committee immediately creates a counterweight to the will of the administration.

To the reformist criticism of bosses of the so-called 'economic royalist' type like Ford in contradistinction to 'good', 'democratic' exploiters, we counterpose the slogan of factory committees as centres of struggle against both the first and the second.

Trade union bureaucrats will as a general rule resist the creation of factory committees, just as they resist every bold step taken along the road of mobilizing the masses.

However, the wider the sweep of the movement, the easier will it be to break this resistance. Where the closed shop has already been instituted in 'peaceful' times, the committee will formally coincide with the usual organ of the trade union, but will renew its personnel and widen its functions. The prime significance of the committee, however, lies in the fact that it becomes the militant staff for such working-class layers as the trade union is usually incapable of moving to action. It is precisely from these more oppressed layers that the most self-sacrificing battalions of the revolution will come.

From the moment that the committee makes its appearance, a factual dual power is established in the factory. By its very essence it represents the transitional state, because it includes in itself two irreconcilable régimes: the capitalist and the proletarian. The fundamental significance of factory committees is precisely contained in the fact that they open the doors if not to a direct revolutionary, then to a prerevolutionary period – between the bourgeois and the proletarian régimes. That the propagation of the factory committee idea is neither premature nor artificial is amply attested to by the waves of sit-down strikes spreading through several countries. New waves of this type will be inevitable in the immediate future. It is necessary to begin a campaign in favour of factory committees in time, in order not to be caught unawares.

TRADE UNIONS IN THE EPOCH OF IMPERIALIST DECAY (1940)

There is one common feature in the development, or more correctly the degeneration, of modern trade union organizations throughout the world: it is their drawing closely to and growing together with the state power. This process is equally characteristic of the neutral, the social-democratic, the communist, and 'anarchist' trade unions. This fact alone shows that the tendency towards 'growing together' is intrinsic not in this or that doctrine as such but derives from social conditions common for all unions.

Monopoly capitalism does not rest on competition and free private initiative but on centralized command. The capitalist cliques at the head of mighty trusts, syndicates, banking consortiums, etc., view economic life from the very same heights as does state power; and they require at every step the collaboration of the latter. In their turn the trade unions in the most important branches of industry find themselves deprived of the possibility of profiting by the competition among the different enterprises. They have to confront a centralized capitalist adversary, intimately bound up with state power. Hence flows the need of the trade unions – insofar as they remain on reformist positions, i.e., on positions of adapting themselves to private property – to adapt themselves to the capitalist state and to contend for its co-operation. In the eyes of the bureaucracy of the trade union movement, the chief task lies in 'freeing' the state from the embrace of capitalism, in weakening its dependence on trusts, in pulling it over to their side. This position is in complete harmony with the social position of the labour aristocracy and the labour bureaucracy, who fight for a crumb in the share of superprofits of imperialist capitalism. The labour bureaucrats do their level best in words and deeds to demonstrate to the 'democratic' state how reliable and indispensable they are in peacetime and especially in time of war. By transforming the trade unions into organs of the state, fascism invents nothing new; it merely draws to their ultimate conclusion the tendencies inherent in imperialism.

Colonial and semi-colonial countries are under the sway, not of native capitalism but of foreign imperialism. However, this does not weaken but, on the contrary, strengthens the need of direct, daily, practical ties between the magnates of capitalism and the governments which are in essence subject to them – the governments of colonial or semi-colonial countries. Inasmuch as imperialist capitalism creates both in colonies and semi-colonies a stratum of labour aristocracy and bureaucracy, the latter requires the support of colonial and semi-colonial governments as protectors, patrons, and sometimes as arbitrators. This constitutes the most important social basis for the Bonapartist and semi-Bonapartist character of governments in the colonies and in backward countries generally. This likewise constitutes the basis for the dependence of reformist unions upon the state.

In Mexico the trade unions have been transformed by law into semi-state institutions and have, in the nature of things, assumed a semi-totalitarian character. The statization of the trade unions was, according to the conception of the legislators, introduced in the interests of the workers, in order to assure them an influence upon governmental and economic life. But insofar as foreign imperialist capitalism dominates the national state and insofar as it is able, with the assistance of internal reactionary forces, to overthrow the unstable democracy and replace it with outright fascist dictatorship, to that extent the legislation relating to the trade unions can easily become a weapon in the hands of imperialist dictatorship.

From the foregoing it seems, at first sight, easy to draw the conclusion that the trade unions cease to be trade unions in the imperialist epoch. They leave almost no room at all for workers' democracy which, in the good old days when free trade ruled on the economic arena, constituted the content of the inner life of labour organization. In the absence of workers' democracy there cannot be any free struggle for influence over the trade union membership. And because of this, the chief arena of work for revolutionists within the trade unions disappears. Such a position, however, would be false to the core. We cannot select the arena and the conditions for our activity to suit our own likes and dislikes. It is infinitely more difficult to fight in a totalitarian or a semi-totalitarian state for influence over the working masses than in a democracy. The very same thing likewise applies to trade unions whose fate reflects the change in the destiny of capitalist states. We cannot renounce the struggle for influence over workers in Germany merely because the totalitarian régime makes such work extremely difficult there. We cannot, in precisely the same way, renounce the struggle within the compulsory labour organizations created by fascism. All the less so can we renounce internal systematic work in trade unions of totalitarian and semi-totalitarian type merely because they depend directly or indirectly on the workers' state or because the bureaucracy deprives the revolutionists of the possibility of working freely within these trade unions. It is necessary to conduct a struggle under all those concrete conditions which have been created by the preceding developments, including therein the mistakes of the working class and the crimes of its leaders. In the fascist and semi-fascist countries it is impossible to carry on revolutionary work that is not underground, illegal, conspiratorial. Within the totalitarian and semi-totalitarian unions it is impossible or well-nigh impossible to carry on any except conspiratorial work. It is necessary to adapt ourselves to the concrete conditions existing in the trade unions of every given country in order to mobilize the masses, not only against the bourgeoisie, but also against the totalitarian régime within the trade unions themselves and against the leaders enforcing this régime. The primary slogan for this struggle is: *complete and unconditional independence of the trade unions in relation to the capitalist state*. This means a struggle to turn the trade unions into the organs of the broad exploited masses and not the organs of a labour aristocracy.

The second slogan is: *trade union democracy*. This second slogan flows directly from the first and presupposes for its realization the complete freedom of the trade unions from the imperialist or colonial state.

In other words, the trade unions in the present epoch cannot simply be the organs of democracy as they were in the epoch of free capitalism and they cannot any longer remain politically neutral, that is, limit themselves to serving the daily needs of the working class. They cannot any longer be anarchistic, i.e., ignore the decisive influence of the state on the life of people and classes. They can no longer be reformist, because the objective conditions leave no room for any serious and lasting reforms. The trade unions of our time can either serve as secondary instruments of imperialist capitalism for the subordination and disciplining of workers and for obstructing the revolution, or, on the contrary, the trade unions can become the instruments of the revolutionary movement of the proletariat.

The neutrality of trade unions is completely and irretrievably a thing of the past – gone, together with the free bourgeois democracy.

From what has been said it follows quite clearly that, in spite of the progressive degeneration of trade unions and their growing together with the imperialist state, the work within the trade unions not only does not lose any of its importance but remains as before and becomes in a certain sense even more important work than ever for every revolutionary party. The matter at issue is essentially the struggle for influence over the working class. Every organization, every party, every faction which permits itself an ultimatistic position in relation to the trade union, i.e., in essence turns its back upon the working class, merely because of displeasure with its organization, every such organization is destined to perish. And it must be said it deserves to perish.

Inasmuch as the chief role in backward countries is not played by national but by foreign capitalism, the national bourgeoisie occupies, in the sense of its social position, a much more minor position than corresponds with the development of industry. Inasmuch as foreign capital does not import workers but proletarianizes the native population, the national proletariat soon begins playing the most important role in the life of the country. In these conditions the national government, to the extent that it tries to show resistance to foreign capital, is compelled to a greater or lesser degree to lean on the proletariat. On the other hand, the governments of those backward countries which consider it inescapable or more profitable for themselves to march shoulder to shoulder with foreign capital, destroy the labour organizations and institute a more or less totalitarian régime. Thus, the feebleness of the national bourgeoisie, the absence of traditions of municipal self-government, the pressure of foreign capitalism, and the relatively rapid growth of the proletariat, cut the ground from under any kind of stable democratic régime. The governments of backward, i.e., colonial and semi-colonial, countries by and large assume a Bonapartist or semi-Bonapartist character; they differ from one another in that some try to orient in a democratic direction, seeking support among workers and peasants, while others instal a form close to military-police dictatorship. This likewise determines the fate of the trade unions. They either stand under the special patronage of the state or they are subjected to cruel persecution. Patronage on the part of the state is dictated by two tasks that confront it: first, to draw the working class closer, thus gaining a support for resistance against excessive pretensions on the part of imperialism; and, at the same time, to discipline the workers themselves by placing them under the control of a bureaucracy.

Monopoly capitalism is less and less willing to reconcile itself to the independence of trade unions. It demands of the reformist bureaucracy and the labour aristocracy, who pick up the crumbs from its banquet table, that they become transformed into its political police before the eyes of the working class. If that is not achieved, the labour bureaucracy is driven away and replaced by the fascists. Incidentally, all the efforts of the labour aristocracy in the service of imperialism cannot in the long run save them from destruction.

The intensification of class contradictions within each country, the intensification of antagonisms between one country and another, produce a situation in which imperialist capitalism can tolerate (i.e., up to a certain time) a reformist bureaucracy only if the latter serves directly as a petty but active stockholder of its imperialist enterprises, of its plans and programmes within the country as well as on the world arena. Social reformism must become transformed into social imperialism in order to prolong its existence, but only prolong it, and nothing more. Because along this road there is no way out in general.

Does this mean that in the epoch of imperialism independent trade unions are generally impossible? It would be fundamentally incorrect to pose the question this way. Impossible are the independent or semi-independent reformist trade unions. Wholly possible are revolutionary trade unions which not only are not stockholders of imperialist policy but which set as their task the direct overthrow of the rule of capitalism. In the epoch of imperialist decay the trade unions can be really independent only to the extent that they are conscious of being, in action, the organs of proletarian revolution. In this sense, the programme of transitional demands adopted by the last congress of the Fourth International is not only the programme for the activity of the party but in its fundamental features it is the programme for activity of the trade unions.

The development of backward countries is characterized by its combined character. In other words, the last word of imperialist technology, economics, and politics is combined in these countries with traditional backwardness and primitiveness. This law can be observed in the most diverse spheres of the development of colonial and semi-colonial countries, including the sphere of the trade union movement. Imperialist capitalism operates here in its most cynical and naked form. It transports to virgin soil the most perfected methods of its tyrannical rule.

In the trade union movement throughout the world there is to be observed in the last period a swing to the right and the suppression of internal democracy. In England, the Minority Movement in the trade unions has been crushed (not without the assistance of Moscow); the leaders of the trade union movement are today, especially in the field of foreign policy, the obedient agents of the Conservative Party. In France there was no room for an independent existence for Stalinist trade unions; they united with the so-called anarcho-syndicalist trade unions under the leadership of Jouhaux, and as a result of this unification there was a general shift of the trade union movement not to the left but to the right. The leadership of the CGT is the most direct and open agency of French imperialist capitalism.

In the United States the trade union movement has passed through the most stormy history in recent years. The rise of the CIO is incontrovertible evidence of the revolutionary tendencies within the working masses. Indicative and noteworthy in the highest degree, however, is the fact that the new 'leftist' trade union organization was no sooner founded than it fell into the steel embrace of the imperialist state. The struggle among the tops between the old federation and the new is reducible in large measure to the struggle for the sympathy and support of Roosevelt and his cabinet.

No less graphic, although in a different sense, is the picture of the development or the degeneration of the trade union movement in Spain. In the socialist trade unions all those leading elements which to any degree represented the independence of the trade union movement were pushed out. As regards the anarcho-syndicalist unions, they were transformed into the instrument of the bourgeois republicans; the anarcho-syndicalist leaders became conservative bourgeois ministers. The fact that this metamorphosis took place in conditions of civil war does not weaken its significance. War is the continuation of the self-same policies. It speeds up processes, exposes their basic features, destroys all that is rotten, false, equivocal, and lays bare all that is essential. The shift of the trade unions to the right was due to the sharpening of class and international contradictions. The leaders of the trade union movement sensed or understood, or were given to understand, that now was no time to play the game of opposition. Every oppositional movement within the trade union movement, especially among the tops, threatens to provoke a stormy movement of the masses and to create difficulties for national imperialism. Hence flows the swing of the trade unions to the right and the suppression of workers' democracy within the unions. The basic feature, the swing towards the totalitarian régime, passes through the labour movement of the whole world.

We should also recall Holland, where the reformist and the trade union movement was not only a reliable prop of imperialist capitalism, but where the so-called anarcho-syndicalist organization also was actually under the control of the imperialist government. The secretary of this organization, Sneevliet, in spite of his platonic sympathies for the Fourth International, was as deputy in the Dutch Parliament most concerned lest the wrath of the government descend upon his trade union organization.

In the United States the Department of Labor with its leftist bureaucracy has as its task the subordination of the trade union movement to the democratic state, and it must be said that this task has up to now been solved with some success.

The nationalization of railways and oil fields in Mexico has, of course, nothing in common with socialism. It is a measure of state capitalism in a backward country which in this way seeks to defend itself on the one hand against foreign imperialism and on the other against its own proletariat. The management of railways, oil fields, etc., through labour organizations has nothing in common with workers' control over industry, for in the essence of the matter the management is effected through the labour bureaucracy which is independent of the workers but, in return, completely dependent on the bourgeois state. This measure on the part of the ruling class pursues the aim of disciplining the working class, making it more industrious in the service of the common interests of the state, which appear on the surface to merge with the interests of the working class itself. As a matter of fact, the whole task of the bourgeoisie consists in liquidating the trade unions as organs of the class struggle and substituting in their place the trade union bureaucracy as the organ of the leadership over the workers by the bourgeois state. In these conditions, the task of the revolutionary vanguard is to conduct a struggle for the complete independence of the trade unions and for the introduction of actual workers' control over the present union bureaucracy, which has been turned into the administration of railways, oil enterprises, and so on.

Events of the last period (before the war) have revealed with especial clarity that anarchism, which in point of theory is always only liberalism drawn to its extremes, was, in practice, peaceful propaganda within the democratic republic, the protection of which it required. If we leave aside individual terrorist acts, etc., anarchism, as a system of mass movement and politics, presented only propaganda material under the peaceful protection of the laws. In conditions of crisis the anarchists always did the opposite of what they taught in peacetimes. This was pointed out by Marx himself in connection with the Paris Commune. And it was repeated on a far more colossal scale in the experience of the Spanish Revolution.

Democratic unions in the old sense of the term – bodies where, in the framework of one and the same mass organization, different tendencies struggle more or less freely – can no longer exist. Just as it is impossible to bring back the bourgeois-democratic state, so is it impossible to bring back the old workers' democracy. The fate of the one reflects the fate of the other. As a matter of fact, the independence of the trade unions in the class sense, in their relations to the bourgeois state, can, in the present conditions, be assured only by a completely revolutionary leadership, that is, the leadership of the Fourth International. This leadership, naturally, must and can be rational and assure the unions the maximum of democracy conceivable under the present concrete conditions. But without the political leadership of the Fourth International the independence of the trade unions is impossible.[1]

NOTES

1. As the Communist International, established in 1919, declined from a revolutionary body into an instrument of Russian foreign policy, it became subservient to Stalin. According to Stalin social democracy was the moderate wing of fascism, that is 'social fascism', therefore there was no question of joining with the social democrats in a united front against fascism. This theory was responsible for profoundly weakening the opposition to the rise of fascism. (Editors).

Part Two
The Revolutionary Tradition

Despite the assumption of orthodox historical analysis that consensus orientated collective bargaining is the dominant tradition in British industrial relations, and the condescending dismissal of those developments which appear to contradict this view, in fact the very birth of the trade union movement occurred during the progress of large-scale strikes, when combinations of workmen developed into permanent organizations, surviving and increasing despite severe legal repression, and each surge in membership growth of the trade unions has been associated with a reawakened militancy in confrontation with employers and government. Finally there is an important tradition of revolutionary philosophy and action which has emerged in strength in particular historical contexts within the British labour movement. The following two readings illustrate the extensive power of this tradition during 1910–20:

> However it is measured – by the sheer growth of the numbers in the unions; by the upsurge of socialist organization, campaigning, ideas; by the intensity and range of debate over the tactics and strategy of the struggle for socialism; even by the victory (albeit the hollow victory) of socialism within the Labour Party in 1918 – these years mark a climax of class-consciousness and self-activity among workers which in Britain has not been surpassed.[1]

Furthermore, the example of the Russian Revolution of 1917 injected into these developments an even greater threat to the established capitalist order.

Yet the political and industrial militancy which had erupted in the strike wave of 1911–13 was, temporarily, deflected by the onslaught of the war in 1914. During the war, however, it became clear that profiteering employers backed by the government were intent on introducing a whole new series of controls over labour:

for example, in the munitions industries, the introduction of 'leaving certificates' – which prevented workers changing their employment without permission – led to gross abuses by employers; secondly 'dilution' of skilled labour was introduced to release more men for the carnage at the front, and the millions of women that were recruited to replace the men were paid at the lowest possible rates. It was the experience of these problems, and the obvious incapacity of trade union officials to deal with them, that stimulated a move towards independent rank-and-file action based on organization at the workshop level. Originating in a strike on the Clyde in 1915, the Shop Stewards' Movement spread to Sheffield and other engineering centres, and was instrumental in organizing the May 1917 strike of 200,000 engineering workers, which was the largest of the war. Initially, the movement had a craft base, but later, 'recovered from its lapse into craft concerns, expanded its base, developed a national leadership, and by January 1918 had moved into the forefront of militant anti-war politics . . . momentarily, the Shop Stewards' Movement had achieved a significant revolutionary presence.'[2]

In the first reading Hinton examines the relationship between revolutionary politics and trade unionism in a time of crisis: 'The catalyst of war, the intolerable demands it placed on the attitudes and practices of skilled engineers, promoted an interaction between the doctrines of revolutionary syndicalism, Industrial Unionism, and the craft tradition of local autonomy. In this interaction the Workers' Committees were born.'[3] The creation of the Workers' Committees was an important practical advance over the syndicalist's insistence on the need for amalgamation of the existing unions on an industrial base, and the Industrial Unionists' policy of total opposition to the existing trade unions as bulwarks of capitalism – advocating the creation of revolutionary unions in opposition to the existing movement.

The Shop Stewards' Movement displayed the unrealistic nature of craft exclusiveness which contradicted the needs of workshop organization, and revealed the inadequacy of the union branch. It provided a significant exercise in participatory democracy at the shopfloor level, and permitted the attempt to press for democratic reform of the official trade unions whilst striving to unite the workers on a class base. Thus the Shop Stewards' Movement was the practical development of syndicalism to communism: the syndicalist conception of trade unions as both the agency of revolution and the basic component of future socialist society placed undue reliance on the trade union bureaucracy and underestimated the problem of sectionalism; the local Workers' Committees based directly on the factories were controlled by the rank-and-file, and were capable of pressing for socialist policies within the trade union movement as well as in wider society, forming the political nucleus of the workers' state.[4]

The second reading, 'Direct Action', was an attempt to develop the Shop Stewards' Movement's ideas on industrial organization into a political instrument of revolutionary struggle, and was published at the crest of the wave of post-war militancy by the National Council of the Scottish Workers' Committees. It was prompted particularly by the failure of the national engineering union officials to support the strike in the West of Scotland for a 40-hour week earlier in 1919. The exasperation of militants with the frequency of the betrayal of their cause by official union leaders, led to the formulation of a policy which espoused direct action as the most effective means to challenge capitalism, and condemned the conservatism inherent in the negotiation and compromise that had traditionally dominated trade union practice.

In opposition to the labour movement constitutionalists who maintained that political change could only come through parliament; and the reformists who argued that direct action was legitimate only to pressure parliament, not to overthrow it (and who usually possessed an implicit faith in the inviolability of the parliamentary institution); Gallacher and Campbell, the authors of the pamphlet, stressed the futility of parliamentary action and the need for a new form of political activity which would represent more adequately the interests of workers. Thus they called for an industrial offensive organized by social and industrial committees which would rival, and eventually replace, the existing political organization of capitalism.[5]

The divergence of these two approaches to the role of parliament in the class struggle, then, as now, is implacable; as a contemporary commentator has observed:

tragically, those who have subscribed to the Parliamentary road to socialism have made it *the* article of their political faith never to encourage, and always to oppose, the emergence of such a radicalized proletariat. They have understood the Parliamentary road to socialism as precisely the *alternative* to this more violent confrontation of class with class, and have accepted a definition of constitutionality in politics which denied to the working class the right to use their industrial power to support their political ends – a right which industrial and financial capital exercise themselves daily in their dealings with the Parliamentary State.[6]

The attempt to implement the ideas of Gallacher and Campbell foundered in the post-war period with the erosion of the Workers' Committees and the mass movement they were built on: 'Within weeks of the armistice, the power of the shop stewards' movement was being crushed by the high levels of unemployment consequent on the run down in munitions production and the widespread victimization of known militants.'[7] The young militant shop stewards of the war, were to become the leaders of the unemployed in the 1920s. Moreover, the economic depression which set in at the end of 1920, threw the whole of the trade union movement on the defensive: trade union membership which had increased dramatically from 2·6 million to 8·3 million in the period 1910–20, slumped to 5·6 million in 1922, as unemployment rose to over 10 per cent in the 1920s and over 20 per cent in the 1930s.

Ironically, the very conditions which diminished shopfloor power, increased the influence of full-time officials within the unions, who consolidated the national trade union bureaucracies during these years. It was the union officials who led the defensive national stoppages of the 1920s, in contrast to the aggressive rank and file organization of disputes in the war era, and it was they who ensured the failure of these desperate efforts to resist the attempt to make the working class pay the cost of the economic collapse of world capitalism.

The groundswell of immediate post-war industrial conflict, including national strikes by the railwaymen and miners, was stemmed by a short-lived profiteer's economic boom and successfully contained by the government in a series of delaying tactics. In particular, the miners who voted in 1919 for a programme of demands including nationalization under joint control were persuaded to accept a commission to investigate this together with the issue of wages and hours. The rhetorical victories of the miners' leaders, who castigated the private owners before the commission, proved fruitless, since the militancy of 1919 was effectively defused: although the commission recommended nationalization, a year later the government handed back control of the mines to private owners. Heavy wage cuts were proposed by the owners, the miners refused, and were locked out. The revived Triple Alliance was invoked, but since the leaders of the railwaymen and transport workers 'were more afraid of its success than of its failure',[8] the miners were ignominiously abandoned on 'Black Friday' April 1921.

The miners campaigned to restore their losses, but the wage improvements they won in 1924 were soon countered by a fresh attempt to cut wages by the owners, whereupon the government again intervened with a commission, and provided a temporary subsidy to the industry, while preparing to defeat the anticipated strike. The scenario was thus set for the 1926 General Strike (originally conceived in the nineteenth century as 'a long strike, a strong strike, and a strike altogether').

The commission supported the owners' demands for longer hours and lower wages, the miners rejected the report and were issued lock-out notices. An attempt by the TUC to prevaricate was defeated since the government was determined on a decisive confrontation; the unions reluctantly instructed solidarity action which was enthusiastically supported by large sections of the labour movement. Collective institutions took over working-class communities and each day the militants grew stronger. And yet, 'After nine days, a majority of the trade union leadership, in collaboration with the Labour Party in London, and conferring with the Government, capitulated, in part fearing its own rank and file. The following day, the strike was a quarter of a million stronger, as if to exemplify the resistance to the new controllers.'[9] The negotiating committee of trade union leaders, none of whom were miners' leaders, attempted to overcome their crumbling control over the strikers in their appeal for a return to work by concealing the fact that it was an unconditional surrender, for instance *The British Worker* carried the deceitful headline 'The Terms of Peace: Miners Ensured a Square Deal'.[10] In fact, the miners were locked out until the end of the year when desperation forced them also to surrender. The government had made extensive preparations (maintained by the previous Labour Government) to combat the expected strike; the TUC – more interested in repressing the struggle than leading it – had made none. It was to take decades for the British working class to recover from this defeat. The failure to build on the practical and theoretical advances of 1910–20, albeit in the difficult economic conditions of the 1920s, consigned the trade unions to gloomy retrenchment and the revolutionary movement to sectarian sterility.[11] Not until the reconstruction of autonomous shopfloor organization and militancy in the late 1950s and 1960s was the rank-and-file of the labour movement once again in a position to advance towards socialist change.

NOTES

1. J. HINTON, *The First Shop Stewards' Movement*, George Allen & Unwin, 1973, p. 13.

2. ibid., pp. 235–6.

3. ibid., p. 333.

4. J. T. MURPHY, *The Workers' Committee*, Reprints in Labour History, no. 1, Pluto Press.

5. A. HATCHETT, introduction to the Pluto edition of *Direct Action*, Reprints in Labour History, no. 3.

6. D. COATES, *The Labour Party and the Struggle for Socialism*, Cambridge University Press, 1975, p. 230.

7. J. HINTON and R. HYMAN, *Trade Unions and Revolution*, Pluto Press, 1975, p. 14.

8. J. T. MURPHY, *Preparing for Power*, Pluto Press, 1972, p. 192. Murphy, a working-class intellectual and leader of the First Shop Stewards' Movement, in 1932 wrote his excellent history, 'to show the evolution of the British working class, from its origins in the industrial revolution of the eighteenth and nineteenth centuries to the present period of capitalist crisis, as a class *preparing for power*'. (p. 23.)

9. N. YOUNG, 'Promethians or Troglodytes? The English Working Class and the Dialectics of Incorporation', *Berkeley Journal of Sociology*, 1967, p. 26.

10. H. PELLING, *A History of British Trade Unionism*, Penguin, 1971, p. 177.

11. The role of the Communist Party in these vital years, which was painfully, but successfully, created in 1920–1 by the rank-and-file leaders who previously had belonged to a variety of revolutionary parties and sects, together with the creation of the National Minority Movement – an industrial arm, with which the early CP enjoyed an uneasy relationship – is critically analysed in Hinton and Hyman, op. cit.

7 The Theory of Independent Rank-and-File Organization

James Hinton

Reprinted with permission from J. Hinton, *The First Shop Stewards' Movement*, George Allen & Unwin, 1973, pp. 275–97.

'Of the eight members of the National Administrative Council elected in August 1917, six [had] joined the Communist Party by the time of the Leeds Unity Convention in January 1921.'[1] Most of these men, and other shop-steward leaders who joined the Communist Party after the war, had served their political apprenticeship under the influence of syndicalist thought, some from within the British Socialist Party (Gallacher, Peet),[2] some in the Socialist Labour Party (MacManus, Dingley), some in the Amalgamation Committee movement (Murphy, and also Peet).[3] Clearly the movement stood, ideologically, at a point of transition between syndicalism and communism. What is surprising, at first sight, is how little the movement in wartime departed from many of the syndicalist notions which it inherited. The tenor of the movement's thinking was organizational; its innovations lay in the field of industrial tactics, not of political strategy as such. Its leaders were practical men whose thinking, so far as it rose above every day concerns, was more concerned to elaborate the tactics than to debate the long-term strategy or ultimate goals of the class struggle. The most intellectually able of them, Jack Murphy, did not, during the war, go beyond tactical thinking, important and often original though that was. 'Humanity,' he wrote, 'is intensely practical,' and he quoted with approval: 'No nation ever yet made itself by theories of social contract or by any other explicit theories; the work was done first and the theories came afterwards; the reason was latent in the fact before it was patent in the explanation.'[4] The object of this chapter is to show how 'latent in the fact' of the wartime shop stewards' movement, though never fully grasped or expounded theoretically during the war, was the development from syndicalism to communism. The next chapter will deal with the post-war period when – paradoxically, in the context of the decline and defeat of the mass movement – this development was made 'patent in the explanation' by Jack Murphy and others.

The syndicalist and communist doctrines are most commonly distinguished by their attitudes towards political action, and more particularly, towards the need for a revolutionary party. Syndicalism is characterized by an exclusive emphasis on social relations at the point of production as the determining factor in the social structure, an emphasis which prevents the syndicalist from appreciating the need for politics, and from grasping the dialectical relationship posited in all communist thinking (with whatever nuances) between the 'spontaneous', economically-based organization of the masses and the political vanguard of the class, the revolutionary party. This aspect of the development from syndicalism to communism is *not* dealt with in this study, and for two reasons. First, it is very doubtful whether, by the time of the formation of the Communist Party in 1920–1, any substantial proportion of its members or leaders had grasped the Bolshevik idea of the party or would have approved of it had they done so. In this sense they carried their syndicalism over into the new party. Second, the contribution of the shop stewards' movement to the ideological development of its leaders had nothing to do with the idea of the party, but it did have a great deal to do with a second, and neglected, aspect of the transition from syndicalism to communism. What the shop stewards' movement implicitly challenged in the syndicalist doctrine was the idea that the trade unions would constitute both the chief agency of transition to socialism and the basic structure of socialist society thereafter. The characteristic and distinguishing feature of communism in Britain during 1919–21 was not the idea of the revolutionary party, but the idea of soviet power. In the communist model of transition the soviet replaced not only the parliamentary part of the state socialist but also the revolutionary industrial union of the syndicalist. The chief ideological significance of the shop stewards' movement is to be found in its contribution to the growth of the revolutionary left who supplied it with leadership.

The chief sources of the ideology of the shop stewards' movement were the French and American doctrines of revolutionary syndicalism and Industrial Unionism, imported into Britain before the war. From its foundation in 1903 the Socialist Labour Party (SLP) had been preaching Industrial Unionism in Britain.

Ferociously sectarian, and its direct industrial influence confined largely to the Clyde, the SLP was nevertheless to make a more important contribution than the much larger British Socialist Party (or any other Marxist grouping) both to the development of the shop stewards' movement and to the subsequent foundation of the Communist Party. The key to this influence, apart from the outstanding ability as leaders of industrial militancy of several of its members, was its pre-war preservation – one might almost say refrigeration – of the clear and systematic De Leonite alternative to state socialism.[5]

The revolutionary syndicalist contribution was a very different one. Tom Mann, who launched a largely French-inspired industrial syndicalism in Britain in 1910, was the perfect personification of the movement. Enthusiasm, rhetoric and ceaseless energy; an unsectarian, unsystematic, eclectic thinker capable of an extraordinary range of responses; above all else an agitator, his life a whirlwind tour of trouble spots (an hour-by-hour itinerary of Tom Mann's life would provide an unparalleled map of the growth points of class struggle over half a century), always there on the platform, in the strike-committee's rooms, directing, speaking, casting the spell of revolution, bringing 'life and health and sympathy and hope into the most sordid of human lives'.[6] 'Syndicalists', writes Pribicevic,

> were generally much more concerned with the burning questions of the day than with the distant future, much more with the methods and tactics of the class struggle than with its ultimate aims. Everybody who was willing to take part in the class struggle, regardless of his organization or his political views, was welcome in the Syndicalist League. They maintained that it would be idle to insist on theoretical distinctions at a time when the main body of the workers were engaged in practical class struggles.[7]

Lacking any systematic doctrine, entirely dependent on the momentum of industrial militancy, the syndicalist movement grew with meteoric speed during the great strike movement of 1910–12 – and fell just as fast in the year before the war. After 1914 its influence was diffuse and difficult to trace, though the syndicalist-inspired Amalgamated Committee movement played an important role in the origins of the shop stewards' movement in England.

The common doctrinal element of industrial unionism and revolutionary syndicalism was their rejection of State Socialism, and their vision of a reconstructed industrial unionism as both the chief agency of class struggle in the present, and as the embryonic administrative structure of the Socialist Commonwealth, 'the skeleton structure of that parliament of socialism wherein the government of men . . . gives place to the peaceful administration of industry'.[8] Both rejected the orthodox social democratic notion of a transition to socialism through the conquest of parliamentary power followed by nationalization, but they differed radically in their attitude to parliamentary politics. The syndicalists, reflecting their French inheritance and the disillusion felt by many active militants with the Labour Party's parliamentary antics, neglected politics and the role of the state altogether. Their strategy of transition rested solely upon the intensification of the class struggle in industry to its logical culmination in the revolutionary General Strike, which would paralyse society, fragment the forces of bourgeois repression, and enable the workers to take over the functions of production, distribution and social administration through the machinery of their industrial unions, trade councils, etc.

The SLP, following Marx, believed that it was only in the arena of politics that the working class could clearly establish its own self-awareness; and it identified political with parliamentary action:

> If we accept the definition of working-class political action as that which brings the workers as a class into direct conflict with the possessing class AS A CLASS, and keeps them there, then we must realize that NOTHING CAN DO THAT SO READILY AS ACTION AT THE BALLOT BOX.

The role of political action was exclusively educative, not the battle but 'the echo of the battle'.[9] The growth of industrial unionism and the SLP representation in Parliament would go hand in hand until the Party was able to form a government; at which point its job would be done. This approach was elaborated during the war:

The SLP enters the political field to capture the political STATE – not with the idea of perpetuating it under socialism, but with one object of wrenching from the capitalist class its power over the ARMED FORCES. The SLP enters the political field to enable Labour to accomplish a PEACEFUL REVOLUTION. With the State in the hands of Labour, the workers functioning through their industrial organization will assume control over the means of production. This being accomplished the STATE will function no more: it will, to quote Engels, die out.[10]

From its origin the Workers' Committee movement was committed to the goal of workers' control of production. During the war, however, it made no significant contribution to the discussion of how this was to be achieved.[11] A constant theme in the discussion of workers' control in the shop stewards' movement was the syndicalist assumption that industrial organization of the workers in production, would, by virtue of its own tremendous weight, displace capital much as a ship displaces water and thereby usher in the Socialist Commonwealth. 'The *ultimate aim* of the Clyde Workers' Committee,' Gallacher had written in January 1916, 'is to mould these unions into one powerful organization that will place the workers in complete control of the industry.' The profound complacency of this formulation derives from its neglect of the role of the state in maintaining the domination of capital.[12] On the question of political action, the shop stewards' movement was no more successful in advancing beyond its pre-war sources. The dispute over parliamentary action continued within its ranks, eventually coming into the open in the spring of 1918 as a split between the CWC (where SLP influence was strongest), and the English movement, especially as represented by *Solidarity*, where revolutionary syndicalism held sway.[13] It was in its attitude towards the existing trade unions that the wartime movement departed fundamentally from both revolutionary syndicalism and the industrial unionism of the SLP.

Both pre-war tendencies saw the existing trade unions as inadequate agencies of revolutionary transition, because of their sectionalism and because of their generally oligarchic and collaborationist character. They disagreed fundamentally on the tactics of reconstruction. The revolutionary syndicalists sought amalgamation of the existing unions on an industrial basis, and believed that the character and goals of the unions could be transformed from within: 'The Trade Unions are truly representative of the men, and can be moulded by the men into exactly what the men desire.'[14] The Industrial Unionists saw no alternative to root-and-branch opposition to the existing unions – bulwarks of capitalism – and the construction of new revolutionary unions. In British conditions 'dual' unionism was a non-starter. A relatively high level of trade union organization, and the existence of general unions willing and able, when conditions were ripe, to recruit previously unorganized workers on a massive scale, left little room for the development of new revolutionary unions outside and antagonistic to the existing movement on the model of the IWW in America. The only success for SLP Industrial Unionism in Britain, the organization of the Singer's works at Clydebank in 1910–11, arose out of quite exceptional circumstances, and was rapidly suppressed.[15]

While the Industrial Unionists strove in vain to establish an alternative leadership to the existing trade unions, the revolutionary syndicalists concentrated on propaganda and education within them. 'It is too early at present to go beyond the educational stage,' Tom Mann told the founding conference of the Industrial Syndicalist Education League in 1910.[16] When in the great battle of 1910–12 masses of workers struck work without the sanction of their trade union officials, the syndicalists were ready to take the lead, as they did most successfully in the Cambrian coal strike of 1910–11 and the Liverpool Transport strike in the summer of 1911. Their main effort, however, was not to construct an alternative leadership to that of the unions, but rather to canalize this militancy into the restructuring of the unions. The lesson drawn by the South Wales syndicalists from the situation of dual power between the unofficial strike committees (which they themselves had manned) and the South Wales Miners Federation Executive during the Cambrian strike, was not that this independent rank-and-file organization provided an important counter to the passivity of the Executive, but that such a dualism divided and weakened the fighting strength of the union. In future the need for independent rank-and-file organization must be eliminated by the reconstruction of the union on a more democratic basis.[17] When members of the various railway unions, together with non-unionists, precipitated the conflict of 1911 by striking unofficially on a very large scale, the syndicalists did not seek to use this rank-and-file revolt against sectionalism and collaboration in order to construct a new industrial union from the bottom up. Instead they devoted themselves to making propaganda for the amalgamation of the existing railway unions.

Amalgamations and greater unity would certainly be essential if the existing trade union movement was to become capable of mounting a revolutionary general strike and of taking control of the means of production. They were also, however, necessary for quite different purposes. The leaders of the railway unions agreed to amalgamate in 1912 because they had, in the strikes of the previous summer, learned that unless the Executives could unite they were likely to be supplanted from below.[18] To many of its founders the Triple Alliance was valued, not as a means of promoting and extending sympathetic strike action, but as a means of preventing spontaneous outbreaks, of controlling and disciplining militancy. James Connolly's characterization of the Triple Alliance contains an important element of truth:[19]

> The frequent rebellion against stupid and spiritless leadership and the call of the rank-and-file for true industrial unity seems to have spurred the leaders on, not to respond to new spirit but to evolve a method whereby under the forms of unity [it] could be trammelled and fettered . . . a scheme to *prevent* united action rather than facilitate it.

No one was more aware than the syndicalists of the dangers of oligarchy, of 'the bad side of leadership', but, eloquent exhortation apart, they could find no satisfactory solution to the perennial problem of combining participatory democracy with large-scale and efficient trade union organization.[20]

In March 1921 Jack Murphy, by then a communist, distinguished two phases 'of our development as revolutionary' agitators in the trade union movement:[21]

> The first phase [pre-war] was that of propagandists of industrial unionism, amalgamation of the unions, ginger groups within the various organizations. The second [wartime phase] was characteristically the period of action, the attempt to adapt industrial-unionism principles to the immediate struggle, and to take on the direct responsibility for the conduct of the fight against the bosses and the State.

The wartime shop stewards' movement carried industrial unionism and revolutionary syndicalism from propaganda to action, from the branch to the workshop. In so doing – though this was not fully grasped at the time – the movement laid the basis in practice for a theoretical solution to the problems of oligarchy and leadership in trade unionism that had eluded the pre-war syndicalists.

The urgency of the problems raised by the impact of war on the workshops, and the failure of the trade union leadership to advance any realistic policy, forced revolutionary engineers to concentrate their attention on throwing up organs of rank-and-file self-defence, capable of immediate and effective action. The long-term goal of industrial unionism – approached by whatever path – could not answer the needs of the moment. Confronted with the spontaneous growth of workshop organization and the fact of its own leadership of rank-and-file militancy on the Clyde, the SLP abandoned dual unionism. 'This is no time for intolerant doctrinaires, this is no place for bigoted critics,' wrote the editor of *The Socialist* in July 1917, urging that the propaganda of Industrial Unionism could now be translated into concrete form, not in antagonism to the trade unions but by building all-grades organizations in the workshops. The Industrial Unions of the future would grow, were growing spontaneously, out of the existing trade unions, not alongside them. 'Our policy,' declared Murphy, newly admitted to the SLP, 'must be a natural development from within the trade union movement.'[22]

The Amalgamation Committee movement had collapsed after the outbreak of war, but from the beginning of 1916 it revived and became increasingly closely linked up with the growing power of the English shop stewards.[23] In November 1916, infuriated by the dilatory attitude of the trade union Executives towards amalgamation, and encouraged by the growing power of the shop stewards, the movement presented the Executive with a three-month ultimatum to amalgamate, failing which a new 'dual' union would be formed. Thus, paradoxically, just as the SLP was abandoning dual unionism owing to its members' experience in the shop stewards' movement, the revolutionary syndicalists were pointing to the power of the shop stewards as their justification for swinging towards dual unionism. When the ultimatum ran out in March 1917, W. F. Watson, since 1910 the leader of the movement, wanted to press ahead with the formation of the new union. The shop stewards, arguing that the time was not ripe for a head-on collision with the trade union Executives, opposed Watson:

> Remember it is not only the amalgamation of unions you require, but the amalgamation of the workers in the workshops ... Let your propaganda take concrete form by transforming the Amalgamation Committee into the Workers' Committee. Make the amalgamation of unions incidental, the amalgamation of the workers fundamental.[24]

The March conference compromised, agreeing to defer, but not abandon, Watson's ultimatum, and, in the meantime, to concentrate effort on forming Workshop and Workers' Committees.[25]

When the deferred deadline passed without visible response from the major union Executives, pressure for the immediate formation of a new union again mounted in the Amalgamation Committee movement. Watson initiated a workshop ballot on amalgamation in August and declared that if the result were favourable the new union would be formed without further delay.[26] For a short while *Solidarity*, closely linked with the English shop stewards, went over to Watson's dual unionist position, declaring in a front page editorial in September 1917: 'Every penny paid into a Craft Union now is a penny given to subsidize and reinforce the power of Capitalism.'[27] When the issue was debated at the Newcastle conference of the Amalgamation Committee movement in October the shop stewards – who appear to have ensured the failure of Watson's ballot by the simple expedient of not conducting it – consolidated their victory of the previous March. A resolution from the Sheffield and Manchester Workers' Committees for the fusion of the two movements was carried by 78 votes to 24: 'That the members of the Amalgamation Committee unite with the Shop Stewards' and Workers' Committees with a view to concentrating activity on the point of production.'[28] The merger finally took place in January 1918.[29] *Solidarity* now gave its whole-hearted support to the shop-steward position. The industrial union, when it came, must be a growth from below and not an imposition from above:

> The very healthy suspicion is abroad, even among the stalwarts

of workshop organization, that any sort of Industrial Union that was set up in the Engineering trade at this moment would not be the real article, such as we hope to develop when education and propaganda have done their work, but only another overlapping and time-serving organization which would crab the genuine and solid achievements of the Workers' Committees.[30]

In building up the Workers' Committees for practical and immediate purposes the leadership of the shop-stewards' movement had registered – though with no sophisticated theoretical explanations – their refusal to accept the assumption that a principled choice must be made between amalgamation and dual unionism. They did not abandon the long-term aim of constructing a revolutionary industrial union. In *The Workers' Committee* Murphy outlined a structure of national industrial unions based on workshop committees integrated with a class unionism based on local Workers' Committees representative of all industries. But in advocating industrial unionism neither Murphy nor the movement as a whole saw any need to plump for one tactic or the other. In 1917 Murphy left it an open question how far in the ultimate process of merging into the 'larger and more powerful structure' of industrial unionism the existing trade unions would be amalgamated or 'thrown off'.[31] Two years later he repeated the same point,[32] as did Gallacher and J. R. Campbell[33] in the pamphlet they wrote for the Scottish Workers' Committees in the autumn of 1919:[34]

The bringing together of the rank-and-file of all trades will create a class outlook amongst the workers that will compel the official organizations to weld themselves together as a compact industrial force, and to remould their internal structure and accept the workshop as the basis of the organization. Either that or they will find themselves ignored in the industrial struggles of the future, functioning merely as sick benefit societies and leaving the actual industrial fighting to be done by the Workers' Committees.

It is in the light of this rejection of the terms of the pre-war syndicalist argument – dual unionism *or* amalgamation – that the attitude of the shop stewards both towards their own organization and towards the existing trade unions can be best understood.

The rejection of Watson's dual unionism necessarily entailed a reluctance to develop any powerful national leadership for the movement. When, in August 1917, a national leadership was eventually established for the movement, the delay and hesitation involved in its evolution was confirmed in its constitution. The National Administrative Council, as its name implied, held no executive power and was intended to function as 'little more than a reporting centre for the local committees'.[35] 'No committee shall have executive power, all questions of policy and action being referred back to the rank-and-file', was a principle accepted throughout the movement.[36] This weakness of the national leadership has, following the subsequent self-criticisms of the leaders of the shop-stewards' movement, been attributed to anti-leadership prejudices inherited from pre-war syndicalism. 'Thus,' wrote Murphy in 1934, 'the first national committee was formed, but held theories which prevented it giving the leadership which the movement needed more than at any time since its foundation.'[37] At the time, however, Murphy justified the weakness of the national leadership not in the language of a doctrinaire blind to the lesson of events, but in terms of immediate practicalities. Any powerful national co-ordination of the Shop Stewards' and Workers' Committees would be indistinguishable from the establishment of a new 'dual' union: 'It must be clearly understood that the National Committee is not to usurp the functions of the executives of the trade unions. Power to decide action is vested in the workshops . . . '[38]

In examining the history of the movement there is nothing to show that its failure to develop an Executive leadership neutralized its potential for action.[39] In the localities the shop stewards seem to have had little reservation about grasping the lead from the officials whenever the opportunity presented itself. On the Clyde 'the most trusted men of the labour movement'[40] had lain in wait for a situation where they could wrest the initiative from the local officials, and had successfully done so late in 1915. The Joint Engineering Shop Stewards' Committee in Manchester did not hesitate to seize the lead from the trade union officials and initiate the national strike movement of May 1917. Nor can the two major fiascos of the movement, the collapse of the May 1917 strike movement, and the failure of the strike call of January

1918, be attributed to any marked degree to a failure of leadership. Of May 1917 Kendall, following Murphy, has argued that:

> The wave of arrests created a crisis, posing an immediate question: what action did the strike committee propose to take in reply? The leadership, feeling themselves responsible to a 'rank-and-file' whose views were unknown, hesitated and proved quite unable to respond with an initiative of its own. In such a situation retreat followed inevitably.[41]

The analysis is misleading: the views of the rank-and-file were far from unknown. The arrests took place precisely because the Government knew that in several key centres the strike had already collapsed. Where the possibility existed, as in Sheffield, the shop-steward leaders were quite ready and able to make the urgent assertion of leadership necessary to keep the men out after the arrests. The collapse of the strike was due to factors largely independent of a failure of leadership. Similarly, it was the rank-and-file, not the leadership, which failed in January 1918.[42]

Murphy's contemporary judgement was more realistic than his later reflection. To have attempted a premature assertion of Executive leadership would not have enhanced the potential of the movement; it would merely have isolated the leaders. The shop stewards' decision to establish a National *Administrative* Council and the subsequent practice of that Council undoubtedly reflected inherited ideology. The leaders were deeply conscious of what *The Miners' Next Step* had called the 'bad side of leadership':

> This power of initiative, this sense of responsibility, the self respect which comes from expressed manhood, is taken from the men, and consolidated in the leader. The sum of *their* initiative, *their* responsibility, *their* self respect become his . . . The order and system he maintains, is based upon the suppression of the men, from being independent thinkers into being 'the men' or 'the mob' . . . Sheep cannot be said to have solidarity. In obedience to a shepherd they will go up or down, backwards or forwards as they are driven by him and his dogs. But they have no solidarity, for that means unity and loyalty. Unity and loyalty, not to an individual, but to an interest and a policy which is understood and worked for by all.[43]

Convinced of the need to wrench the rank-and-file from unthinking loyalty to old-established institutions, the leaders set out to build a movement which substituted 'organized expression on the part of the mass', for the deeply ingrained principle of reliance on representatives.[44] 'Whereas we used to be plagued with the collectivists, who gloried in the production of a special class of officials to regulate the workers and do things for them, nowadays we take pleasure in the growth of the capacity in the rank-and-file to do things for themselves.'[45]

These attitudes stemmed not only from the leaders' ideological inheritance[46] but equally from their assessment of the character of the movement they were leading. Syndicalist concerns merged naturally with craft traditions of local autonomy and democratic control. Moreover, as Pribicevic has observed:

> The power of the movement did not depend on the number of members, on contributions, or on solid organization – all of which were decisive in the case of trade unions – but rather on the capacity of the local leaders to interpret the desires, demands and grievances of the main body of the workers. To ascertain when this main body of workers wanted action on any particular issue and then to place themselves at the head was the correct policy for a movement of this kind.[47]

A movement springing up so rapidly did not possess the institutional inertia that makes it so difficult to decide in the case of an old-established organization how far, in any particular action, the rank-and-file is pursuing its own conscious purpose or how far it is responding loyally but blindly to the instructions of respected leaders operating with a legitimacy sanctioned by tradition. The leadership of the shop stewards' movement, almost all young men unknown before the war, whose names carried no charisma, could only lead the rank-and-file where it positively wanted to go.

While rejecting dual unionism the shop stewards' movement equally refused to 'centre its activity' on capturing the existing trade unions.[48] The need for independent rank-and-file organization was argued (as indeed it was felt) from the structural inadequacies of engineering trade unionism. As dilution advanced and the interdependence of all crafts and grades in production became a matter of daily experience, the multiplicity of sectional societies stood in growing contradiction to the needs of the workshop community. Sectional trade unions appeared positively anti-social, 'maintaining distinctions which the social processes are rapidly making artificial', and tending to split up the spontaneous unity of the workers in modern socially organized production.[49] In this situation it was folly to expect that 'by the capturing of official positions we can change the nature of the organization . . . A craft organization conserves a craft psychology or outlook and everything is determined in similar terms.'[50] At the same time, as the extent and power of organization at the workplace increased, the inadequacy of a trade unionism based in residential branches became ever more apparent. 'In a large industrial centre half of the men in the branch will work outside the neighbourhood from which the branch draws its members, and the other half are scattered amongst a number of shops in the neighbourhood.'[51] The inability of the branches to deal with the immediate problems of the workshop; the low level of attendance at branch meetings and the absorption of the branches in the routine administration of friendly benefits, made them unfit organs on which to base a militant organization.[52]

> In so far as the branch of any organization corresponds to the grouping of the workers in their industrial activity, so far can it reflect directly the wishes of the members as a whole, check oligarchical tendencies, and act organically. In so far as the branch deviates from this primary principle it ceases to reflect the membership efficiently, develops caucus rule, and becomes involved and cumbersome in action.[53]

In the absence of fundamental structural reform which replaced branch by workshop as the formal basis of the union, or, failing this, of a strong and independent rank-and-file movement based in the workshops, any full-time official, whatever his original opinions, would in this situation find it difficult to resist the pressures of bureaucratic rationality, and collaboration.

Given such a critique, which owed little to syndicalist doctrine and much to immediate wartime experience, the value of participation in the official union machinery necessarily appeared limited. No organized effort was made to capture full-time trade union office, though this was never ruled out in principle by the movement. Sam Bradley, the secretary of the first national conference of Workers' Committees, became full-time district secretary of the London ASE in 1917. George Peet, leader of the Manchester shop stewards and secretary of the movement from August 1917, had stood unsuccessfully for full-time office in the ASE early in 1917.[54] The shop stewards believed that the growth of all-grades workshop organization and of Workers' Committees, might force the existing officials 'to remould their internal structure and accept the workshop as the basis of the organization', but they did not intend to encourage this process by capturing official positions and fighting for such a reconstruction of trade unionism from above as well as from below. They were content to rely on putting pressure on the trade union officials from the strongholds of independent rank-and-file organization, confident that if the officials failed to respond to this pressure the existing unions would eventually be 'thrown off' and replaced in all their essential functions by the Shop Stewards' and Workers' Committees. 'We did not conduct the fight so much against the officials, but rather ignored them and fought the employing class directly.'[55] This refusal to campaign directly for full-time union office has been widely attributed, following Jack Murphy's later comment, to an irrational, childish 'rank-and-file-ist' prejudice on the part of the movement's leaders.[56] There is some truth in this criticism, but its significance should not be exaggerated.

In so far as the task of capturing the existing trade unions presented itself as an alternative to the construction of independent rank-and-file organization (as would tend to be the case in any movement lacking an unlimited supply of able militants) it would be rightly rejected, *firstly* as not answering to the urgent immediate needs of the workers, *secondly* as worthless by itself. Only on the basis of an independent rank-and-file movement in the workshops could even a sympathetic trade union official hope to build the revolutionary Industrial Union. Moreover, despite Murphy's later optimism on this score, it is far from certain that the revolutionary shop stewards could have made any very substantial inroads into trade union officialdom had they tried.[57] In most areas the appeal of their distinctive policies was limited to a small minority of the more militant workers. Only in situations of extreme and temporary crisis, if at all, did they gain general support. Trade union elections cannot be expected to occur only, or even predominantly, at such moments.

Given this minority position as leaders of an advance guard of the movement, it would always seem more important to the shop stewards to concentrate their energies on enlarging the effective size of this vanguard (which could only be done in the workshops), than to build an electoral machine which, because of its branch base, would be valueless for fighting purposes.

While the movement may be criticized for its failure seriously to contest full-time trade union office, it is quite wrong to suggest that it refused to participate in the official trade union machinery at a local level.[58] In Glasgow, where in 1915–16 the Workers' Committee represented only a minority of the engineering workers and consequently could not control the local District Committees, the rank-and-file movement tended to stand outside and in antagonism to the official structures of trade unionism. In Sheffield, on the other hand, the Workers' Committee, representing the great majority of local engineering workers, worked closely with the ASE District Committee, the two structures acting as 'legal' and 'illegal' wings of a single organization. One of the most prominent members of the Sheffield Committee, Ted Lismer, was also a local official of his union, the Steam Engine Makers. Murphy, in *The Workers' Committee*, which draws heavily on the Sheffield experience, naturally stresses the possibilities of working within the unions, proposing shop-steward rules for adoption by the District Committees which would make it possible for the workshop committees to operate as 'part of the official movement . . . The means are then assured of an alliance between official and unofficial activities by the official recognition of rank-and-file control.'[59] In January 1918 the movement adopted Murphy's pamphlet as its official statement of policy.[60] 'Branch and workshop activity has always been our rule,' wrote Campbell in 1922. 'The emphasis we place on either line of action depends on conditions.'[61]

During the late summer of 1918, in the aftermath of January and the context of defeat and inactivity, there was a temporary hardening of attitudes towards the existing trade unions. When the national conference assembled in Birmingham in September 1918 delegates from Liverpool, which had a long record of official activity to 'counteract the non-official anti-trade union movement', advanced a scheme of organization which had been formulated locally following a militant wage movement in July. They argued that local General Councils, representative of the

District Committees as well as the workshops, and closely analogous to the organization of the Coventry Engineering Joint Committee, should be established as the new 'basis of the movement'.[62] This motion provided the occasion for a vigorous attack upon the 'officialization' of the movement. Unrepentant dual unionists reasserted their position.[63] More important, J. T. Murphy now took his own pamphlet, *The Workers' Committee*, to task for having exaggerated the possibilities of working in the unofficial movement: 'We must be prepared to profit by experience and realize the impossibility of the Workers' Committees working with the unions.' The experience he had in mind was that of Coventry. This had shown that attempts to reconcile all-grades workshop organization with the existing trade union structure by the construction of local Joint Boards of union District Committees to which the shop stewards were responsible led only to the preservation of sectionalism.

The continued existence of the separate unions in the joint body provided 'centres round which can gather elements of discontent, which can easily break away . . .' as occurred in Coventry during the Embargo strike.[64] Most of the delegates agreed with Murphy and the Liverpool scheme, identified as being 'better suited for adoption by an Allied Trades Conference', was rejected by 40 votes to 9. 'The feeling of the conference was against trying to square with the official movement.' The retreat into dual unionism was, however, neither complete nor permanent. While the conference repudiated the Liverpool scheme, and with it any attempt as in Coventry to *fuse* the shop stewards' movement with the local official structures, it did not close the door on the policy of *alliances* with the local officials from an independent, 'unofficial' basis. Arthur MacManus, in the chair, was careful to block any attempt to formally commit the movement to a dual unionist position. Steering the delegates away from any 'specific resolution' of their attitude to the unions, he re-emphasized that the primary object of the movement was neither amalgamation nor Industrial Unionism: 'The crucial point had been missed. The discussion had concentrated around organization outside the shop, whereas we should be discussing shop organization.'[65] This left the way open for the explicit reassertion of the movement's flexible attitude towards the local official structures of trade unionism during 1919.[66] Like *Solidarity* earlier in the year MacManus had successfully invoked the 'solid and genuine

achievements of the Workers' Committees' against any precipitate rush to dual unionism.

At the height of its power the rank-and-file movement co-
ordinated and led militancy through a local Workers' Committee
representative of the organization in the workshops. Because of
their delegatory character these committees were capable of
initiating and carrying through stike action independently of the
trade union officials. It is this independence that primarily
defines the rank-and-file movement:

> We will support the officials just so long as they rightly repre-
> sent the workers, but we will act independently immediately
> they misrepresent them. Being composed of delegates from
> every shop and untrammelled by obsolete rule or law, we claim
> to represent the true feeling of the workers. We can act im-
> mediately according to the merits of the case and the desire of
> the rank-and-file.[67]

The movement did not seek, for the time being, to replace the
existing structures of trade unionism, but to co-exist with them
while working (with more or less energy) for constitutional
reform and – most important – to 'erect a structure inside and
outside the trade union movement, which will unite the workers
on a class basis', and thus to place the workers 'in a position to
act independently in case of faulty leadership'.[68] Not the suppression of sectional and collaborationist trade unionism, but the
establishment of a situation of 'dual power' between trade union
officialdom and independently organized militant sections of the
rank-and-file – this was the essence of the wartime practice of the
shop stewards' movement.

The shop stewards' movement pursued neither dual unionism
nor amalgamation, but attempted to straddle and go beyond the
two tactics. Inevitably such a movement laid itself open to
criticism for the incompleteness of its attention to either or
both of the tactical legs upon which it stood, and much criticism
of this nature has been levelled against it. It is true that the
movement 'failed to capture any major trade union': it is also
true that the shop stewards failed to create any overall alternative
organization to the existing trade unions.[69] Because, during the
war, the movement achieved no theoretical elaboration of its
practice, it was easy to see it merely as an evasion of those

ultimate problems about the role of trade unionism in the transition to socialism which had exercised the imagination of Industrial Unionists and revolutionary syndicalists before the war. It was not until 1919 that the movement's leadership was able to draw out the full implications for the theory of socialist revolution of the wartime practice of 'dual power' between trade unionism and independent rank-and-file organization. Only in the light of this later theoretical development can the 'failure' of the wartime movement to adopt a 'consistent' position of dual unionism or amalgamationism be fully evaluated.

NOTES

1. W. KENDALL, *The Revolutionary Movement in Britain, 1900–21*, 1969, p. 164. Moreover it was the SLP group in the leadership of the shop stewards' movement – MacManus and Murphy (together with Tom Bell and William Paul) – who 'became the dominant figures in the Communist Party during its first four years': L. J. MACFARLANE, *The British Communist Party*, 1966, p. 28.

2. Syndicalist ideas gained extensive influence in the BSP before the war: KENDALL, *The Revolutionary Movement in Britain*, pp. 38–45, 56–60.

3. Other organizations were also of importance in spreading syndicalist ideas in the industry, especially the Herald League and the Plebs League. For the sake of simplicity this chapter concentrates on the influence of the SLP and the Amalgamation Committees as representing the two major schools of syndicalist thinking in Britain. The best history of British syndicalism is E. BURDICK, 'Syndicalism and Industrial Unionism in England until 1918' (Oxford D. Phil., 1950).

4. *The Socialist*, September 1917. See also J. R. CAMPBELL, in *The Worker*, 10 January 1920.

5. 'Marxism, which the SDF had interpreted as an exclusively political doctrine, was turned by the SLP into a justification for concentration on the industrial scene. In so doing it did a great deal to provide an ideological basis for the industrial militancy and the shop stewards' movement which developed both during and before the war.' KENDALL, *The Revolutionary Movement in Britain*, p. 76. Daniel De Leon (1852–1914) was leader of the American Labour Movement from the 1890s; he was a founder member of the Industrial Workers of the World in 1905 (eds.).

6. T. MANN, writing in *Industrial Syndicalist*, September 1910.

7. B. PRIBICEVIC, *The Shop Stewards' Movement and Workers' Control*, Oxford, 1959, p. 17.

8. *The Socialist*, February 1910; cf. *Industrial Syndicalist*, December 1910, p. 45.

9. J. CONNOLLY, *Socialism Made Easy*, 1907, p. 24.

10. *The Socialist*, December 1916.

11. It was only on Clydeside that any systematic thought was given to problems of workers' control during the war, first in the dilution programme of 1915–16, which was in theory and in practice a complete abortion, secondly by GALLACHER and J. PATON in their pamphlet, *Towards Industrial Democracy*, 1917. This is remembered chiefly for its 'unrivalled lack of realism'; PRIBICEVIC, *The Shop Stewards' Movement and Workers' Control*, p. 153. It is the inadequacy of these programmes that vitiates Pribicevic's attempt to discuss the movement primarily in terms of the articulation of the demand for workers' control.

12. *The Worker*, 29 January 1916; see also PRIBICEVIC, *The Shop Stewards' Movement and Workers' Control*, pp. 129–30. As the postwar communist critics of syndicalism were to delight in pointing out, encroaching control, 'the wringing of step by step concessions from the capitalists' in the workshops would, as it approached success, inevitably come up against the armed might of the state. W. GALLACHER and J. R. CAMPBELL, *Direct Action*, Glasgow, 1919, p. 27.

13. PRIBICEVIC, *The Shop Stewards' Movement and Workers' Control*, p. 92. See also *Workers' Dreadnought*, 9 March, 20 April 1918; *Solidarity*, May 1918.

14. T. MANN, in *Industrial Syndicalist*, November 1910.

15. *The Socialist*, October 1910, April–July, December 1911; *Forward*, 10 February 1917.

16. *Industrial Syndicalist*, September 1910.

17. *The Miners' Next Step*, Tonypandy, 1912, pp. 10–11.

18. P. S. BAGWELL, *The Railwaymen*, 1963, pp. 289–91, 325–7.

19. *Workers' Republic*, 12 February 1916; quoted in B. PEARCE, *Some Past Rank and File Movements*, 1959, p. 38.

20. *The Miners' Next Step*, pp. 13–15.

21. *The Worker*, 19 March 1921; cf. J. R. CAMPBELL, in *The Worker*, 10 January 1920.

22. *The Socialist*, September 1917. PRIBICEVIC, *The Shop Stewards' Movement and Workers' Control*, p. 86, is very misleading about the SLP attitude, quoting an article of June 1917, but not that of July which marked a decisive shift in the Party's position. The SLP had never opposed working within the existing unions at a grass-roots level, but members were forbidden to stand for trade union office on the grounds that the existing unions were bulwarks of capitalism and must eventually be destroyed rather than taken over by the left. T. BELL, *Pioneering Days*, 1942, p. 42.

23. The Amalgamation Committee themselves were purely propa-

gandist organizations with no foothold in the workshops.

24. J. T. MURPHY, in *Solidarity*, March 1917.

25. *Solidarity*, April 1917; *The Herald*, 31 March 1917; PRIBICEVIC, *The Shop Stewards' Movement and Workers' Control*, pp. 74–7.

26. *Fusion of Forces, Report of the Fifth National Rank and File Conference*, Newcastle upon Tyne, 13–14 October 1917, *passim*.

27. *Solidarity* had been founded by the leading central group of revolutionary syndicalism, Tom Mann, Will Hay, W. F. Watson, J. V. Willis, in 1913, after their original paper, *The Syndicalist and Amalgamation Committee News*, had been taken over by the anarcho-communists. The paper collapsed on the outbreak of war, but in December 1916 it was revived by a group of London Industrial Unionists allied to the Chicago (anti-political) IWW rather than the Detroit (De Leonist) section. Despite intimate relations with the shop stewards, on whom the paper rapidly became dependent for its workshop sales, E. C. Pratt and S. A. Wakeling, the editor and manager, remained unrepentant dual unionists. Ultimately they were forced to resign, and in the summer of 1918 were replaced by Jack Tanner, leader of the west London engineers who was much closer in outlook to the dominant sections of the shop stewards' movement. After the war *Solidarity* was formally adopted as the organ of the English shop stewards' movement. In May 1921, when the shop stewards decided to concentrate their resources on the Scottish *Worker*, the editorial team of *Solidarity* announced their intention of continuing the paper under the new name *The Liberator*.

28. *Fusion of Forces*, pp. 19–21.

29. BELL, *Pioneering Days*, pp. 302–3.

30. *Solidarity*, January 1918.

31. J. T. MURPHY, *The Workers' Committee*, Sheffield, 1917, p. 14.

32. A. GLEASON, *What the Workers Want*, New York, 1920, p. 199.

33. J. R. CAMPBELL (b. 1894). Shop assistant and member of BSP. Volunteered for service in war. Organizer for Scottish Workers' Committees, 1919–21. Founder member of Communist Party and editor of *The Worker* from 1922.

34. *Direct Action*, pp. 20–21. PRIBICEVIC, *The Shop Stewards' Movement and Workers' Control*, p. 90, draws a contrast between *The Workers' Committee* and *Direct Action*, arguing that while the former assumed that the growth of the rank-and-file movement would ultimately be bound to disrupt rather than amalgamate the existing unions, Gallacher and Campbell laid exclusive emphasis on the task of re-moulding the existing unions. This constitutes a misreading of both pamphlets; throughout it remained an open question how far trade unionism would be superseded or remoulded. In so far as there was a change in emphasis between 1917 and 1919, however, it was in the reverse direction to that suggested by Pribicevic.

35. J. T. MURPHY, *New Horizons* (1941), p. 61.

36. *Solidarity*, February 1919. Cf. MURPHY, *The Workers' Committee*, pp. 4–5: 'The functions of an Elected Committee, therefore, should be such that instead of arriving at decisions *for* the rank and file they would provide the means whereby full information relative to any question of policy should receive the attention and consideration *of* the rank and file, the results to be expressed by ballot.'

37. J. T. MURPHY, *Preparing for Power*, 1934, p. 152, also pp. 97, 146, 159; W. GALLACHER, *Revolt on the Clyde*, 1936, pp. 220–21; PRIBICEVIC, *The Shop Stewards' Movement and Workers' Control*, p. 99; KENDALL, *The Revolutionary Movement in Britain*, pp. 142, 165.

38. MURPHY, *The Workers' Committee*, p. 14.

39. As Kendall argues in *The Revolutionary Movement in Britain*, p. 142.

40. *Vanguard*, October 1915.

41. KENDALL, *The Revolutionary Movement in Britain*, pp. 160–1; cf. MURPHY, *Preparing for Power*, p. 141.

42. Both Kendall (p. 166) and Pribicevic (p. 102) assume that the NAC's decision to ballot the workshops early in January 1918 was responsible for a delay in the call for strike action which prevented any decision being made until the German spring offensive had been launched. This is, of course, quite untrue. The threat of strike action against the war had collapsed long before the German offensive.

43. *The Miners' Next Step*, pp. 13–14. This pamphlet was very influential among the shop steward leadership: MURPHY, *Preparing for Power*, p. 152. There is an article by J. R. Campbell in *The Worker*, 1 January 1920, which repeats the above quotation almost word for word without acknowledgement.

44. *Solidarity*, July 1917.

45. J. T. MURPHY, in *The Socialist*, 26 June 1919.

46. This would be a difficult thesis to sustain in any case since the syndicalist tradition was far from single-minded on the question of leadership. One would still have to explain why the shop stewards chose to emphasize the 'bad side of leadership', rather than the equally 'syndicalist' insistence on the need for centralized, executive authority. See, for example, W. F. Hay's important statement of this characteristic of syndicalism in *Solidarity*, September 1913.

47. PRIBICEVIC, *The Shop Stewards' Movement and Workers' Control*, p. 99.

48. *Solidarity*, June 1918.

49. J. T. MURPHY, in *The Socialist*, 8 May 1919. See also *The Workers' Committee*, pp. 5–6.

50. J. T. MURPHY, in *Solidarity*, September 1918.

51. *Consolidation and Control* (1921), published in *The Worker*, 27 August 1921.

52. The level of attendance at branch meetings can be judged from the percentage of members voting in the major wartime national ballots:

	Membership voting
	%
Treasury Agreement, 1915	11·5
Election of general secretary, 1916	15·6
Munitions Bill, 1917	21·7
Secession from Federation, 1918	13·0
Amalgamation scheme, 1918	10·0

ASE, *Monthly Journal and Report, passim.*
Significantly, in the only postal ballot of the period which did not require members to make the effort to attend a branch meeting – the vote on the Man Power proposals early in 1918 – over 50% of the membership took part.

53. J. T. MURPHY, in *The Socialist*, 10 April 1919: *The Workers' Committee*, p. 5. Murphy, quoted in K. COATES and T. TOPHAM, *Industrial Democracy in Great Britain* (1967), pp. 84–5.

54. *Solidarity*, January 1917; ASE, *Quarterly Report*, March 1917, election addresses. Both Pribicevic (p. 91) and Kendall (p. 167) give exaggerated prominence to the movement's reaction against 'officialization' in the summer and autumn of 1918. As we shall see, this represented only a partial and temporary deviation from the more flexible position which characterized the movement.

55. J. T. MURPHY, in *The Worker*, 10 January 1920; 'The official unions will have to come together and democratize their government or leave the actual fighting to be done by the Workers' Committees.'

56. MURPHY, *New Horizons*, p. 81; PRIBICEVIC, *The Shop Stewards' Movement and Workers' Control*, pp. 91–2; KENDALL, *The Revolutionary Movement in Britain*, p. 167.

57. MURPHY, *New Horizons*, p. 81.

58. Contrast KENDALL, *The Revolutionary Movement in Britain*, p. 294: 'The shop stewards . . . refused to participate in official union machinery beyond shopfloor level.'

59. *The Workers' Committee*, pp. 8–9. The West London Workers' Committee in 1918 adopted a similar position, allowing branch delegates to attend its meetings in a non-voting capacity: *Solidarity*, May 1918.

60. *Solidarity*, February, May 1918.

61. *The Worker*, 4 February 1922.

62. *Mun.* 2. 28, 20 October 1917; *Mun.* 2. 16, 13 July 1918: *Solidarity*, October 1918, March 1919. The motion was seconded by H. King, the National Council member for Coventry.

63. Cf. *Solidarity*, June 1918, 'Should we Capture the Trade Unions?'

64. *Workers' Dreadnought*, 21 September 1918; *Solidarity*, Septem-

ber 1918. The dual-unionist implications of these remarks were, for Murphy, only a temporary deviation. In 1919 he was again reiterating the orthodox shop steward formula: 'We must be in the unions, of the unions, but not determined by their limitations.' *The Socialist*, 18 December 1919. See also PRIBICEVIC, *The Shop Stewards' Movement and Workers' Control*, p. 91. There was, however, one permanent change, both for Murphy and for the movement as a whole. The disastrous effects of the December 1917 shop stewards' agreement, which recognized the stewards only of individual unions, led Murphy to abandon his previous careful insistence that the separate representations of each grade on the shop stewards' committee was necessary if the interests of the less skilled were not to be subordinated to those of the craftsmen. The danger of craft domination now seemed less than the danger of sectionalism and disintegration. The earlier position is expounded in *The Workers' Committee*, p. 8; *Firth Worker*, May 1918; the later attitude in *Solidarity*, August 1918; *The Socialist*, 18 May 1919; and the 1919 rules of the shop stewards' movement.

65. *Solidarity*, October 1918; *Workers' Dreadnought*, 21 September 1918.

66. At the national conference of January 1920: 'D. Ramsey, on behalf of the NAC. explained at length the position of the shop stewards' movement in relation to the official Unions. So far as that was concerned, there was no need to change the policy of the movement.' *The Worker*, 14 February 1920. According to Jane Degras, the *Communist International, 1919–1943, Documents*, vol. I, 1919–1922 (1955), p. 145, Gallacher put a dual-unionist position at the second congress of the Communist International in August 1920. This is a misreading of his position. Cf. J. KLUGMANN, *History of the Communist Party in Great Britain*, vol. I, London, 1968, p. 52. This misunderstanding occurred also in Moscow. See J. T. MURPHY's complaint in *The Reds in Congress*, London, ? 1921, pp. 19–20; and contrast RILU, *Labour's New Charter*, Glasgow, 1922, p. 37.

67. *Bev.* iii, p. 96, 'Fellow-workers', the CWC's first leaflet (? November 1915).

68. J. T. MURPHY, in *Solidarity*, April 1917, November 1919.

69. PRIBICEVIC, *The Shop Stewards' Movement and Workers' Control*, p. 91; KENDALL, *The Revolutionary Movement in Britain*, p. 169.

8 Direct Action

W. M. Gallacher and J. R. Campbell

From W. M. Gallacher and J. R. Campbell, *Direct Action*, National Council of the Scottish Workers' Committees, 1919.

THE LABOUR UNREST

There is not a country in the world today where the position of the working class in industry is not the foremost theme for discussion amongst those interested in the social question. The press and the politicians discuss it unceasingly, without however contributing anything of value either to an understanding of the unrest or of the means which might be adopted towards its removal.

The fact that this unrest bulks so largely in the public eye indicates to all who look beneath the surface of things that the struggle between the workers and the employers is reaching a point of intensity never before experienced in the history of capitalism.

We do not mean to say labour unrest is an entirely new thing. Discontent has always been smouldering amongst the workers throughout the entire period of the industrial system. But discontent in the past did not wear the menacing aspect that it does today. If we except the stormy days of the Chartist movement, and the heroic if premature attempts made by Owen, Docherty and others to achieve class unionism about the same period, working class discontent in Britain has up to within recent years expressed itself in petty struggles for the fraction of a penny per hour increase in wages. Those struggles seemed to have little significance for anyone except the groups of workers and employers immediately concerned. They did not ruffle the surface of our social life. Not so, however, the industrial struggles of today. The industrial wars of today are taking place on a constantly larger scale, which threatens social dislocation, thereby making the labour unrest the most outstanding social feature of our time.

It is obvious to anyone that the existing industrial system is in a truly desperate state. The order of industry which, previous to the war, seemed destined to last for ever, is now tottering in every country of the world. In spite of all the efforts of the capitalists and their subsidized politicians to induce the workers to co-operate with them in rebuilding the industrial system, the gulf between the classes grows wider, and the labour unrest manifests itself in a constantly larger scale. The workers are realizing that the part they have to play in co-operation with the capitalists in rebuilding the industrial system has been carefully mapped out for them by the capitalist politicians. The workers' part in industrial reconstruction, according to the prophets of reconstruction, is to submit to increased exploitation in order that a greater mass of taxable wealth will be created which can be drawn upon by the politicians in order to liquidate the capitalists' war debt.

Efforts have already been made to induce the workers to increase production without any appreciable measure of success. The worker cannot be so easily fooled by the panic stunts of the press on matters that affect him intimately in his daily life in industry. He knows fairly well that the only effect of increased production would be to increase the wealth flowing into the lives of the plundering classes in the country. He therefore asks why he should slave harder to encourage social parasitism.

It is questionable if all the sermons on increased production inflicted on the workers during the past years by the parasitic classes and their hirelings have resulted in a pennyworth more wealth being created by the workers.

But the necessity of the capitalists increasing the exploitation of labour is too imperative to be abandoned at the first set back. A greater mass of wealth has got to be created to liquidate the war debt or the financiers themselves will have to make sacrifices by allowing a levy on capital to take place. They are not in a mood for making renunciations at the present time. They will try every means to increase the robbery of the workers rather than forego their ill-gotten gains. If they cannot *induce* the workers to increase production, then they will use their economic power to *force* the workers to increase production. Wherever the workers are weakly organized, there will newer and more vicious schemes of speeding up be imposed. Thus the labour unrest will grow in volume.

In those industries such as the railways where speeding up is hardly practical, attempts will be made to break the workers' standard of wages down to a lower level. Here also the workers will be stimulated to offer the most determined resistance to the encroachments of their exploiters. Not only so, but the latest developments of capitalist industry are running counter to the demand of the workers for a greater control of their working conditions. Under the guise of 'scientific management' the capitalists are introducing into industry schemes for dividing operations, and making the labour of the workers more automatic. The result of this tendency is to deny the worker responsibility, rob him of initiative, and reduce him to the level of some ghastly, inhuman, mechanical puppet.

The capitalist idea of more 'automatic' workers is bound to conflict with the workers' aspirations for greater responsibility, greater initiative and the democratic control of industry. The two are absolutely incompatible. There can be no compromise between them. Either we submit to capitalism and 'automatization' or go forward to industrial democracy and freedom.

The struggles of the capitalists to impose their ideal on the workers will be met by the workers increasing their efforts to get rid of the tyranny that is crushing them. The result, therefore, of the tendencies operating in industry, will be to intensify the class struggle, and make social peace impossible until the capitalists are finally overcome.

THE NEW OBJECTIVE

But not only is the outward aspect of working-class discontent more menacing, but it is challenging the existing industrial order in a more fundamental manner. Formerly all labour troubles were centred upon wages and hours. If the employer met the workers' demands on these points there was little disaffection, and he was generally allowed to manage his industry as he thought best. The idea that the capitalist possession of the tools of industry should be challenged by the industrial organizations of the workers would have seemed outrageous to the men who formed the existing national trade unions in the middle of last century. Their ideal was a fair day's wage for a fair day's work, and so far from challenging the despotic rule of the capitalist in industry, their ambition was to make that despotism a little more benevolent, thereby bringing about harmony between employers and employed.

Yet it is this capitalist ownership of industry that is being challenged today. The intelligent worker today understands that the factory he works in, the marvellous machinery he operates, while it is the private property of a group of capitalists, is nevertheless the embodiment of the labour of workers in other industries. He has no respect for capitalist property, because he recognizes that that property is the fruit of the past robbery of the workers. He has still less respect for it when he discovers that it is a means for robbing him in the present; robbing him not merely of material wealth, but robbing him of manhood.

Today the worker in industry is merely a living tool. He has no voice in the conduct of the industry his labour sustains. He has no voice in determining the purposes, for which industry is carried on. He is on a level with the inanimate machine he works, or the raw material which he changes into the finished produce. Indeed, has not a well-known reconstructionist said: 'Labour is our most precious raw material.'

It is against this industrial degradation that the workers are beginning to struggle. They are realizing that the right to vote for parliament, once in five years, is of little value compared with the right to vote on the way industry should be carried on. Consequently, the demand is arising that the brain and manual workers in industry shall, by electing their own controlling bodies and their own officials, democratically manage the industry in which they work. This movement for industrial self-government has already gained sufficient power on the continent of Europe to shake the capitalist system to its foundations. It is rapidly acquiring similar power in Britain. In the industries where the mass of the workers are enrolled in one union, as in the mines, the railways, and the Post Office, the demand for self-government in industry is beginning to figure on the programmes of the official unions. In the other industries, where craft unionism prevails, it finds expression in the demands of the unofficial Workers' Committee movement.

THE ROAD TO INDUSTRIAL FREEDOM

The problem of attaining self-government in industry can only be solved by the development of the workers' power in industry. It cannot be solved by the workers remaining passive and expecting an assembly of political supermen to change the world for them. No great social change has ever been brought about by people, who desired to see that change, being content merely to express pious opinions on the matter. A drastic social change, such as the taking of industry from the control of the capitalists and placing it in the control of the workers, demands that the workers shall exercise initiative, and assume responsibilities, in the everyday struggle with the functionaries of the employing class in the workshop. The workers' power rests upon the circumstances that it is they who keep the wheels of industry turning round, without which an ordered social life is impossible, and it is they who are the most numerous class in the country. It is by organizing the workers' power of numbers, in the place where that power can be applied most successfully, namely, in industry, that we will be able to break the power of the employers and their puppet government, and acquire the power to control the industrial forces of the country in the interests of the working class. To enable the workers to acquire the requisite power a re-modelling of the workers' industrial organizations is imperative. The bulk of the trade unions of the country have been built up to attain the ideal of a fair day's wage for a fair day's work, and in power and organization they are totally unfitted to bring about a change of social and industrial structure. Indeed, it may be questioned if they would be able to defend the existing wage standard of the workers against a concerted attack from the employers!

THE STRUGGLE FOR CONTROL

We pointed out at the beginning of the pamphlet that intelligent workers have got beyond mere wage and hour questions, and are beginning to advocate that the industrial struggle should be waged to oust the capitalists from the control of industry. *This involves a revolutionary struggle for power*. We do not believe it is possible to any great extent to win control by wringing step by step concessions from the capitalists.

The capitalists are going to put up a terrific struggle before they will relinquish any of the authority they possess in industry, and we are therefore convinced that their power must be broken once for all by the mass action of the workers before real control becomes possible.

It would strengthen the workers greatly in their struggle for control if they could command the allegiance of the technical staff in industry. It has been the habitual policy of big businesses in America to buy off the skilled workers with concessions, thereby driving a wedge between skilled and unskilled, making solidarity impossible, and enabling them to exploit the unskilled all the more ruthlessly.

A similar policy will doubtless be tried in Britain as the unrest intensifies, though its success here would be more doubtful. But if the capitalists are able to maintain the traditional separation between the staff and the ordinary manual workers, the power of the workers will be impaired. It is, however, becoming increasingly difficult for the bosses to do so. The technical staffs are beginning to organize to fight the employer for better conditions. The manner in which they were slighted by the bosses during the war has taught the salaried workers that there is no livable future before any section of the working class who refuse to organize and fight. And so organizations of technical workers are springing up everywhere. That there is a tendency on the part of these organizations to stand aloof from the general movement of the workers is apparent. But this is merely temporary. It is due largely to the hostile attitude of the manual workers and the fear of victimization. But with the development of the struggle for control the manual worker will realize the necessity for getting the staff on his side, while the growth in strength of the workshop movement will afford the technical workers adequate safeguards against victimization.

It is inevitable that the struggle should develop with constantly increasing bitterness on both sides. Industrial struggles will cease to be struggles of isolated trades, or even isolated industries, and will tend to become of a class nature. Every such struggle has revolutionary potentialities which should be exploited to the utmost.

It is essential, when such a struggle arises, that the industrial power of the workers shall be capable of being mobilized quickly.

Trade union branches meeting once a fortnight or once a month, attended by an infinitesimal fraction of the membership they represent, hampered by constitutional procedure, cannot move with the rapidity that alone can ensure success in a time of social crisis. Such rapidity can only be secured by the workshop organization above outlined.

Immediately a crisis, like the late railway strike arose, workshop meetings in the industries not immediately affected could be held, the facts of the situation put before the workers, and the whole industry be prepared for action if necessary. The District Committees and District Councils would sit in permanent session. The Social Committees would elaborate ways and means of feeding the workers, the National Committees of Particular Industries, and the National Council of All Industries would prepare for action. This would increase the workers' power and confidence enormously, and would enable a crisis to be exploited to the limit of its revolutionary possibilities.

A FINAL WORD

In placing this sketch of organization before the workers it is not our business to criticize trade union leaders, or to waste further time dealing with the obvious fact that the present form of trade-union organization is totally unfitted for the struggle now going on between the workers and those who live on their labour.

Neither do we wish to enter into such a controversial question as to whether politicians and parliament are useful, or otherwise, in the fight for working-class emancipation. What we do wish to emphasize is that only by a complete change in the method of production and distribution can there ever be any hope for the future. That change can only be brought about by industrial organization. Even the most devoted adherent of political action would never dream of suggesting that the House of Commons was the foundation of society. Everyone knows that it is merely a part of the super-structure, and whatever changes may take place in its personnel, and however desirous they might be to aid a revolution, the revolution can only be brought about by a form of organization that will place the control of the product in the hands of the workers themselves.

Why have we a few people living in idle luxury, while millions are continually faced with the spectre of want? Because of our method of production and distribution. Why have we un-employed men and women walking the streets by the thousands? It is not because of parliament, but the result of our insane method of production and distribution. So we might travel over every form of social inequality, and the cause is always the same. It is this that causes the crushing of the Indian and Egyptian, that necessitates an armed force in Ireland. It is this problem we must face if we would be free.

At the same time it must be understood that we do not offer our outline of organization as a hard and fast scheme. We do not present it with an air of finality. Like all active workers who are in close contact with industrial developments, we realize that the present form of industrial organization is obsolete, and we have outlined a constructive policy, whereby the industrial strength of the workers can be exerted to the utmost in any struggle that takes place. But we are not above learning, and we therefore invite constructive criticism from all sections of the labour movement.

It was never so necessary as it is now for the workers' movement to submit itself to the most ruthless self-criticism. Old tactics and old methods of organization have to be overhauled and brought up to date to enable us to meet and overcome the latest developments of organization from the employers' side. Delay spells disaster. Everywhere the organization of the employers and their cats-paw government is being improved to meet all eventualities. If we do not counter these developments with improved organization, then the existing organization will be no more able to deflect the employers from imposing industrial serfdom on us than a match-box placed in the path of a steam roller could deflect it from its path.

The servile state or industrial and social democracy? That is the choice that circumstances are presenting to the workers. We do not idealize our class. We know its prejudices and its limitations. But recent developments have encouraged us in the belief that the faces of the workers are turning towards the goal of industrial freedom. The way to that goal will not be traversed easily. It will be strewn with all the barriers that a privileged class playing on the fears of the timid, and the ambition of the unscrupulous, can erect. There will be defeats and heart-breaking set backs on the way. But with courage and persistence we will triumph over every obstacle, and will finally attain to the industrial Republic of Labour, where the workers will cease to be mere living tools and become free men; where the gates of opportunity will be thrown open to everyone, and the workers of hand and brain will finally enter into possession and enjoyment of the heritage which the labours of former generations have bequeathed to them.

Part Three
Sociological Analysis

The academic analysis of industrial relations has been traditionally dominated by pragmatism and pluralism, perspectives in
which trade unions are viewed as a means of marginal reform
within the existing social structure, not a means of transcending
the structure. The primary orientation of this approach is
towards the normative and institutional regulation of the
collective bargaining relationship between employers and unions
within capitalism, ignoring the element of conflict and opposition
inherent in unionism to the very existence of capitalism. As
Goldthorpe infers, beneath the veneer of neutrality, 'the liberal-
pluralist approach to industrial relations is managerial in its
priorities and conservative in its implications'. Nevertheless, the
work of this school has not only achieved predominance in the
academic world; but has also been adopted by the state, and –
even more significantly – by large sections of the labour movement, as the most adequate analysis of contemporary industrial
relations. A convincing explanation of this occurrence, provided
by Allen, is that, 'A social theory achieves acceptability and
hence predominance not through its capacity to explain reality
alone, but through its capacity to explain reality in the context of
a given power structure.'[1] A theory which questions the acceptance of the existing power structure, even if closer to the
reality experienced by the majority of people, is destined for
dismissal and obscurity to the extent that the powerful may effectively enforce it. Despite this difficulty, the repeated failure of the
palliatives of liberal-pluralist analysis, when constantly confronted by entrenched industrial conflict, has stimulated a resurgence in radical sociological analysis, a selection of which is
contained in this section, which removes some of the obfuscation
of the dominant perspectives.

In the first reading, it is singularly apposite that Fox, having
once offered a major defence of pluralism in industrial relations,
should now present a penetrating critique of the pluralist ethos.

He explores various possible ideological interpretations of the distribution of power between labour and capital in society and industry, and the relationship of such interpretations to the behaviour of the two sides: the pluralist takes an optimistic view of the business enterprise, assuming a roughly equal balance of power between employers and workers organized in trade unions, and, therefore, that workers have a responsibility to observe agreements, with any outstanding differences resolved by the formal procedures of collective bargaining; in his 'autocritique' Fox challenges this pluralist reliance on collective bargaining in capitalist society, and offers a radical alternative as a more convincing analysis. Thus collective organization of workers in trade unions does not equalize the balance of power between employers and workers, since collective bargaining does not deal with fundamentals, but with restricted issues, which in themselves pose no threat to the established order. Were trade unions ever to pose such a threat, the state would intervene in support of the employers to restore the existing system.

Collective bargaining therefore is not an effective means of social change, or social justice, and imposes on workers no binding moral commitment to comply with negotiated agreements. The extent to which workers do conform to agreements is often determined by expediency, in particular their perception of the capacity of management to impose greater sanctions, and whenever this power disparity, temporarily, is eliminated, workers feel free to break agreements which were never a true reflection of their interests. Fox's analysis explains the demonstrable failure of capitalist industry to secure the loyalty of workers which they amply display in other contexts, and reveals how the creation of a new normative order is dependent upon a fundamental reconstruction of industry and society rather than minor changes in collective bargaining.

Hyman and Fryer, in the second reading, attempt to overcome the aridity of conventional organizational analysis of trade unionism, which is insensitive to the different purposes and special character of trade union organization compared with other formal organizations. In particular they stress that: 'To understand trade unions it is essential to analyse the environing institutions of power with which they interact: an adequate analysis of trade unions and trade unionism must also be, in large measure, an analysis of the political economy within which they operate.' The most prominent feature of this power relationship they recognize is the massive economic, political and ideological power imbalance between capitalists and workers; and they detail the objective and subjective determinants which enable unions to exercise a limited countervailing power to capital.

Turning to an examination of the internal power relationships of labour unions (which are themselves greatly influenced by the external power distribution), they show how the capacity of union leaders to determine the primary 'needs' of the union – in particular the 'need' for security, solvency, absence of dissent, and administrative efficiency – may displace the overt objectives of the union to protect and advance the interests of the membership. The informed participation of the membership is essential to the prevention of such displacement of union goals, but Hyman and Fryer point out the factors which may inhibit union democracy, especially how a narrow conception of union function provides little incentive for membership participation. It is in this situation that the growth of the contemporary shop steward's movement and the increase in domestic bargaining has occurred, developing rank-and-file involvement in the shop floor organization rather than the union: thus in present-day unionism the 'official machinery is often of very little significance to the ordinary member'. However, shop stewards are not immune to the incorporative pressures which afflict union officials at a higher level: shop stewards may alternatively provide a counterbalance to bureaucratization, or, if successfully incorporated, become the first line of union bureaucracy.

Looking further at trade union democracy, Eldridge summarizes some of the academic theories that have evolved analysing and legitimizing bureaucratic control of trade unions. Most of these theories exhibit a profound pessimism, concentrating on those factors which restrict democracy, and largely ignoring counteracting tendencies:[2] for generally, those democratic pressures which led to the formation of unions antagonistic to the rule of capital, ultimately will engender effective opposition to union oligarchy. The disclosure of the limitations of the democratic process in contemporary unions is a vital task, but a sterile one unless it is wedded to an exploration for, and analysis of, those forces which create an 'iron law of democracy'.[3] The rooted opposition between the interests of workers and capitalists, will result in an incorporated union oligarchy servile to capital's interests being met – in one form or another – by rank-and-file revolt.[4]

In the final reading Goldthorpe takes serious issue with the branch of the liberal-pluralist school which heavily influenced the work of the Donovan Commission on industrial relations of 1965-8.[5] The commission recognized that there had been a shift in the bargaining strength of trade unions from the bureaucratic official structures to the shopfloor and the failure to accommodate the formal collective bargaining machinery to this shift had led to pathological industrial militancy and wage drift, the commission argued. The solution to this problem, the commission suggested, was that shopfloor representatives should be incorporated into the bargaining structure, by the development of formal plant-level industrial procedures with government encouragement, and union official-management supervision.[6] But as Goldthorpe precisely explains, both the theoretical presuppositions of the pluralist approach, and the policy recommendations which flow from it, are inherently unsound: though professing to extend the pluralist process, the actual achievement would be to preserve the heavy concentration of power in the hands of industrial management. The liberal-pluralist prescription is, in essence, enlightened managerialism, permitting the regulation and channelling of shopfloor action and demands in a predictable fashion thereby enhancing managerial control: therefore, Goldthorpe suggests, 'the liberal-pluralist approach to industrial relations policy is in its implications fundamentally conservative . . . the changes which it seeks to promote are ones designed to bring about the more effective integration of labour into the existing structure of economic and social relations, in industry and wider society, rather than ones intended to produce any basic alteration to this structure.'

The central weakness of the pluralist analysis is the diagnosis of industrial relations problems, such as unofficial strikes, protective practices, and wage drift, as pathological, rather than as legitimate expressions of social conflict intrinsic to the economic and social relations of capitalism. One reason for this weakness is the exclusive focus on the immediate institutions and processes of industrial relations to the neglect of wider concerns: 'Nowhere . . . in the entire literature of academic industrial relations . . . is there to be found any systematic consideration of how the functioning of the economic system as a whole and of its constituent units is founded upon, and sustains, vast differences in social power and advantage . . .' On the contrary, Goldthorpe concludes, the reform of industrial relations is only possible as part of a more general understanding and restructuring of wider society.[7]

NOTES

1. V. L. ALLEN, *The Sociology of Industrial Relations*, Longmans, 1971, London.

2. R. HYMAN, *Marxism and the Sociology of Trade Unionism*, Pluto Press, 1971, pp. 20–5, 35–7.

3. A. W. GOULDNER, 'Metaphysical Pathos and the Theory of Bureaucracy' in L. A. COSER and B. ROSENBERG (eds.), *Sociological Theory*, 1964.

4. A graphic account of one such revolt is T. LANE and K. ROBERTS, *Strike at Pilkingtons*, Fontana, 1971. This also analyses the present difficulty in creating a more militant breakaway union, placing the onus upon the struggle to make the *existing* unions more democratic.

5. Royal Commission on Trade Unions and Employers' Associations, Report, Cmnd. 3623, 1968.

6. The 'voluntarism' implied in the Commission's proposals and which had previously distinguished the British industrial relations system is deceptive, as Hyman has maintained, 'In Britain, "voluntarism" in industrial relations shared with laissez-faire ideology in general an essentially practical basis: the confidence of employers in their own ability to exercise control without outside assistance. This meant in turn that trade unions should lack either the power or the will to interfere excessively with managerial objectives.' R. HYMAN, *Industrial Relations: A Marxist Introduction*, Macmillan, 1975, p. 135.

7. It is imperative to distinguish clearly the 'radical-pluralism' of Fox and Goldthorpe from a Marxist analysis. Though Fox and Goldthorpe have elaborated the profound weaknesses of the liberal-pluralist explanation of capitalist society, they seem to lack a conception of the *agency* for the transformation of capitalism, beyond the gradual spread of socialist enlightenment, which departs little from traditional Fabian thinking. Some limitations of Fox's radicalism are presented in S. Wood and R. Elliot, 'A Critical Evaluation of Fox's Radicalisation of Industrial Relations Theory', *Sociology*, Vol. 11, no. 1, 1977. A Marxist critique of pluralism is R. Hyman, 'Pluralism, Collective Bargaining and Procedural Consensus,' *BJIR*, 1977.

9 The Myths of Pluralism and a Radical Alternative

Alan Fox

Reprinted with permission from A. Fox, *Man Mismanagement*, Hutchinson, 1974, pp. 10–25.

A PLURALIST PERSPECTIVE ON THE BUSINESS ENTERPRISE

The pluralistic interpretation of the industrial organization probably represents the received orthodoxy in many Western societies, even if it comes in a variety of versions. By this is meant not that it commands universal assent but that it is the view favoured, either explicitly or implicitly, by probably most persons of power, authority, status and influence who can be said to manifest a view at all.

Just as the pluralist perspective takes an essentially benign view of Western industrial society, so it takes a similar view of the work organization. It sees the organization as a coalition of interest groups presided over by a top management which serves the long-term needs of 'the organization as a whole' by paying due concern to all the interests affected – employees, shareholders, consumers, the community, the 'national interest'. This involves management in holding the 'right' balance between the sometimes divergent claims of these participant interests. The possibility exists, however, that management, under pressure, say, from market competition or from shareholders, might pay insufficient heed to the needs and claims of its employees if they were not able to bring those needs and claims forcefully to its attention. Through collective organization in trade unions, therefore, employees mobilize themselves to meet management on equal terms to negotiate the terms of their collaboration. The pluralist does not claim anything approaching perfection for this system. In some situations, imbalances of strength as between employers and unions or between management and particular work-groups may be such that for one side or the other justice is distinctly rough. They are not seen as so numerous or severe, however, as generally to discredit the system either from the unions' point of view or from management's.

We come here upon an implication of considerable importance that will recur at several points in our analysis. This is that the system of employers and unions, or management and unionized work-group, jointly negotiating terms and conditions of employment depends to some extent for its stability and health upon neither side feeling that it is being overly subjected to coercive dictation by the other. We can explain this by recalling a well-established proposition about power and promises. If someone extracts a promise from us by holding a pistol to our head, neither a legal nor a moral judgement regards that promise as binding in honour, and it is certain that we ourselves do not so regard it. As soon as the immediate threat is removed we feel justified in ignoring the promise, since it was extracted from us 'under duress'. Of course, were the threat to be maintained continuously – which might prove difficult and costly – we would continue to observe the required behaviour, but this observance would follow not from our recognition of a moral obligation but from expediency – from prudent calculation in the interests of avoiding punishment. Commitments and agreements which we feel to have been extracted from us under compulsion as a result of extreme weakness on our part do not evoke our sense of obligation so far as observance is concerned. What kinds of commitments and agreements *do* evoke such a sense of obligation? Only those in which we feel ourselves to have enjoyed adequate freedom in undertaking the commitment or concluding the agreement. And the sense of obligation is the greater the more nearly we approach a position of complete equality with the other party. When we accept the terms and conditions of an undertaking, not from any sense of being pressured or coerced, but from a sense of voluntarily agreeing to obligations whose nature and consequences we fully understand, we are conscious of a moral obligation bearing upon us. To be sure, we may sometimes be tempted to evade it, but when others appeal to us that the obligation exists – and seek to keep us to the line of duty by threatening penalties if we default – we do not consider the moral appeal to be irrelevant or the threatened penalties to be an offence against natural justice.

What is the relevance of all this to relationships between management and rank-and-file, and to the pluralist perspective on these relationships? First of all it casts light on those situations where rank-and-file employees are not collectively organized. Here the employee stands only in an individual contract relationship with his employer. The employer's superior economic power in this contract gives him, in many cases, correspondingly disproportionate ability to determine its terms. This was the predominant pattern during the earlier phases of industrialization and has by no means disappeared. Yet men of substance were apt to defend this system with the palpable fiction that it represented free contract between master and man bargaining as equals in the labour market, and as such called for full and honourable discharge by the employee of his obligations towards the master. Whether or not particular employees saw this situation as fair and as calling for scrupulous observance, the passage of time saw a growing number of outside observers who regarded this degree of power disparity as socially unjust, and of course the trade unions were propagating this message from the start. As they gained in strength the notion spread that, by mobilizing themselves collectively and presenting a united force, employees were gradually eliminating the acute imbalance of power between themselves and their employers. Collective bargaining developed through which both sides committed themselves to certain terms and conditions of employment, including procedures which defined the method of handling claims and grievances without resort to strikes, lockouts, or other forms of disruptive action.

The significance of our 'ethics' argument now emerges. To the extent that the terms and conditions of the employment contract are seen as being settled, not by the coercive power of the employer, but by free and equitable negotiation between parties of roughly comparable strength, employees can fairly be required to offer honourable observance of the agreements that result. Organized collective relations in industry have therefore developed to the accompaniment of the widely propagated assertion that both sides have a moral obligation to observe the agreements negotiated by their representative agencies. As we have already noted, this is not to say that a sense of moral obligation is, or need be, the only motive for observing agreements. Men may be punctilious in observance for reasons of expediency – or, in the phrase used earlier, prudent calculation. They may, for example, consider that it will serve their interests best in the long run ('Honesty is the best policy'); or that to default would expose them to penalties and give the other side a good excuse for defaulting also. But because these expediency motives rest on men's calculations of their own self-interest they are a somewhat uncertain basis for observance in a complex and constantly changing world, for men's views of where their self-interests lie may fluctuate during the span of an agreement, and in any case there may be differences between the perceived self-interests of a group of union members on the shopfloor and the calculation made and negotiated on their behalf by union officers. A sense of being under a *moral* obligation to honour agreements can therefore help to sustain consent despite these fluctuations and differences – and if the outside observer sees the negotiation arrangements as fairly balanced he will be the readier to see employees penalized if they default.

We can illustrate this pluralist perspective by relating it to what is felt by many to be one of the major issues of industrial relations today. For many years now employers in Britain have been bitter in their denunciations of the so-called 'unconstitutional' strike – the strike undertaken by a work-group, with or without tacit support from union officers, in transgression of the official disputes procedure negotiated by union and employers. The written evidence submitted by the Confederation of British Industry to the Royal Commission on Trade Unions and Employers' Associations (1965–8) asserted that 'For many years employers have felt that the greatest single contribution which could be made to the better working of the industrial relations system would be better observance of agreements.' The attitudes taken by the pluralist on the moral issue here are clearly shaped by his assumptions about the distribution of power in society and industry. The belief that the powers of employers' associations and trade unions, and of management and unionized work-groups, are as fairly matched as can reasonably be hoped for in a complicated world, leads to the assertion that employees should always act 'responsibly' (i.e., in accordance with their obligations) by observing the terms of the agreements negotiated on their behalf. Some of those making this assertion argue that where employees flout agreements 'society' would be justified in penalizing them in some way until they respect them. From this view, transgressors are seen either as lacking all sense of responsibility and obligation, or as having some psychological quirk which renders them anti-authority on principle, or as holding subversive political views which require them to render present institutions unworkable.

The general picture of industrial relations that could be drawn from this pluralistic approach is one which, though hardly free of conflict, contains mechanisms enabling the contending parties, not too unevenly matched, to negotiate their mutual accommodations in a manner appropriate to a society which aspires to industrial as well as political democracy. Within this framework, employees would be assumed to see management as simply discharging its necessary functions and receiving its rewards like any other group in the organization. In carrying out its job it tries to apply certain principles which appear to rank as inevitable facts of life – for example, that those doing more responsible work must receive larger incomes than those doing less responsible work, that those wielding authority should earn more than those under their command, and that the managerial function is of self-evidently higher status than manual labour. In performing its co-ordinative, directive and innovatory functions for society, management has to control and contain the possibly divergent, possibly excessive aspirations of the various subordinate groups which make up the enterprise. These efforts inevitably involve it in friction and dispute. Yet these are not unhealthy conflicts which rock the fundamentals of the system (about which men are taken to be generally agreed), but understandably divergences of the sort only to be expected in a free society. Collective bargaining enables most of them to be resolved in a tolerable manner, though to be sure it creates problems, as in all industrial countries, still to be resolved.

It is some such picture as this that we derive from applying a pluralist perspective to the work organization. As already suggested, probably many of the more favoured members of our society find it, or some variant of it, a convincing and satisfying interpretation. Again, this is to say not that they interpret their experience in any ordered and articulated way, for people rarely arrange their beliefs so comprehensively unless pressed to do so, but rather that such a view can be said to be implicit in their attitudes and behaviour. If we ask, however, how many rank-and-file employees think, feel and act by such beliefs and assumptions the answer must be that we do not know, for we have remarkably little hard evidence as to how they see their world. What is certain is that there exists a variety of 'social images' of which this, or some approximation to it, is one. Another is the radical perspective now to be presented. Between them they illustrate the sharply contrasting views men may hold of the social and industrial scene, and the way in which these views affect their interpretation of events and consequently their behaviour.

A RADICAL PERSPECTIVE ON THE BUSINESS ENTERPRISE

The starting point for examining the radical view relates to the distribution of power. Like the pluralist interpretation, it emphasizes the gross disparity of power between the employer and the individual employee. Lacking property or command over resources, the employee is totally dependent on being offered employment by owners or controllers – and a dependence relationship is a power relationship. From this position of weakness he has little ability to assert his needs and aspirations against those of the employer, who can therefore treat him not as an end in himself but as a means to the employer's own ends: as a commodity-resource to be used for purposes about which he is not consulted and which he may not share. Unlike the pluralist, however, the radical does not see the collective organization of employees into trade unions as restoring a balance of power (or anything as yet approaching it) between the propertied and the propertyless. He may well agree that it mitigates the imbalance and thereby enables employees to challenge some kinds of management decision on issues of special and immediate importance for them. But a great imbalance remains, symptomized by the fact that there are many other types of management decision which employees might aspire to influence were they conscious of having the power to do so, but from which they are presently completely excluded.

The radical would agree, however, that appearances may sometimes suggest to the casual eye that, on the contrary, the imbalance is in the employees' favour – and certainly this is a widespread and popular impression. Is not management sometimes forced to its knees by a powerful union or organized work-group? But, says the radical, examine the issues which are and are not at stake even in the most titanic-seeming clash. The former revolve around wages, who does what work and under what conditions, who should join what union, and other matters which, though of great significance for both sides, do not touch the basic fundamentals of the system. Trade unions strive to effect marginal improvements in the lot of their members and to defend them against arbitrary management action. They do not – and here we come to the crucial point of what issues are *not* at stake in management/worker relations – attack management on such basic principles of the social and industrial framework as private property, the hierarchical nature of the organization, the extreme division of labour, and the massive inequalities of financial reward, status, control and autonomy in work. Neither do they try to secure a foothold in the majority of decisions made within the organization on such issues as management objectives, markets, capital investment, and rate of expansion. Very rarely do they seriously challenge such principles as the treatment of labour as a commodity to be hired or discarded at management's convenience.

Why, asks the radical, do they not challenge management on all these issues which may clearly have major significance for the work experience, rewards and life destinies of their members? The answer he offers is twofold. First, employee collectives (unions and organized work-groups) realize that while they can deploy enough economic power (i.e., the collective control of their own labour) and enjoy enough support from government and other sections of society to enable them to offer an effective challenge to management on a limited range of issues where their participation in decision-making is seen as legitimate, they would need to mobilize far more power than is customary at present if they were to achieve significantly larger aspirations. For, faced with demands which in effect struck at the foundations of management power, privilege, values and objectives, management would draw not only upon its own full reserves of strength but also upon the support of other managements, employers' associations and sympathetic sections of society (including government), which were concerned to defend the *status quo*. Such a basic clash would soon reveal where ultimate power lay, and the present capacity of the rank-and-file for a mass mobilization against the *status quo* would have to increase enormously for it to lie with the unions.

This leads into the second aspect of the radical's answer. A mobilization of power on this scale would require great resources of will, determination, confidence and aspiration. Why are these resources not presently available to the unions? Because their members, quite apart from being conscious of having something to lose from such a clash, are still too much under the influence of social conditioning to venture a bid of these dimensions. To some extent they accept as valid the principles on which the work organization is constructed and the conventions by which management operates it. If they doubt them at all it is certainly not with the universal unquestioning conviction that would be required for a successful onslaught against the full power of property and resource-control. But, says the radical, this acceptance, total or partial, of the principles and conventions of work organization cannot realistically be seen as a free and informed choosing situation in which employees rationally examine alternative possibilities and make an unforced choice. As we saw, the vast majority who are without resources must seek access to resources owned or controlled by the few, and such is their relative weakness and dependence that they are constrained, for the most part, to accept the essential nature of work organization as they find it. Power counts, too, in many indirect as well as direct ways. It was noted earlier that the values of wealth, position and status shape much of the content of public communication in newspapers, magazines, radio, television, advertising, public relations, education and training, all of which manifest either explicitly or implicitly these dominant ideas and assumptions and, equally important, define the terms and limits of current controversy and debate. Recognition of this does not require us to accept a conspiracy theory of history, simply to acknowledge that in a thousand different ways powerless men survive and possibly prosper by serving the interests, values and objectives of powerful men, and can usually find some method of salvaging their self-respect while doing so.

All this suggests that the approach of many rank-and-file employees probably consists of a low-key acceptance of the organization's essential characteristics. They are encouraged to see them not only as necessary and inevitable but also as legitimate and right, and while they may be keenly conscious of grievances these are not so overwhelming as to drive them to condemn the system *in toto*. Yet their subordinate and inferior position generally precludes them from participating in it with enthusiasm and commitment, for they cannot help but see it as having been imposed on them. Cynicism and distrust of 'them' may not be far below the surface, coexisting with a disposition to make the best of things, to reflect that they could be worse, and to conclude that since hierarchy, subordination and inequality are so universal and enduring they are probably in some mysterious way inevitable. If these ideas are changing it is only very slowly. Meanwhile they probably play an important part in maintaining the relative passivity which so many among the lower ranks extend to the major features of the system in which they find themselves.

When the employees 'accept', therefore, as they almost invariably do, the basic structure, principles and conventions of the work organization, they do so not from free considered choice, but partly because they are aware of the superior power which supports that pattern of organization and makes it seem inevitable, and partly because their social environment induces them in any case to see it as 'natural', 'realistic', and 'only to be expected'. They limit their union and work-group aspirations to influencing such managerial decisions as are immediately important to them and which experience has taught them are within reach through the medium of collective bargaining.

How do they themselves see this negotiating method? We have already noted one view of it as a process of joint regulation by parties of roughly comparable strength who agree the terms of their collaboration and who acknowledge the imperative of moral obligation as well as of self-interested expediency in the observance of the resulting agreements. Employees with a radical perspective cannot hold this view. For them, collective bargaining is at worst a mere façade behind which the employer continues to dictate terms, at best a means by which organized employees can get marginally to grips with their masters on some issues although still leaving the latter with the real reserves of power. These reserves they rarely need to use because society and its institutions and values continue to retain the configuration necessary for their interests. For employees with this view of the social and industrial scene, the severe inequalities of power which subject rank-and-file employees to an inferior and subordinate position exempt them from moral obligation to observe organizational rules which run specially counter to their own needs and interests. This applies no less to those rules which have been jointly negotiated, for even in this process the employees are seen as being at a great disadvantage.

As we have noted, the radical agrees that appearances may suggest the contrary. Do not wage and other settlements sometimes lie nearer the employees' preferred position than to that of the employer? The radical's reply would be that, quite apart from the fact that bargaining tactics and gamesmanship complicate, even for the participants, the issue of what their preferred positions are, the aspirations of employees are themselves shaped by their awareness of the employer's power and the need to be 'realistic'. Employees try to achieve what they feel to have some chance of achieving given the prevailing power relations. Their claims take into account their awareness of the employer's superior position. Thus, says the radical, appearances are misleading and in no way contradict the proposition that employees, even when unionized, remain in a greatly inferior power situation. Similar arguments can be turned upon those negotiated procedures for settling individual or group claims and grievances – procedures which, by ruling out strikes, overtime bans or other forms of direct action, seek to guarantee to management that no disruption of work occurs. Through such procedures, management commits itself, in effect, to hearing appeals against its decisions. But to secure this concession, employee groups (and their unions) must forego such tactical ability as their position may afford them to put pressure upon management during the process. In this matter too, then, says the radical, management's superior power is able to shape arrangements to its liking.

Thus, while employees may be able to secure from the employer certain marginal improvements in their relatively lowly position and its rewards, that position is essentially imposed upon them by these great structural inequalities of property ownership and economic power, officially sanctioned and supported by the coercive forces of the state, and by Labour as well as by Conservative governments. What moral obligation, asks the radically-minded employee, does he owe the employer to obey organizational rules, when even those that are 'jointly agreed' have been negotiated within what is in fact a highly unequal power relationship? Rather does he feel justified in pressing every minor advantage, manipulating every rule, exploiting every loophole, harrying every managerial weakness or leniency in his continuous struggle against those whom he sees as exploiting his economic weakness for purposes about which he is not consulted.

MOTIVES FOR COMPLIANCE: EXPEDIENCY AND OBLIGATION

Whether the radically-minded employee (or work-group) does or does not flout agreements and refuse to extend to the employer a spirit of give and take (the spirit which, in fact, to varying degrees characterizes most work situations) depends on his calculations of expedience. Our preceding argument suggests why he may feel no sense of obligation in his relations with the employer or management. But expediency may induce him to behave in much the same way as someone who does. Relevant factors here can include a calculation that this will serve his long-term interests best, an awareness that to maintain a permanent guerrilla campaign against management may goad it into a massive retaliation exercise which it feels it has to win, and knowledge that sharp practice on his part deprives him of effective argument against similar behaviour by management. Yet, as we know from experience and observation, work-groups do not necessarily calculate that their net interests point in this direction. They may, for a variety of reasons, resort to very different behaviour.

The significance of a purely calculative or expediency approach to the procedures, disciplines and restraints associated with a stable collective bargaining situation is that, whereas an established and accepted moral obligation remains unvarying in what it admonishes us to do, the dictates of calculative expediency vary according to circumstances, mood, and who is making the assessment. An example can be offered which illustrates these differences. Let us suppose that a certain work-group and the appropriate full-time district officer accept that the disputes procedure of the company concerned, having been, as they see it, fairly negotiated, deserves the fullest possible moral observance. While this conviction holds, the group's adherence to procedure can be expected to take a certain amount of strain. Some decisions emanating from the procedure may be unpopular and men grumble, but the predominant opinion supports faithful observance of the agreement. But if their reading of the situation is that the disputes procedure in question, or the circumstances of its origins, are such that they cannot offer it their moral adhesion, their behaviour with respect to its provisions will be governed by expediency. They may, for example, observe them when in a weak position where they feel unable to do otherwise, and flout them when in a strong position where they are conscious of enjoying a temporary advantage over management on the issue in question. We would also expect the group's acceptance of the decisions or awards issuing from the procedure to be uncertain for, lacking moral adhesion to the system, their attitude is less likely to be able to take the strain of unfavourable outcomes. Finally, we must note the possibility that the work-group and the full-time official may make different calculations of expediency. The latter may work to what he considers a higher-order expediency than that shaping the responses of the rank-and-file. He may look beyond their immediate personal interests to the union's long-term relationship with the company, perhaps with an employers' association, or to its institutional interests *vis-à-vis* rival unions. The possibilities of conflict are apparent, for the officer may find difficulty in convincing his members when they ask why his reading of the situation should prevail over theirs.

One of the characteristics of an expediency approach is that any relevant participant can claim his assessment to be as valid as anyone else's. Divergences are equally sharp if rank-and-file members insist on an expediency approach while the full-time officer endorses the approach of the Trades Union Congress in its written evidence to the 1965–8 Royal Commission, where it declared that 'The General Council acknowledged, as would every responsible trade union leader, that procedure agreements embody promises and therefore should not be broken by any union representative.'[1]

The threat presented to authority, control and leadership when rank-and-file react to rules, agreements and contracts only from an expediency calculation unsupported by any sense of obligation renders understandable not only that *management* should be found urging the moral sanctity of agreements and commitments 'freely and voluntarily' entered into, but also that trade union leaders too, in their concern for observance, should sometimes feel the need to reinforce expediency with the un-equivocal ethical message that agreements embody promises which ought to be kept. In this they are like all rulers who seek to control their subjects' behaviour. We are, for example, threatened with detection and punishment if we rob banks. But if authority relied on this expediency argument alone the numbers of those who fancied their chances of evading detection would probably rise. We are taught, therefore, that it is also morally wrong to rob banks. With a combination of these two arguments authority hopes to keep us under control.

The reasons why trade union leaders have normally been concerned with their members' observance of negotiated agreements will be examined later. Meanwhile we can note that for anyone wishing to urge the moral sanctity of an agreement of any kind it is crucial, in most Western cultures at least, to be able to assert convincingly that the agreement in question was negotiated between parties of roughly comparable strength. For, as we have noted, to the extent that it is seen, or felt, to have been imposed by a markedly stronger party upon a weaker, the moral obligation bearing upon the latter will be felt to be that much the less. The significance for industrial relations of a belief that the negotiating parties are not so unequal in strength as to exempt the weaker from obligation is therefore apparent. It plays a useful supportive role for those concerned to promote stability and order in work relations. Insofar as employees themselves accept the belief, their observance of agreements is reinforced by their sense of obligation. Insofar as that vague and ill-defined entity, 'public opinion', accepts it there may be political support for coercing employee defaulters into what is seen as their moral duty. With this kind of support within reach, those anxious to maintain stability are less dependent upon employees' calculations of personal expediency.

It is understandable, therefore, that interpretations of society based on the assumption of an approximate balance of power between the principal interest groups tend to be popular among those concerned to ensure that existing institutions work as smoothly as possible. Again, no conscious calculation need be postulated, only a tendency for men to be attracted by doctrines and interpretations which accord with, and support, the preferences, values and objectives they already hold. Conversely, those strongly critical of the prevailing social and economic order are likely to be found rejecting interpretations which appear to support a view of society as composed of balanced interest groups fairly negotiating the terms of their collaboration.

The author has already indicated that he finds the radical view, or some version of it, more convincing than the one with which it has been compared. But vastly more important for the manager is to gauge the views held by his own labour force, and to bring to the level of conscious inspection the views he holds himself. Only when he realizes that his attitudes and behaviour implicitly contain assumptions about society and organization is he in a position to examine them and decide whether he finds them convincing. It can, of course, safely be repeated that only a tiny minority of us formulate our views in any conscious, articulated manner. Nevertheless, in our attitudes, responses and behaviour, we all express a general orientation of whose fuller implications we may be unaware. In this sense, some employee groups may display a general orientation carrying the implications labelled here as pluralist. But equally likely – and in the absence of reliable evidence this can be no more than an impression – is that many employee groups, unionized or not, consider themselves in a greatly inferior power position *vis-à-vis* their remote and impersonal top management, and that their observance of rules and agreements owes more to expediency than to any sense of obligation (though this does not imply that the latter is wholly absent).

What happens when such a group becomes specially frustrated or resentful while at the same time conscious of a modicum of strength is exemplified in those industries where management complains of unruly and disruptive behaviour in defiance of agreed procedures for the peaceful handling of issues in dispute. The groups in question are clearly, on those occasions, no longer defining expediency for themselves in terms of observing the formal procedures agreed by management and unions (designed as they are to restrain or delay the groups from using such strength as they can muster). While they may choose leaders with a clearly defined social philosophy based on rejection of the *status quo*, they themselves may be conscious only of resentment and frustration in a work situation which affords them little or no satisfaction apart from the pay packet; which subjects them to subordination, discipline and control for purposes they have not chosen and do not share; and which dominates them through decisions made remotely and impersonally on the assumption that they are instruments to be used and not ends in themselves.

Men with feelings like these often behave according to the implications of the radical view whether they consciously hold it or, as is more likely, not. Whether they act on these feelings in such ways as to cause difficulties for management depends on their aspirations, their job situation and how far it affords them scope for bringing pressure to bear, and on the éxtent to which they have the will to mobilize and exercise that pressure. The higher their score on these counts – which of course interact with each other – the greater the strain on any expediency calculation they may have made (or that has been made for them) to the effect that agreements should be punctiliously observed.

When men's adherence to constitutional procedure breaks under this strain they often come under moral condemnation for failing to honour the commitments signed in their names. A crucial question which such critics might well put to themselves here is whether the men concerned are capable of honouring *any* moral commitment. The simplest enquiry will usually reveal that in their other roles most of them are dutiful husbands, devoted fathers, loyal friends, steadfast workmates. Why, then, does this capacity for moral commitment sometimes appear to fail them in respect of their agreements with the company? The one answer which management seems determined to avoid is that, while other claims and other situations *can* command their moral adhesion, the company cannot. Yet the company does command the moral adhesion of many in the upper ranks of the hierarchy. Where it most demonstrably fails is in its appeal to the rank-and-file. Unless there is evidence that the rank-and-file are incapable of extending moral adhesion to anything, we must surely look for explanations of their defaulting behaviour in the very nature of their work situation as they experience and perceive it. We shall find ourselves driven back again and again in subsequent discussion to this widespread failure of the industrial enterprise to evoke the full moral involvement of the rank-and-file. We shall have occasion to note again, too, the overwhelming tendency among members of the favoured classes to explain this away by blaming the moral infirmity of manual wage-earners or lower salary-earners, rather than considering the possibility that the enterprise is so structured as to be largely incapable, in Western culture, of attracting strong rank-and-file commitment.

NOTES

1. Among those leaders who have chanced to make this acknowledgement explicit in recent times is Mr Jack Jones, general secretary of
the Transport and General Workers' Union. After drawing attention
to the difficulties of guaranteeing absolute observance by the rank-and-
file, he asserted that all 'a trade union leadership can do is bind itself
in honour to try to observe the agreements it concludes with employers and this I believe in absolutely. In general the assurance we give
to management is that we bind ourselves in honour – we will do our
very best to see that the agreement is observed' (quoted in *Working for
Ford*, by HUW BEYNON, E. P. Publishers, 1975, p. 302)

10 Trade Unions: Sociology and Political Economy

R. Hyman and R. H. Fryer

Reprinted with permission from R. Hyman and R. H. Fryer, 'Trade Unions: Sociology and Political Economy', in J. B. McKinlay, *Processing People: Studies in Organizational Behaviour*, Holt, Rinehart & Winston, 1975, pp. 160–3, 182–91.

One final peculiarity of trade unions requires special emphasis. Because of their secondary nature – the fact that they represent workers' response to the deprivations inherent in their role as employees within a capitalist economy – opposition and conflict cannot be divorced from their existence and activity. They constitute a constant challenge to the 'rights of capital': first, to hire labour in the cheapest market; second, to deploy, manage and control labour irrespective of workers' own wishes and aspirations. Individually, few workers have the power to assert their interests against those of the employer. Collectively, they can exert greater influence.

Trade unions – workers' collective organizations – are thus first and foremost a source and medium of power: and processes of power are central to their internal and external relations. This fact must recur throughout our analysis. The notions of power, control and dependence which are essential for any proper understanding of trade unionism are of course the subject of intense theoretical controversy. While this is not the place to pursue at length the conceptual debate over the nature and meaning of power, we must state explicitly how we propose to employ the concept. First, we would emphasize that any definition which focuses on a distinction between 'power' and 'authority' seems to us of secondary importance. Second, we are unimpressed by attempts to interpret power relations as relationships of exchange: for the latter presuppose the *prior* existence of rules, rates and currency of exchange, and the determination of this prior framework is itself typically the outcome of power relations. In our view the critical focus of any analysis of power must be *the differential distribution of control over and access to resources and sanctions, both material and ideological.* This methodological presupposition, which distinguishes us from most writers on the sociology of organizations, should be evident in much of our argument.

A power relationship between individuals or groups with competing or opposing goals and interests necessarily generates conflict, overt or latent. Conflict in industry – the outcome of the pursuit by employers and workers of incompatible demands and objectives – can assume a wide variety of forms.

Its means of expression are as unlimited as the ingenuity of man. The strike is the most common and most visible expression. But conflict with the employer may also take the form of peaceful bargaining and grievance handling, of boycotts, of political action, of restriction of output, of sabotage, of absenteeism, or of personnel turnover. Several of these forms, such as sabotage, restriction of output, absenteeism, and turnover, may take place on an individual as well as on an organized basis and constitute alternatives to collective action. Even the strike is of many varieties. It may involve all the workers or only key men. It may take the form of refusal to work overtime or to perform a certain process. It may even involve such rigid adherence to the rules that output is stifled.[1]

Only those forms of conflict which assume an organized form are normally associated with trade unionism, at least when it has achieved any strength and viability. Moreover, different unions may prefer different methods – pure industrial action to political involvement, peaceful bargaining to militancy: such differences, underlie in part the typologies produced by such writers as Hoxie.[2] As is shown in a later section, there exist pressures which often induce trade union officials to moderate and contain the conflictual aspects of their activity. Nevertheless, the conflict inherent in industrial relations can never be wholly suppressed.

Because of the centrality of power and conflict to their functions and activities, there is only limited value – far less, probably, than in the case of any other kind of organization – in studying trade unions simply as 'formal organizations' wrenched from their social context. To understand trade unions it is essential to analyse the environing institutions of power with which they interact: an adequate analysis of trade unions and trade unionism must also be, in large measure, an analysis of the political economy within which they operate. For the same reason, theories of trade unions as organizations are intimately related to broader theories of industry and society: thus we shall need to examine the dominant theoretical perspectives on both in some detail. First, however, we will summarize very briefly some of the determinants of the power which unions can exercise and that which is deployed against them.

The starting point for any realistic analysis must be the massive power imbalance between capital and labour. This derives from the very fact that the productive system is, in the main, the private property of a tiny minority of the population, and that profit is its basic dynamic. Confronting this concentrated economic power, the great majority who depend on their own labour for a living are at an inevitable disadvantage.[3] Marshall's classic argument remains valid: 'labour is often sold under special disadvantages, arising from the closely connected group of facts that labour power is "perishable", that the sellers of it are commonly poor and have no reserve fund, and that they cannot easily withhold it from the market.'[4] Put simply, the employer can normally survive without labour for longer than the worker can survive without employment. How overwhelming this purely economic predominance may be depends in part on the state of the labour and product markets. A single employer (or tightly knit group of employers) in an isolated community may be able to exercise almost feudal power. In periods of heavy unemployment, workers' ability to influence their terms and conditions of employment even by collective action may be minimal. By contrast, in a context of relatively full employment and a variety of alternative job opportunities, the imbalance may be considerably reduced. Whatever the economic climate, moreover, workers with scarce technical skills or professional qualifications will be in a stronger position than those lacking such assets. The state of the market for the employer's products or services may affect the balance of power by raising or reducing the cost to him of a withdrawal of labour or other forms of conflict. Yet despite all these qualifications, the economic imbalance remains real and pervasive. In the last resort, the employer can threaten to shut up shop and take his capital elsewhere; but while the individual employee may move home and family to a different labour market, a labour force collectively has no such option.

Moreover, this economic predominance is doubly reinforced. First, capital normally has privileged access to the coercive sanctions of the state. In the everyday relationship between employer and worker, the law underwrites a contract which authorizes the former to give orders and obliges the latter to obey. In less routine circumstances, where the collective power of labour seriously threatens employer interests, governments typically intervene to restore the normal imbalance. This is a point to which we return in more detail. Second, unequal economic and political power gives capital a crucial influence over processes of *ideological* formation: legitimating its own predominance and inhibiting effective challenge on the part of labour.

The countervailing power of union organization, at its most successful, can only partially redress this imbalance. The main determinants of union power are of two types: objective and subjective. Of the former, the most significant are the strength or density of organization among the potential membership, and the strategic importance of the workers covered. The importance of intensive organization is obvious: when a significant proportion of the relevant employee group are outside the union and unlikely to follow its policies and instructions, or where there exists an alternative labour force of non-unionists, the ability to exert effective pressure on the employer is considerably reduced.[5] Strategic importance increases the impact of any forms of overt conflict in which union members engage. Thus a group of assembly-line workers may be able to disrupt an integrated production process; or newspaper printers may be able to cause immediate and substantial damage to the employer because of the perishable nature of their product. Such groups as dockers or electricity supply workers, whose work is vital to the entire economy, may have the power to oblige the government to intervene in any dispute to achieve terms acceptable to them.

While such objective factors as intensive organization and strategic importance are among the preconditions of powerful unionism, power also depends on the manner in which workers perceive their situation and interests, and the solidarity and determination with which they pursue their objectives. Workers who perceive no major conflict of interests with their employers are unlikely to organize effectively. Those who define their interests primarily in narrow sectional terms may succeed in winning improvements in relation to other groups; but the consequence may be division and disunity at a broader collective level, and hence a weakening of workers' power as against that of their employers.[6] In practice, there are powerful ideological pressures inducing workers to conceive their interests, on the one hand in limited and parochial terms, on the other as merely part of some all-embracing 'national interest'; consciousness on the part of wage- and salary-earners that they have substantial common interests *as employees* is systematically inhibited. The solidarity and resolve with which workers engage in open industrial conflict – particularly if they possess significant strategic strength – is also commonly exposed to powerful ideological onslaught.[7] A notable example was provided during the electricity workers' dispute of 1971: the disruptive potential demonstrated by even limited industrial action provoked so hostile an ideological reaction by politicians and the media that the Electrical Union ended the dispute with what at the time appeared minimal gains.[8]

INSTITUTIONAL PRESSURES AND UNION POLICY

The wide range of potential union goals, and the absence of any general consensus on their proper objectives, create particular scope for the process of goal displacement. It is a commonplace of organizational analysis that the original purposes of organizations often tend, over time, to become supplemented and extended; procedures devised for the efficient attainment of these goals become sanctified as ends in themselves; and those in charge of the organization become committed to 'institutional' goals which are considered necessary for its security and stability but may conflict with its overt purposes. That such tendencies are particularly evident in trade unions has been emphasized by Ross:

As an institution expands in strength and status, it outgrows its formal purpose. It experiences its own needs, develops its own ambitions, and faces its own problems. These become differentiated from the needs, ambitions, and problems of its rank-and-file. The trade union is no exception. It is the beginning of wisdom in the study of industrial relations to understand that the union, as an organization, is not identical with its members, as individuals.[9]

It is worth repeating that the notion that institutions have needs, ambitions and problems – like the idea that organizations act – is a reification which carries with it a serious danger of obfuscation of the actual social processes involved. The concept of 'institutional needs' is a metaphor which makes sense only to the extent that it is based on an implicit reference to the wants and interests of real people. In one sense, the 'needs' of trade unions might be understood in terms of those of the members themselves. In so far as a union exists to serve the interests of its members, they have at least an instrumental interest in its organizational strength and survival. Yet there are three important reasons why such institutional needs may conflict with the actual wishes of trade unionists and hence the manifest purposes of the union. First, workers as individuals may be able to benefit personally from policies or actions which, if pursued by members generally, would result in a reduction in collective union strength and hence be to the ultimate disadvantage of all.[10] Second, the benefits of strong organization may accrue only in the long term, and may be obtained only at the expense of members' short-term wishes. A simple example might be a proposal to increase membership subscriptions. Where such conflict exists, the priority to be assigned to long-term institutional as against immediate membership interests is itself an important policy issue. And third, policies oriented towards organizational needs may become ends pursued for their own sake rather than through any calculation of long-term membership interests. This is especially likely where organizational interests become intrinsically linked with the fate of a union's leaders; for them, the demands of union strength and security will acquire major salience, and may come to provide a simple rationalization for any policy against the wishes or immediate interests of the rank-and-file.

There are four main types of institutional goal which can readily displace the overt objectives of a union: security and stability; financial solvency and strength; unity and cohesion; and administrative efficiency.

The problematics of institutional security and survival, important in any organization, are particularly salient within trade unionism: for unions by their very nature represent a challenge to the structure of power within the political economy of capitalism. Their purely economic objectives conflict with the capitalist's desire to minimize costs of production; their involvement in a struggle for control challenges his managerial autonomy; while any connection between trade unionism and socialist politics is a potential threat to his very existence. The more ambitious and extensive a union's objectives, the more likely it is to attract the hostility of those in positions of economic and social dominance. Hence the formative period of trade unionism in many countries has been marked by violent employer opposition, and often governmental repression – which has in turn rendered union organization itself precarious. Conversely, if a union can curb those of its objectives which seriously challenge the *status quo* it may be able to win the acquiescence and even goodwill of employers and the state, in a manner which considerably enhances its security. In practice, unions which have become firmly established have typically been drawn inexorably towards policies which are relatively acceptable to these significant others. Thus it is rare indeed for trade-union commitment to major social change to be an operational one, in the sense of influencing day-to-day industrial policies or serious long-term strategies: the socialist attachments of British unions are in general confined to the rhetoric of rulebook preambles and conference speeches.[11] Similar pressures normally affect industrial policies in such manner that interference with managerial control does not go 'too far',[12] while economic demands are characterized by 'moderation'.[13] Where unions are willing to confine their objectives within these comparatively innocuous limits, far-sighted managements have little reason to resist, and much reason to welcome, union involvement in job regulation. For by articulating the many discontents generated by the workers' role within capitalist employment a union makes their behaviour more predictable and manageable. Resentment is not permitted to accumulate explosively, but is formulated in a manner which facilitates at least temporary solution; and union involvement in any settlement increases the likelihood that its members will feel committed to the agreed terms.[14]

An accommodative relationship between union and employer – in which the former acts, in Wright Mills' famous phrase, as a 'manager of discontent'[15] – thus has obvious pay-offs for the employer. He may thus be keen to reciprocate in a manner which assists union security. The closed shop is one such response. 'The union shop, or other forms of compulsion, are highly important to the strength and stability of labour unions. It is the union as an organization, not the worker directly, that needs the "job control".'[16] It follows that a trade-off between union moderation and employer goodwill may appear particularly attractive to union officials, even where the advantages for the ordinary member are far less obvious. The future of the bargaining relationship forms an important consideration whenever demands are formulated or strategies devised. In some circumstances such long-term concerns may impose so severe a constraint on union action that, like a miser who refuses to enjoy his wealth, the potential achievements of union strength are never realized.[17]

The importance of financial solvency as an organizational objective is clearly shown in the history of British unionism. In the earliest associations financial administration and control largely devolved upon the individual branches. Yet these tended to exhaust their funds in over-liberal benefits or injudicious strike action; it was impossible to accumulate sufficient funds to support an effective long-term industrial strategy, and at times the existence of the organization itself was threatened by bankruptcy. Hence there was an inexorable trend towards the centralization of financial control, which extended – since strike pay could constitute a major drain on union funds – to centralization of power to authorize strike action and central co-ordination of industrial policy.[18] Yet the pursuit of financial solvency and strength easily became an end in itself: a policy originally justified as a prerequisite of effective militancy could be used as an argument *against* militancy. It was a common complaint against the late nineteenth-century British craft unions that their leaders were preoccupied with accumulating massive bank balances; they were reluctant, their critics alleged, to support strike action or even pursue demands which involved a risk of confrontation, for fear of reducing the financial reserves. In contemporary industrial relations there is little evidence that such considerations induce a 'peace-at-any-price' attitude among union leaders; nevertheless, they can exert a noticeable influence on industrial policy.

'Unity is strength' is a common trade-union maxim, and

internal unity and cohesion is thus a natural organizational goal. Conversely, division and dissension within a union may well be regarded as undesirable and even dangerous. Yet a concern to maintain unity may conflict with the democratic control which overtly characterizes trade unions: for criticism of leadership actions and decisions, or attempts by sectional groups to obtain greater attention to their special interests, may be suppressed as disruptive and subversive.[19] Unity is most likely to be assigned priority over democracy where a union's membership is heterogeneous: for there may be no strong feeling of common identity, while bargaining strategy may require a judicious balancing of divergent sectional interests. In such a context, 'excessive' internal democracy may be viewed by its leaders as a threat to the integrity of the whole union. On the other hand, the open articulation of opposing viewpoints is far more likely to be tolerated in societies with a homogeneous membership: these often constitute what Turner has described as 'exclusive democracies'.[20]

The goal of efficiency has been at least part of the rationale of most of the changes in the internal organization and functioning of trade unions since the early nineteenth century: centralization, the rise of the full-time organizer, the gradual professionalization of many of the leadership functions.[21] Again, as is discussed in the following section, there is an apparent conflict with the democratic character of trade unionism. Union leadership, it need hardly be said, would be in many ways a simpler task if the wishes of the members themselves could be ignored – or at least, if the scope for their articulation could be as narrowly circumscribed as possible. And it is significant that many of the most vocal critics of trade union 'inefficiency' (often themselves associated with employer interests) are in reality attacking trade-union democracy.[22]

The theory that institutional pressures divert trade unions from their overt objectives and confer on their policies 'a profoundly conservative character' was first explicitly stated by Michels in his *Political Parties*.[23] The original goals, he argued, 'are, whenever requisite, attenuated and deformed in accordance with the external needs of the organization. Organization becomes the vital essence . . . More and more invincible becomes its aversion to all aggressive action . . . Thus, from a means, organization becomes an end.'[24] For Michels, such goal displacement was inevitable: an intrinsic element in an 'iron law of oligarchy'. Yet while Michels' sociological insight was of immense theoretical importance, we would deny the operation of any 'iron law'. The pressures which formed the stimulus for the emergence and growth of union organization – which are rooted in the experience of workers within capitalist wage-labour – inevitably set limits to the process of goal displacement.[25] The relative strength of conservative and oligarchic tendencies on the one hand, and countervailing pressures on the other, itself varies between unions and may be seen as in large measure situationally determined. But before pursuing this argument further it is necessary to turn explicitly to the question of union democracy on which we have already commented briefly.

UNION POLICY AND UNION DEMOCRACY

Implicit in any analysis of goal displacement, as we have seen, is the appreciation that trade unions develop 'official' policies which can diverge from members' conceptions of their own interests. The danger is that the membership may become merely the object, rather than the prime beneficiary, of job regulation. Thus our previous discussion leads naturally to a consideration of problems of internal union government.

One theme pervades the voluminous literature on this topic: the conflict between the goals of efficient and effective organization on the one hand, and membership control of union policy and its implementation on the other: a conflict which becomes manifest as soon as a bureaucratic hierarchy of full-time officials is established.[26] A related finding often emphasized is the fact of rank-and-file apathy: in most situations only a small minority participate in the official processes of union government.

Michels' famous (or notorious) conclusion was of course that democratic control is in practice, impossible.[27] While the primary concern of his *Political Parties* – as the title indicates – was with the political organizations of the working class, he insisted that 'in the trade union movement, the authoritative character of the leaders and their tendency to rule democratic organizations on oligarchic lines, are even more pronounced than in the political organizations'.[28] Unions, he argued, could not operate on the basis of 'direct democracy'; for the conduct of negotiations and disputes required an organization, led by officials with specialized experience and knowledge. The privileges of office naturally led union leaders to cling to their positions; even if subject to re-election, the experience and political skills which they developed constituted an overwhelming advantage over any rivals. Social isolation from the rank-and-file led to ideological differentiation, undermining any socialist commitment the officials might originally have had: 'their own social revolution has already been effected'.[29]

Thus far, Michels' argument is in line with the earlier analysis of the Webbs (with which he was himself familiar). Historically, they noted, 'with every increase in the society's membership, with every extension or elaboration of its financial system or trade policy, the position of the salaried official became ... more and more secure'. By the turn of the century, when they were writing, chief officers of trade unions had come to enjoy a 'permanence of tenure exceeding even that of the English civil servant'. They added that 'the paramount necessity of efficient administration has co-operated with this permanence in producing a progressive differentiation of an official governing class, more and more marked off by character, training and duties from the bulk of the members'.[30] In these circumstances, the Webbs insisted, any attempt to maintain the traditional procedures of 'direct democracy' would lead 'straight either to inefficiency and disintegration, or to the uncontrolled dominance of a personal dictator or an expert bureaucracy'.[31]

For the Webbs, though, specific institutional arrangements could safeguard trade unions against this sad fate. (Their Fabian political philosophy made them fervent if disingenuous advocates of quasi-parliamentary representative institutions as the key to union democracy.) Michels, by contrast, brushed aside such qualifications to his 'iron law'. 'Uncontrolled dominance,' he insisted, was inevitable; and the leaders' power permitted them to impose their conservative policies, even where these were 'disapproved of by the majority of the workers they are supposed to represent'.[32] Such 'abuse of power' in general provoked little resistance. Lacking adequate information or experience on which to base any serious criticism of leadership policies, most members accepted that their officials had a 'customary right' to their positions and were willing to allow them to take the difficult decisions. Thus oligarchic control was reinforced by mass apathy.[33]

Any study of contemporary trade unionism which examined

only the official mechanisms of internal government would appear to offer considerable support for Michels' diagnosis of an 'iron law of oligarchy'.[34] Where unions require the regular re-election of officials, 'the defeat of the incumbent is a relatively rare event';[35] and there has been a discernible trend in recent years for several unions to limit or remove even the formality of election. Hence the emergence of a leadership caste is repeatedly emphasized:

> In sum, whether we consider the objective pattern of organizations, recruitment and reward or the subjective orientations and career expectations of the staff experts or the characteristics of those who are selected for high influence, the picture is one of slowly growing yet embryonic bureaucracy.[36]

By contrast, the formal processes of union democracy seem frail indeed. Most union conferences, as we saw in the introduction, are dominated by the leadership 'platform' and thus fail to function as a genuine means of rank-and-file determination of policy. The branch, the one formal link between the ordinary member and his union, is more often concerned with routine administration than with decision-making on issues which might encourage membership involvement. Thus it is not surprising that membership apathy is regularly documented:[37] in most unions only some 5–10 per cent of members are in any sense active participants in the official processes of union democracy, regularly attending branch meetings and voting in union elections.

Undoubtedly the general factors discussed by Michels provide part of the explanation for this state of affairs. But in addition it is possible to mention a number of more specific influences on the degree to which internal union government deviates from the democratic ideal.[38] Perhaps the most important of these is membership composition. As was seen in the previous section, the degree of membership homogeneity is likely to affect internal democracy. Where a union represents a variety of occupational groups with divergent and in some respects even conflicting interests, open articulation of these sectional interests may threaten organizational unity; where membership is more homogeneous this is far less a danger. Moreover, members of a diverse union may lack any real basis for judgement on those aspects of policy which do not affect their immediate interests. (Some unions – notably the Transport and General – attempt to overcome this difficulty by means of separate 'trade groups' which determine the industrial policy for the various sections of membership.)

Membership participation and control are also affected by such factors as skill, status, educational qualifications, and strength of occupational identity. Higher-skilled groups, or those that form cohesive occupational communities, are often associated with a high degree of union democracy. Conversely, lower-skilled occupations, women, and occupations marked by casual employment or high labour turnover, are often organized by unions which fit Turner's category of 'popular bossdom' – strong leadership control and little rank-and-file participation.[39] Where a union contains both types of membership, the former normally dominates its internal government. Hence in the Engineers, a disproportionate number of activists and officials come from the skilled section. Or in most unions in which women form a large majority of the membership – the Public Employees, the Teachers, the Shopworkers, the Tailors and Garment Workers, the Civil and Public Services Association – most leading positions are occupied by men.

Union democracy is also affected by the size and distribution of membership. The scope for direct participation and control by the rank-and-file in central decision-making is clearly greatest where membership is small and geographically concentrated. The larger and more dispersed the membership, normally, the larger is its bureaucratic apparatus and the more fragmented its rank-and-file. Either the individual branch is very large, and itself prone to oligarchic control; or the branch is only one of many striving to influence higher union policy – and co-ordination of initiative from the various branches is then difficult (and may even be prohibited by union rules); or there exist several intermediate levels between branch and national executive, so that the central leadership is particularly remote from the rank-and-file.

Union government is affected not only by the nature of the membership but also by the prevailing conception of union *purpose*. The more restricted a union's objectives, the less likely it is to manifest extensive democratic control. This relationship was noted by Hoxie in his original characterization of business unionism: 'in harmony with its business character it tends to emphasize discipline within the organization, and is prone to develop strong leadership and to become somewhat autocratic in government'.[40] If the function of a union is merely to provide its members with a limited economic service, it is less unreasonable to judge its operation by the standards of an ordinary commercial enterprise, and the case for democracy is accordingly weakened. Where union goals are so narrow and thus so unproblematic, technical expertise is the most important requirement on the part of the union official: and it follows from this perspective that 'trade union wage policy is inevitably a leadership function'.[41] This is to advocate the radical division between leadership and membership which was condemned by the authors of *The Miners' Next Step*: 'this power of initiative, this sense of responsibility, the self-respect which comes from expressed manhood, is taken from the men, and consolidated in the leader. The sum of *their* initiative, *their* responsibility, *their* self-respect becomes his'.[42]

Not surprisingly, then, a narrow conception of union function provides little incentive for membership participation.

Participation in any organization appears to be related to the number and saliency of the functions which it performs for its members and the extent to which they require personal involvement. In most cases, trade unions perform only one major function for their members – collective bargaining, which can be handled by a more or less efficient union administration without requiring any membership participation, except during major conflicts. In such unions, we would not expect continuous participation by more than the handful of members who are involved in administration.[43]

Hence an attempt by union leaders to confine activities to the pursuit of limited economic improvements may, by encouraging membership apathy, reinforce their own predominance. This would seem to represent the vicious circle diagnosed by Michels: oligarchy, mass apathy and narrow and conservative policy each stemming from and at the same time perpetuating the other.

Yet we would deny, as against Michels, that there is any inevitability in such a vicious circle. Indeed, recent developments in industrial relations demonstrate the absurdity of such an assumption: for neither oligarchy, nor apathy, nor conservatism can be regarded in any simple fashion as characteristic of trade unionism. Structural pressures inhibiting democracy are not irresistible; they can be counterbalanced, for example, by a union constitution which facilitates rank-and-file control, a tradition of democracy, or the existence of rival factions each ready to mobilize opposition to autocratic action on the part of the other. The Engineers is one example of a union in which all three of these factors are important. Union leaders themselves may hold a genuine commitment to democracy and extensive union functions, and hence encourage rank-and-file participation. There has certainly been a tendency in this direction in Britain in recent years, particularly in the two largest unions. And perhaps most important of all, membership apathy in respect of the formal machinery of union government may coexist with rank-and-file involvement in other forms of organization and activity. The importance of shopfloor organization in a wide area of British industry is a case in point: and its significance for the whole operation of trade unionism is immense. It is to this that we now turn.

SHOP STEWARDS AND DOMESTIC BARGAINING

'Britain has two systems of industrial relations,' wrote the Royal Commission on Trade Unions and Employers' Associations in its *Report* (the Donovan Report). 'The one is the formal system embodied in the official institutions. The other is the informal system created by the actual behaviour of trade unions and employers' associations, of managers, shop stewards and workers.'[44]

The official structure of collective bargaining, established in most industries for at least half a century, normally involves regular negotiations at national level between officials of the union or unions concerned and the relevant federation or association of employers. The resulting national agreements specify rates of pay, hours of work, and other conditions of employment for the industry. In theory, this process determines all important aspects of the employment relationship that are negotiable: all that is left for discussion at local or workplace level are questions of the implementation of national agreements, and minor problems of domestic concern.

The reality is very different: in most industries with strong organization the national agreements set a bare minimum standard for wages and conditions; the worker relies primarily on domestic bargaining to win acceptable terms. The clearest evidence of the impact of shopfloor bargaining is the gap between officially negotiated wage rates and workers' actual earnings. The Donovan Report contrasted basic rates in engineering in October 1967 – £9.37 for a labourer and £11.08 for a fitter – with actual average earnings of £21.39 for men in engineering and electrical goods and £24.42 in vehicle manufacturing.[45] This striking difference derives from three main sources. Systems of payment by result, or piecework, apply to roughly a third of all wage-earners,[46] and provide considerable scope for domestic bargaining; strong shopfloor organization may be essential if workers are to achieve acceptable earnings. Overtime, for which payment is made at an enhanced rate, is extensively worked – an average of roughly 6 hours a week for male manual employees.[47] Its amount and allocation are often controlled by shopfloor bargaining. Finally, the nationally agreed rates may be increased by straightforward supplements negotiated at workplace level.

Domestic bargaining has less obvious but nevertheless important consequences in respect of control over the process of production. Formally and legally, employers possess almost unlimited authority over their labour force. Trade union attempts to achieve constraints on these 'managerial prerogatives' through official negotiations have rarely achieved significant success. As a protection against arbitrary managerial control, and a means of winning an element of autonomy within their working lives, trade unionists are obliged to act collectively at the point of production. Where shopfloor organization is strong, workers can indeed impose important limitations on managerial autonomy: affecting such issues as who shall be employed or dismissed, how machinery shall be manned, what shall be the rate of production, whether men shall be moved from one job to another.

The prevalence of informal shopfloor bargaining, and the strength of organization at the place of work, are reflected in the British strike pattern. For most of the postwar period at least 95 per cent of all strikes have been 'unofficial', in the sense that they occur without the formal approval of the union executive (though this is sometimes accorded retrospectively). An unofficial strike is not necessarily one of which the union leadership disapproves (though this is indeed true in some cases); often the workers merely see no need to seek official support before stopping work. Most stoppages are small and short, and occur relatively spontaneously; and even in a major dispute, official support is of limited value since strike pay in most unions is so small (often about £5 a week). In addition, such actions as over-time bans and going-slow may be even more common than actual strikes, and are probably even more overwhelmingly un-official.[48]

The pattern of unofficial action is directly related to the pattern of industrial relations in Britain. Since the most important issues concerning workers' employment are settled at the place of work, it is natural that sanctions should be applied at this level when the results of negotiation are unsatisfactory. Since the official representatives of the national union are rarely involved in negotiations at workplace level, it is hardly surprising that workers should commonly see no reason to seek official approval before stopping work. This is obviously of central importance when we evaluate the significance of 'apathy' or 'oligarchy' in the official union machinery; for given the structure of British industrial relations, this official machinery is of very little direct significance to the ordinary member.

'The Shop Steward is for most rank-and-file members their first and only contact with the Union. To them the Shop Steward rather than the Branch is the Union.'[49] The rise of the shop steward to his key position in British unionism has been a slow one. Since the nineteenth century, some unions have had representatives at the workplace to carry out such functions as checking that all workers are paid-up members, collecting subscriptions, and reporting to the branch or district on conditions within the factory. Such stewards came gradually to act as representatives of their fellow-workers when urgent issues arose within the workshop, and this function became particularly important during the 1914–18 war. The danger of victimization by employers limited their negotiating role during the interwar depression; but in the past three decades there has been a great expansion in their number and influence. Today there are probably over 250,000 shop stewards in Britain, about a third of these in engineering.

By definition the steward is a shopfloor employee, typically chosen directly by his fellow-workers because he enjoys their trust. His authority as a negotiator does not derive from the union of which he is a member; until very recently, few union rule books even mentioned the steward's bargaining functions. Nor, in the main, does it derive from formal procedure agreements: most of these define the steward's role in a manner far more restrictive than occurs in practice. His powers stem primarily from the fact that he shares the aspirations of his members, is personally involved in their experiences and grievances at the point of production, and is expected to represent their interests closely in negotiation with management. Should he fail to do so adequately, it is relatively easy for the rank-and-file to reassert control, through shopfloor meetings or less formal pressures. In the last resort, workers can replace a steward whose competence or integrity they doubt by one in whom they have greater confidence.

There are thus very important differences between the worker's relationship with his shop steward and with his full-time union official; yet at the same time these differences should not lead us to ignore certain similarities. In some situations, particularly in the largest factories, the shop-steward organization can itself display considerable bureaucratization. Management will often permit one or more chief stewards (or convenors) to act full-time as union representatives, even though they may be nominally employed in a specific shopfloor job. Important negotiations may be largely monopolized by a committee of leading stewards and convenors, who may make little effort to maintain effective contacts with the rank-and-file or even with the remaining stewards. Highly bureaucratic shop-steward organization may be made possible by and in turn encourage membership apathy. Thus there is rarely much competition for the steward's position: most are elected unopposed, or else 'emerge' without the formality of an election.

In addition, shop stewards are subject to the same institutional pressures in microcosm as affect union officers. Despite popular stereotypes, the Donovan Report insisted that 'it is often wide of the mark to describe shop stewards as "troublemakers" ... Quite commonly they are supporters of order exercising a restraining influence on their members in conditions which promote disorder.'[50] For the steward, as for the full-time official, the bargaining relationship with management is necessarily a salient consideration during negotiations. In addition, a number of specific facilities may be dependent on management goodwill: permission to carry out shop-steward duties without loss of pay;

provision of office and telephone facilities; opportunities to recruit members, collect subscriptions and hold meetings; above all, perhaps, the mere readiness to allow access to discuss any issue or grievance arising. Not surprisingly, then, most stewards are reluctant to act in a manner which might alienate management goodwill; the natural predisposition is to seek a mutually satisfactory outcome to issues which arise – to view them, like management, as 'problems' to be resolved rather than as disputed ground in a continuing relationship of conflict.[51]

Necessary as these qualifications are, however, it remains true that the shop steward is, potentially at least, far more closely attuned to the wishes of his members and subject to their control than is normally the case with the full-time official. Yet the steward is himself involved in a relationship with the official, and this relationship may exercise a considerable influence on the activities of each.

NOTES

1. C. KERR, *Labor and Management in Industrial Society*, New York, Doubleday, 1964, p. 171.

2. For another classic analysis of trade union methods see the WEBBS' *Industrial Democracy*, Longmans, 1897; also the critique by FLANDERS in *Management and Unions*, Faber, 1970.

3. Only 4 per cent of the adult population in Britain own shares, and 1 per cent own 81 per cent of all privately owned shares. For data and an important analysis of the inequality of economic power and its implications, see R. BLACKBURN, 'The unequal society' in R. BLACKBURN and A. COCKBURN (eds.), *The Incompatibles: Trade Union Militancy and the Consensus*, Harmondsworth, Penguin, 1967. While any analysis of the power of private capital must take account of the existence of a 'public sector' of employment, major qualification is unnecessary: for to a large extent it functions to service the private sector and it is subject to policy norms which parallel those of private capitalism. And while the power of capital is mediated by the existence of a professional, often 'propertyless' managerial hierarchy, its basic nature remains unaltered (see in this connection the powerful critique of 'managerialist' and 'post-capitalist' ideologies by T. NICHOLS, *Ownership, Control and Ideology*, London, Allen & Unwin, 1969).

4. A. MARSHALL, *Principles of Economics*, 8th ed., London, Macmillan, 1920, p. 567.

5. It is worth noting that size in itself is probably a less important source of union power than membership density: intensive organization may well be more powerful than extensive. Thus a small but tightly knit union of strategically located workers may be more powerful, for some purposes at least, than a larger body with less intensive coverage. Many trade union amalgamations seem to make little significant contribution to the power of their members *vis-à-vis* their employers; but they may well enhance the personal positions of union leaders (particularly within the inner councils of such bodies as the Trades Union Congress).

6. As D. LOCKWOOD has noted (*The Blackcoated Worker*, London, George Allen & Unwin, 1958, p. 137), trade unionism may well represent a consciousness of sectional rather than class interests. For an illuminating discussion of the interrelationship of sectional and broader collective consciousness and action see R. K. BROWN, P. BRANNEN, J. M. COUSINS and M. L. SAMPHIER, 'The contours of solidarity: social stratification and industrial relations in shipbuilding,' *Br. J. Indust. Relat.*, 10 (March 1971). The question of levels of rationality involved in various perceptions of interests and the related strategies is discussed by R. HYMAN, *Strikes*, London, Fontana, 1972, pp. 132–9.

7. Solidarity action by workers not directly involved in an industrial dispute is viewed as a particularly serious threat by employer interests; and most actions of this kind were (at least in theory) outlawed by the Industrial Relations Act of 1972.

8. Trade unions also attempt to exert ideological influence: arguing, for example, that 'good employers' must observe certain minimum conditions and practices. Such arguments have certainly achieved some effect – particularly in government employment, where unions have traditionally felt inhibited from engaging in overt conflict. But on balance, `the ideological influence of unions on their opponents is limited, and by comparison with that exerted in the reverse direction it may well be declining.

9. A. M. ROSS, *Trade Union Wage Policy*, Berkeley, University of California Press, 1948, p. 23.

10. For a discussion of this point see M. OLSON, *The Logic of Collective Action*, Harvard University Press, 1965. He suggests (p. 87) that many members' attitude to their union is 'analogous to the characteristic attitude of citizens towards their government. Voters are often willing to vote for higher taxes to finance additional government services, but as individuals they strive to contribute as little as the tax laws allow (and on occasion even less).'

11. It is interesting that while most American unions have explicitly disavowed socialist objectives and embraced the ideology of business u ionism, this has not occurred in Britain. But their broader overt aims

do not appear to make a significant difference to the actual policies of British unions.

12. This is discussed by HYMAN, *Strikes*, pp. 95–7.

13. This point is strongly emphasized by ALLEN, *Militant Trade Unionism*, Merlin, 1966, pp. 29–30.

14. As we have seen, the stabilization of capitalism resulting from this process of 'antagonistic co-operation' has fascinated writers in the functionalist-pluralist tradition.

15. C. WRIGHT MILLS, *The New Men of Power*, New York, Harcourt Brace, 1948, pp. 8–9.

16. OLSON, *Logic of Collective Action*, p. 87.

17. The process of goal displacement in a specific British union is examined by R. HYMAN, *The Workers' Union*, Oxford, Clarendon Press, 1971, pp. 195–205.

18. The classic discussion of this trend is in S. and B. WEBB, *Industrial Democracy*, Longmans, 1897.

19. See for example J. R. COLEMAN, 'The compulsive pressures of democracy in unionism', *Am. J. Sociol.*, 61 (May 1956), reprinted in W. GALENSON and S. M. LIPSET (eds.), *Labour and Trade Unionism*, New York, Wiley, 1960.

20. TURNER, *Trade Union Growth, Structure and Policy*, London, George Allen & Unwin, 1962, pp. 289, 304–5.

21. Again, the classic analysis is provided by the Webbs.

22. A clear example is M. SHANKS, *The Stagnant Society*, Harmondsworth, Penguin, 1961.

23. R. W. E. MICHELS, *Political Parties*, 1915 (original German edition 1911). Reprinted, New York, Dover, 1959.

24. ibid., pp. 369–73.

25. This argument is developed in detail in R. HYMAN, *Marxism and the Sociology of Trade Unionism*, London, Pluto Press, 1971.

26. Our discussion in this section focuses principally on problems associated with the development of professional trade union *leadership*. The relationship between rank-and-file and lower-level full-time officials is considered in a later section.

27. The proper definition of the concept of democracy is as contentious an issue in industrial relations as in political theory. In particular it is persistently debated whether active participative control by the rank-and-file is a prerequisite of union democracy, or whether passive membership consent, supplemented by the occurrence of periodic elections, is a sufficient condition. For a consideration of this issue see HYMAN, *The Workers' Union*, pp. 206 ff.

28. MICHELS, op. cit., p. 143.

29. ibid., p. 305.

30. *Industrial Democracy*, p. 16.

31. ibid., p. 36.

32. *Political Parties*, p. 143.

33. Elsewhere Michels characterizes the attitude of rank-and-file members to their leaders not as apathy but as virtual hero-worship: they felt they owed them a 'sacred duty' of loyalty. A strong sense of personal loyalty towards officials is certainly a notable feature of the British trade union movement, and one no doubt deliberately cultivated by many leaders. But conversely, the bureaucratic aspects of modern union leadership may tend towards the 'routinization of charisma' analysed by Weber.

34. Only one empirical study has claimed to provide an important counter-example to MICHELS: S. M. LIPSET, M. A. TROW and J. S. COLEMAN, *Union Democracy*, Glencoe, Ill., The Free Press, 1956. This examination of the International Typographical Union in the USA emphasizes the two-party system which has allowed alternating control of union government for over half a century, and also the high degree of rank-and-file participation. But the authors add that there are many features of this union which make it virtually unique.

35. H. A. CLEGG, *The System of Industrial Relations in Great Britain*, Oxford, Blackwell, 1972, p. 82.

36. H. L. WILENSKY, 'The trade union as a bureaucracy' in A. ETZIONI (ed.), *Complex Organizations: a Sociological Reader*, New York, Holt, Rinehart & Winston, 1961, p. 223.

37. Findings are summarized by CLEGG, *The System of Industrial Relations* and HYMAN, *The Workers' Union*; see also Government Social Survey, *Workshop Industrial Relations*, London, HMSO, 1968.

38. Among general discussions of these influences see, for America, W. SPINRAD, 'Correlates of trade union participation', *Am. Sociol. Rev.*, 25 (1960); S. M. LIPSET, 'The political process in trade unions: a theoretical statement' in GALENSON and LIPSET, *Labour and Trade Unionism*; and A. S. TANNENBAUM, 'Unions' in J. G. MARCH (ed), *Handbook on Organizations*, Rand McNally, 1965. More recent British discussions are TURNER, *Trade Union Growth, Structure and Policy*; J. HUGHES, *Membership Participation and Trade Union Government*, Royal Commission Research Paper 5 (part 2), London, HMSO, 1968; and R. MARTIN, 'Union Democracy: an Explanatory Framework,' *Sociology*, 2 (1968).

39. *Trade Union Growth, Structure and Policy*, pp. 290–1.

40. R. F. HOXIE, *Trade Unionism in the United States*, Appleton, 1917, p. 47.

41. ROSS, *Trade Union Wage Policy*, p. 39.

42. Unofficial Reform Committee (of the South Wales Miners' Federation), *The Miners' Next Step*, 1912, Tonypandy: Davies, pp. 13–14.

43. LIPSET, in GALENSON and LIPSET, p. 226.

44. Royal Commission on Trade Unions and Employers' Federations, HMSO, 1968, p. 12.

45. ibid., p. 15.

46. National Board for Prices and Incomes, *Report 65: Payment by Results Systems*, Cmnd 3627, London, HMSO, 1968, p. 7. The proportion of workers paid by results may have declined more recently, with the introduction by a number of employers of forms of measured day work.

47. E. G. WHYBREW, *Overtime Working in Britain*, Royal Commission Research Paper 9, London, HMSO, 1968.

48. For a more detailed discussion see HYMAN, *Strikes*. In recent years there has been a revival of large-scale official strikes.

49. J. GOLDSTEIN, *The Government of British Trade Unions*, London, Allen & Unwin, 1952, p. 241.

50. pp. 28–9. The findings of the survey conducted for the Commission are revealing: 46 per cent of managers thought their stewards were less militant than ordinary members, only 16 per cent that they were more militant; while 70 per cent preferred negotiating with shop stewards to full-time union officials; only 3 per cent thought stewards 'unreasonable' (Government Social Survey, *Workplace Industrial Relations*, pp. 85–6).

51. A number of recent publications discuss shop-steward activities and organization, and consider factors underlying variations in stewards' influence. See for example W. E. J. MCCARTHY, *The Role of Shop Stewards in British Industrial Relations*, and MCCARTHY and S. R. PARKER, *Shop Stewards and Workshop Relations*, Royal Commission Research Papers 1 and 10, London, HMSO, 1966 and 1968; CLEGG, *The System of Industrial Relations in Great Britain*; J. F. B. GOODMAN and T. G. WHITTINGHAM, *Shop Stewards in British Industry*: McGraw Hill, 1969; W. A. BROWN, *Piecework Bargaining*, London, Heinemann, 1973.

11 Trade Unions and Bureaucratic Control

J. E. T. Eldridge

Reprinted with permission from J. E. T. Eldridge, *Sociology and Industrial Life*, Michael Joseph, 1971, pp. 175–82.

It might be argued, as writers such as Schumpeter and Galbraith have done,[1] that democracy in industrial societies, if it is to be realized at all, must be expressed in a situation of competition between bureaucratically organized interest groups. Leaving aside the important question as to what kind of competition actually takes place between interest groups in terms of effective power and accomplished actions, there is another significant question which relates to the internal organization of the bureaucracy. Putting it into the context of our discussion of alienation the question is: are we to regard the modern trade union as an organization over which the individual worker has no effective control, such that having been set up in his name it remains to dominate him, rather than express his real interest? To answer in the affirmative is to suggest that the masses are alienated from power which is exclusively exercised by an élitist governing group. And this of course was the contention expressed in Michels' 'iron law of oligarchy' and specifically applied by him to political parties and trade unions.[2] His study, first published in 1911, with its key theme – 'who says organization says oligarchy' – has played a continual if controversial part in academic work and debate since then. Michels' research strategy is to take the apparently least favourable situation for his thesis and then to indicate how it still appears to hold:

> The study of the oligarchical manifestations in party life is most valuable and most decisive in its results when undertaken in relation to the revolutionary parties, for the reason that these parties . . . in respect of origin and of progress, represent the negation of any such tendency and have actually come into existence out of opposition thereto. Thus the appearance of oligarchical phenomena in the very bosom of the revolutionary

parties is a conclusive proof of the existence of immanent oligarchical tendencies in every kind of human organization which strives for the attainment of definite ends.[3]

In discussing trade union organization Michels emphasizes the increasing need for a bureaucratic organization staffed with technically competent men who become better educated, and separated in life-style, from those they represent. Leadership and authority tend to get increasingly centralized and it becomes possible for the leadership to initiate actions not approved of by the majority of their members. Indeed Michels held the oligarchical tendencies of trade unions to be more pronounced than in the sphere of political organization. It might be thought that union leaders coming from a working-class background would identify with their membership and represent their true interests. But what actually happens, Michels maintains, is that the proletarian leader is assimilated into the existing order. 'What interest for them has now the dogma of social revolution? Their own social revolution has already been effected.'[4] Michels cites the example of English trade unionists entering into sliding-scale agreements in which wages were related to the selling price of the product, as a case of a technical organizational solution which played down class antagonisms. American trade union leaders are, if anything, more strongly indicted:

. . . not a few labour leaders are altogether in the hands of the capitalists. Being uneducated parvenus, they are extremely sensible to flattery . . . In many cases they are no more than paid servants of capital . . . Among the best organized unions there are some which enter into regular treaties with the capitalists in their respective branches of industry in order to exploit a consumer and to effect with the capitalist a friendly division of the spoils. In other cases, the leaders of a federation of trade unions, bribed by one group of employers, will organize strikes among the employees of another group. On the other hand, many strikes which are progressing favourably for the workers come abruptly to an end because the employers have made it worth the leaders' while to call the strike off.[5]

Despite Michels' comments on the conservative tendencies of bureaucratic organizations – administrations tending to become ends in themselves rather than means to achieve the known ends of the membership – it would be incorrect to interpret his study as an anti-democratic tract. Rather he was concerned to destroy illusions and claims made in the name of democracy which were a charade. Moreover, one could put the question: how could the iron law of oligarchy be checked? Democracy as an ideology could certainly act as a check in its own right: the very act of labouring to produce a greater measure of democracy provides a force for criticism and control of oligarchical tendencies. The unmasking of illusions is part of such action. Perhaps most important is Michels' stress on the role of education as a factor for diminishing the gap between the leaders and the led, and increasing the capacity for the masses to exercise control in consequence:

> Taken in the mass, the poor are powerless and disarmed *vis-à-vis* their leaders. Their intellectual and cultural inferiority makes it impossible for them to see whither the leader is going, or to estimate in advance the significance of his actions. It is, consequently, the great task of social education to raise the intellectual level of the masses, so that they may be enabled within the limits of what is possible to counteract the oligarchical tendencies of the working-class movement.[6]

The Webbs, writing about English trade unions before Michels, came to similar conclusions. Indeed they are cited by Michels as confirmatory evidence in his own study.[7] The trade unions presented for them 'an unrivalled field of observation as to the manner in which the working man copes with the problem of combining administrative efficiency with popular control'.[8] They argued that 'if a democracy means that everything which "concerns all should be decided by all" and that each citizen should enjoy an equal and identical share in the government, trade union history clearly indicates the inevitable result. Government by such contrivances as Rotation of Office, the Mass Meeting, the Referendum and Initiative, or the Delegate restricted by his Imperative Mandate, leads straight to either inefficiency and disintegration or to the uncontrolled dominance of a personal dictator or an expert bureaucracy.'[9] They pointed to the substitution of these features of primitive democracy by 'the typically modern form of democracy, the elected representative assembly, appointing and controlling an executive committee under whose direction the permanent official staff performs its work.'[10] They pointed at the same time to the 'extreme centralization of finance and policy which the Trade Union has found to be a condition of efficiency',[11] which was at the root of an apparent paradox: 'the constant tendency to a centralized and bureaucratic administration [which] is in the Trade Union world accepted, and even welcomed, by men who, in all other organizations to which they belong, are sturdy defenders of local autonomy'.[12]

Looking at the question of trade union administration in Britain much later, V. L. Allen[13] argues that the increasing size and complexity of functions together with the need for efficiency has led to a bureaucratic form of administration (in the Weberian sense) because in his view trade unions derive power from efficient organization. They have adopted the bureaucratic form of organization at the expense of 'self government'. He argues that this is scarcely surprising since 'the end of trade union activity is to protect and improve the general living standards of its members and not to provide workers with an exercise in self-government'.[14] In so far as they are 'delivering the goods' for their members however, Allen suggests that union leaders and executives have not deserted democratic principles, since they are, typically, genuinely representing their members' interests. For him it simply illustrates 'the tendency for democracy to have a preference for the authoritarian solution of important problems'.[15] For Allen, unrepresentative union leadership leads to membership dissatisfaction and decline. 'Membership fluctuates frequently and substantially in trade unions in response to the kind of service they are expected by their members to provide. Membership fluctuations, therefore, represent fairly clearly the changes in the conditions of trade unionism.'[16]

Lipset has suggested that the union career of John L. Lewis gives some support to Allen's view. In the late 1920s and early 1930s he followed conservative union policies in leading the united Mine Workers of America. But confronted with a rapidly declining union membership and the growth of left-wing opposition, Lewis then proceeded to adopt a much more militant policy.[17] And C. Wright Mills has concurred in this judgement that labour leaders in the United States who fail to 'deliver the goods' are at risk.[18] At the same time he portrays successful union leaders as seeking to act within and as part of the national power élite. As union leaders they do not seek radically to transform the social structure but to achieve a more advantageous integration of their members into the existing framework:

> The drift their actions implement in terms of the largest projection, is a kind of 'precapitalist syndicalism from the top'. They seek, in the first instance, greater integration at the upper levels of the corporate economy rather than greater power at the lower level of the work hierarchy, for, in brief, it is the unexpressed desire of American labour leaders to join with owners and managers in running the corporate enterprise system and influencing decisively the political economy as a whole.[19]

Whether this is acting in their members' interests is perhaps not something that can be empirically easily ascertained. Wright Mills appears to draw the conclusion that effective control of such leaders by the membership is made more difficult because many of their actions are invisible to the membership. This in itself implies that membership allegiance is based on ignorance rather than knowledge and is perhaps not well described positively as satisfaction. There is rather a zone of indifference among the membership based on lack of interest or lack of knowledge which gives the union leader what in the strict sense is power without accountability. The argument appears to shift, therefore, to one in which, while the union leader's insecurity may be related to expressions of discontent from the membership, his security does not rest upon positive satisfaction with his work by the majority of members. However, the matter may be seen to be further complicated by the fact that membership fluctuations can only in a very guarded sense be treated as an indicator of membership satisfaction or dissatisfaction. The fluctuations may be caused by quite other factors, such as the general level of employment and the particular fortunes of the industries in which the union operates. Furthermore, a union may have established negotiating rights in a firm or industry which make it very difficult for dissatisfied members to set up alternative arrangements. There are great problems in bringing into being breakaway unions, as the Pilkington glass workers have recently discovered, notwithstanding their expressed disenchantment with their official union, the NUGMW.[20]

The situation is made much more difficult by the general drift, certainly in the UK, towards a more rationalized trade union situation of fewer and larger groupings. There, in any case, agreements between trade unions, such as the Bridlington principles operating in the UK, are of the 'no poaching' variety and can effectively control reductions in union membership arising from discontent. Factors of this kind lead one to pose again the question: what constitutes union democracy? They have led Martin to argue that union democracy hinges on the existence of factions within a union: 'union democracy exists when union executives are unable to prevent opposition factions from distributing propaganda and mobilizing electoral support . . . The survival of faction limits Executive ability to disregard rank-and-file opinion by providing the *potential* means for its overthrow . . . faction is an indispensable sanction against leadership failure to respond to membership opinion.'[21] The empirical question then becomes: what are the determinants of effective opposition with a union? Martin lists a range of factors including, for example, decentralized collective bargaining arrangements, a decentralized trade union structure with sub-structural autonomy, extensive and constitutional power in the hands of lay members and an indirect electoral system, unions operating in the sphere of craft technology, well-educated union members, and unions with a high level of membership participation. But he explicitly recognizes that much more empirical work needs to be done before an adequate theory of union democracy can be formulated.

Turner's recent discussion of trade union democracy emphasizes that the position of the worker in Britain can vary considerably.[22] This may be schematically summarized in the following way:

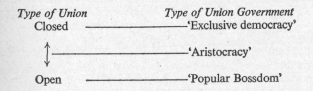

Type of Union	*Type of Union Government*
Closed	'Exclusive democracy'
↕	'Aristocracy'
Open	'Popular Bossdom'

The closed unions in Turner's distinction are characterized by a restrictionist outlook which seeks to control the supply of labour to particular occupations and maintain an exclusive claim to employment within those occupations, whereas open unions are expansionist, relying on strength of numbers for their bargaining power. Turner discusses in detail the factors which both predispose a union to belong to one type rather than another, and which may lead it to move from an open to a closed position or the converse. 'Like most categories in the real world the borderline is blurred by mixed types and by transfer across it.'[23] The interesting point in this context is that the three types of union government can be located at different points on the closed/open continuum. The 'exclusive democracies' occur in closed union situations and are marked by: high membership participation in union affairs and management, and relatively few full-time officials – whose expertise and status is little different from that of the lay member (e.g., the London Typographical Society). The 'aristocracies' emerge where, essentially, one has, so to speak, first and second class citizens within a union – as, for example, when the Spinners recruited piecers, and the AEU non-craft engineering operatives. The skilled men who maintained control over the supply of labour to their occupations constitute a lay aristocracy, filling to a disproportionate extent full-time as well as unpaid union positions. The 'popular bossdoms' exist in open union structures. Here we get a low level of membership participation in union affairs (as Goldstein has illustrated with regard to the T & GWU),[24] a marked gap between the laity and the professionals in terms of expertise, and, commonly, a dominating General Secretary. Turner notes that in practice popular bossdoms may be characterized by different leadership styles: they may be radical or conservative, militant or conciliatory in their bargaining stances. This of course has different implications for the rank-and-file membership. The entrenched bureaucratic authority of the General Secretary and his District Officers can however be challenged despite apathy in many sectors; one of the most clear-cut examples of this is to be found in the chequered relations existing between the T & GWU and the dock workers.[25]

Notwithstanding Allen's earlier discussion which was an attempted partial refutation of Michels, he has more recently expressed views on the British trade union situation which essentially re-echo part of Michels' argument. Thus he points out that strikes are defined typically in the wider society as irresponsible, against the interests of the community, and so on.

Union officials are particularly prone to the anti-strike environmental influences because they are frequently made out to be responsible for the behaviour of their members. Once they are committed to a strike call, union officials tend to become defensive, apologetic and concerned about taking avoiding action. When they are actually engaged in a strike they are frequently motivated by a desire to end it quickly irrespective of the merits of the issue.[26]

NOTES

1. J. A. SCHUMPETER, *Capitalism, Socialism and Democracy*, Allen & Unwin, 1943. J. K. GALBRAITH, *American Capitalism*, Penguin, 1967.

2. R. MICHELS, *Political Parties*, Collins, 1962.

3. ibid., p. 50.

4. ibid., pp. 283–4.

5. ibid., p. 289.

6. R. MICHELS, *Political Parties*, p. 369.

7. ibid., p. 67.

8. S. and B. WEBB, *Industrial Democracy*, London, 1911, pp. v and vi.

9. ibid., p. 36.

10. ibid., p. 37.

11. ibid., p. 102.

12. ibid., p. 103.

13. V. L. ALLEN, *Power in Trade Unions*, Longmans, 1954.

14. ibid., p. 15.

15. ibid., p. 25.

16. ibid., p. 206.

17. S. M. LIPSET, in his introductory essay to MICHELS' *Political Parties*, op. cit., p. 29.

18. C. WRIGHT MILLS, 'The Labour Leaders and the Power Elite' in A. KORNHAUSER, R. DUBLIN and A. M. ROSS (eds.), *Industrial Conflict*, McGraw-Hill, 1954.

19. ibid., pp. 151–2.

20. For further examples see S. W. LERNER, *Breakaway Unions and the Small Trade Union*, Allen & Unwin, 1961.

21. RODERICK MARTIN, 'Union Democracy: an Explanatory Framework' in *Sociology*, II, no. 2, 1968.

22. H. A. TURNER, *Trade Union Growth, Structure and Policy*, Allen & Unwin, 1962.

23. ibid., p. 267.

24. J. GOLDSTEIN, *The Government of British Trade Unions*, Allen & Unwin, 1952

25. On this point see: V. L. ALLEN, *Trade Union Leadership*, Longmans, 1957 and J. WOODWARD *et al.*, *The Dock Worker*, Liverpool University Press, 1954.

26. V. L. ALLEN, *Militant Trade Unionism*, Merlin Press, 1966, p. 27.

12 Industrial Relations in Great Britain: A Critique of Reformism[1]

J. H. Goldthorpe

Reprinted with permission from J. H. Goldthorpe, 'Industrial Relations in Great Britain: a Critique of Reformism', *Politics and Society*, 1974.

Arguments for the reform of industrial relations in Britain are advanced at the present time from a number of different standpoints: one cannot, therefore, without undue simplification, speak of 'reformism' *tout court*. What is, however, possible is to describe, in broad terms, a set of industrial relations 'problems', from consideration of which the arguments of virtually all advocates of reform begin. Furthermore, one may trace, if not the first recognition, then at least the dominant formulation of these problems and of their interrelations to a particular intellectual source: namely, that of the 'Oxford' school of industrial relations which developed in the 1950s and which reached the height of its influence with the work of the Royal Commission on Trade Unions and Employers' Associations (the 'Donovan' Commission) between 1965 and 1968.[2]

The problems in question may be stated briefly as follows.

(i) The strike problem: the increase from the later 1950s onwards in the frequency of unofficial and unconstitutional strikes in all major industries except mining,

(ii) The restrictive practices problem: the relative inefficiency in labour utilization in British industry, traceable in some important part to over-manning, rigid job demarcation, the systematic control of output and other forms of work regulation upheld by groups of rank-and-file employees with, or more often without, the official support of their unions.

(iii) The wage- or earnings-drift problem: the uncontrolled upward movement of earnings, and thus of labour costs, which results from bargaining at plant level producing increases in earnings much in excess of those which would follow simply from increases in nationally negotiated wage rates.

Arising from the wide acceptance of the foregoing as central problems of British industrial relations, two main lines of argument may then be discerned on the origins and causes of these problems which are quite clearly divergent. One view, which may perhaps be best labelled as 'Tory', is the relatively simple and straightforward one that all three problems reflect the greatly increased, and now excessive, power of organized labour in a society committed to high levels of employment and social security. From this diagnosis, the claim has then followed that essential to any solution of Britain's industrial relations ills is new legislation designed to restrict what is regarded as oppressive, selfish or irresponsible trade union activity.[3] The other view, which could in turn be labelled the 'liberal' or 'liberal-pluralist' one[4] – and behind which the authority of the Oxford school is ranged – is that the problems in question stem from deficiencies and contradictions which have accumulated in the post-war period in the entire system of British industrial relations institutions, so that the system itself now tends to generate confusion and disorder, and in particular at workplace level. Thus, effective reform must mean a programme of far-reaching institutional reconstruction, and of a kind which will have to be accomplished primarily by managements and unions themselves; the role of the law should be restricted, as it has traditionally been in British industrial relations, to providing a helpful framework within which 'voluntary' action by the parties directly concerned may proceed.

It was this latter view which was substantially taken over, and indeed in certain respects developed, in the Report of the Donovan Commission,[5] and in this way it achieved a clear intellectual ascendancy. From what might be termed a governmental standpoint, on the other hand, its credibility and appeal would seem to have been rather less evident. The Labour government which set up the Commission accepted most of its findings but still wished, until overwhelmed by union opposition, to provide for new forms of ministerial intervention in industrial crises in which the 'national interest' appeared to be threatened. The Conservative government which succeeded Labour in office in 1970 had within months produced an Industrial Relations Act which, while in some part based on the Commission's diagnosis of the sources of disordered industrial relations, obviously implied rejection of its belief in the capacity of the 'voluntary' system to reform itself adequately without external stimulus, and which also in part accepted the Tory view that 'responsible' trade unionism would require some degree of legal enforcement.[6] However, subsequent experience with the Act cannot be said to have lent much support to the philosophy underlying it. The sanctions which back up its more restrictive provisions have not, so far at least, been used very frequently, and there is little indication that the Act is in any way operating as a positive inducement to more rational and efficient industrial relations practices. On the contrary, defenders of the liberal-pluralist position have been able to argue cogently that the attempt implicit in the Act to combine the objectives of reform and union restraint was fundamentally mistaken, and that, in so far as the Act is having any appreciable effects at all on the day-to-day conduct of industrial relations, these are ones making more for the persistence of excessive disorganization and 'irresponsibility' than for their diminution.[7]

In other words, then, far from being superseded by a policy of 'giving Donovan teeth' through legislation, the liberal approach to industrial relations problems could be said to have gained a good deal in credibility on account precisely of the difficulties which such a policy has encountered. It is, therefore, primarily towards liberal analysis *and* prescription that any relevant critique of reformism must at the present time be directed, and the present essay will proceed accordingly.

In the liberal view, as already implied, the unsatisfactory state of British industrial relations is seen as the outcome of what might be termed 'institutional lag'.[8] In the economic and social conditions of the post-war period, it is argued, not only has the bargaining strength of industrial labour been greatly enhanced but, moreover, a steady expansion has occurred in workers' wants and expectations from their employment: it has become taken for granted that real incomes should continuously rise and, in addition, new and more demanding standards have developed in regard to such matters as security, welfare provisions, fringe benefits and status. Thus, throughout this period there has been more or less constant pressure from workers for the improvement of their wages and conditions of service – and pressure which has been exerted in the main directly from the shopfloor. In turn, then, this has had the effect of greatly increasing the significance of collective bargaining conducted at the level of the individual enterprise, plant or workshop: groups of workers have sought, in a relatively autonomous fashion, to extract whatever advantages and gains appeared possible to them in the specific circumstances of their own work situations, and local managements have usually been obliged to treat with them. The assumption underlying the established or 'formal' system of industrial relations institutions in Britain is that most, if not all, matters appropriate to collective bargaining can be covered by industry-wide agreements negotiated between representatives of trade unions and employers' associations. But it is now evident that this assumption has been rejected over large areas of industry in that within the framework set by such 'national' agreements, a great deal more 'informal' bargaining is carried on between workers, shop stewards and managers in particular workplaces; and, indeed, much bargaining too which goes *beyond* the scope of national agreements into areas which had previously been ones of managerial 'prerogative' – for example, work practices, discipline, recruitment and redundancy policy.

Thus, the conclusion reached is that at the present time there are in fact *two* systems of industrial relations operating in British industry – the formal and the informal – which are unco-ordinated or indeed in conflict. Moreover, it is emphasized in the liberal analysis that the latter system, which for most workers is now the more consequential, remains nonetheless in an often inchoate – that is, inadequately institutionalized – state. What is meant by saying that workplace bargaining is informal is that it is to a large extent carried on within a context of 'custom and practice' rather than being guided by explicit procedural rules, and gives rise to understandings and arrangements which are mostly tacit, or at any rate rarely set down in a systematic, written form. Such a manner of conducting industrial relations may in the short term appear a convenient and comfortable one for the parties concerned; but in the long term, it is held, it is also one likely to lead to serious trouble. For in the rapidly changing conditions of modern industry, circumstances inevitably occur which informal agreements do not cover, or in regard to which they are unclear or uncertain; and even if such situations can to some extent be dealt with 'as they arise' – that is to say, in an *ad hoc*, piecemeal fashion – discrepancies and anomalies in procedural and substantive matters alike will tend in this way to be produced, and will constitute further threats to orderly workplace relations. Many unofficial strikes can be traced back to confusion over what management does or does not have the right to do, or to inadequately worked out disciplinary codes or grievance procedures; and many more originate in discontent generated by chaotic pay structures and differentials which have emerged from numerous unrelated 'deals', adjustments and accommodations.

Finally, the liberal analysis would represent the disorder which is typically associated with the informal system as indicative of a serious crisis of authority in workplace relations. Managements, it is argued, when confronted with the greater bargaining strength of labour, have too readily allowed their control over both work and payments systems to be eroded. For instance, they have viewed too passively the operation of irrational and inefficient manning practices, or of 'decayed' piece-rate and bonus schemes which make production costs unpredictable and are a major source of earnings drift. At the same time, it is pointed out, the increase in informal workplace bargaining has undermined the role in the bargaining process of full-time union officials; and, correspondingly, their authority over their memberships within particular establishments has greatly declined. In many plants bargaining is either highly fragmented or else effective control on the side of labour is in the hands of multi-union shop stewards' committees, responsible to no one but themselves. The general effect is, then, that of the extensive breakdown in the normative regulation of industrial life – or the creation of what Flanders and Fox have referred to as a state of *anomie*.[9] Throughout a large part of British industry at the present time no authority prevails at workplace level which is capable of establishing and maintaining coherent normative systems to govern relations between employers and employees. There exists only a proliferation of generally unrelated, small-scale systems of doubtful effectiveness, whose inconsistencies serve often to intensify disorder and conflict.

From this understanding of the origins and causes of Britain's industrial relations problems, the liberal-pluralist programme for reform then follows with some consistency. It is recognized that the trend towards workplace bargaining stems from social changes which are irreversible; any realistic appraisal of the modern industrial situation requires that the increased bargaining strength and expanding demands of the shopfloor be taken as givens. The aim of effective reform must therefore be not that of curtailing or impeding the power of organized labour by legislation, but rather that of bringing into being, by largely voluntary means, a more adequate institutional context within which workplace bargaining may go on. That is to say, one which is capable both of reflecting, and at the same time of regulating the situation which *de facto* prevails.

To achieve this aim, it is seen as necessary for managements and unions to accept, first of all, that the problem of the loss of authority in the workplace is one which they have in common; and secondly, that the only way in which they can overcome it is by committing themselves to the idea that the regulation of both work and payments systems within the enterprise should be their *joint* undertaking.[10] From the side of management this would mean abandoning strict adherence to doctrines of employer's 'reserved rights' or of managerial 'prerogative' and acknowledging the right of unions to seek to exert influences in all areas of decision-making. In other words, it would have to be recognized that the scope of collective bargaining is in principle unlimited. From the side of labour, it would correspondingly need to be conceded that under a system of joint regulation practices with no more than a 'customary' basis or ones established by unilateral shopfloor action could be properly called into question; and that in appraising work and payments systems generally, technical rationality and cost effectiveness must become dominant criteria. Finally, both sides would be required to move from their present reliance on excessively informal and fragmented workplace bargaining to recognition of the need for formal – that is, written and signed – plant agreements determining the relationship between work and pay in a comprehensive fashion and linking in with the terms of agreements made at higher levels. Both sides would thus lose some degree of freedom of action: managements would become more extensively involved in negotiations with workers, and unions would be less able to react 'tactically' to pressures from the rank-and-file. But in return managements would gain the advantage of greater order and stability in workplace relations, and the possibility of taking effective action in regard to labour utilization and cost control; while for the unions formalization, as well as confirming a significant extension in the scope of bargaining, would increase the involvement in workplace affairs of their full-time officials and thus help them re-establish their control over their stewards and rank-and-file.

In sum, then, what is in effect proposed is a further development in a historical process already well established in advanced capitalist societies: that of the containment of the inherently conflict-laden relations between employers and workers within institutional arrangements which, while perhaps themselves reflecting significant shifts in the balance of social power and advantage, are at the same time designed to prevent industrial conflict taking on what would be disruptive or destructive forms from the standpoint of the existing social order.[11] In this connection, it is important to add that the liberal reformers emphasize that the new institution building which they urge cannot, and is not intended to, *eliminate* industrial conflict; and that they indeed see great merit in the persistence of a pluralist industrial relations system in which some degree of conflict has to be accepted as normal and legitimate. For example, they also make clear that while they see their proposals as representing a way of substantially increasing industrial democracy, they are not ones aimed at producing an integrated enterprise under 'worker control'. By accepting collective bargaining as the major instrument of industrial democracy, the liberal approach seeks to preserve the independence of unions from management, so that, in the last resort, the possibility of unilateral action remains open to labour. Correspondingly, therefore, no challenge is raised against management's ultimate responsibility for the conduct of the enterprise and for the definition of its goals.[12]

The liberal-pluralist position is, thus, one which displays a considerable *esprit de système*: analysis and prescription are capable of being explicitly and closely related. Consequently, any effective critique of the position must begin at a fundamental level: it must be directed in the first place towards its, often implicit, assumptions and presuppositions before more specific issues can usefully be taken up.

As earlier noted, the liberal, in common with other reformist arguments, starts from the identification of a number of industrial relations problems. It is, however, developed from this basis in a manner which reveals a rather distinctive strategy of liberal reformism generally: that is, the case for the changes which are being sought is made out on the grounds that they are the necessary means of removing, or at least of containing, a state of affairs which may be regarded as a form of social pathology or breakdown. In this way, then, by assuming the stance of the social physician or engineer, the advocates of reform can attempt to play down the *ex parte* aspects of their proposals and to mobilize support for them as either 'common sense', or essentially technical measures designed to serve the common good.[13]

As strategy, it must be recognized that this approach has often proved successful, as the history of social reform movements in Britain or other Western societies would show. However, the danger is that its very attractiveness may result in the strategy being allowed, as it were, to 'contaminate' the analysis which should be prior to and independent of it: that, in other words, would-be reformers may let their preference for an effective style of political rhetoric persuade them that the situation to which they would apply it corresponds more closely with the assumptions of that rhetoric than is in fact the case. Specifically, they may be disinclined to confront the crucial issue of whether what they represent as a 'problem' is in fact recognized as such by all the parties involved, or whether it may not be but one facet of a more complex situation in which the difficulties experienced by one party tend to be no concern of others or even perhaps to be *their* advantages and opportunities. To the extent that the latter interpretation is the more valid, it is difficult for reformers to avoid the awkward questions of just *whose* are the problems to which they are offering solutions and, where conflicts arise, of just whose side they are on. But, at the same time, to ignore or underplay aspects of a given situation so as to make it easier to employ the rhetoric of 'problem solving' is also likely to prove discomfitting in the end. For even if they gain a wide measure of political approval, attempts at reform based on inadequate analysis will still face rebuff by the social reality on which they are intended to act.

In the case of British industrial relations, this dilemma would appear to be one which exponents of liberal reform have in some degree appreciated, but have not avoided. Rather, it may be argued, deficiencies in their analysis – and ones which threaten the viability of the liberal reform programme – are brought about in a number of respects precisely because the analysis is conducted in such a way as to obscure the point at which political – and ideological – divisions must become manifest.

If one returns to the three industrial relations problems which, it was suggested, are the source of reformist arguments generally – those of strikes, restrictive practices and earnings drift – it would seem hard to deny that these are, primarily, problems of *management*. This is not to say that only management is adversely affected by them, but simply that within the industrial enterprise it is managers who are likely to have the major concern and interest in overcoming them, while other groups may conceivably be little troubled by them or even believe that they have an interest in their continuation. If this is granted – and liberal reformers seem prepared to accept at least that these problems are primarily management's *responsibility*[14] – then the question may be raised of how the liberal analysis contrives to start from such problems and yet to arrive at the conclusion that they must be seen as indicative of some more fundamental and general malaise which involves all parties to industrial relations alike, but which, if its true character were to be understood, could be dispelled largely by voluntary action and to the general benefit. This *tour de force*, it will be maintained, is accomplished only by exploiting shortcomings in the analysis first of the nature of social control within both the enterprise and the union and, secondly, of the work orientations and motivations of rank-and-file employees.

The claim that the increased bargaining strength of labour and the growth of the informal system of workplace relations have resulted in a serious loss of authority and condition of *anomie* in industrial life is one which involves a good deal of conceptual uncertainty. To begin with, exponents of this argument appear to make no clear and sustained distinction between *authority* and *power*, and this confuses, in particular, the discussion of management's control over labour. If authority is understood, in the manner of Max Weber, as referring to the 'legitimate exercise of command' (*legitime Herrschaft*), it is in fact by no means evident that the authority of management *has* been reduced in any dramatic way. Managerial authority in the industrial enterprise is, to continue with Weberian terminology, essentially authority of a 'rational-legal' kind; that is to say, the legitimacy of command that management has derives from its performance of a delimited function under the regulation of the law. Specifically, its authority over workers stems, on the one hand, from the manager's status as the agent of the employer and, on the other, from the contract of employment in which workers have engaged. In this sense, then, managerial authority must be seen as still at the present time largely intact: it has not been ceded, and indeed has not had to face any major challenge – as, for example, through widespread demands for radical changes in managerial accountability or for 'worker control'. Management, in other words, still retains its right to plan and conduct the affairs of the enterprise in the interests of the employer and, to this end, to issue orders to employees.[15]

However, the important point here is that the employment contract is typically, indeed almost invariably, of an incomplete and inexplicit nature. While it gives management the right of command, it does so only in a generalized way. It does not itself determine just what tasks an employee is required to undertake, just how he shall do them, just how much effort he shall expend on them, just what work rules he shall obey, and so on.[16] Thus, for the exercise of detailed control over employees in the actual performance of their work tasks and roles, it has always been a necessary feature of the industrial enterprise that managerial authority should be supplemented by the managerial exercise of power: that is, by management's use of various resources at its disposal in order to impose a work discipline. Chiefly, of course, one refers here to economically-based or 'remunerative' power deriving from the employer's position of advantage within the labour contract; but one may note too the importance in some cases of 'symbolic' power as expressed through management's superior social prestige.[17] To the extent, then, that in the economic and social context of the post-war period management's control over labour has been weakened, the correct interpretation of this change would appear to be that it indicates a decline, not in management's authority, but in its purely *de facto* capacity to secure the compliance of workers with its specific requirements. Because of the improved market situation of industrial workers, because of their more effective organization at shopfloor level, their greater self-confidence and heightened wants and expectations, management has become less able than before to, as it were, fill in the 'silences' in the employment contract to its own advantage. Workers can now often prevent management from using its power in an entirely arbitrary or summary fashion; they can compel managements to negotiate and bargain with them on a widening range of issues; and, in these and other ways, they are able to call into question managerial 'prerogatives', the exercise of which in the past must be seen not so much as an act of legitimate command but rather as the expression of a superior power position.[18]

Furthermore, the sense in which it may be said that the unions are involved along with management in the crisis of authority in the workplace is also one which requires critical examination. In arguing thus, liberal reformers seek to imply that management and unions are in a broadly similar situation: both have difficulty in maintaining control over the actions of men on the shop floor. Hence, it appears reasonable to suggest that they should move towards a common solution of their problems by creating a new basis for their authority in their 'joint regulation' of work and payments systems. However, just as it may be held that management's problem of control should be understood as one of power rather than of authority, it may similarly be argued that the unions' problem is one in which the question of authority is, at all events, much less central than is that of *influence*.

The authority which union officials can claim over men on the shopfloor is a limited one: it is that of the elected or duly appointed leadership of a protective association over its members. Union officials, one might say, can claim legitimate command over workers insofar as co-ordinated action is required in the pursuit of the union's objectives of defending and furthering the interests of the membership as a collectivity. Thus, where a union bureaucracy finds that it has little control over the activities of a group of its members who have discovered that they can best serve their interests in the regulation both of work and payment by bargaining in a more or less autonomous way, or through a multi-union shop stewards' committee, this cannot in itself be taken as implying a challenge to, or a failure of, union authority. It could be said to do so only if the activities in question were contrary to union rules or had come under some kind of official union ban – as, for instance, have a number of attempts by militants at linking up stewards' committees on an industry-wide basis. For the most part, though, what is indicated is essentially a failure of the union as an organization – a failure to adapt to the changing realities of market and work situations, so that, in the eyes of the rank-and-file, the bureaucracy has become increasingly irrelevant to the conduct of industrial relations in their particular workplace.[19] Consequently, the 'leverage' that full-time officials can exert on the rank-and-file – the officials' ability to advise, guide and persuade them into preferred courses of action – is greatly diminished.[20] As theorists of social exchange have pointed out, influence and dependence are intimately related.

Viewed in this way, then, the unions' problem of control is seen in fact to be of a very different nature from that of management: rather than being one of the effectiveness of the power of superiors over subordinates within a hierarchial organization based on contract, it is one of the responsiveness of leaders to lead within an organization which claims to pursue its members' interests on the basis of a democratic constitution. Moreover, it can now be appreciated that in situations where the two problems co-exist, the possibility of a 'common' solution being achieved is, to say the least, a good deal less obvious than liberal reformers would pretend. To the extent that union officials are involved, or are felt by workers to be involved, in attempts by management to reassert its control over the shopfloor, their difficulties in maintaining *rapport* with their rank-and-file can only be increased.[21]

In sum, if one regards the present disorder in industrial relations as having little to do with questions of authority *stricto sensu*, and views the breakdown in normative regulation as largely epiphenomenal to shifts in patterns of power and influence, the appropriateness of the 'problem-solving' approach to industrial relations policy is at once called into doubt. The increased economic and organizational strength of workers on the shopfloor and their readiness to use it to pursue a widening range of demands has surely given rise to problems of order – that is to say, of control – for managements and union bureaucracies alike. But in the perspective which has been suggested as an alternative to the liberal one, it is readily seen that these are not similar, nor in any meaningful sense shared problems. More importantly still, the further issue which clearly emerges is that of how far one may regard the problems of either managements or union bureaucracies as being ones that are of great concern to the men on the shopfloor themselves. If these problems originate chiefly in a shift in bargaining advantage towards the latter, why should it be thought that they too will regard the existing state of affairs as being in evident need of reform?

This question is one which in fact seems never to have been squarely faced by exponents of the liberal-pluralist position. For the most part, it has been simply concealed under the blanket assumption that the removal of disorder in industrial relations must constitute a general good. Only occasionally and fleetingly has the attempt been made to justify this assumption by explicitly considering the experience and interests of rank-and-file workers in relation to some particular aspect of 'disorder'. However, for present purposes, these instances are of some interest, since they serve to reveal the generally inadequate treatment of the 'view from below' which characterizes both the Oxford tradition of industrial relations research and, hence, the liberal analysis of present-day problems.

For example, one may take the case of overtime working – the regular practice of which is viewed by liberal reformers as both a serious manifestation and cause of unruly workplace relations and of inefficient production. The level of overtime to be worked and its distribution between individuals and groups, it is pointed out, are now more often than not determined through negotiations or, rather, informal consultations between lower-level managers – quite possibly foremen – and shop stewards. The decisions which emerge tend thus to be unco-ordinated, often from one work group or department to another, and to become a major source of anomalies in earnings, and hence of grievances and disputes, within the labour force. Even where attempts have been made to develop a planned pay structure, overtime earnings are likely to distort and disrupt it, and to generate 'drift'. Moreover, it is also claimed that the systematic working of overtime is regularly associated with practices designed to ensure that the overtime is there; that is, ones which involve some kind of deliberate time-wasting during standard working hours. In short, systematic overtime is indicative of disorder in both work and payments systems alike.[22]

This totally negative assessment, it may be remarked, is a questionable one even from a strictly managerial standpoint. A Report of the National Board for Prices and Incomes has argued that there are often quite sound economic grounds for overtime working, and that where inefficiencies in the use of manpower co-exist with systematic overtime – which is not always the case – it still cannot be assumed that they are invariably a consequence of this.[23] However, the crucial issue in the present context is that of how far, even if one accepts that overtime *is*, or ought to be, a problem for management, it is one also for the workers involved.

What appears to be the strongest argument for regarding it as such is that the practice of overtime working is likely to be damaging both to the health of employees and to their family and social lives. But this claim is not so obviously valid as it may at first seem,[24] and moreover it is not altogether to the point. For the available evidence clearly shows that industrial employees often actively seek overtime, even if their attitudes towards it may to some extent remain ambivalent. To understand this 'quest for overtime', as one writer has called it,[25] it is clear that one must begin with the individual's situation outside the workplace – especially with his responsibilities and aspirations in his familial roles – and with the way in which these influence his orientation to work.[26] But so far as the work situation itself is concerned, it is important to note that the attraction of overtime becomes easier to understand precisely where it is linked with time-wasting – that is to say, with a reduction of effort – during the normal working day. For in this way, given the premium rates that are paid for overtime, workers may well feel that they can gain an improvement in the terms of the 'money for effort' bargains which they make with their employer. Furthermore, where workers are thus able to regulate their effort and to 'create' overtime, it must be recognized that they are better placed to prevent the fluctuations in earnings which, it is claimed, overtime often produces.

Proponents of reform typically argue that if time-wasting were ended and working methods were generally made more efficient, it would be possible for hours to be greatly reduced while earnings remained at their previous level – to the advantage of management and workers alike. But this is to disregard the fact that such a change would, other things being equal, require workers to raise the intensity of their effort; and it is also to underestimate the possibility that time-wasting at the employer's expense may in itself be gratifying to workers. Flanders has written that 'One must take a very poor and cynical view of humanity to believe that this [deliberate time-wasting to create the need for overtime] can be a source of human happiness . . .'[27] The obvious reply is, however, that one is not here concerned with humanity *sub specie aeternitatis*, but with men in the role of wage worker within a modern industrial enterprise. There is ample evidence to show that such men do often view their relationship with their employing organization in essentially calculative, 'money for effort' terms. Where this is so, it would then seem perfectly understandable that, under certain conditions, they might prefer to gain a certain level of earnings through a longer period of lower effort rather than through a shorter period of higher effort; or, at very least, there would seem no reason why, from their point of view, a shift from the former arrangement to the latter should be regarded as an entirely cost-less one. Furthermore, there is also extensive evidence of workers' concern to maintain their autonomy in the performance of their work tasks and roles and, to this end, to exert control of their own over basic features of the work situation – control over *time* being seen in various ways as highly important.[28] In the case, then, of groups of workers who conceive their relationship with their employer in either a calculative or some more directly antagonistic manner, it is not difficult to appreciate that being able to apply such control *against* management could be found inherently rewarding. In addition, in the particular instance of time-wasting, it needs also to be appreciated that 'time out' may sometimes serve a significant social function for the work group; that is, it may provide opportunity for various activities through which the solidarity of the group, and the shared beliefs and values of its members, are daily reinforced.[29]

Finally, in this connection, one may note that the view of systematic overtime as a generally undesirable outcome of dis-ordered workplace relations is also controverted by the difficulty which is experienced when attempts are made to eradicate it. If the view in question were correct, one would suppose that in cases where management had sought to get to grips with the situation and a reduction in overtime, together with the ending of any associated restrictive practices, had been successfully negotiated, then the 'problem' would tend not to recur. In other words, if the demand for overtime that had existed did not in fact reflect workers 'real' interests, but merely a misguided opportunism in the face of managerial slackness, then once a more orderly and rational state of affairs had been brought about, one would expect little pressure from workers for a return to the *status quo ante*. However, according to the NBPI Report, the tendency is for agreements on the reduction of overtime to be followed by just such pressure, and within a relatively short period of time. The main, if not perhaps the only, reason for this is fairly obvious once the assumption is abandoned that overtime always is, or ought to be, undesirable from the worker's point of view. As the Report points out, 'if [workers'] preferences as between hours of work and earnings were reasonably well-suited before the agreement – which is likely on the whole to be the case – then they will not necessarily be so well-suited after the agreement, despite the benefits the latter confers'.[30]

A second illustration of the way in which the liberal case for reform is founded upon an unsatisfactory treatment of the orientations and motivation of rank-and-file workers can be taken from the – highly critical – attention which is given to 'payment by results'. Although the operation of PBR systems is not seen, as is systematic overtime, as *necessarily* indicative of a pathological condition of workplace industrial relations, such systems are regarded as being in fact a very frequent source of disorder. Unless kept under strict control by management, it is argued, PBR systems tend to 'decay' or 'degenerate'; that is to say, the link between effort and pay which they are intended to establish is attenuated, so that their incentive effect declines and pay is increasingly determined by factors other than effort. In some part, this degeneration tends to be produced by what are termed 'autonomous mechanisms' – such as the natural improvement over time in workers' skills. But often too it is brought about as the result of direct bargaining over piecework at shopfloor level, between managers, foremen and work study engineers on the one hand, and work groups or individual employees on the other. Where this latter influence is allowed to become a powerful one, it is observed, degeneration is likely to be rapid and extreme. The determination of piece-rates becomes essentially a political, rather than an economic or technical process, and one which is governed by rules that derive largely from 'custom and practice' rather than from actual negotiation and agreement between management and workers' representatives. Given, then, this prevalence of highly fragmented and informal bargaining, the usual consequences are to be expected: anomalies and inequities in pay structures, spiralling unit costs, uncontrolled movements of earnings, and so on. If such disorder is to be avoided, it is held, a particular need arises for formal workplace agreements which comprise explicit 'transactional' rules to govern the operation of PBR. The alternative, preferable perhaps in many cases, is to abandon piecework altogether in favour of 'measured day work' or some other kind of time-based method of payment.[31]

It is appreciated in this analysis that the probability of PBR systems being disrupted through workplace bargaining reflects a fundamental change in the bargaining situation: that brought about by the greater 'bargaining awareness', the stronger economic position and the more effective organization of men on the shopfloor. It is also recognized that, in this changed situation, a general effect of informal bargaining is to reduce the area of job regulation which is subject to managerial prerogative and to increase that under the control of workers themselves. The result is, then, that it is in this case scarcely possible for liberal reformers to avoid altogether the difficulty which arises in attempting to maintain a purely 'problem-solving' approach. The inappropriateness of this would seem to be indicated by much of their own argument, which may readily be taken as bringing out the extent to which management and workers are here in a relationship of conflict – with the latter having now frequently achieved a position of relative advantage. In other words, the implications cannot be overlooked that the disorder found often to be associated with piece-rate working might most accurately be seen as in fact the turning of PBR systems against their makers. Devised as instruments of managerial control over labour, it may be argued, these systems have now, with a shift in the balance of power in workplace relations, become in many cases the means through which rank-and-file employees are able to improve their effort bargain and to expand their own control over the work situation.

This alternative interpretation has not been accorded any full and explicit attention by members of the liberal-pluralist school, but two claims intended, it would appear, as objections to it have been advanced. First, it has been maintained that although informal bargaining has the *effect* of bringing job regulation increasingly under workers' control, this is not the *intention* of the workers who engage in such bargaining; it is an unlooked-for outcome, reflecting no concern with, or strategy for, greater control on their part. Secondly, it is held that it should not in any event be supposed that workers will prefer to have unilateral control over aspects of their work situation rather than to engage, via their union representatives, in joint regulation with management, since such joint regulation would reduce the area over which they, and perhaps also management, exerted no control at all.[32]

These arguments have at least the merit of being counter-intuitive – that is to say, they seem in certain respects to lack inherent plausibility. But more to the point is that they also lack any systematic evidence in their support. The major study made of piecework bargaining from the standpoint of liberal reformism – in which both arguments are to be found – is remarkable for the fact that in the course of it, the author conducted interviews with managers, foremen and shop stewards but *not* with rank-and-file workers.[33] The basis of his remarks concerning the intentions and preferences of the latter remains therefore obscure. Scepticism is, moreover, reinforced by the fact that such evidence as is available on the response of workers to piece-rate payment does indicate a general awareness of the advantages that arise in regard to autonomy and control – even though this evidence sometimes comes from studies made in bargaining situations less favourable to labour than those now common.[34] Where labour's position is strong and piecework bargaining is extensive, it may be that the consequences of this can build up in ways not entirely intended, or even perhaps desired, by workers; but it remains nonetheless difficult to accept that a concern to widen the range of their freedom of action is not an important element in workers' motivation, and that the achievement of this goal is not a major source of satisfaction.[35]

Finally, it may be observed that if piecework is widely experienced as a cause of unwelcome disorder by those employees engaged in it, it is surprising that this is not more clearly reflected in the answers given by workers when asked directly about their preferences as between piece- and time-rates. For example, in an enquiry undertaken on behalf of the Donovan Commission, those members of a sample of trade unionists who were paid by results were asked if they would favour replacing this system by some other, such as time-rates. The proportion saying that they would favour such a change was 33 per cent. This result may then be compared with that obtained when respondents not paid by results, but whose work would allow this, were asked if they would favour moving over to piece-rates. In this case, the proportion in favour of the change was 54 per cent.[36]

It is, one hopes, evident that the purpose of the foregoing paragraphs is not to claim that PBR will always and in every respect be to the advantage of labour – any more than it was previously the aim to contend that systematic overtime is an unalloyed good. That piece-rate working can operate so as to be in various ways seriously disadvantageous to workers is not in question. What *is* being suggested is, to repeat, that under certain conditions which now seem quite frequently to prevail, it is in fact possible for workers to exploit PBR so as to increase the extent of their control over both work and payment systems and in ways which clearly serve their interests – just as they may also do through being able to exploit arrangements for the working of overtime. Consequently, it is argued, to represent the situations thus created as being simply ones of 'disorder' is seriously misleading.

The attraction of such an interpretation to liberal reformers is understandable enough in terms of their preferred political rhetoric. But their strategic concern to make out that industrial relations policy can, and should, be approached in an essentially problem-solving, technocratic fashion – that it is primarily a matter of devising the right kind of regulatory institutions – involves them in weaknesses and evasions in analysis which cannot be concealed. Furthermore, as the remainder of this paper will seek to show, these deficiencies have consequences which in fact threaten to be politically damaging to the liberal case in two rather different ways.

First, it may be noted that, in the recent past, the ideological basis and implications of the liberal-pluralist position have attracted an increasing amount of critical scrutiny. Attacks on this position have indeed always come from the Marxist Left, but these have been often of little effect, either intellectually or politically, since their usually perfunctory and dogmatic character rendered them vulnerable to mere disregard. Of late, however, not only have more seriously argued challenges been presented by certain Marxist authors but, further, questions and objections of a kind which it is difficult simply to ignore have come from, as it were, nearer home, and most notably in the writings of Alan Fox, once a prominent member of the Oxford school.[37]

The main significance of this more recent criticism is that it attacks liberal reformism on its own ground: that is, it queries whether the liberal approach is one likely to bring about the greater pluralism in industrial relations and in the wider society which is its professed ideal – or, rather, one which will in effect help to preserve a heavy concentration of power, both within and outside the enterprise, in the hands of a business and managerial elite.

As Fox has pointed out, the commitment of liberal reformers to pluralist values is not unlimited: it does not extend, for example, to giving support to the activities of 'would-be self-determining work groups' in the pursuit of their perceived interests, or at least not where these activities come into conflict with the objectives of management. At this point, a diagnosis of 'disorder' is introduced and the first priority is taken to be that of restoring managerial control.[38] To achieve this, the joint regulation of work and payments systems by management and unions is held to be necessary. However, in this connection it has to be noted that (as liberal reformers acknowledge) joint regulation is not joint management; and further that (as they are less ready to concede) the involvement of unions in formalized rule-making and rule-enforcing procedures cannot be taken as guaranteeing the acceptability of these means of control to the rank-and-file. For this would be to assume, as Hyman has observed, that workers are positively engaged in the political and organizational processes of their unions – which is clearly not the typical case. Although not necessarily 'undemocratic' bodies, unions clearly 'do not function as agencies for the active involvement of workers generally in the control of their industrial destinies'.[39] Moreover, the more serious inroads into managerial control tend to be made through the spontaneous action of rank-and-file workers and to be maintained through their own shopfloor organization, towards which the attitudes of union officialdom are often, to say the least, ambivalent. Thus, proposals for formal company or plant agreements which would bring full-time officials back into a closer involvement with the affairs of the workplace must be seen as threatening to the autonomy of the shopfloor. Indeed, liberal reformers, in stressing the common 'challenge from below' facing employers and unions alike, are led to imply that formalization will give unions the possibility of keeping their stewards in check and of re-establishing official 'authority' at workplace level.[40] Hence, when Flanders writes that managements 'can only regain control by sharing it', the question which must arise is that of whether those with whom control is to be shared and those over whom control is to be reimposed are in fact the same people.

It may therefore be persuasively argued that if the liberal programme for reform were to be realized, the most probable outcome would be not an expansion of industrial democracy but rather, whether intended or not, the consolidation of managerial capitalism – the essence of what is proposed being in effect the extension of the principles of rationalization and bureaucratization to the labour relations field. As both liberal and Marxist economists have recently observed, increases in the scale of production, advancing technology and more integrated and competitive markets place mounting pressure on industrial enterprises to engage in the long-term planning of their activities. It is no longer sufficient for managements simply to seek to adapt to new business conditions as they arise: they must attempt to foresee and, as far as possible, to control these conditions.[41] In this attempt, however, the factor of labour represents, at least potentially, a source of major difficulty. For labour cannot be disassociated from the individuals who provide it, and thus, as Kidron has put it, 'It has a will of its own and more or less independent organizations. It can, and does, take advantage of its own scarcity.[42] Moreover, labour problems may be expected to be especially acute where, as in Britain, the market position of many groups of workers is strong, and where local, shopfloor organization has relatively high autonomy. Thus, in such a context, the liberal prescription for the reform of British industrial relations can, as Fox points out, be readily interpreted as representing 'a high point in enlightened "managerialism".'[43] It appears expressly conceived to give managements the advantage of, if not a docile labour force, then at all events one whose demands, and action in pursuit of such demands, will be institutionally regulated and channelled to a high degree: so much so, in fact, as to be more or less predictable by management or, alternatively put, so as to be deprived of much possibility of strategic timing or tactical surprise.

Indeed, in what may be regarded as the latest version of the liberal programme – that of McCarthy and Ellis – one finds the argument explicitly advanced that in order to meet the 'challenge from without', the 'challenge from below' will need to be 'directed at managers in a more precise and predictable way' than hitherto. Management-union negotiations at plant and company level should, it is urged, become increasingly future-oriented in character, so that a link may be established between collective bargaining of a 'predictive' kind and corporate planning. And from this proposal there then follows, logically enough, the suggestion that the present tradition of 'open-ended' agreements, which go on until, and only until, one side wishes to renegotiate, should give way to a system of 'fixed term' agreements. It is recognized that agreements of this latter type would mean that there would have to be a 'closed season' for demands made by labour against the enterprise, but this is accepted as only reasonable: 'Corporate plans cannot be changed overnight, and attempts to monitor and assess the impact of all aspects of the wage-work equation on other parts of the business take a considerable time.'[44]

There is here, then, clear enough confirmation of Fox's argument that the liberal-pluralist approach to industrial relations policy is, in its implications, fundamentally conservative – that the changes which it seeks to promote are ones designed to bring about the more effective integration of labour into the existing structure of economic and social relations, in industry and the wider society, rather than ones intended to produce any basic alteration in this structure. Given the reality of increased economic and organizational power on the part of industrial workers, the interest of liberal reformers is not primarily directed towards institutional developments which would reflect this change in any radical fashion: as, for example, by confirming workers' autonomy in regard to certain features of their immediate work situation; or by giving them an effective voice in policy-making, rather than simply the opportunity to react to policy once made by management; or by enabling them to raise questions about the basic principles which should guide the organization and conduct of the enterprise.[45] Rather, the institutional reconstruction which is envisaged appears to be aimed chiefly at the *containment* of shopfloor power, by the extention – but at the same time formalization – of collective bargaining, and, in its more advanced features, at 'bringing home to workers the extent to which their claims are dependent upon the firm's ability to surmount and exploit the challenges posed by the external environment'.[46]

As, therefore, the ideological aspects of liberal reformism are revealed by its critics (and also by its exponents, impelled by critical probing into greater candour about their value commitments and assumptions) so is its political strategy undermined.

That is to say, the attempt by liberal reformers to present themselves in the role of, as it were, institutional engineers, investigating generally recognized 'problems' and devising the best 'solutions' to them, must become increasingly called into question. The fact that they are themselves protagonists in the political and ideological arena, albeit perhaps highly sophisticated ones, is less capable of being masked; and once it is evident that in their analyses and prescriptions expertise is combined with a distinctive political and ideological stance, then acceptance of the former is likely to become in some degree conditional on sympathy with the latter.[47]

Threatened thus, the response that liberal-pluralists might most readily make to defend their position would, it seems, be an appeal to pragmatism. They might claim, for example, that if their approach is 'managerial', then this is because in present-day society industrial management is of crucial importance: the achievement of more orderly labour relations and of a more efficient use of manpower is essential to the control of inflation and to the rising productivity on which the future well-being of all groups in the community, workers included, must ultimately depend. Or again, they might argue that if their programme for reform is one conceived within the limits of the existing social order, it has at the same time the merit of being aimed at feasible changes, and ones from which workers, as well as managers and employers, would derive at least sufficient benefits to outweigh any costs entailed. As already noted, experience with the 1971 Industrial Relations Act has enabled liberal writers to reply forcefully to their critics from the Right that Tory reformism, however plausible it may sound in theory, simply does not work in practice. And correspondingly, as against their critics on the Left, they might contend that visionary schemes for worker control or the socialization of production hold out in fact far less promising prospects of real gains for labour, whether material or otherwise, than do their own more modest, but more considered proposals for 'joint regulation', based as these are on the tried and proven methods of collective bargaining.

Such a counter-attack could, in principle, be a powerful one. But its effectiveness must of course depend on it being shown that the liberal programme for industrial relations reform *is* as 'realistic' and 'workable' as its advocates would wish to imply –

that, in comparison with other approaches, it results from a more valid appraisal of the existing situation and from a sounder judgement of the potentialities for change that are inherent in it. However, in this respect again, it may be held, the liberal-pluralist position is seriously weakened by the effects of sub-ordinating analysis, if not to overt ideology, then at all events to the requirements of political style. It is in fact by no means established that the liberal programme can claim any special merit on pragmatic grounds: so far at least, it may be argued, progress towards its implementation is not impressive. And furthermore, a major source of difficulty would seem to lie precisely in its exponents' concern to treat industrial relations problems as a form of social pathology, rather than as ex-pressions of social conflict, and in their neglect of the importance of the orientations and motivations of the actors involved at grass-roots level. For illustration of this argument, one may best turn to the Report of the Donovan Commission itself – as the most detailed working blueprint thus far prepared for the re-construction of British industrial relations on liberal-pluralist lines.

As already noted, the Donovan Report largely accepted the liberal view that Britain's industrial relations problems stemmed from the inadequacy or malfunctioning of regulatory institutions, especially at the level of the workplace. To overcome these problems, it was then held, new institutional arrangements would need to be developed on a company or plant basis in order to complement those operating on a 'national' or industry, basis. What primarily was recommended was that representatives of management and labour should come together to negotiate workplace agreements of a formal, comprehensive and authori-tative kind which could provide a clear substantive and pro-cedural basis for their collaboration in the work of the enterprise. In other words, then, the Commission also underwrote the liberal argument that the chief *medium* of the reform of workplace relations should be the process of collective bargaining itself – and in this way it accepted too the virtual corollary that the part to be played by the law should be a decidedly secondary one. The furthest, in fact, that the Commission was prepared to go in the direction of legal compulsion or inducement to reform was to propose an Act which would require companies of over a certain size to register collective agreements with the Department of Employment and Productivity (or to explain why they had not done so), and which would also set up an Industrial Relations Commission with investigatory and advisory functions. Otherwise, the achievement of the new order was to be left to the initiative and efforts of the parties directly concerned.[48]

However, what might seem a strong indication that such faith in the 'voluntary principle', and in the analysis underlying it, could prove to be misplaced was already present in findings produced by the Donovan Commission's own research programme. In the main, the research undertaken reflected the 'institutionalist' preoccupations of the Oxford school, and no detailed studies were made of the conduct of workplace industrial relations from the point of view of the participants themselves. However, in multi-purpose interviews carried out with samples of managers, foremen, union officers, shop stewards and rank-and-file employees, a number of questions were asked aimed at assessing their degree of satisfaction with existing arrangements and procedures at workplace level. What was revealed was that satisfaction was widespread, and appeared to be greatest of all among those groups likely to be most immediately involved in the 'informal' system – that is, foremen, stewards and shopfloor workers. The only groups in which sizeable minorities expressed dissatisfaction on any of the issues raised were the full-time union officials and personnel (but not works) managers.[49]

Although given less prominence in the Donovan Report than their significance would appear to warrant, these findings were inevitably a source of some embarrassment to the Commission. For one thing, if the liberal diagnosis was correct, and over a large part of British industry workplace relations were in a seriously disorganized and anomic state, it might have been expected, as the Report indeed admits, that existing arrangements 'would be unpopular with large numbers of those who work under them'. To accommodate the fact that this was not the case, the Commission was obliged to acknowledge that these arrangements must have 'some important advantages which impress themselves upon the participants'. But it then went on to argue that they were nonetheless still to be condemned because while no doubt 'comfortable' and 'flexible' to operate and conducive to 'a very high degree of self-government in industry', their benefits were outweighed by their shortcomings: 'the tendency of extreme decentralization and self-government to degenerate into indecision and anarchy; the propensity to breed inefficiency; and the reluctance to change – all of them characteristics which become more damaging as they develop, as the rate of technical progress increases, and as the need for economic growth becomes more urgent.'[50]

At this point, therefore, the Commission was forced to accept that its definition of a situation as constituting a 'problem' could be far from coinciding with the experience of the individuals involved in it. However, what was *not* accepted was what might seem a direct and crucial implication: that if disorder in workplace relations, albeit detrimental in its effects on the national economy, is not generally seen as a problem by participants, then the portents for a voluntarist approach to industrial relations reform can scarcely be promising. In such circumstances, it may be asked, how are those interests that are rooted in existing arrangements to be counteracted? How is one to overcome the understandable reluctance of managers and union leaders to disrupt a system which, even if less than perfect, they do not find it impossible to operate, and with which lower-level participants appear largely content? If the use of the law is to be ruled out, as either undesirable or in the end impracticable, what other way exists to persuade those in industry who see little desperately wrong in the present situation that the need for reform is in fact urgent and that they should direct their energies accordingly?

The answer that the Donovan Commission offered to such questions was one, indeed the only one, consistent with the general position that it had espoused. If industrial relations problems can be understood essentially as symptoms of something having 'gone wrong', in a largely technical sense, with the regulatory institutions of industrial life and as being thus to an important extent of common concern to all parties to industrial relations, it is then possible to regard the promotion of reform as calling not for compulsion but chiefly for instruction and enlightenment. Thus, what the Commission represented as the principle means to the implementation of its proposals was not detailed legislation designed to push employers, managements and unions willy-nilly into reform; but, rather, efforts to inform and educate them so that they would come of their own accord to see the deficiencies of existing arrangements and the importance – and advantages – of changing them. Prevailing difficulties, the Commission declared, were 'primarily due to widespread ignorance about the most sensible and effective methods of conducting industrial relations, and to the very considerable obstacles to the use of sensible and effective methods contained in our present system . . .'[51] Many of these obstacles were themselves ones raised by an undue fixity of ideas and attitudes; much basic rethinking of positions was required on both sides of industry and 'time-honoured assumptions would have to be abandoned'.[52] In other words, then, the key to the achievement of reform on the basis of voluntary principles was taken to lie at a psychological – and, primarily, at a cognitive – level. As Clegg, writing as a member of the Commission, has put it: 'The job to be done, therefore, was educational, beginning with the Donovan Report itself, and subsequently to be carried on by the new Commission [i.e., the Commission on Industrial Relations]. When managers and trade unionists saw that current ideas were out of touch with reality, and had become a prop for outworn institutions, they would be ready to carry out the reforms that were needed'.[53]

In fact, however, such a view of the possibilities of reform has by now been revealed as being as *simpliste* as the sociological analysis from which it sprang. In the first place, there is little to suggest that the arguments of the Donovan Commission or of its various academic outriders have proved capable of transforming ideas and attitudes in industry to the extent of creating widespread motivation to engage in reform where none had existed before. In this connection, one may note, for example, the case of productivity agreements, regarded by the Donovan Commission as offering 'solutions to many of the typical problems of industrial relations' – and, indeed, by some liberal writers as nothing less than 'a principal means for creating a new social order in industry'.[54] In the later 1960s the popularity of productivity bargaining was such that it could well have appeared to be transforming management-union relations in Britain. But from the standpoint of the present, it can be seen that its acceptance in these years was in fact to a large extent superficial, the idea of productivity agreements being prompted (but also frequently distorted) by the constraints of a statutory incomes policy. In more recent economic and political circumstances, which have offered few external incentives to productivity bargaining, its decline has been remarkable. It would appear, in other words, that the changes which Flanders has deemed essential to genuine productivity bargaining – in management and union organization and 'most difficult of all, modifications of established, even traditional, beliefs and patterns of behaviour on both sides' – have not been forthcoming on any major scale.[55]

Secondly, where efforts at reform of workplace relations have been made, it has become evident enough that somewhat more is involved than simply the availability of information on 'the most sensible and effective methods' of conducting them. Even in liberal-pluralist quarters it is now acknowledged that a basic weakness in the Donovan Report was the underlying assumption that once 'widespread ignorance' had been dispelled, then employers, managers and unionists would find themselves at one on the ends that they wished to pursue through reform, and that these would be in accord with the particular requirements urged by the Commission – to reduce the fragmentation of bargaining units, to maximize the precision and formality of agreements, to extend the scope of bargaining, and so on.[56]

From studies that have so far been undertaken of attempts at reform, it is indeed evident that a consensus of this kind is improbable, and that changes proposed in any aspect of workplace bargaining are likely rather to give rise to issues of conflict between management and labour. Moreover, these may well include ones which set strict limits to the extent to which reform is possible: as, for example, where unions refuse to move on the enlargement of bargaining units, or managements on the reduction of their prerogatives. In this respect, a report on research carried out by the Department of Employment in eleven companies in which attempts had been made to restructure workplace bargaining is of particular interest.[57] Although the report is presented as seeking to 'make a case for reform', it arrives nonetheless at conclusions which indicate a significant withdrawal from, and undermining of, the Donovan position. As well as suggesting that the comprehensive 'single-step' agreements favoured by the Commission may not always be the best approach to clearing up 'disorder' and that a degree of informality may well serve useful functions, the authors of the report are also concerned in a more general way to dispel the idea that reform is essentially a matter of knowing the right prescription. There is no reason to suppose, they argue, that 'the mere taking of an initiative, however well designed, will result in agreement, let alone the recognition of an identity of interest between management and unions'; indeed, they would reject the possibility of there being *any* pattern for workplace industrial relations which is likely to win general acceptance 'because it is, in some sense, "in everybody's interest".' In so far as the Donovan Report implied that such an ideal pattern could be specified, it must be regarded as mistaken: 'Certainly this study does not support the view that there is any single "model" for bargaining reform that is universally appropriate, and which would be readily acceptable by the parties once they saw where their "real" interests lay.'[58]

Thus, the kind of workplace agreements which the Department of Employment report would recommend as a practical proposition appears likely to fall a good way short of realizing the reform of collective bargaining on the lines envisaged by the Donovan Commission – let alone the yet more ambitious 'prescriptions for change' that have been offered in liberal-pluralist attempts to 'go beyond' Donovan. And even then, it must be added, it remains entirely to be seen just how effective reform in this more limited sense will prove to be in producing greater 'orderliness' in workplace relations. Evaluative, as opposed to descriptive, studies of the introduction of new bargaining structures are still to be made, and one possibility which must obviously be considered is that the working of the new institutional forms will tend more to reflect the pre-existing situation than to change it in any basic way.[59]

The connection between the inadequacies of the Donovan Commission's scheme for reform and those of the analysis which underlay it is then fairly apparent. Because the starting point is with industrial relations problems, which are taken as indicating some failure of regulative institutions, there is little concern to go, as it were, behind these problems and to enquire into the social relationships and modes of action *which throw strain on such institutions* in the first place; that is, which create, and express, social conflict. Nowhere in the Donovan Report, or in the entire tradition of academic industrial relations writing on which it drew so heavily, is there to be found any systematic consideration of how the functioning of the economic system as a whole and of its constituent units of production is founded upon, and sustains, vast differences in social power and advantage; nor of how there are then generated – in undoubtedly complex ways – on the one hand, objective oppositions of interest and, on the other, subjective responses of frustration, resentment and antagonism, and also in some degree aspirations and movements towards an alternative dispensation. Nevertheless, despite this vast omission, some warrant is still assumed for confident assertions as to which patterns of thought and action on the part of those in industry, and in particular of industrial workers, are 'out of touch with reality', 'outmoded' or 'irresponsible', and which 'enlightened', 'progressive' and 'mature'. On what basis of evidence or argument such judgements are supposed to rest remains unstated. But it is difficult to resist the conclusion that the main criterion applied is simply that of whether or not the ideas and behaviour in question are compatible with the institutional engineering that is being projected. The blueprint for the new institutional machinery is drawn up, and those patterns of response which are necessary to energize it are then distinguished from those which will obstruct its working by the use of appropriately coloured adjectives.[60]

But to proceed thus, whatever rhetorical advantage it may offer, is not best calculated to lead in the end to reform of an effective kind; and especially not where reliance is placed chiefly on voluntary action, and the whole question of motivation has then to be treated as one of spreading the requisite degree of enlightenment *de haut en bas*. Moreover, even if some measure of institutional change in industrial relations is brought about from above, through the initiative of duly instructed managements and union leaders, it will be unlikely to achieve its intended goals without support from the grass roots. Exponents of liberal reform often present their case in terms of creating 'new normative codes' in industry: yet they have paid far too little attention to the matter of compliance with norms. As argued elsewhere, the reform of collective bargaining according to the Donovan, or similar, proposals might for a time endow its procedures and outcomes with greater formal rationality. But this is not to say that a *stable* normative order would thereby be arrived at.[61] Unless the norms implicit in the new regulative arrangements were ones to which the mass of those regulated felt some degree of moral commitment – which, on the evidence, would scarcely seem likely[62] – then the acceptance that the reformed institutions could command would be of no more than a pragmatic, provisional kind; that is to say, these arrangements would in turn be exposed to distortion and 'decay' as they were found to conflict with the values and interests of those subject to them, and 'order' would once again become problematical.

While, then, there is much justification for the charge that the liberal-pluralist approach to industrial relations is managerialist in its priorities and conservative in its implications, there is also, it would seem, the danger that critics on the Left may regard it too seriously as a threat to the freedom of action of industrial workers. For if the liberal-pluralist conception of a new order in industrial relations is ideology, it is also, in a sense, utopia. The liberal commitment to voluntary reform is one which would be appropriate to a society in which there *already existed* some broad consensus on the principles governing the organization of production and the distribution of the product: that is to say, a society in which any disorder in industrial relations could correctly be attributed to institutional malfunctioning, and in which a general interest could then be assumed to exist in devising and implementing those institutional forms which would maintain order by, as it were, providing the channels through which the underlying consensus could best emerge. Given, however, an actual society which falls far short of this consensual model, and in which economic life is a matter of individuals and groups exploiting as best they can their positions within a generally unprincipled structure of power and advantage, the divergence of interest and value among the parties to industrial relations will tend always to militate against the possibility of their concerted action towards 'reform'. In pursuing the goal of 'agreed normative codes regulating the production and distribution of wealth', liberal reformism must be regarded as assuming precisely that which it seeks to create.

In this perspective, then, the Tory approach to reform would appear, up to a point, to be decidedly the more realistic. Its exponents in effect accept that it is scarcely possible to envisage a transition from the existing situation in industrial relations to one of greater order by which all interests involved would be best served. Thus, they would doubt the idea that such a process of reform could be carried through primarily by voluntary action guided by 'expert' instruction and advice. The issues that arise are recognized as being not merely technical but also, in a broad sense, political. Any significant change in the existing situation must entail a change in the relations of power among the parties concerned, and it is therefore unlikely to be brought about other than by the exertion of some still greater power – namely, that of the law.

However, the difficulty with the Tory approach lies in the contention that the major source of disorder is the now excessive power wielded by the trade unions. To begin with, this misidentifies the crucial change that has occurred: it is not, at least at the level of the workplace, the power of the unions that has increased, but rather the economic and organizational strength of the workers on the shopfloor – in consequence of which, the degree of effective control that can be exercised over them by either managements or unions has been significantly diminished. Moreover, once this fact is accepted, the viability of the use of the law as an instrument of industrial relations reform is called into question. If unions were hierarchical organizations which did possess the power to impose a tight discipline on their rank-and-file, then the closer legal regulation of the conduct of union officials and representatives might give some purchase on industrial relations at workplace level. But since in fact the actions of union members on the shopfloor do not for the most part follow directives from above but are determined rather in a largely autonomous fashion, the possibility of any such regulation achieving its intended effects is seriously undermined, and the far more likely outcome is that of the law being brought into disrepute.

The conclusion to which one is led is, then, that reformism in the field of industrial relations is at something of an *impasse*. Neither the Tory nor the liberal approach appears capable of accommodating the hard facts that the resolution of current problems of disorder in workplace relations can only be achieved with the co-operation of workers from whose point of view these 'problems' will often represent situations of relative advantage in terms of autonomy and control; and that neither attempts to coerce them into greater 'responsibility' nor to educate them into a more 'enlightened' understanding of their interests than they presently possess seem likely to have any extensive success. Indeed, the further, more radical, conclusion may be suggested that at the present time British industrial relations are simply not in any far-reaching way reformable – other than, perhaps, as part of some more general restructuring of British society as a whole: that is, either in an authoritarian and corporatist direction, so that far more drastic sanctions than are at present conceivable could be applied against workers; or in an egalitarian and socialist one, so that a more effective basis for workers' collaboration might be created. Within the existing form of society, however, a disordered state of industrial relations may best be understood not as a pathological, but as a normal condition.

NOTES

1. The original version of this paper was prepared for a conference on 'Sources of Discontent and Institutional Innovation in Advanced Industrial Societies' held under the auspices of the Institute on Western Europe of Columbia University. I am indebted to participants at the conference for many useful comments and also, among my British colleagues, to John Eldridge, Alan Fox and Mike Terry, for detailed criticisms.

2. The leading figures in the Oxford school were all in one way or another heavily involved in the affairs of the Commission. H. A. Clegg was one of the Commission's twelve members, and is believed to have played a major role in drafting its Report. Allan Flanders submitted lengthy written evidence, which would seem to have been highly influential, and was subsequently appointed a member of the Commission on Industrial Relations set up on the recommendation of the Donovan Commission. W. E. J. McCarthy was the Commission's Research Director, and others in the Oxford group – including Alan Fox, A. I. Marsh and G. S. Bain – were authors of Research Papers prepared for the Commission.

3. See in particular, Inns of Court Conservative and Unionist Society, *A Giant's Strength*, London, 1958, and Conservative Political Centre, *Fair Deal at Work*, London, 1968.

4. Although in this paper both terms are used interchangeably, the latter, though cumbersome, is the more accurate. If 'liberal' alone is used, it must be understood in the American rather than the European sense. On the other hand, to describe the view in question simply as 'pluralist', as is most often done, is to obscure the important point that other versions of pluralism than that here represented are conceivable. Cf. J. E. T. ELDRIDGE, 'Industrial Conflict: some problems of theory and method' in JOHN CHILD (ed.), *Man and Organization*, London, 1973.

5. Royal Commission on Trade Unions and Employers' Associations, *Report*, Cmnd 3623, 1968.

6. For a brief analysis of the very complex terms of the Act, see H. A. CLEGG, *The System of Industrial Relations in Great Britain*,

2nd ed., Totowa, N.J., 1972, ch. 12.

7. See in particular W. E. J. MCCARTHY, and N. D. ELLIS, *Management by Agreement: an alternative to the Industrial Relations Act*, London, 1973. Prior to the General Election of February, 1974, some leading industrialists and even backbench Conservative MPs were openly voicing dissatisfaction with the working of the Act and discussing the possibility of its amendment. The Labour Party, which regained power at the Election, is committed to repeal of the Act. (The Industrial Relations Act was repealed by the Labour government later in 1974 – editors.)

8. The following account of the liberal position draws primarily on the Report of the Donovan Commission: ALLAN FLANDERS, *Management and Unions: the theory and reform of Industrial Relations*, London, 1970; and CLEGG, *The System of Industrial Relations in Great Britain*.

9. ALLAN FLANDERS and ALAN FOX, 'The Reform of Collective Bargaining: from Donovan to Durkheim', *British Journal of Industrial Relations*, vol. VII, 1969. (Reprinted in FLANDERS, *Management and Unions*.)

10. See in particular on this point FLANDERS, *Management and Unions*, pp. 109–13, 171–3, 196–7, and 'Productivity Bargaining as a Rule-Changing Exercise' in D. C. ALEXANDER (ed.), *A Productivity Bargaining Symposium*, London, 1969.

11. For discussions of this process, see CLARK KERR, *Labor and Management in Industrial Society*, New York, 1964, and RALF DAHRENDORF, *Class and Class Conflict in Industrial Society*, London, 1959. A crucial difference between Kerr and Dahrendorf is that while Kerr appears to have assumed that the extent to which industrial conflict was (up to the mid-1960s) institutionally contained represented a permanent achievement of Western capitalist societies and indeed formed part of an evolutionary trend towards their greater integration, Dahrendorf, with some foresight, explicitly rejected such a view: '. . . it is never possible simply to extrapolate social developments. The fact that industrial conflict has become less violent and intense in the last century does not justify the inference that it will continue to do so . . . It is certainly conceivable that the future has more intense and violent conflicts in store.' op. cit., pp. 278–9.

12. For the major statement of the liberal-pluralist view on industrial democracy, see H. A. CLEGG, *A New Approach to Industrial Democracy*, Oxford, 1960. Cf. FLANDERS, *Management and Unions*, pp. 148–53; and MCCARTHY and ELLIS, *Management by Agreement*, pp. 106–8.

13. See further on this point, JOHN H. GOLDTHORPE, 'Theories of Industrial Society: reflections on the recrudescence of historicism and the future of futurology,' *Archives Européennes de Sociologie*, vol. XII, 1971.

14. Cf. Donovan Commission, *Report*, paras 182–4, 318–29; FLANDERS, *Management and Unions*, pp. 56–62. It is also relevant in the present connection to note how in this passage, and in various other places, in Flanders' writing on industrial relations reform, medical analogies are introduced. Industrial relations problems are said to be 'symptomatic' of a 'sickness' in industry (p. 57), and elsewhere we hear, for example, of 'diseases' in industry and of their 'remedy' (p. 67) or of 'contagious disorder' (p. 272).

15. The only systematic discussion of the concept of authority by a member of the Oxford school appears to be that provided by Fox. Authority, he suggests, is to be distinguished from power as being legitimate command rather than command that is *imposed upon* subordinates. In other words, the criterion of legitimacy is taken to be subordinates' *acceptance* of the norms and related sanctions involved in their superior's exercise of command. See ALAN FOX, *A Sociology of Work in Industry*, London, 1971, pp. 34 *et seq*. This view (which is, of course, by no means peculiar to Fox) does, however, give rise to some difficulties. For one thing, it implies that the same command – as, say, embodied in a law or formal regulation – can vary in its legitimacy, that is, may or may not constitute 'authority' – depending on the subjective dispositions of those to whom it relates. The position adopted in the texts is that the extent and nature of the legitimacy of any exercise of command is best indicated by the answer to the question 'by what warrant'? Acceptability to subordinates in the above sense is only one of various conceivable answers – that is, only one possible, and not a necessary, source of legitimacy. Depending on the nature of the organization, legitimacy may come 'from above' – for example, from the law – rather than 'from below'. From this point of view, therefore, one can speak of legitimate command which does not have the acceptance, or even secure the compliance, of subordinates; and conversely of the exercise of power which is accepted by those on whom it bears, but which is not necessarily legitimate – as, say, in the case of 'manipulation'.

16. Cf. W. BALDAMUS, *Efficiency and Effort*, London, 1961, chapters 3 and 4 esp.; and also A. W. GOULDNER, *Wildcat Strike*, London, 1955, pp. 162–3.

17. Cf. AMITAI ETZIONI, *A Comparative Analysis of Complex Organizations*, New York, 1961, pp. 5–6, 31–3.

18. This point is perhaps best brought out in accounts of the efforts of early industrialists to establish a detailed work discipline within their enterprises – and of the resistance offered, even if to a large extent unavailingly, by their employees. See, for example, PAUL MANTOUX, *The Industrial Revolution in the Eighteenth Century*, London, 1928, pp. 384–6; N. MCKENDRICK, 'Josiah Wedgwood and Factory Discipline', *Historical Journal*, vol. 4, 1961; S. POLLARD, 'Fac-

tory Discipline in the Industrial Revolution', *Economic History Review*, 2nd series, vol. XVI, 1963–4, and *The Genesis of Modern Management*, London, 1965, ch. 5; and E. P. THOMPSON, 'Time, Work-Discipline and Industrial Capitalism', *Past and Present*, no. 38, 1967. Although subsequent generations of workers may have become increasingly habituated to the demands of large-scale, mechanized production, attempts on their part to weaken managerial control and to increase their own autonomy within the work situation appear regularly ɔ have occurred whenever conditions were at all favourable. Particularly significant in this connection is the 'workshop movement' of the period 1910–20. See, for example, CARTER GOODRICH, *The Frontier of Control*, London 1920; and G. D. H. COLE, *Workshop Organisation*, Oxford, 1923. In historical perspective, the 'challenge from below' of the years following the second world war appears as the continuation of this earlier movement after two decades in which high levels of unemployment undermined labour's strength.

19. Cf. JOHN H. GOLDTHORPE, DAVID LOCKWOOD, FRANK BECHHOFER and JENNIFER PLATT, *The Affluent Worker: Industrial Attitudes and Behaviour*, Cambridge, 1968, ch. 5; and RONALD DORE, *British Factory – Japanese Factory*, London, 1973, pp. 160–2.

20. As Clegg has recognized, by the 1960s 'a hierarchical model of organization was no longer applicable to the unions, if it ever had been', *The System of Industrial Relations in Great Britain*, p. 443. To take again a historical view of the matter, it could be argued that it is the ascendancy of the full-time officials in the inter-war period that is best regarded as unusual – this reflecting the importance of industry-wide bargaining under conditions calling for an essentially defensive union strategy.

21. For example, as Whittingham has pointed out, even in the case of shop stewards there is the likelihood that in acting as 'policemen' in regard to the terms of formal workplace agreements, they may lose rank-and-file support and, perhaps, have their position usurped by unofficial shopfloor leaders. 'Productivity Bargaining, Full-time Officials and Shop Stewards' in B. TOWERS, T. G. WHITTINGHAM and A. W. GOTTSCHALK (eds.), *Bargaining for Change*, London, 1972, pp. 76–7. Arising out of such situations in the car industry, the phenomenon of 'unofficial unofficial' strikes has been noted. See H. A. TURNER, G. CLACK and G. ROBERTS, *Labour Relations in the Motor Industry*, London, 1967, pp. 214, 222.

22. See FLANDERS, *Management and Unions*, pp. 56–8; CLEGG, *The System of Industrial Relations in Great Britain*, pp. 182–5, 276–80, and *How to Run an Incomes Policy*, London, 1971, p. 73; also E. G. WHYBREW, *Overtime Working in Britain*, Royal Commission on Trade Unions and Employers' Associations, Research Papers, No. 9, 1968.

23. National Board for Prices and Incomes, Report No. 161, *Hours of Work, Overtime and Shiftworking*. Cmnd 4554, 1970, ch. 4. See also the critical comments on Whybrew's paper cited in the previous note in H. A. TURNER, 'The Royal Commission's Research Papers', *British Journal of Industrial Relations*, vol. 6, 1968.

24. The increase in overtime working since the second world war has not been associated with any increase in the average number of hours actually worked in British industry, nor does this average appear out of line with those recorded for other Western industrial countries.

25. FERDYNAND ZWEIG, *The Worker in an Affluent Society*, London, 1961, pp. 70–6.

26. Cf. SYLVIA SHIMMIN, 'Extra-mural Factors Influencing Behaviour at Work', *Occupational Psychology*, vol. 36, 1962, and other studies cited therein. It is also of course relevant that an inverse correlation exists between the level of overtime working and the level of basic rates of pay. However, liberal concern with the 'problem' of overtime has centred less on this correlation than on the lack of (managerial) control over the amount and distribution of overtime work.

27. *Management and Unions*, p. 57.

28. On workers' concern for autonomy generally, see, for example, the enormous amount of material brought together in GEORGES FRIEDMANN, *Ou va le travail humain?*, Paris, 1950; *Problèmes humains du machinisme industriel*, Paris, 1955; and *Le travail en miettes*, Paris, 1963; and in ROBERT BLAUNER, *Alienation and Freedom: the Factory Worker and his Industry*, Chicago, 1964. On control over time, specifically, see also D. ROY, ' "Banana Time": Job Satisfaction and Informal Interaction', *Human Organisation*, vol. 18, 1959–60; JASON DITTON, 'The Problem of Time: Styles of time-management and schemes of time-manipulation amongst machine-paced workers', *Working Papers in Sociology*, No. 2, University of Durham, n.d.; and THOMPSON, 'Time, Work-Discipline and Industrial Capitalism'.

29. For an excellent illustration of this point, see RICHARD BROWN, PETER BRANNEN, JIM COUSINS and MICHAEL SAMPHIER, 'Leisure in Work: the "occupational culture" of shipbuilding workers' in MICHAEL SMITH, STANLEY PARKER and CYRIL SMITH (eds.), *Leisure and Society in Britain*, London, 1973. Shipbuilding is an industry noted for both its 'restrictive practices' and large amounts of overtime working.

30. *Hours of Work, Overtime and Shiftworking*, para. 118.

31. See FLANDERS, *Management and Union*, pp. 76–81, 199–202 and 'Measured Daywork and Collective Bargaining', *British Journal of Industrial Relations*, vol. XI, no. 3, November 1973; CLEGG, *The System of Industrial Relations in Great Britain*, 266–76; and WILLIAM BROWN, *Piecework Bargaining*, London, 1973.

32. See in particular Brown, *Piecework Bargaining*, pp. 146, 153–4.

33. ibid., p. 2.

34. See D. ROY, 'Work Satisfaction and Social Reward in Quota Achievement: an analysis of piecework incentive', *American Sociological Review*, vol. 18, 1953; J. P. DAVISON, P. SARGANT FLORENCE, BARBARA GRAY and N. S. ROSS, *Productivity and Economic Incentives*, London, 1958, pp. 123–4, 266–9; T. LUPTON, *On the Shop Floor*, London, 1963, chs. 10–11. It is notable that managerial advocates of the ending of PBR stress the way in which piecework gives employees a potentially large measure of control over their work situation and a justification for exerting it. See, for example, WILFRED BROWN, *Piecework Abandoned*, London, 1962.

35. In addition to the intrinsic aspects of this satisfaction, it is important to note that, as Eldridge has pointed out, a 'decayed' PBR system may entail a shift in the distributive pattern of the reward system – to the advantage of workers and to the detriment of management and shareholders. *Sociology and Industrial Life*, London, 1971, p. 60.

36. Government Social Survey. *Workplace Industrial Relations*, London, 1968, para. A.54. In his most recent paper, Flanders omits to mention these figures, referring only to the finding that stewards with some members on PBR showed a slight majority in favour of some other method of payment, and expressing the hope that stewards' 'influence would enable them to win workers' co-operation in moves to measured daywork'. 'Measured Daywork and Collective Bargaining', p. 374.

37. The transition in Fox's thinking and the accompanying *autocritique* which is to be found in his writing is of considerable interest. See his *Industrial Sociology and Industrial Relations*, Royal Commission on Trade Unions and Employers' Associations, Research Paper No. 3, 1968; the paper co-authored with Flanders, 'The Reform of Collective Bargaining: from Donovan to Durkheim'; his book previously cited, *A Sociology of Work in Industry*: and finally, 'Industrial Relations: a social critique of pluralist ideology' in Child (ed.), *Man and Organisation*. In an as yet unpublished paper, 'Collective Bargaining, Flanders and the Webbs', Fox questions the validity of Flanders' attempt to undermine the Webbs' notion of unions as 'bargaining agents' and to further the idea that the essential role of collective bargaining is to enhance the status and dignity of workers by allowing them to share in job-regulation, as opposed to achieving any significant redistributive advantage.

38. 'Industrial Relations: a social critique of pluralist ideology', p. 213. Cf. FLANDERS, 'Productivity Bargaining as a Rule-Changing Exercise'. (Fox's paper, 'Collective Bargaining, Flanders and the Webbs', was published in the BJIR, vol. XIII, No. 2, 1975 – editors.)

39. RICHARD HYMAN, *Strikes*, London, 1972, pp. 96–7.

40. Cf. FLANDERS, 'Productivity Bargaining as a Rule-Changing Exercise' and also FLANDERS and CLEGG, 'Productivity Bargaining and the Unions', unpublished paper, January, 1965, p. 16.

41. Cf. ANDREW SHONFIELD, *Modern Capitalism*, London, 1965; J. K. GALBRAITH, *The New Industrial State*, London, 1967; MICHAEL KIDRON, *Western Capitalism Since the War*, London, 1968.

42. ibid., p. 16.

43. 'Industrial Relations: a social critique of pluralist ideology', p. 212.

44. MCCARTHY and ELLIS, *Management by Agreement*, pp. 96–9, 102–9, 183–6.

45. As already noted, liberal reformers show little concern for methods of extending industrial democracy other than through collective bargaining. See, for example, Flanders' brief and unenthusiastic comments on the possibilities of changing the nature of managerial accountability through the reform of company law (*Management and Unions*, pp. 138–9); or what Turner has aptly described as 'the Donovan Commission's quite summary – almost contemptuous – treatment of the movement for "workers' participation in management".' (*Report*, ch. xv). Turner points out that the Commission acknowledges the high degree of self-government in industry allowed by the 'informal system': 'And,' he goes on, 'its own proposals for company agreements would appear to involve a reduction of this facility, and a new concentration of authority at the level of company managements and full-time trade union officials. One would have thought some compensation in other directions would at least have been indicated.' 'The Donovan Report', *Economic Journal*, LXXIX, 1969. Finally, in this connection one may note McCarthy and Ellis' rather strange reading of Paul Blumberg's work which enables them to enlist Blumberg in support of their idea of participatory decision-making through collective bargaining while ignoring Blumberg's powerful critique of essentially this idea as expressed by Clegg. See *Management by Agreement*, pp. 100–1. Cf. PAUL BLUMBERG, *Industrial Democracy: the Sociology of Participation*, London, 1968, ch. 7.

46. *Management by Agreement*, p. 101.

47. Cf. FOX, 'Industrial Relations: a social critique of pluralist ideology', pp. 223–4.

48. See paras. 188–206. The main responsibility for reform was placed on Boards of Directors (para. 168). A 'Note of Reservation', arguing for a greater role to be given to the law, was written by one member of the Commission, Andrew Shonfield.

49. See *Workplace Industrial Relations*, paras. 2.150, 3.82, 4.94, 5.69 and A.69; and also W. E. J. MCCARTHY and S. R. PARKER, *Shop*

Stewards and Workshop Relations, Royal Commission on Trade Unions and Employers' Associations, Research Paper No. 10, 1968, paras. 223–32.

50. *Report*, paras. 123–30.

51. ibid., para. 204. Cf. *Shop Stewards and Workshop Relations*, para. 230.

52. *Report*, para. 206.

53. *The System of Industrial Relations in Great Britain*, p. 454.

54. *Report*, para. 325, also paras. 158–9; FLANDERS, 'Preface' to TOWERS, WHITTINGHAM and GOTTSCHALK (eds.), *Bargaining for Change*, p. 14, and cf. FLANDERS and FOX, 'The Reform of Collective Bargaining: from Donovan to Durkheim'.

55. FLANDERS, 'Preface', p. 14. Other members of the Oxford Group, it should be added, appear to have become in any event somewhat disillusioned with productivity bargaining as a means of industrial relations 'problem-solving', or at all events wish to rather radically redefine its functions. See for example, CLEGG, *How to Run an Incomes Policy*, pp. 64–5 and 'The Reality of Productivity Bargaining' in P. SEGLOW (ed.), *The Future of Productivity Bargaining*, Brunel University Management Programme, London, 1973.

56. Cf. MCCARTHY and ELLIS, *Management by Agreement*, pp. 82–6. It may also be noted that on the particular problems earlier discussed arising out of overtime and piece-rate working, some shift from a voluntarist to an interventionist position is evident. For example, Clegg now favours legislation both to restrict overtime and to make it possible to freeze the level of earnings in workplaces where the rate of increase in piece-work earnings is above a given figure and management and labour are unwilling or unable to negotiate a new and 'acceptable' pay structure, *How to Run an Incomes Policy*, pp. 73–4.

57. Department of Employment, *The Reform of Collective Bargaining at Plant and Company Level*, Manpower Papers, No. 5, 1971.

58. ibid., pp. 86–8. Also relevant on the – very limited – extent to which reform on Donovan lines has been, or is likely to be, implemented is A. I. MARSH, E. O. EVANS and P. GARCIA, *Workplace Industrial Relations in Engineering*, London, 1971, pp. 58–67 esp.

59. An obvious analogy here is with 'joint consultation', an institutional development which has but rarely been shown to have any significant independent impact on workplace relations. One supposedly immediate effect of the reform of workplace bargaining which, it appears, has not occurred is the increased involvement of full-time union officials in workplace affairs. See, for example, WHITTINGHAM, 'Productivity Bargaining, Full-Time Officials and Shop Stewards'; Department of Employment, *The Reform of Collective Bargaining at Plant and Company Level*, pp. 84–5.

60. Even McCarthy and Ellis, who generally take a more hard-

headed view of the problems of industrial relations reform than most liberal writers, conclude an outline of their 'prescription for change' as follows: 'Finally, it must also be stressed that inherent in the notion of management by agreement is the assumption that both sides will be willing to change their bargaining habits. Unless this is possible what is being proposed here simply cannot work.' *Management by Agreement*, p. 108. Elsewhere, the habits to be abandoned and those to be adopted are characterized as 'traditional' or 'customary' on the one hand and as 'progressive', on the other.

61. JOHN H. GOLDTHORPE, 'Social Inequality and Social Integration in Modern Britain' in D. WEDDERBURN (ed.), *Poverty, Inequality and Class Structure*, Cambridge, 1974.

62. And still less so, it may be added, in the industrial relations 'climate' of Great Britain at the present moment. Government attempts to impose a rigid incomes policy, and the resulting series of major confrontations with unions, appear to be having the general effect of increasing rank-and-file militancy. In this way, the point that, whether for analytical or policy purposes, *anomie* in workplace industrial relations cannot be considered separately from the anomic condition of economic life generally is well brought out. Cf. GOLDTHORPE, 'Social Inequality and Social Integration in Modern Britain'.

Part Four
Workers, Unions and Job Control

The tendency of official union organizations to tacitly accept the
economic rules of capitalism, and the long-term interests of employers as of paramount importance, encourages shopfloor
workers – who suffer the consequences of such policies – to
evolve their own independent defensive organizations. The
official union focus on formal wage negotiation frequently
abandons workers to endure harsh working conditions, since
control of these is part of the supposed 'managerial prerogative'.
However, many groups of workers have rejected the arbitrary
control of management, the representatives of capital at the point
of production, over the nature of their working lives, and have
clawed back control of conditions, manning and work effort in
many industries, which enables them to ensure some content-
ment and freedom in their work. But once formalized, job
control may itself be subject to the collaborationist inclinations
of union officials and become little more than a form of standard-
ization of personnel administration, of greater benefit to the
management than to the union members: in the last analysis,
unofficial militancy remains the only effective safeguard of
working conditions in the face of unresponsive union and autocratic management.

The first reading in this section, a pioneering study of workshop
politics written in the period of the First World War by a young
American, Carter Goodrich, reveals how, though recorded in no
formal agreements, workers extended 'the frontier of control' on
a whole range of managerial and production questions: employment and dismissal; promotions; methods of payment; organization of work; changes in technology; and so on. Thus by autonomous organization at the point of production workers provided
a constant check to managerial autocracy: in this instance, not
only the choice of foreman and their organization, but also
standards of foremanship were effectively enforced by workers
who insisted that they were 'not to be controlled disagreeably'.

At other times, when labour was more plentiful and union organization weaker, foremen – 'the corporals of capitalism' – have had a reputation for the brutal disregard of the feelings and interests of workers, particularly in industries with casual labour:[1] to a great extent however, foremen are simply the medium through which market demands and managerial domination are imposed. Therefore workers' control over first line management may ultimately involve combating also the forces of the market, and although the militancy Goodrich describes was primarily defensive in nature, it was a foundation upon which the demand for workers' control of industry could be developed.

Beynon provides, in the second reading, a colourful and emotive analysis of industrial conflict in a modern car plant that highlights the contradictions in both trade unionism, and the economic system within which the unions operate. Thus beneath the veneer of normality, mass production in advanced capitalism involves management-worker relations punctuated by 'naked aggression being met with violent defiance'. Beynon documents at length the imaginative guerrilla tactics of the rank-and-file confronted by a systematic attempt of their employers to economically exploit them. The inhuman conditions of work that prevail on the assembly line are revealed, which destroy the possibility of workers gaining intrinsic satisfaction from their jobs. In response to a demand by a senior academic that technology was the determining factor in the high level of alienation and conflict experienced in the motor industry, Beynon once disturbed the sacrosanct air of a post-graduate seminar with the retort, 'No! It's not technology – it's fucking capitalism!' It is, perhaps, regrettable that the rigorous candour of his analysis is rare in academic discussion. The determinism of those who view technological development as a neutral impersonal force ignores the human agency and interests involved in such processes, and the power relations which determine their outcome: 'the primary determinant of basic choices with respect to the organization of production has not been technology – exogenous and inexorable – but the exercise of power – endogenous and resistable.'[2]

In fact, central to the conflict Beynon describes is a fundamental opposition between management rationality and worker rationality on how plant production should be organized: 'It is in this way, in disputes over control at work, that the class struggle has been fought out by the British working class during this century.' However, though the job control established by workers is subject to external market forces and government intervention, which may seriously erode it – or even destroy it – at any time, the consciousness of workers as to the nature of their predicament rarely extends beyond the factory boundary: as Marx declared, 'They fail generally from limiting themselves to a guerrilla war against the effects of the existing system, instead of simultaneously trying to change it.' Beynon expresses eloquently the passionate but confused response of workers battered by an economic system, the alternative to which they are not aware of, and, therefore, are incapable of fighting for in any coherent fashion.

Continuing this theme, in a monumental work Herding offers an incisive analysis of industrial conflict at the plant level in the United States. Shopfloor organization has contradictory implications he implies: combating the collusion of union bureaucracies with management and the prevailing economic system, shopfloor organization around offensive job control develops militancy out of workers' immediate experience of the contradictions of the industrial system; but shopfloor militancy stimulates 'job' rather than 'class' consciousness, and may promote the sectionalism typical of official union action: if primarily defensive, job control has conservative rather than radical implications.

The American practice of exclusive bargaining agents makes union democracy of vital importance Herding reveals, and the impediments to the achievement of democracy are analysed. In contrast to liberal commentators' ostensible belief that union democracy encourages industrial peace, Herding points out that there is evidence that more democratic unions are more militant in their bargaining and that democratic unionism is detrimental to 'responsible' relations with management; moreover, 'most of the celebrated cases of union-management co-operation are ominously associated with undemocratic practices.'

Thus the 'apathy' commonly found among union members is a product of the union leadership induced stalemate of labour-management conflict, and there is a current need for worker militancy to be directed against the union as well as management, as Herding concludes: 'The emerging failure to achieve even the "economic" objectives of American labour under representative union government, "expert" advice, and top-controlled bargaining – as experienced in the revolts – is producing the insight that labour's goals are incompatible not only with the existing capitalist structure, but most important, with the avenues and mechanisms for change and conflict resolution it provides.' Within the degenerated American labour movement the first task is to 'rescue the potential of resistance from bureaucratic restraints'. Hence, even in America, the institutionalization of industrial conflict is in a state of precarious instability.

NOTES

1. For an account of such practices in one industry, see, D. F. WILSON, *Dockers*, Fontana, 1972, ch. 1.

2. S. A. MARGLIN, 'What Do Bosses Do? The Origins and Functions of Hierarchy in Capital Production', *Review of Radical Political Economics*, Summer 1974, vol. 6, no. 2, p. 112 (reproduced in A. GORZ, *The Division of Labour*, Harvester Press, 1976.) A modern Marxist critique of the capitalist mode of production of major importance is H. BRAVERMAN, *Labour and Monopoly Capital*, Monthly Review Press, 1974. Braverman's analysis of how the imperative of capital accumulation provides the dynamic for the transformation and degredation of labour in capitalist society is a powerful refutation of the orthodox explanations of bourgeois social science. For comment on various managerial strategies in response to worker resistance see A. FRIEDMAN, 'Responsible Autonomy Versus Direct Control Over The Labour Process', *Capital and Class*, No. 1, 1977; also the discussion of 'The Capitalist Labour Process', by the Brighton Labour Process Group in the same issue of *Capital and Class*.

13 The Frontier of Control

Carter L. Goodrich

Reprinted with permission from C. Goodrich, *The Frontier of Control*, Pluto Press, 1975, pp. 135–45. First published: Bell, 1920.

THE STANDARD OF FOREMANSHIP

Workers' choice of foremen is rare; the effect of organization of foremen on workers' control is real but indirect. The most important means by which workers exercise control over their supervisors is simply that of the strike or threat of strike when supervision becomes unbearable. The effective power of this form of control is usually underestimated since it is difficult to detect and define and can hardly be embodied in a formal agreement. But in proportion to the strength of the trade union, it represents a real veto, if not actually over the choice, at least over the retention of foremen – and a real regulation of their actions.

Mr R. H. Tawney sums up the situation as 'autocracy checked by insurgence'; the present point is that there is a great deal of insurgence. Some sense of this may be gained by going through the official *Reports on Strikes and Lock-outs*. In 1912 there were thirty-two disputes reported as caused by objections to certain foremen; in 1913, twenty-five disputes involving 10,500 workers. The reports of causes read like these: 'alleged harassing conduct of a foreman', 'alleged tyrannical conduct of an under-forewoman', 'alleged overbearing conduct of officials'. The award in a recent arbitration case details the charges against an unpopular under-manager as 'indifference to and want of consideration of suggestions made to him by workers in connection with their work and improvements; uncivil, inconsiderate, harsh and autocratic treatment, and neglect to properly consider their claims as regards both employment and remuneration; and the preference of friends and relatives'. And among the results of the strikes, along with numerous dismissals and resignations of the officials in question, there are occasional agreements that, 'the men must be treated with proper respect and threats and abusive language must not be used', or 'tyrannical acts to cease'.

The number and the frequent success of these strikes indicates a considerable trade union veto over the choice of foremen. The 'right of rejecting as fellow-workers' may often become the right of rejecting as foremen. This alone, however, does not sufficiently emphasize the amount of trade union pressure effective in setting a standard of decent foremanship. The rules of the British Steel Smelters provide that members leaving on account of 'unjustifiable abuse or ill-treatment from employer or foreman' are entitled to dispute pay. The secretary of a union which had never succeeded in securing the dismissal of a bullying foreman was nevertheless sure that its protests were effective as warnings to foremen. And in some trades a definite standard is so much a matter of course that the issue rarely arises. The Compositors, for example, will not stand for what is known as 'policing' by foremen and managers and any violation of the code is immediately reported to the union for action. A story was told me by a former miners' agent in Lanarkshire illustrating a similar standard on the part of the Scottish Miners. In a case arising under the Minimum Wage Act, the overman was called upon to testify whether or not a certain workman did his work properly. The examination was as follows (in free translation from the original Scotch):

Overman: 'I never saw him work.'
Magistrate: 'But isn't it your duty under the Mines Act to visit each working place twice a day?'
'Yes.'
'Don't you do it?'
'Yes.'
'Then why didn't you ever see him work?'
'They always stop work when they see an overman coming, and sit down and wait till he's gone – even take out their pipes if it's a mine free from gas. They won't let anybody watch them.'

An equally extreme standard was enforced for a part of the war period at a Clyde engineering works. The convenor (chairman) of shop stewards was told one morning that there was a grievance at the smithy. He found one of the blacksmiths in a rage because the managing director, in his ordinary morning's walk through the works, had stopped for five minutes or so and watched this man's fire. After a shop meeting the convenor took up a deputation to the director and secured the promise that it should not happen again. At the next works meeting the convenor reported the incident to the body of workers – with the result that a similar standard came into effect throughout the works, and the director hardly dared stop at all on his morning's walk.

Much of the feeling in struggles for the recognition of unions (long since secured in the better-organized trades and conceded in principle at least for all by the unanimous recommendations of the National Industrial Conference) was due to the workers' desire to have someone outside the control of the immediate employer to represent them on just these questions. This finds very definite expression in the dispute that occasionally arises over the trade union officials' claim of the right to enter the works in order to investigate disputes. This has been paralleled during the war by the frequent claim of the shop steward or of the convenor (chairman) of shop stewards or of the chairman of the Works Committee for freedom to go into any department of the works to investigate a grievance. An amusing story was told me of the way this right was won in one of the Clyde ship-building works: The convenor had begun to exercise the right – and to go freely from shop to shop as disputes arose – without the permission of the management. The manager then ordered him to stop and to stay at his own machine. The convenor obeyed, but arranged for a grievance to occur the next morning in the shop furthest from his own. The steward from that shop came to him with word of the grievance. 'I can't leave my work.' – 'But it's important.' – 'How many men involved?' – '200.' – 'I don't dare leave my machine. Tell them to come to me.' And so the 200 men walked the length of the works, gathered round the convenor's machine while he kept on with his work, and discussed the dispute. The result – in the prevailing shortage of labour – was the concession of the privilege. But the fighting of the same issue in another works, with Mr David Kirkwood[1] as the shop steward in question, led to the deportation of the Clyde strike leaders in 1916. The shop stewards' agreement of December, 1917, between the engineering employers and certain of the engineering unions provided that:

In connection with this agreement shop stewards shall be afforded facilities to deal with questions raised in the shop or portion of a shop in which they are employed. In course of

dealing with these questions they may, with the previous consent of the management (such consent not to be unreasonably
withheld), visit any other shop or portion of a shop in the
establishment. In all other respects shop stewards shall conform to the same working conditions as their fellow-workmen.

The *Works Committees* report of the Ministry of Labour states
that, 'from the experience of several works . . . it would appear
that this freedom of movement is found to be an essential condition of the success of a committee.' The various elaborate
methods of procedure for the presentation of grievances by trade
union officials or shop stewards, whether embodied in long-
standing collective agreements or in recent constitutions of
works committees (as well as the various provisions for securing
for the aggrieved individual the 'principle of the open door' to
the higher management) are beside the present point. The
interesting thing for our purpose is that they involve a recognition
that grievances of this sort are within the field of action of the
workers' representatives. An editorial in *The Post* (the journal of
the Postmen's Federation)[2] of 8 March 1918, emphasized as one
of the chief functions of the shop steward his duties in 'a case of
petty spite or constant bullying from an overseer or a foreman'.
'It would appear,' said the *Works Committees Report*, 'that a
Works Committee, if it is to be of any value in ventilating and
removing grievances, must be in a position to ventilate grievances
arising from the conduct of foremen and overlookers. Such
grievances touch the worker most closely in his daily work.' The
case already referred to at Reuben Gaunt's, Ltd, in which a foreman charged with bullying was tried by a joint body representing
the management and the workers, is a definite embodiment of
this principle.

These are still only partial indications of the importance of
grievances against foremen in trade union activity. The union
may try to secure the discharge of an arbitrary foreman; the
union may secure consideration of its grievances against him by
peaceful means. But frequently the resentment merely smoulders
and breaks out on other issues. This feeling, whether or not it
appears on the face of the workers' demands, is undoubtedly, as
the secretary of an employers' association told me, 'at the bottom
of some of the bitterest strikes.' A correspondent writing to *The
Times* during the railway dispute of 1907 declared that:

The whole cause of these continued disturbances is due to the authority and petty tyranny exercised by the foremen, who are nothing less than despots and slave-drivers.

And the Commission on Industrial Unrest in 1917, in analysing the unrest in South Wales, said:

We must also recognize the fact that the Welsh collier, even though possibly addicted to bluntness of speech in conversation with his fellow-workmen is quick to resent any ebullition of temper or violence of language towards himself on the part of those placed in authority over him . . . Much avoidable friction is due to lack of self-control in language and temper and want of tact generally on the part of officials, though circumstances may often be such as to test them severely in this respect.

The control exercised by trade unions over the actions of foremen is a real and continuous thing, though it gains public notice only when it is fought for in a strike. It is not of course argued that this control is wholly different from the modicum of control exercised by any body of men under supervision, whether organized or unorganized. The manager who sees that a certain foreman fails to get the best work out of his men because he is unpopular and so replaces him is to that extent 'controlled' by the dislikes of the workers. Moreover, any group of men, no matter how helplessly situated, enforces, if only by nagging and sulkiness, some sort of standard of treatment from its overseers – a standard which I was made to feel very definitely in a few days' service as a prison guard. The most accurate literary expression of this group-standard, in *The Code* by Robert Frost, is written of the completely unorganized 'hired men' of the New England farms:

The hand that knows his business won't be told
To do work faster or better – these two things.

But from the individual hired man, working alongside the small farmer in the hurry to get in the hay before a rain and defending his 'code' by simply thrusting his pitchfork into the ground and marching himself off the field, it is a long way to the action of the whole body of workers in a great engineering establishment or in a group of coal pits scattered up and down a Welsh valley, no individual of whom is of any particular importance to the employer, nevertheless enforcing by their collective power a certain level of personal treatment when one foreman has violated the code in respect to one worker. No one claims that trade unionism is mere knight errantry, that a high recklessness over obscure and delicate points of honour leads to lack of caution in regard to trade union funds or the interests of trade union members. Even the authors of the *Miners' Next Step*, for all their insistence on fighting individual grievances that involve principles, recommend as a point of tactics that:

> Whenever it is contemplated bringing any body of men out on strike, demands must be put forward to improve the status of each section so brought out.

But the extent to which decent foremanship may be felt to be a matter of union and inter-union concern is suggested by the description, in the annual report of the Furnishing Trades Association for 1917, of joint action by the metal and wood-working trades in an aircraft factory:

> A mass-meeting of all sections made it quite clear that they were determined to insist that any attempt to treat any group of men without regard to their feelings or self-respect would be treated as a challenge to all the unions, and as such would be taken up and replied to by a general stoppage of work. They demand the right to work under a manager who will treat them as men inside the shop.

A standard of foremanship, or at least a standard of manners in foremen, enforced in the more spectacular cases by striking for the foreman's dismissal but also by other methods of steady pressure, is as real – though less definite and possibly less universal – a subject of trade union regulation as the standard of wages itself.

NOTES

1. David Kirkwood (1872–1955) was convener of shop stewards at the Parkhead Forge in Glasgow, a member of the ILP, and one of those deported in 1916. He ended his career as a Labour Peer. (Note by R. Hyman, Pluto edition.)

2. The Postmen's Federation was the main component of the Union of Post Office Workers formed in 1920.

14 Controlling the Line

Huw Beynon

Reprinted with permission from H. Beynon, 'Working For Ford', E. P. Publishing, Wakefield, 1975, Chapter 6.

Most workers endure supervision while they are at work. Many of them resent it and have built up defences against the supervisor. Coal mining perhaps provides the most well-known examples of the sort of controls that workers have developed at work. Writing in the 1920s Carter Goodrich describes a court case which arose out of the Minimum Wages Act. An overman was asked whether a particular miner did his job properly: 'I never saw him work,' he replied. 'But isn't it your duty to visit each working place twice a day?' asked the magistrate. 'Yes,' replied the overman, but 'they always stop work when they see an overman coming, and sit down till he's gone . . . they won't let anybody watch them' (Goodrich, 1920, p. 137). Particular features of mining, not least the danger involved in the work, have contributed to the proliferation of quite extensive job control by the miners. While such controls are not highly developed in every work situation there is every reason to expect that, in a society where most people have only their labour to sell, a conflict over control will be a feature of work situations. Although the syndicalist call of 1911 – 'the mines for the miners' – has died away, the idea of worker control still exists within the British working class. On the shopfloor of many factories the division between the supervisor and the men can be characterized as a 'frontier of control' – management's rights on the one side and those of the workers on the other. It is in this way, in disputes over control at work, that the class struggle has been fought out by the British working class during this century. At the lowest, and most fundamental level, it has involved a conflict over how much work the men do and how much they get paid for it. At its most developed level it has produced an ideological conflict over who runs the factory and why, to a questioning of the essential nature and purpose of production within a capitalist society.

The unionization period at Halewood was marked by very

severe conflicts along the frontier of control. It involved the workers in a major struggle for a degree of job control within the factory, and this struggle was based upon the relationship between the worker and his supervisor. Victories in these struggles were far from hollow ones, for in their defeat of the supervisor the workers and their stewards laid down the essential basis for a say in the way their lives were to be regulated while they were in the plant. These struggles were of crucial importance for the development of the shop-stewards' committee and in examining them it will be useful to begin by drawing upon the experiences of the small-parts section of the Paint Shop.

Eddie Roberts was the shop steward for the section, George was his stand-in and Kenny was their close friend. All three of them had been on the section from the early days. Kenny was a militant.

> I don't know what I am, or what I want to do. I hate Ford's. I'd give up a wage increase to have Henry Ford on this section and give him a good kick up the arse. I'd thought of going to Australia. Of opening a shop. Can you be a socialist and own a shop?

Kenny hated Ford's and loved a fight. He hated having to get up early in the morning. He hated being told what to do. He hated having to work his balls off for nothing. He arrived on the section from the Wet Deck. Bert (the Wet Deck steward) couldn't handle him. 'I spotted him so I thought I'd unload him on to Roberts . . . It worked out good.' Kenny was amazed by the small-parts section.

> I came there and I was put on the front of the line. There was all these hooks and they *all* had to be filled with bits and pieces. I tell you Huwie it was murder. I'd get home and I'd go straight to bed. I couldn't stand it. So I decided that I'd had enough. I started to fill every other hook – to leave big gaps. The foreman went mad. Berserk he went. He started jumping on and off the line, running down the shop filling up the hooks. I ask you. He was shit-scared. 'You *must* fill them all' he kept screaming. Well the lads caught on and they started leaving empty hooks. He was going crazy. Then we got hold of Eddie to

complain that the foreman was working. We did that every day.

The situation is a lot better now. In fact we've got one of the easiest sections in the plant. It can be done see. You can control it if you have a go.

The Paint Shop is the earliest process that the car shell passes through in the PTA. Stoppages of work there will stop production and lay off the rest of the workers in the PTA within a matter of hours.[1] The Paint Shop workers were aware of this and during periods of market boom when they were working high schedules they pressed their advantage. Certain sections were able to establish and maintain control over line speeds and the allocation of work. In the small-parts section the advantages of their position in the production process had been exploited to the full by a high level of solidarity and cohesion amongst the men on the section and an audacious, gifted leadership. As a result of this, and the decline in through-put of the section which accompanied the new fascia panels, the manning of the section in 1968 was almost twice as high as management considered reasonable. Eddie explains:

We've just had to destroy the foremen. When we were here first the foremen really threw their weight around and it took a bit of time to sort things out. Kenny was up at the end of the line. He did a great job. Since then they've tended to send weak foremen down to us. They leave us alone and we leave them alone. One or two of them have tried to get on top but they're easy to beat. There are lots of things you can do to make it bad for them. The lads would do half the job, and play around with them. I'd set him up for cases and destroy him in the office. Every time I was in the office I'd say something about him. That's what we *had* to do. We *had* to destroy the foremen.

We've got it pretty easy now. The blokes are told what has to be done at the beginning of the shift and they work out the speeds, and the times when they're going to take their breaks for tea and cards. Occasionally the foreman will come on to the section during the shift and tell me or George that they want some more parts done quickly – so will the lads do it, as a favour? He goes on about how appreciative he is and that, and the lads do it for him. They just take longer breaks.

I don't know what it is. Some sections like this one are good sections with all good jobs. It's because you've had blokes like myself and Kenny and George who've come to stay I suppose. We've decided not to be beaten down by Ford's or to leave. On other sections the jobs are really bad. I can't understand it. I've been down to talk to the lads on one of those sections, to try to persuade them to do something. They just say they'll be leaving soon. At the other extreme you get the daft buggers in the boiler house who've been here since the start-up and still haven't done anything. For all we say though, there's no easy job in this plant. We're going to have to give way on manning on this section soon. We've just been fortunate with the change in the fascia panels. Most jobs in this plant, even the easy ones, are pretty bad really. There's no joy in putting things on hooks.

In the small-parts section of the Paint Shop the method of work, along with the strategic position of the section in the plant, assisted the organized attempts of the workers to obtain strong areas of job control. The fact that they were able to maintain these controls during a period of declining work schedules was largely due to the influence that Eddie – the steward and deputy convenor – was able to exert over the supervisor and plant manager. It has already been suggested that bluff plays an important part in negotiations between shop stewards and representatives of management. Periods of months can go by without either side calling the other's bluff. In some factories the bluff is never called. In a period of expanding output it would not be worth it for management to challenge the areas of job control in the small-parts section because this carried the risk of a stoppage. In the long-term, however, the bluff would be called and Eddie knew this; he also knew that when that happened they would have to settle for a reduction in manning.

The extent and durability of job controls are subject to the market. Fluctuations in the sales of cars, in the rate of capital investment, soon reveal themselves in the social relations on the shopfloor. It is in this sense that unionism and workplace organization can be seen as a direct consequence of economic forces. Workers who restrict their output, who 'malinger' at work, frequently justify themselves by their need to regulate the supply of labour. 'If we all worked flat out it would be dead simple what would happen. Half of us would be outside on the stones with our cards in our hands.' The Labour government's notion of 'shake out' is but a euphemism for the fact that by maximizing the return on capital working men are put out of a job. The idea of maximizing returns and cutting labour costs is instilled into the minds of modern managers, particularly those who have attended courses in business economics in our universities. Yet a similar understanding is denied to workers because they are in a position to see beyond it. Maximizing returns makes sense only if you're not going to be maximized into the dole queue. Workers who understand this are called 'bloody-minded' because they have come to understand something important about how the economic system operates.

We are left with arguments about 'fairness'. 'A fair day's work for a fair day's pay.' But what is fair? Fair for whom? What sort of fairness commits some men to a life on the line while others write books about them? It's not a fair world and there is no way of deciding what is a fair day's work from these men. The very act of asking them to work there *at all* is manifestly unfair. People who sit in offices, ride in lifts and Company cars have no right to demand that the lads on the line work harder, because to ask the same thing from themselves would be unthinkable.

It's got nothing to do with fairness. What it has to do with is economics and power. In these terms it is important to examine the strengths and vulnerabilities of the job controls established by the Halewood workers, and in doing so I shall now concentrate upon the experiences of the workers in the Trim and Final Assembly Departments. The situation in these departments differed in a number of important respects from the Paint Shop. In these departments the assembly line exerted an even greater pressure upon the nature of work and work relationships. In these departments the operator, the steward and the foreman were under a greater, and more continuous, pressure than that experienced by their counterparts in the Paint Shop. Here thousands of components are assembled around the painted body shell, which moves upon a line that never stops. To miss a job means the threat of chaos because someone further down the line has a job which depends upon your job. In the small-parts section an empty hook was an important act of defiance which laid the ground for a movement towards job control, but it did not involve the *sabotage* of the job. On the assembly line a missed job could mean precisely this. Although this means that the individual operator has a greater amount of power at his disposal, in the early days of the plant this power was essentially superficial and illusory. Unless you were sure of the support of your steward and work mates, to miss a job on the line at this time meant that you took on the whole world.

One of the most firmly held policies of the Ford Motor Company has been its opposition both to piece-rates and to negotiations over job manning and individual workloads. The company has held consistently to its right to manage its factories as it thinks fit – to employ whom it likes and to use those in its employ as it likes. In 1969 I had a conversation with a senior Labour Relations Executive of the company, who made clear to me his objections to 'mutuality agreements' with the trade unions over such things as the timing of jobs and the allocation of work. Such an agreement would make the management and the trade unions jointly responsible for ascertaining the time for a particular job, the organization of work, speed of the line and so on.

No. We cannot accept mutuality at this time. Where the trade union movement fails to see these areas of common interest we are inhibited from going down the mutuality road. The first duty we have to our employees is the business. We're not going to be a loss maker. People can look at Ford's, look at its assets and think that the company is safe. Ford's can go to the wall like any other company. If we're not competitive, we make losses and we go to the wall. It's in their interests – shareholders, customers and workers – for us to stay competitive.

Clearly, therefore, any move towards 'mutuality' or the establishment of extensive job control by the workers through their union is seen to involve a direct threat to the competitive position and profitability of the company. It was not felt that this insistence upon the manager's right to manage and pursue efficiency should of necessity give rise to conflict. To quote from the same conversation:

No: I may be naïve over this but I can't see that at all. Management don't set difficult work standards. All we want is maximum use of the plant; we can do this in a number of ways – overtime, shift working. All we want then is the plant to produce *the number of cars that we know it can produce* – we're simply asking for *good continuous effort.* And it's here that we need a good working relationship between the foreman and the shop steward in order to achieve these standards. On the track for example there may be a work allocation on the basis of three two-doors followed by one four-door followed by three two-doors and then a mistake occurs and three four-doors come down together. Now it's in these sort of situations that a good working relationship with the steward is vital. If the relationship is good they can work out whether to put men in on the line or to let the bodies go down the lines and gradually move them back again. In these sort of cases co-operation becomes so important.

The unions have taken the wrong turning over this. They seem to think that increased efficiency means that we are asking the men to sweat blood. We're not doing this at all. We aim to set standards that can reasonably be met.

In spite of this, however, it would be true to say that there was no common agreement in the Halewood plants over what constituted 'good continuous effort' or a 'reasonable' workload. The management's insistence that it was its right to make the vital decision on these issues, in itself produced mistrust. The question of job timing and job control was the source of very severe conflict in the Halewood assembly plant throughout the 1960s.

On the assembly line each worker is termed an operator, he works at a particular station and work is allocated to him at that station. He is surrounded by stacks of components and maybe a man is sub-assembling these for him. His job is to attach his component to the body shells as they come to him. Obviously the faster the line runs, the less time he has on any particular body shell, and consequently the smaller the range of tasks that he is able to do. If the line is running, for example, at thirty cars an hour, he is allocated two minutes work on each car that passes him. The allocation of the two minutes work is done on the basis of the times recorded for each operation by the Works Study Department of the Ford Motor Company. Most of the assembly-line workers I talked to were suspicious of the timings. It wasn't so much that they thought that the times were rigged but more that they thought the whole idea of timing jobs to be a questionable one – both ethically and scientifically. As two of them put it:

> They say that their timings are based upon what an 'average man' can do at an 'average time of the day'. That's a load of nonsense that. At the beginning of the shift its all right but later on it gets harder. And what if a man feels a bit under the weather? On night shift see, I'm bloody hopeless. I just can't get going on nights. Yet you've always got the same times: Ford's times. It's this numbering again. They think that if they number us and number the job everything is fine.

> *They* decide on *their* measured day how fast *we* will work. They seem to forget that we're not machines y'know. The standards they work to are excessive anyway. They expect you to work the 480 minutes of the eight hours you're on the clock. They've agreed to have a built-in allowance of *six minutes* for going to the toilet, blowing your nose and that. It takes you six minutes to get your trousers down.

The 'science' of the stopwatch was conceived in America at the beginning of the century. Much of it emerged from the factories of men like Ford, but the chief publicist of 'scientific management' was Frederick 'Speedy' Taylor. Like Ford he was an eccentric. As a boy he insisted when he played with his friends that their games conform to detailed, rigid rules. The longer he lived the less he slept, for he had perfected a device that woke him if he dozed in his chair. His mission was to make labour scientific. To work out the most efficient means of working through detailed timings of physical movements, and by related incentive payment schemes. His schemes met with considerable opposition and eventually in 1912 a Congressional Committee was set up to investigate his methods.

Men still claim scientific status for work-study methods. Usually, however, such claims come from those who are not on the receiving end of the stopwatch. (The extent to which the 'professional classes' support increased rationalization and productivity on the shopfloor yet deny the applicability of such criteria to their own work is one of the more interesting phenomena of modern society.) Unbiased opinion rarely disagrees with Professor Baldamus's contention that the whole work-study operation hinges upon 'intuitive guesses as to what is in fact a normal, reasonable, fair, average or right degree of effort for any particular task.' Even writers closer in their identification with the aims of management are reluctant to make sweeping claims for science and objectivity in work study. One of the books written for students of management on methods of payment makes it clear that 'the allocation of points encourages one of the major fallacies about Job Evaluation',[2] that it is 'a scientific or at the very least an objective technique which introduces definitive criteria into the emotive and subjective matter of determining levels of remuneration'. It goes on to conclude that 'the measurement is spurious', and overwhelmingly laden with subjective evaluation 'as any examination of the way factors and their weightings are determined will reveal' (North and Buckingham, *Productivity, Agreements and Wage Systems*, Gower Press, 1969, p. 197).

The work-study engineer, the man with the clock, bore the brunt of much of the antagonism engendered by job timings in the PTA plant.

The work-study men themselves had to put up with this. A lot of them were young men. Their dads were workers and they'd been to grammar school, got a few O levels and jacked it in. They didn't believe in the Ford Motor Company either. It was just their job.

Some of them were attending evening classes, for a qualification in works management, or personnel management. A bit of work study and a bit of industrial sociology and psychology. They didn't like it much. 'It's all a load of baloney tha'. As far as I can see it's all about manipulation. And the lecturer's only there for the cash. I don't blame him, like, but it's a bit difficult to take it seriously. I'm going to pack it in and go to India.' The few that I spoke to were sympathetic towards the workers, one of them in particular even more dubious about the science of job timings than the lads themselves. Tony coped with it all through jokes and a heavy irony – by laughing and calling himself 'the workers' friend'.

Apart from the timings themselves, the main problems faced by the operatives on the assembly line related to *speed-up*. The history of the assembly line is a history of conflict over speed-up – the process whereby the pace of work demanded of the operator is systematically increased. This can be obtained in a number of ways, the most simple involving a gradual increase in the speed of the line *during* a shift. In other words a man may start a shift with a work allocation of two minutes to coincide with a line speed of thirty cars an hour and then find that he is working on a line that is moving at thirty-five cars an hour. He gets suspicious after a bit because he finds that he can't make time on the job. He can't get those few stations up the line which allow him a break and half a ciggie now and then. We have already seen that this practice was common in the pre-union era of the American motor industry and also at Dagenham. The long-serving stewards and workers at Halewood insist that plant management made frequent use of this type of speed-up in the early days of the plant. Production managers out to make a name for themselves can only do it through figures – through their production and their costs. They abuse their supervision to this end. To serve the god of production is also to serve yourself and in this climate a few dodges are all part of the game. These dodges could be controlled though. They provoked a number of unofficial walkouts on the trim lines. 'The lads said "Sod you. We're not doing it, we're just not doing it." It worked as good as anything else y'know. We just said no and if they pushed it we went home.' No procedure could sort out issues like these. This was naked aggression being met with violent defiance. Management was trying to force the lads to do the unthinkable and they weren't having it. An agreement had to be reached and management conceded to the stewards the right to hold the key that locked the assembly line. Little Bob Costello had the key on the A shift, and the line speeds were changed with great ceremony, watched and cheered by the workers on the line. This wasn't enough for some sections. Some stewards had been able to obtain an additional safeguard. The first man on these sections was given an extra time allowance for counting the cars that entered the section. If the number of cars in any hour exceeded the stipulated line speed he was able to stop the line.

Some control then was obtained by a straightforward refusal to obey – by rebellion. Instances such as this one were commonplace in the plant before negotiated agreements had been made over the control of the work. Individual acts of sabotage were also common at this time. Men pulled the safety wire and stopped the line. These acts were part of a general movement towards job control and in substance differed only slightly from the formally articulated acts of defiance just mentioned. In an organized plant, however, sabotage takes on a different significance.

In the late 1960s the management at Halewood was forced to lower the minimum age of recruitment to eighteen, letting in a flood of lads who couldn't believe their eyes. What a place this was. These lads wanted the money. They dressed well, lived it up, with girls and music. The PTA plant at Halewood had nothing to offer them but money. They wanted to take their Fridays off and have a good time. They didn't want to put petrol tanks in motors. A gang of these lads worked together on the high line. They started by peeling the foreman's orange, carefully, removing the fruit and filling the skin with Bostik. The new remoulded orange was returned to the supervisor's bag. And they watched him trying to peel it. Bostik is a marvellous substance. It sticks and it burns. Bostik bombs were manufactured and hurled into the steel dumper rubbish containers. Explosions . . . flames twenty-feet high. Someone could have been killed. On the trim lines they started pulling the safety wire. On one shift after the 1970 strike the line was stopped on thirty-six occasions. Foremen were restarting the line without checking.

In one respect incidents like these involve a fundamental challenging of the whole thing because these lads just didn't want to produce motors. This denial is so fundamental that it has nothing whatsoever to do with trade unionism. In the summer of 1969 for example the Convenor met the works manager who asked him if there was any dispute outstanding, that they could sort out. There wasn't, but the weather was beautiful – hot and sunny. The lads kept coming in late from their dinner breaks. 'If they can play football they can work. They're just a lazy bunch of bastards.' It got hotter and hotter, it was too hot to work. 'But they played football . . .' They weren't going to work – take the roof off. Senior plant management went into the Paint Shop to check the complaint. One of them was streaming with sweat. 'What did the lads want?' They wanted iced lime juice. This unfortunately couldn't be supplied but would orange be all right? Yes, orange would do fine. They drank it and went home.

Trade unionism is about work and sometimes the lads just don't want to work. All talk of procedures and negotiations tends to break down here. The lime juice incident illustrates this well. It could be coped with, it was good fun but it had little to do with conventional union-management relations. There comes a point, however, where certain sorts of individual action come into direct conflict with the very nature of trade union collectivism. The steward organization was developed to protect the members against management and as such an important part of its function was to obtain a degree of internal discipline within the work force. Bostik bombs could kill someone. The lads *had* to stop. They had to be sorted out and the convenor had to do it. Once more that was all. Just one more Bostik bomb and they'd be outside the gate.

All right Eddie. We'll take it from you Eddie. We'll not take it from him [the supervisor] though. We'll not take it from him. Treating us like little kids. We're not at school y'know.

They're not bad lads. It's just working in this fucking place.

Controlling the membership is part of the steward's job. The nature of the relationship between the union and the employer can mean that the steward rather than the manager disciplines individual workers for not working properly. This is one side of the picture. In an organized shop individual acts of defiance or 'laziness' can threaten the unity and organization achieved by the mass in collective action. But although individual acts of sabotage *can* be antipathetic to unionism, not all sabotage need be.

In the Paint Shop the car, after an early coat of paint, passes through the Wet Deck where a team of men armed with electric sanders – 'whirlies' – sand the body while it is being heavily sprayed with water. From the Wet Deck the car shell goes right through the painting system and emerges finished some three hours later. In 1967 Bert Owen was the steward for the Wet Deck. The lads on the Deck played in a football team, went away on coach trips, drank together in the pub. They had their own nicknames for each other. A lad called John Dillon worked there. So they all took Magic Roundabout names. Dougal, Florence, Zebedee – 'Did you see it yesterday?' 'It's clever mind – how they do it.' There was also Mumbles, Big Ears and Uncle Fester. And Bert. They sang songs. Played about.

If there was a problem on the Wet Deck, a manning problem, speed-up, if the foreman had stepped out of line, they always had a comeback. They could sand the paint off the style lines – the fine edges of the body that give it its distinctive shape. And nobody could know. The water streaming down, the whirlies flailing about, the lads on either side of the car, some of them moving off to change their soaking clothes. The foreman could stand over them and he couldn't spot it happening. Three hours later the finished body shell would emerge with bare metal along the style lines. They *knew* it was happening.

'The bastards . . . now look here, Bert, this has gone far enough. I've taken as much as I'm going to from them fuckers. You tell them to stop.' Stop what? Bert was always prepared to urge them to improve their work but really it was the equipment, or the paint, or the metal. 'All right, Bert, they can have what they want.' They'd sing then. After a victory. They'd stand there with their whirlies – singing. In the wet. 'Walk on through the wind, walk on through the storm, and you'll n – e – ver walk a – lone . . .' For the rest of the shift.

Few sections had this degree of cohesion or such assistance from the means of production. Things were quite different on the trim lines where the car assembly workers at Halewood met speed-up in its most developed form. While little Bob's key foiled the more flagrant excesses of management, other, more sophisticated, means of increasing the work content were more difficult to combat. These derive from the fact that fluctuations in the market demand for cars result in the speed of the line, and the mixture of models (and therefore jobs) coming on to the line, varying from week to week and even from day to day. As a consequence of this both the allocation of jobs and the number of men employed on a particular section has to be altered and renegotiated with each change of speed or model mix. In this situation speed-up can be obtained by an increased rationalization of work allocation at the higher speeds, i.e., a less than proportionate increase takes place in the number of men employed on a section and this manning ratio is maintained when lower speeds are returned to. For example, a hundred men might work on a section with a line speed of thirty cars an hour; with an increase in the speed of the line to forty cars an hour (by 33 per cent) the manning might be increased to 125 (or only 25 per cent) and then when the speed is dropped again to thirty the manning might be cut to ninety-five. Again the stewards maintain that such practice was commonplace in the early days of the plant.

The establishment of controls over speed-up achieved through variations in the manning ratios was obviously difficult to obtain given the company's principle of refusing to negotiate the allocation of work – a principle formally recognized in the Agreement signed by the company and the trade unions. In spite of this, however, several sections had established unwritten agreements as to the manning ratios that would operate at the various speeds. By 1968 most of the sections in the Trim and Final Assembly Departments had established a code of custom and practice which governed the allocation of work and it is important to look at some of the ways in which these controls were established.

By 1968 the shop stewards' committee was in a position to establish a level of consistency in the job control exercised by each of its stewards on their section. Its ability to secure this consistency derived from the actual controls over job regulation that had been built up unevenly throughout the plant. Within the Trim Department areas of strongly developed job control co-existed with sections where such control was quite rudimentary. These strong areas of control were invariably associated with the fact that sometime in the past, the steward, or another operative on the section, had stuck his neck out and opposed the supervisor. One steward describes what happened on his section:

I've told you that it was pretty bad when we came here first. The supervisors used to treat you like dirt. I've always been able to stick up for myself like, they knew that if they messed me about they'd have some trouble on their hands, so it wasn't too bad for me. You see I don't think any man, any supervisor, should consider himself above another man. I don't think he should ask another man to do what he wouldn't do himself. A lot of the lads who came here first were given a really bad time. I've never been able to sit back and watch another man take a beating. To see a man struggling with a job. So I started telling the supervisor that he was out of line. Then the lads asked me to represent them – to be the steward – and I've done that ever since.

Such opposition frequently produced situations of severe conflict and sometimes this conflict developed into a personal battle between the steward and the supervisor. In order to establish controls over the supervisor's decisions, the stewards resorted to a number of different tactics. One of the most successful stewards on the trim sections obtained his autonomy by restricting his negotiations with the supervisor to a torrent of abuse and a recorded 'failure to agree'. Les explains:

I expect everyone has told you how bad it was down there in the beginning have they? It was murder. We had no representation. We were just supposed to do exactly as we were told. Well I started shouting my mouth off and the lads asked me to be the steward. That started it. I was working on the line. A member would have a dispute with the foreman and ask for me, but the foreman wouldn't get me a relief. I'd have to wait he said. So we stopped the job. Yes it was really bad then. You had no say in anything – in who did what or how much work or nothing.

Anyway we stopped the job a few times and things got a bit better but not much. They still thought that we hadn't to be listened to. So I thought sod this, we won't listen to you. I used to swear blind at them all the time – I still do a bit, it's the only way sometimes – swear blind and 'fail to agree'. Then we'd go up the office and I'd abuse him again. Call him a stupid bastard in front of management. It was the only way on my section. I had forty 'failure to agree's' going at one time.

The bitterness in this situation exploded when one of the supervisors attempted to plant a component in Les's haversack which was subsequently searched by a security guard. Les, however, had been forewarned. Another steward tells the story:

Yes that did happen. Les used to curse the supervisors all the time on the trim. He used to cuss them up in heaps. He used to call them everything. I can't remember what his favourite one was now but he had some beauties. They're not supposed to lose their tempers see, the supervision, and they're definitely not supposed to hit a man. So there wasn't much they could do except put it in procedure. And they were a bit afraid of that, because Les was no fool and they knew that he could make them look stupid. Les had a tough job down there on the trim at that time and he did a hell of a lot of good work. A lot of the stewards didn't like the way he carried on, but he was the only steward on the trim on his shift who got anywhere.

'Failure to agree' we used to call him.

Anyway, he drove the supervision to distraction. They just couldn't handle him. So one of them put a flasher unit in Les's rucksack, and tells the security guard on the gate to look out for him. You couldn't miss Les. He used to wear this lumber jacket with a big sheepskin collar. Fortunately one of the lads on the section spotted this and told Les – 'Look out for your bag mate.' So anyway Les goes through the gates and the security bloke grabs him. Les throws up his arms – he's brought a few witnesses like – and shouts 'It's a frame-up'.

It was a pretty nasty situation. Paul Roots came up from Warley and didn't believe any of it. He knew Les like, and Les was for the sack. Anyway little Jimmy stuck to his story. They questioned him for hours, tried to catch him out and all sorts. It was like the SS. But little Jimmy didn't change his story once, and I think Roots suddenly saw that he was speaking the truth. He gave the foreman a bit of a grilling. It lasted all night long. In the end he broke down . . . in tears he was. He said he couldn't stand hearing Les cursing one of the older supervisors.

After that of course Les couldn't go wrong. He was the man they tried to frame.[3]

While this incident is obviously an extreme example, it should not be readily dismissed as an entirely misleading and atypical one. Many of the stewards experienced periods of perpetual confrontation with their supervisors. During the autumn of 1967, for example, the issue of job control became important within the material handling sections of the plant. These sections had previously been relatively unorganized, but had by this time produced two active shop stewards. The material handling department receives and stores components, and then distributes them to the stations on the lines. The workers in these departments were part storeman, part clerk and part fork-lift driver. They were split up all over the plant, and organization was difficult. Jack Jones was another of the young stewards on the A shift. He was smart and a bit cheeky. Like so many others he'd come to Ford's for the cash and with some idea that he might 'get on a bit'. He had been a distance lorry driver and then a storeman at English Electric. Ford's made him into a unionist. 'It was so obvious when I came here. It was obvious that you had to have an organization. Everyone was getting screwed. This place without an organization would be lost.' Bill Brodrick who was a mate of his encouraged him to take on the steward's job. Jack became a steward in 1964. He had a lot of trouble organizing the section. His job made him isolated. It was impossible for him to be on the spot with a grievance. He had to be told of the problem and relieved from his job. Frequently he had up and downers with the foreman and the superintendent. In 1967 one of these culminated in Jack being sued for libel. In building up an organization on the section the steward enforces unwritten agreements from his supervisor. When the supervisor is placed under pressure by his superiors he often breaks these secret understandings. Jack committed his feelings to print. He filled in a procedure report calling the supervisor a 'perpetual liar' and a 'deceitful bastard'. The supervisor went to law, but he wasn't allowed to push it too far. Higher management persuaded him that the case was better dropped and Jack Jones escaped his chance to testify in the dock.

The right of the shop steward to have freedom of access to his members on a section, and his right to negotiate with the supervisor over allocation of work and the like were therefore established in the main by way of periods of severe conflict between the stewards and supervision. These rights were minimal requirements for a degree of job control by the men on the assembly line, and they had to be fought for. Once they were obtained the steward and the shop stewards' committee was able to build upon them.

This conflict over 'rights' is a fundamental one and permeates union–management relationships. It is not restricted to the shopfloor. During a meeting of the Ford NJNC in 1970, the Company's Director of Labour Relations, Bob Ramsey, clashed with the Committee's Secretary, Reg Birch, of the AEF. The basis of the clash appeared trivial. They were arguing about the men who worked in the Ford plants; Ramsey claimed that they were Ford workers who happened to be members of the AEF, the TGWU or whatever, Birch that they were first and foremost union members who happened to be working for the Ford Motor Company. There is no doubt that Birch and Ramsey were touching the nerve end of quite fundamental differences in principle. This clash of principles reveals itself on the shopfloor in the conflict along the frontier of control. It is these principles that are at stake when the foreman starts to allocate work and the steward retorts,' 'Hang on a minute. *You* tell us what's to be done and *we'll* decide who does it.' It is a direct clash over management's right to manage. A clash of power and ideology.

The position of the steward in the car plant is rooted in this clash. In the early years at Halewood the day to day life of the plant was virtually one endless battle over control. The establishment of a steward in a particular section was clearly related to the attempt by the workers to establish job control in that section. If the steward wasn't up to the job he was replaced, or he stood down leaving the section without a steward for a while. Where a steward stuck with the job, he and the men on his section were involved in a perpetual battle with foremen and management. Even in 1967 the stewards felt that the overwhelming majority of the problems that they had to deal with on their section were related either to speed-up or 'the blue-eye system', the favouritism practised by foremen in allocating work and overtime or in moving men from one section to another.

The problem of overtime is an important one. Initially it can be seen as a point of tension between the steward and his members. The stewards didn't like overtime. As I was writing down one steward's comments he remarked, 'That looks bad tha', going down there like tha' – "overtime". But it is my biggest headache.' Another steward made the situation quite clear:

> What causes me the most trouble? It's a sore point with me but it must be overtime. The distribution of overtime, insufficient notice, etc. I detest overtime but it's my job to represent the lads and if I wouldn't sort it out they'd soon get someone who could. Overtime and the movement of labour cause most disputes on my section.

This tension between the steward and his members over overtime is part of a general ideological struggle and is taken up later. At the moment it is important to recognize issues of overtime allocation as part of the conflict over control which the workers are involved in on the shopfloor. Assembly-line workers work for money and they want overtime because it gives them more money to pay off hire-purchase debts, mortgages, and the like. The foreman allocates overtime. He says who works when. This is part of his prerogative. His right to manage. The individual operator can exercise no control over the supervisor's decisions – apart, that is, from buying him pints in the local. On the assembly line one man is as good as the next man. The operator can stake no claims on the basis of ability or expertise. He is in the supervisor's pocket. If he doesn't behave, or if the supervisor just doesn't happen to 'like' him, he can lose his overtime for a week or forever. In a skilled work situation things are slightly different. At the Rolls-Royce factory in Bristol, for example, men can control their rights to overtime on certain jobs by virtue of the fact that they control the tools, or the knowledge, vital to the completion of the job. The foreman *has* to ask *them*. The assembly-line foreman can ask *anyone*. The emergent shop stewards' committee was a response to this situation. On many sections, the allocation of overtime was taken out of the hands of the supervisor and replaced by an overtime rota, administered by the steward.

Men became stewards in their battle with supervisors over injustices, over the workers' rights as opposed to management's indiscriminate right to manage. Frequently their response was crude. The vulnerability of their situation defied subtlety.

We just said 'No. We're not doing it.' It was as good as anything else at the time. They'd say: 'You've got a complaint?' We'd say: 'No, we're all right. We've not got any complaints.' They'd say: 'But what about the line speed, the work allocation. I thought you were complaining about that.' We'd say: 'No, it's all right now. We're happy as it is. We're only complaining if you try to change it.' They'd say: 'Oh, but we are going to change it. The speed must be changed.' We'd say: 'Well we're not doing it. Y'er not on.' Richie Rowlands had a classic. He'd say, 'All right off we fucking pop'. It used to drive them to distraction. We used to say to some of them 'All right, put it in procedure' and y'know the stupid buggers would.

As part of the logic of management's 'right to manage' the supervisor can expect his instructions to be obeyed. In case the operator objects to the order a procedure exists whereby he can object personally and then through his steward. Where no agreement can be obtained it is assumed that the man will obey the order until a decision has been reached at a higher level in the procedure. The procedure, therefore, assumes that the supervisor has authority. It exists to safeguard the worker from a wrong decision. It makes no sense for the *supervisor* to put a complaint in procedure for such an act negates management's authority and the very nature of the procedure. In a climate where the 'right to manage' was being perpetually challenged by the 'rights' of the workers it is not surprising, and certainly revealing, that many supervisors became confused about what was theirs 'by right'.

As the organization developed the stewards presented more subtle challenges to management and supervision. In order to deal with disputes over work allocation most of the stewards (thirty-four) had had some training in the techniques of work study. Several of them (twelve) had in fact decided to become work-study experts and had attended an advanced course on the subject that had been organized by the WEA. By virtue of the expertise gained on such courses, and also by their length of service in the plant, a number of the stewards had developed a far greater understanding of these techniques than had their supervisors. This had a number of consequences. For example, it meant that if an operator complained that he was being asked to do too much work, the steward was able to base a case upon the efficacy of the job timings which often served to drive a wedge between the supervisor and the work-study department. In these arguments the steward usually had to rely upon intuition, but one steward who had been bought a stopwatch by the men on his section was able to make more accurate checks upon the timings. It was through negotiations of this sort being carried out by individual stewards on their sections that the shop-stewards' committee was able to establish an agreement for the whole PTA plant which prevented management retiming any job without the prior agreement of the steward involved. Controls that were established within certain sections could therefore be extended through the committee to other sections which previously had not achieved such controls. Certain sections, however, still demonstrated greater worker control over job allocation than others, and the expertise and experience of the steward was one of the factors which explained this uneven development. Given the timings of the jobs that had to be manned on a particular section, there were any number of ways in which these jobs could be allocated to the men who worked on the section. As with most things there is an easy way and a hard way, and on several sections of the Trim and Final Assembly Departments the steward was more likely to know the easy way than the supervisor. A combination of this expertise and support from the men on their sections resulted in the steward's allocating work on at least six of the eighteen sections of the Trim and Final Assembly Departments in 1967. Given the speed of the line and the model mix, these sections functioned almost autonomously, with all the co-ordinating tasks being performed by the shop steward.

One of the stewards described the situation in this way:

I'm always in early. This means that I can check with the supervisor on line speeds and the model mix. Then I walk up and down the section to show the lads that I'm in. I talk to all the lads to make sure that everything is all right. I explain to them the manning changes if there are any. I discuss things with them to make sure that they are right in the picture.

You see I've been working on this section for six years and I know the jobs much better than the supervisor can. The other thing of course is that the lads trust me more than him. So it's easier all round.

These controls over the job gained the operative a degree of autonomy from both supervision and higher management. Through their steward they were able to regulate the distribution of overtime, achieve a degree of job rotation within the section, and occasionally sub-assembly workers, in particular, were able to obtain 'slack' work schedules. But there were quite precise limits to the way in which workers can run the section. An example of these limits was revealed on the Wet Deck. The lads didn't like working in the plant. They looked forward to the weekends. The Friday shift was the worst. Particularly on nights, because it messed up your Saturday as well. So the Magic Roundabout lads decided to have a rota. Eight of them contributed to a pool. Every eighth week one of them took the Friday shift off, and got paid a shift's money from the pool. It became too regular, too open and was noticed by management. Friday absenteeism is a problem in a car plant. Perpetual absenteeism, like lateness, is a sacking offence. So management intervened with threats and the pool was abandoned. Not a few managers found examples of working-class collectivism such as this one emotionally attractive. A member of the Central Industrial Relations staff at Warley, for example, explained the militancy of the Halewood plant in terms of Liverpool's working-class tradition:

> They say that there are a different type of people in the North. They're not as materialistic as the people in the South. They've not got their own houses or their own cars. They're much more easy going altogether. They don't take life so seriously. Apparently if they go in for a claim that is just not on, they prefer to be told to 'fuck off out of it'. That's how labour relations are conducted up there. Now in Dagenham they'll come in with a claim that you know and they know is hopeless and you'll argue round and round it all day. In Halewood you'd just say 'fuck off' and that would be the end of it. They're much more easy-going there; the men are much more independent of their wives; they drink more; go and watch the football . . . I suppose they'll change. When they get into debt with buying a house they'll have to go to work I suppose.

Do you think that that would be a good thing?

> Ah, now that's a *philosophical* question not a *business* question. It's like those questions on class we were discussing earlier; they make life very complicated if you think too much about them. I can see that it wouldn't be a good thing. I can see that there's something attractive about that way of life; but it's not much good for business. And business is what counts I suppose.

And business *is* what counts. However things *should* be, that certainly is how things are. The need for capital to produce a surplus, a profit, is an inexorable need. It is this which structures the world of the shop steward in an assembly plant. The stewards may be able to prise away some of management's controlling rights but they can hang on to these for only as long as the needs of business dictate. Essentially the controls obtained over the job by shopfloor union activities involved little more than a different form of accommodation to the more general controls imposed by management. Johnny saw this very clearly:

As I've said, I don't like Ford's. I don't like what they do, what they stand for, or what they've done in the past – in this country and America. I can see the time when the bomb goes up, you know. I can see myself leading the lads off my section and just destroying this place. I can see that happening. But you've got to cope with this plant as it is now, you've got to come in every day and represent the lads. That means you've got to set up some relationship with the supervision and with management. Sometimes I think 'what the hell are you doing? you're just doing management's job.' But I think it's better for the lads if I do it. It *is* better for the lads if I allocate the jobs and the overtime because if I do it it will at least be done fairly.

While the controls established within the sections may not have involved a very radical challenge to management's organization of the plant, they were radical enough to reveal conflict between a worker rationality and a management rationality, and it was at times when this conflict became manifest that the vulnerability of worker control over work was cruelly exposed. While the stewards were able to exert a degree of influence over the way in which jobs were timed, and a strong degree of control over work allocation, they had not established any control over the market, and its expression in the variations in the speed of the assembly line.

A district secretary of the NUGMW, an ex-convenor of the MSB plant at Halewood, explained how the absence of piece-rates increased the vulnerability of the steward's position when alterations took place in line speeds.

They're killing themselves up there in that plant. A steward on that estate is on a hiding to nothing. They just won't be able to last. It's different with piece-rates. A steward's job is a lot easier then. He can negotiate the rate and then let the lad make his time. If management want to change anything the steward can start talking about the rate. Now up there the rate is fixed so the steward's got nothing to bargain with. He spends all his time arguing about workloads. They set a line speed and they get things sorted out and then they change the speed and he's back where he started. It's heart-breaking and back-breaking. They're killing themselves up there in that plant.

With severe variations in the speed of the line, even the most well-organized sections had difficulty in maintaining and re-establishing 'traditional' areas of job control. One of the senior stewards concurred with the union officer. 'We're mad,' he said, 'we're crazy I think, sometimes I don't know why we do it. We're running flat out all the time and just to stay in the same place.'

The effect of the market upon the controls established by workers in the factory deserves further treatment, and in discussing the problems of job security in a car plant it will be possible to examine this and the vulnerabilities of the shop steward's position a little further . . .

NOTES

1. This power is not without its responsibilities. A fiercely fought issue within the shop stewards' committee was over 'sectional' as opposed to 'plant' interests.

2. A detailed Job Evaluation scheme was introduced by the Ford Motor Company in 1967 which gave rise to severe conflict on the shopfloor.

3. Les was a very complicated individual who eventually had his steward's credentials removed. He asked to be moved off the trim and eventually became a foreman.

15 Job Control and Union Structure

Richard Herding

Reprinted with permission from R. Herding, *Job Control and Union Structure*, Rotterdam University Press, 1972, pp. 10–12, 42–7, 51–5, 299–304.

JOB CONTROL AS A MEANS OF CAPITALIST INTEGRATION OF THE WORKING CLASS IN MARXIST VIEW

However the Marxist views differ among themselves, they do not adopt these lines of interest conflict (of the pluralist and functionalist analysis of job control and union representation*) at face value. Unions in a capitalist system which they accept, serve as tools of 'capitalist integration'[1] to channel and administrate labour protest in forms tolerable for the system. The expression of workers' interests is, in the first line, distorted by the division of the working class in various competing groups.[2] This division, boldly obvious in American society through a racially defined subproletariat, providing cheap labour, an industrial reserve army, and strikebreakers[3] pays off not only for employers, but must, under capitalist conditions, be upheld by the different workers' strata themselves in their short-run interest.[4] Secondly, in an intra-organizational view, as the representation of workers interests is pursued from bottom to top, the requirements for integration in the capitalist system are better understood, and 'collusion and alliance'[5] between business and organized labour increases. This distortion in interest representation is the basic socio-economic content of 'labour oligarchy'. Since in a private enterprise economy labour as a class inevitably has to pay for whatever gains a specific labour organization may enjoy, 'responsible' leadership in a union,[6] 'business-like' behaviour,[7] and collusion and oligarchic distribution of decisive power come up to the same: pursuing labour's long-term interests within an accepted capitalist economy means to abide by the economic rules of the system, and thus, if necessary, to suppress the 'short-sighted' demands voiced on the grass roots. Since essentially labour unions cannot change or at least have not succeeded in

* Editors.

changing labour's share in national income, but merely shift its distribution from one temporarily privileged stratum of the working class to the other, leaving profit margins untouched at best,[8] the very first goal of unionism – influence on wage determination – requires a competitive attitude, oriented at partial privileges rather than at general improvement. Nearly everything organized labour can gain in economic terms, but possibly also 'qualitative' changes such as in authority structure, if they constitute a potential threat to profitable operations, has to be paid for in losses of real incomes, drops of employment level, in preserving 'substandard' conditions elsewhere, or, in the last analysis, in external surplus realization through militarism and imperialism.[9] All a particular group or stratum in organized labour can do is passing the negative effect to others, trying to minimize the adverse consequences for themselves.[10]

Shopfloor organization and shop-level union-management relations in American society, therefore, have necessarily contradictory implications in the Marxist argument. On one hand, they root in workers' dissatisfaction with whatever aspects of the capitalistic organization of production may be at stake, and should be the more important for building class-consciousness as they focus on production rather than on income distribution. Wildcat strikes, slowdowns, restrictions of output and militant on-the-job leadership battle concrete phenomena in areas such as technological unemployment, increased physical or mental exploitation, and supervisory power. They do so in a fairly naïve, straightforward way, with little distortion of immediate interests through a more sophisticated, adjustment-oriented upper-level bureaucracy.[11] Precisely because interests are claimed in a blind, 'irresponsible' way at this level, this could verify Engels' early notion of trade unionism that its very one-sidedness and limitation compel it to proceed to ever larger demands, lest it fall back behind its own achievements.[12] Thus, shopfloor organization provides fundamental exigencies for militant unionism out of the immediate experience of the contradictions in the industrial system.

On the other hand, shopfloor militancy remains essentially within the framework of 'job' rather than 'class' consciousness, of selling labour aggressively on a given market. Gains made in collective bargaining or through grievance processing and pressure tactics on the plant or shop level[13] normally tend to strengthen the better situated plant, or the more strategic group within the plant,[14] at the expense of others. Successful union leadership at this level has to utilize competitive advantages, resulting in some sort of hierarchical order and widening gaps between the strata.[15] It will thus rather encourage the concept of 'private' bargains and confine the consciousness of those participating in the process, than contribute to wider material solidarity and the translation of the economic contradictions experienced into political ones. The resort to legal formalism in the contractual structure of the relationship would indicate this development.[16]

I have elaborated the Marxist view beyond the scarce writing on union-management relations that adopts this point of view to arrive at a full spectre of arguments. However, the detailed empirical analysis by Marxian social scientists of the American socio-economic system has been confined to macro-economic data, and occasional accounts of problems like those implied in 'job control' are rather impressionistic . . .[17]

The need for 'offensive' job control

Our discussion so far suggested that the pattern of management initiative and union veto, contract and grievance, joint policy-codification and unilateral execution, is geared to particular objects of union influence, namely, off-job rewards and bureaucratically controlled policies affecting employment rules and stability. For every-day job-control measures, from the application of the seniority rule to more ambitious aims such as autonomous organization at the work place, it is far less suitable, and the practice tends to deviate significantly from it. On-the-job conditions require some initiative for the union, some fusion of policy-making and execution, and elimination of time lags in enforcement. At the same time, from a purely organizational point of view, all this is far easier to accomplish at this level than at any other, since distortion through representation is technically less likely, and can fairly smoothly be corrected, at the grass roots. To some degree, the arrangements and practices I have mentioned, pre-empted such a structure without official recognition.

One feature is common, however, to the official and the 'underground' structure of job control by organized workers,

and is not overcome by informal qualifications of the countervailing power conception: job control is conservative. It is
geared to 'preserving' jobs, to 'preclude changes' in operations,
to retain 'restrictive' rules. Shopfloor representatives have
seldom come up with proposals for restructuring employment,
or, in connection with it and even more important, for reshaping
the work process of a firm or an industry. This is a reason why
things probably cannot be done with an unintended 'division of
labour' between the official and the unofficial system. Wherever
'positive' humanizing changes have taken place – normally in
capital-intense, rapidly growing industries with little pressure on
labour productivity increases in the short run – it was initiated
unilaterally by management – for instance, in the case of job
enlargement[18] – and naturally kept within the limits of management interests. Otherwise, autonomous work groups were part of
a traditional setting, or of an incentive system; normally both.[19]
Today, drawing on the auto and steel contracts' letter, a production standard may not be changed to the employee's detriment, or a new one may be challenged; respectively, locally prevailing norms are protected against unilateral change. But it is
completely out of the scope of the Steelworkers' union to make
proposals how to reorganize a mill, as Paul Jacobs quotes an
official of that union, and the Auto Workers have given up
earlier plans of this kind[20] for more and better 'real life' that
begins after work.[21] It is hard to develop plans for a redesigned
work process either on a negative basis, such as the grievance
machinery, or in the tug-of-war of contract administration
practice. Imaginative reorganization of working conditions falls
prey to the combined pressure of the centralized unions' adjustment to management's drive for individual productivity and
stable employment, the countervailing-power conception of
unionism, and the resulting defensive shape that even the unofficial job-control organization has retained. As Bell puts it,
quite aware of the disruptive forces that 'offensive' job control
has in store for the economic system:

In the challenge to the work process itself, the unions have
failed . . . For the unions to challenge the work process would
require a radical challenge to society as a whole: for to
question the location of industry or size of plant is not only to
challenge managerial prerogatives, it is to question the logic

of a consumption economy whose prime consideration is lower costs and increasing output. Moreover, how could any single enterprise, in a competitive situation, increase its costs by re-organizing the flow of work, without falling behind its competitors?[22]

We might conclude that for 'offensive job control' neither the concept of 'countervailing power' nor that of 'joint participation' alone provide an adequate institution framework. The conflict-conscious American industrial relations system has not precluded collusion, in an objective sense, between management and union bureaucracies on the general trend the employment relationship is following, against both rank-and-file and those excluded from organized labour. The all-embracing authority of the productive enterprise, as envisioned by the liberal pluralists,[23] may well come about in spite of the eroded safeguards of formally conflicting organizations. But at the same time, the American system has put forward the challenge of job control, local autonomy, and dispute-involving conflict solutions. These institutions have been able to respond from the bottom to the collusion on the top, but not to tackle the problems offensively. From the links between the formal institutions of union influence and their substantive contents and effects, we conclude that although under conditions of removed productivity pressure, the institutions of job control tend to combine, in a unique way, 'countervailing' power with issue-oriented 'joint management', the adequacy of this arrangement to the shopfloor has its limits in the 'defensive' nature of the policies embraced. Since shopfloor practice tends to dissolve the dogmatic alternative of joint management and countervailing power, the American experience makes the problem of codetermination redesigned by job control (including strike enforcement) appear in a new light.[24] Beyond that surface alternative, the question it raises for labour is the combination of issue-oriented participation with dispute-involving machinery to arrive at 'offensive' job control.

MATERIAL DETERMINANTS OF JOB CONTROL: UNION DEMOCRACY AND ORGANIZING POLICIES

The need for a unified approach to job control

The state of democracy within a trade union has an obvious and crucial impact on the job-control rights the union will demand in the bargaining process, and on the distribution and meaning of these rights for its members. Devices regulating intra-union competition, which is one aspect of seniority, can vary tremendously in their effects depending on the relative power that groups such as skilled workers, or a particular seniority unit, or blacks, wield in the respective union. Instruments controlling – and intended to alleviate – human effort in work, such as work rules or procedures for challenging production standards, depend a great deal on the responsiveness of the union leaders in question to the demands and complaints of the membership. The same is true with regard to the pursuit and enforcement of 'rationalizing' devices: written vs unwritten rules of discipline, for instance, may not be an issue in a local dominated by an entrenched group of employees indispensable because of their skills, and thus leave the constraint of arbitrary supervision entirely to management, resulting in a disadvantaged position for the unskilled workers. The American set-up of industrial relations, characterized by the absence of legislative regulation of most shop conditions, and by exclusive representation of the bargaining unit by one union, virtually cuts off recourse to the judicial process as well as to challenge from outside against a union irresponsive to the membership's interests. Democratic unionism, therefore, is even more vital than in countries without these two features. Legislation has recognized the need for implementing collective bargaining by regulation of internal union affairs.[25] However, these remedies are hardly effective and can only in extreme cases be used by the individual;[26] in addition, they embrace contract administration and representation, but not bargaining itself. There is no legal substitute for the social processes conducive to democratic unionism.[27]

The relevance of union democracy, that is, of the relationship between rank-and-file and union leadership, for job control is matched by a second one that commands far less public attention. It is the relationship between organized labour and the entire working class as its potential of recruitment. Again, this is particular to American industrial relations: the legislative principles of the exclusive bargaining agent and the bargaining autonomy of each unit make it almost possible to organize large industrial units 'from within', by way of 'selling unionism' to a gradually growing membership. As a union represents 'all or nothing', cost and effort of organizing a complete unit can only be afforded by an outside organization. 'Workers in no . . . basic industry have been able to organize without assistance from other unions.'[28] Given both inducement and necessity to organizing from outside, the access to effective unionism is open only to the degree that an already existing, powerful organization decides to organize an unorganized unit. Will there be an organization at all to make this decision? To whom will 'they' give preference in their organizing efforts? These questions are the more crucial for the unorganized worker since, as a rule, the union wage has a far stronger tendency to spill over to non-unionized establishments under competitive pressures in a tight labour market, than do job rights, whether job-security measures or the host of practices that employers term 'featherbedding' or 'restrictive practices' and consider the specific *faux frais* of unionization.[29] In fact, wages in excess of comparable union scales have been offered to workers as a counterpoison to unionization attempts, whereas this is hardly true with job rights that would restrain management's discretion and flexibility.[30]

Reversely, the size of a union's membership is affected by its collective bargaining policies (and these, in turn, by the state of internal democracy): a union can, in effect, service members out of the organization. The most obvious instance is furnished by some craft unions, such as the Printers' and Carpenters' (and building crafts in general), whose wage policies have allowed a non-union sector with lower wages and benefits to develop in their industries. More closely related to job control (and to intentional policy), the Mine Workers' consent to automation after 1945 put many of their members out of work altogether, and forced others into marginal mines under substandard conditions. In one of the first deals of co-operative productivity bargaining[31] – concerning elimination of jobs as well as placing output ahead of safety[32] – the loss in membership could be engineered without fear of internal problems in the union: Under exclusive bargaining representation, a worker loses, for all practical purposes, his influence in the union once he is dropped from the company's payroll, especially, where dues check-off applies. In most cases the union constitution bars him from active membership.[33] Once he has started to work in a marginal, non-union shop, his membership is worthless even if continuing. In brief, unless the decision to concur with technological progress eliminating jobs is prevented beforehand (which is a question of effective union democracy), it is hardly possible to influence it for those who experience its consequences as they get displaced to the unorganized sector (which shifts it to a question of organization policy). The virtually free discretion of union leadership to decide on the boundaries of their organization, to 'service in' or to 'service out', to manipulate the constituency for which union government is to be established and maintained,[34] is closely tied to the substantive meaning of 'union democracy' itself, although it is hardly ever treated in a common framework. Formal exclusion from membership, e.g., of members of a coloured race, have been analysed,[35] but not decisions to organize or not to organize, which lead to the same effects.[36]

With the Mine Workers' 'special relationship' to automation, we have already touched on the meaning of union democracy, combined with organizing policies, for union-management relations.[37] From the research evidence on union democracy we will try to establish a pattern on the following issues: just what groups tend to have power in unions? Can we identify any – along occupational, racial, or what other lines – or is union democracy a play with empty boxes, the 'ins' versus the 'outs'?[38] What effect is working democracy in a union likely to have on its relations with employers? Are democratic unions more or less militant, 'restrained', 'responsible' in their attitudes towards management? And on organizing policies: Whom will unions tend to organize, and who is bypassed (or 'serviced out')? Some of these questions, at first sight, seem to answer themselves, but on examining the literature, we will find scarce attempts to identify the substantive forces behind the bearing of union structure on labour-management relations . . .

Union democracy: Class interest and democratic organization

The conceptions of union government we have examined differ much more conclusively in their normative reasoning than in the substantive results of the research. When we examine the first of the questions formulated above – just what groups generally tend to have the power within unions – we are getting very few, scattered answers. If it is 'one group which controls the administration' and 'usually retains power indefinitely',[39] and such is the diagnosis in which most of the divergent therapies concur, then who is this group? What are the characteristics of the recruitment potential of 'activists' who are likely to become union leaders? Most of the literature has the 'ruling class' of a union form only after its rise to power; members are active, rise to office positions, acquire a monopoly of administrative skills, and keep control: such is the classical argument developed by Michels and resumed by Lipset. But a few things can be said beforehand on the power group, some of them apparently too obvious to be noted for most observers, and yet by no means self-evident. One of them is the rule of the senior members. Lipset by implication,[40] and Tannenbaum and Kahn more systematically,[41] note that seniority and activity in union affairs tend to correlate.[42] Observation of union politics confirms that 'having been around for a while' is required of any aspirant for office. Excessive requirements of prior office holding, such as those that in 1968/69 bent the Labor Department's attention to the National Maritime Union elections, fall in line with this general tendency.

A second factor that characterizes the would-be and actual leader is satisfaction with his job and company: he displays a 'double loyalty' to union and company.[43] Third, it is the skill level that distinguishes those who control unions which encompass members of different skills. The recruitment of most of the UAW leadership and the *de facto* veto power which the skilled trades managed to obtain in that union is a case in point, although political and ideological forces in the UAW served to check the skilled workers' influence for a long time.[44]

Finally, unions tend to be dominated by racial 'majority' groups, as current language puts it. Kornhauser's model of 'sponsorship and control'[45] applies to the pattern of co-optation at the local as well as national levels of leadership. The failure of the Auto Workers' union to establish adequate black representation on the international level – despite black majorities in some of the areas in question – suggests that things are considerably worse in unions with a less integrationist tradition.

The research findings, though inconclusive, do show that

union leadership potential and actual leaders are likely to be selected from those favoured by job security and labour-market position within the work force, rather than from 'underdogs' who would not, without union organization, achieve a strong position. As a union secretary put it, 'It's no use getting a good committeeman, next day they make him foreman.' What makes union leaders push for an equalitarian policy, for militant bargaining behaviour – defined as pressing demands beyond what the market position would furnish – is a 'specific socialization' inherent to the union leader's task through the pressure from below,[46] rather than their own experience and interests.

There is a bit more attention, and slightly less consensus, in the research examined about the effects of union government on bargaining behaviour *vis-à-vis* management, on whether a democratic or an autocratic set-up makes for militancy. Clearly, part of the discussion on the Landrum-Griffin Act assumed that stronger internal dissent would weaken unions. This belief backfired, if not in terms of increased union 'strength' but of stepped-up pressure for militancy from dissenting ranks of labour organization.[47] As Benjamin Aaron warned in 1960,

Contrary to assumptions so often expressed by Congress, union members are frequently more radical and irresponsible than their leaders in the conduct of collective bargaining. The attempt to overcome a deficiency of democratic procedures by injecting massive doses of guaranteed new rights may result, for a time, in an increase of a primitive type of democracy, characterized chiefly by the disregard or overthrow of present leaders and the vigorous pursuit of collective bargaining demands formulated by local majorities, without regard to the broader aims of their national organizations. The inevitable result will be more industrial strife.[48]

It seems that the 'fight-for-my-cause' pressure on the leadership, who had long accepted a judicial rather than a political view of grievance handling, gained new momentum to the extent that government authorities assisted in stabilizing collective bargaining relationships.[49]

The case of the printers' union that provided the material for *Union Democracy* suggests that more democratic unions will be more militant in their bargaining, especially for issues so dear to the membership that neither party can afford to let them down. Lipset *et al* view the relationship as mainly shaped by management attitude:

> The more secure a union is in its relationship with management – i.e., the less it is obliged to behave like a military organization – the greater the chance for internal democracy. This does not rule out the possibility that democratic unions may be more militant on the average than oligarchic unions but if they are, it is more the result of internal political pressures than of sustained external challenge from management.[50]

The ideological cleavages between the parties in the ITU are clearly related to collective bargaining issues such as the closed shop and unemployment,[51] and the New York newspaper strike of 1962 has been taken to be the result of this very internal pressure. It involved the bogus rule and other safeguards against technological unemployment: restrictive practices it has become as fashionable for 'labour statesmen' to sell as for the rank-and-file to cling to.[52] The historical evidence as presented in the Printers' case is not pressed too far with the observation that democratic unionism is detrimental by itself to 'responsible' relations to management.[53] Clark Kerr does not concern himself much with the collective bargaining effects of internal democracy in unions. But in at least one case he describes in the *Causes of Industrial Peace* – one of these causes was supposed to be that 'the union is strong, responsible, and democratic'[54] – the union leadership was actually 'discharged' and subsequently replaced as bargaining agent.[55] The issue was indifference to local problems,[56] and the break in the union was made final by a contract rejection by the rank-and-file that defied the joint recommendation of union leadership and management. Kerr did not really fail, however, to notice that the apparent harmony of industrial peace with democratic unionism was 'deceiving'.[57]

He notes:

> It is a sad commentary on industrial relations that the situations which further local democracy and autonomy seem to work against peace . . . Factionalism is often the only vehicle for protest against the incumbents under the one-party system

which characterizes most unions . . . In some of the cases
studied, a reduction of independence has been accompanied
by an increase in peace – a triumph of union-management
fraternity over worker liberty.[58]

But his picture of 'industrial peace' happily wedded to democratic unionism was not spoiled in the last analysis where we find
local autonomy listed under factors favourable to 'peace' even
though 'factionalism' is expelled here.[59]

Similarly, Galenson reports escalation of demands among rival
European unions as part of the competitive arrangement.[60] Only
Holland presents itself as a deviant case:

Since there are three major labour federations, every company
is confronted with three separate grievance agencies, each
representing its membership only. The potentially disastrous
competition that might result from this arrangement is averted
by the fact that the unions do not attempt to outbid one
another.[61]

This seems not to be the rule in rival unionism, and the mutual
escalation hypothesis can be supported, in addition, by what
little experience West Germany had after World War II in this
respect.[62] Another case in point is Ivar Berg's distinction, in a
comment on public reactions to internal rifts in unions, between
purely intra-union struggles between leadership and ranks, and
those which adversely involve the public by labour disputes. One
of the instances[63] is the American Motors-UAW profit-sharing
agreement: a substitute for the short work week then called for
by the union membership in the fierce battles around the 1958
convention, and hailed as a major co-operative 'breakthrough'
in collective bargaining.[64] It was at that time, to the public's outrage, turned down by a notoriously rebellious Wisconsin local.
The one instance of solely intra-union revolt Berg cites, the
Cincinnati milk drivers' disaffiliation from the Teamsters in
1961, may be ambiguous. As *The Wall Street Journal* observed,

in the locals that have deserted, the reasons are fairly clear –
and they do not stem from sudden disenchantment with
Jimmy Hoffa. Mr Luken (President of the Joint Council of
Teamsters in Cincinnati, R.H.) has fought him for years and

has negotiated better contracts for his dairy drivers than Mr Hoffa gets in most of the surrounding territory with his area-wide agreements.[65]

When another small local was cut out of the parent union, bold reference was made to contract negotiations ahead.[66] Maybe, under close enough scrutiny, the 'other kind of union democracy' that 'makes trouble only for union leaders'[67] disappears altogether. At this point, the case touches on the enigmatic issue of militancy or acquiescence in the Teamsters,[68] which can only be discussed by linking their internal government to their organizing policy. Adding to this picture the fact that most of the celebrated cases of union-management co-operation in collective bargaining are ominously associated with undemocratic practices,[69] it seems that we can with good evidence establish an association between union democracy and aggressive relations to management, with high emphasis on job rights and local conditions. A closer examination of the qualifications put forward by authors who essentially agree with this point,[70] indicates that their exceptions detract little from the basic relationship between militancy and democracy. As American 'public' opinion firmly insists on union democracy as a means to achieve industrial peace, harmonious labour-management relations, and so forth, it need not surprise that the liberal defenders of democratic unionism do not stress its incompatibility with those objectives.[71] Problems of 'false' consciousness in terms of class interest, at this level, occur in two types[72] of consensus achievement: by charismatic leadership, and by specific combinations of union government with organizing policies that allow manipulation of the size and composition of the membership . . .

THE POLITICAL IMPLICATIONS OF LABOUR REVOLT

Certain sociological theories have held for a long time that industrial workers' 'apathy' was the result of their integration into a 'middle mass' society,[73] and apathy again the reason why a progressive political role by the working class in the advanced countries of the West was an illusion of the past. Apathy might be defined in this context as a world view focused on off-work rewards, lack of interest in the system which determined the work lives, and social mobility to move away from, rather than political activity to change the work situation. Robert Dubin declared,

> The industrial workers' world is one in which work and the work place are not central life interests for a vast majority,[74]

in short, the 'real world begins after work'; community, not class (nor even job) is the adequate unit of analysis. Apathy might express objective, but no more than latent, alienation.[75] The confrontation between the theories of industrial mass society, apathy, and leisure-orientation (and authoritarian or totalitarian inclinations of the 'middle mass'), and of capitalistic class society, latent protest, alienation in work (and revolutionary potential of the working class)[76] parallel the unfortunate bifurcation between industrial sociology and industrial relations.[77] Industrial relations research, more frequently than industrial sociology, has taken notice of the conflicts in spite of institutionalization, and of the revolts against institutionalization, which key groups of industrial workers actually engaged in – although there was little sediment of intransigence or even of the relevance of industrial conflict, in their reactions to survey questions. One of the tasks the phenomenon of labour revolts points up is the restoration of a unified perspective of industrial relations and industrial sociology. This perspective would contribute to resolve the paradox of in-plant militancy versus integrated consciousness in the American working class: first by focusing on the significance of collective behaviour in contrast to isolated communication for the measurement of class-conflict potential; it would still relate one to the other, but in a less naïve or unilateral way than either discipline did before. Second, it would have to perceive the difference in the results of industrial relations and industrial sociology, on militancy and apathy, in terms of historical changes. The basic lines of such an analysis would recognize that labour unions articulated, formalized, and seized, the protest of a minority – a minority which comprised the segments of the labour force most capable for and advanced towards an active political role. After an initial period in which the authority of management as a class was challenged, organized labour in the post-war economic upswing diverted its militancy (and the appeal of a record of success) towards a policy of wage and consumption goals, and came to adopt the neo-feudalistic employment pattern (permanent, high-paid, long-service core versus temporary, low-paid, casual fringe) – all the same maintaining the form of institutionalized struggle against the employers. The picture of apathy, to the degree it applied to the unionized rank and file at all (and it seems it never buried anti-management challenge at Ford Rouge, or Chrysler's Highland Park, or US Steel at McKeesport, or American Motors in Kenosha), might rather have been the result of conflicting pressures than a consistent phenomenon in its own right: the unionized workers' political energy was diverted towards consumption goals, a form of the wage struggle ever more functional in the new stage of capitalism and hence ever less political; after reaching a point of relative satisfaction,[78] they made the experience that in order to make progress at the level of command over the work place, they had to fight the union (which they still identified as holding their side in labour-management conflict in any issue) either before or along with the company.[79] Labour revolt in the 1960s may have resolved the union-effected stalemate of labour-management conflict, whose social-pathological reflection used to be called 'apathy'. On behalf of organized labour, militant language, official strikes, the ritualistic drama of bargaining tended to further the illusion of an ongoing struggle long after it lost momentum. Battling the union at one time or another, is the tall order facing the revolts; even when overcoming the barrier, they have to retain, not to lose, the gains of the past and bargaining power for the future. The problem is familiar; it shows up in each of our cases above. When asked about referendum elections of international officers, once a hot issue in the steelworkers and now in the UAW, a shop chairman said,

'I don't go for referendum election. I'm totally against it with international representatives, and not with international officers either. This local pumped a lot for referendum, but I began to see it was wrong. Look at the steelworkers: they had a split right at the eve of negotiations. That's insanity. That could elect somebody with no concept, no background, no way to do in office, he wouldn't learn in two years. He has to have experience. And staff, that's especially different. It would result in chaos, no representation at all. I'm for democracy but within a framework to operate. They could elect a sweeper right away.'[80]

Besides and behind any 'working-class authoritarianism' exhibited in this statement, stands the fundamental task not to lose bargaining power, efficiency, and past accomplishments, with which the revolters in labour are saddled. In the McDonnell case, the vexing question of how to wield sufficient power when facing a nationwide corporation as a local all on its own, drove the independent rebel union into the arms of the Teamsters.[81] And I described the painstaking process by which the striking black workers at Second Auto made sure they had no choice but to act without and against the union. When a vote on forming a 'real' picketline was taken, a speaker from the floor stated:

D 13 (to the chairman): 'Listen, we aren't stupid. We may be slow to come over to the big war against industry and society. Bear a while with us. Be patient. Don't blow your cool. We are amateurs, you may be a professional. (D 13 obviously did not know the chairman, who dressed in Afro-garb, was a fellow worker.) We're family supporters . . .'

The need of current militancy to direct itself against the union as well as against management, is a retarding factor in the revolts. A rebellion cannot propose to start something new from scratch; in order not to 'lose' anything it must, in what seems to be a vicious circle, prove as strong *vis-à-vis* management as the union it is challenging. But this need may also be a politicizing element. Traditional 'economic' wage and conditions disputes, are bound to expand towards a specific political dimension when they have to cope, on whatever level, with a restraining labour organization. The reorganization of the working class through rank-and-file movements takes at least the degree of broader social and political consciousness than was necessary at the end of the 1930s for a similar reorganization, the formation of the CIO.[82] The emerging failure to achieve even the 'economic' objectives of American labour under representative union government, 'expert' advice, and top-controlled bargaining – as experienced in the revolts – is producing the insight that labour's goals are incompatible not only with the existing capitalist structure, but most important, with the avenues and mechanisms for change and conflict resolution it provides. These means have effected change, if at all, at an other-determined pace, and with a series of self-defeating trade-offs, the dominating of which was the one between 'rights' and 'benefits', between authority at the place of work and off-work rewards.

Unlike the 1930s, the insight into the futility of immanent change is being promoted in addition by the independently originating insurgencies waged in the black and student communities.[83]

Blacks and students have reminded union members of their own standards as to what are available (if drastic) means of protest. A member of the steering committee in the above-mentioned wildcat stoppage, when a sit-in in the labour-relations office was discussed, commented:

> D 1: 'We've got to kick asses. Look, today, students knock the principal out of the window.'

It is this kind of tactical model and alliance,[84] rather than a horizon of common consciousness, which serves as cement between labour 'revolts' and the black and student movements. The latter's political-cultural consciousness differs principally from the workers', which in the definition of goals – but not in the selection of means nor in the assessment of institutional avenues of change – fails to reach beyond traditional unionism. The impact to the 'technology of revolt', however, should not be discounted as merely superficial: in the labour movement, the problem is rather to rescue the potential of resistance from bureaucratic restraints, than to formulate new demands; to push for militant interest representation 'within the system' by the unions, at a time when expectations of a coherent anti-capitalist policy by the degenerated movement would be illusory. Here, the forms of revolts observed elsewhere obtain a crucial function of provocation and liberation.

A realistic assessment of the 'labour revolts' would have to emphasize their instrumentalist nature. The growth in rank-and-file behaviour adverse to the bureaucracy is most visible in those points – such as union shop de-authorizations, or contract rejections – in which the leadership, based on traditional patterns of identification, demands loyalty while offering meagre rewards.

Its growth in the areas of decertifications and disaffiliations has been slow and essentially dependent on the availability of organizational alternatives. The political strikes (or those which refused to leave the economic battleground for the sake of the prevailing 'patriotic' political consensus) did not centre around issues formulated by labour; they have been reflections within labour of the nationwide unrest. With regard to wildcat (and/or 'unwanted') strikes, the 'plant guerrilla' pattern seems to spread from the vanguard industrial sectors to the rest of the economy, while in the 'old' militant unionized industries, strike activity shifts from union sponsorship and traditional union issues to shopfloor articulation: Thus, it is the more advanced sectors of industry in which the anti-bureaucracy component is gaining along with a sustained high level of anti-management activity. By any standard, the means and ways of the revolts were nowhere considered legitimate by established union government; on the other hand, wherever feasible, they did not leave the ground of the formal rules of collective bargaining, union constitutions, and the legal environment (which on the contrary they use effectively against its intentions). Due to this formal adaptability, as well as to their instrumentalism, successful revolts have in some cases been susceptible to the very same routine and ritualism of collective bargaining they had fought – even though on a higher level. This observation, too, would emphasize the insistence by the revolts on vigorous interest representation by the unions; the revolts appear as indicating organized labour's falling back behind its stated goals, rather than pushing it beyond them. The growth of the 'revolts' in quantitative terms has been less significant than their accumulated appearance in the conflict history of individual unions and (or) industrial plants. This derives not just from the distortions through selective reporting by the mass media,[85] statistical insufficiencies, and the harmonistic preoccupations of academic industrial relations research, but roots in the focus of class struggle in American history: relevant conflicts centre around plants (resp. corporations) and issues of strategic meaning to union policy in economic, technological, and organizational respects. In the tremendous diversity and differentiation of the plant-level conflicts, the inherited racial, ethnic, skill and other splits which were hardly overcome in the process of unionization of the working class, merged with the new process of differentiation by managerial strategies at the work place. Qualitative-historical analyses fit the nature of this process better than do quantitative assessments: the respective methodologies parallel the distinction of class versus parliamentary politics, strikes versus the ballot. It is in these analyses (which necessarily proceed in single case studies with no claims to generalization, but receive limited support from the large-scale data) that the more fruitful explorations into the explanatory factors of the revolts can be pursued. We have found that wage-restraint policies and neglect of working conditions by the union leadership underly the revolt movement: more generally speaking, substantive collusion with the established system by those supposedly bearing the standard of social change.

In historical context, the interpretation of the revolts as instrumentalist and failing to transcend 'pure and simple unionism' would be thoroughly static. It is not by accident that the unions under capitalism are forced to either align with the system or proceed to greater intransigence; in different realms, both the discussion of the constancy of labour's share in national income and our research on stagnation in job-control bargaining point to this dilemma. Enforcement of abstractly 'system-conforming' union goals by the membership today is thus not a step backwards but expresses a more advanced level of the class struggle. Reconsidering the substance and process of the revolts: the growth of the job-autonomy conflict, increasing self-organization of the membership, decentralization of the issues and alternative co-ordination of the procedural weapons, and the intrinsic combination of anti-bureaucratic and anti-management struggle, imply a clearer focused power antagonism in industry; most of all, with the belief in the unions as a recognized avenue of gradual change, the prevailing ideology of quasi-automatic progress in society without changing power relations is threatened.

Even in this interpretation, it is not suggested that a revolutionary potential would unfold from the labour revolts, unless the country's militancy and economic power in the context of its imperialist world position is dealt a defeat serious enough to remove the heaviest mitigating and integrating impact on the internal contradictions of interest in the class structure. What the revolts do indicate, however, is that there are domestic forces along the reshaped lines of 'institutionalized' class conflict which might well be expected to unleash in such a situation what now simmers as conflictual background resources under precarious containment. The time when it was fashionable to write off American organized labour wholesale, as a conservative, stabilizing force in society,[86] is past . . .

GLOSSARY

AER	American Economic Review
AFL–CIO	American Federation of Labor–Congress of Industrial Organizations
AJS	American Journal of Sociology
CUF	Columbia University Forum
HBR	Harvard Business Review
HLR	Harvard Law Review
IBT	International Brotherhood of Teamsters
ILIR	Institute of Labor and Industrial Relations
ILRR	Industrial and Labor Relations Review
IR	Industrial Relations
ISJ	International Socialist Journal
LLJ	Labour Law Journal
MLR	Monthly Labour Review
MR	Monthly Review
Proceedings NYU . . . ACL	Proceedings of the New York University Annual Conference on Labor
SP	Social Problems
WSJ	Wall Street Journal

NOTES

1. HERBERT MARCUSE. *One Dimensional Man*, London: Routledge, 1964, p. 21.

2. PAUL A. BARAN, PAUL M. SWEEZY, *Monopoly capital: An essay on the American economic and social order*, New York, London: MR Press, 1966, pp. 263f.

3. BARAN, SWEEZY, *Monopoly capital*, pp. 261, 264.

4. This does not necessarily pertain to privileged strata only: for

instance, negro workers in the South got their first chances of promotional mobility through segregated seniority units, as reported in F. RAY MARSHALL, *The negro and organized labor*, New York, etc.: Wiley, 1965, p. 146.

5. MARCUSE, *One Dimensional Man*, p. 19.

6. SEYMOUR MARTIN LIPSET, 'The political process in trade unions: A theoretical statement', in WALTER GALENSON and S. M. L., *Labor and Trade Unionism: An Interdisciplinary Reader*, New York, London: Wiley, 1960, p. 217.

7. E. BAKKE, *Mutual Survival*, p. 3 and *passim*. Hamden, Conn., 1946.

8. BARAN, SWEEZY, *Monopoly Capital*, p. 77.

9. See S. H. SLICHTER *et al.*, *The Impact of Collective Bargaining on Management*, Brookings, 1960, pp. 37, 41 on long-range effects; the entire argument of BARAN, SWEEZY, *Monopoly Capital*, on the relationship between internal and external surplus realization: 'Labor looks at labor: A conversation. Some members of the United Auto Workers undertake a self-examination', (Santa Barbara, Cal.) Center for the study of democratic institutions, 1963, p. 21, on the anticipated employment effect of disarmament.

10. The basic underlying argument is, of course, by no means confined to Marxist social scientists: see e.g., ABBA P. LERNER, *Economics of Employment*, New York, etc.: McGraw-Hill, 1951, p. 201.

11. STANLEY WEIR, 'A new area of labor revolt: On the job vs official unions', Berkeley, Cal.: Independent Socialist Club, 1965 (mim.), p. 22. (See also S. W. ,'U.S.A.: The labor revolt,' *ISJ*, yr. 4, no. 20, April 1967; no. 21, June 1967.)

12. FRIEDRICH ENGELS, *Die Lage der arbeitenden Klasse in England*, (1892), Berlin, 1952, p. 436.

13. The crucial threshold between 'upper-level' bureaucracy and 'shopfloor' organization may well be located within the local union itself.

14. On leverage techniques applied by strategically favoured working groups in the rubber industry, of JAMES W. KUHN, *Bargaining in Grievance Settlement*, New York, London: Columbia University Press, 1961, p. 153.

15. On the political advantage (veto power) that skilled workers were able to secure from their labour market position, see WEIR, op. cit., 'U.S.A.', *ISJ*, pp. 201 f.

16. A valuable discussion, though unconcerned about broader theoretical perspectives, is provided in SEYMOUR MELMAN, *Decision-making and Productivity*, Oxford: Blackwell, 1958, p. 182. Reporting on a major showdown between management and a militant work force in Coventry, Melman advises the British workers, who in an ideological commitment, took the stand that management should be prevented from conducting any layoffs, they had better adopt seniority

rules so that layoffs could be conducted in an orderly manner and hardships were avoided. Cf. also the discussion of seniority rules in MILTON DERBER, 'Labor-management relations at the plant level under industry-wide bargaining: A study on the engineering (metal-working) industry in Birmingham, England' (Champaign, Ill.), ILIR, University of Illinois, 1955.

17. Cf. WEIR, 'New era': his 'U.S.A.', *ISJ*: some *MR* contributions, e.g., 'The steel strike in perspective', 11/10, Feb. 1960, pp. 353–62.

18. Cf. GEORGES FRIEDMAN, *Le travail en miettes* (1961), (Paris), Gallimard, rev. 1964; A. R. N. MARKS, 'An investigation of modifications of job design in an industrial situation and their effects on some measure of economic productivity', Berkeley: UC 1954 (Ph.D. Diss.); C. R. WALKER, 'Experience at IBM Corporation', in his *Modern Technology and Civilisation*, 1962, pp. 119–27.

19. Cf. MELMAN, *Decision-making*: E. L. TRIST, G. W. HIGGIN, H. MURRAY, A. B. POLLOCK, *Organizational Choice*, London: Tavistock, 1963, on the group system at the coal face. RAY COLLING, 'Abteilungssystem und Arbeiterkontrolle: Kritik,' *AH*, nos. 6–8, April 25 1965, challenges 'democratic self-regulation' of work groups under incentives as futile.

20. *Labor Looks*, pp. 14f., 20. See also TOPHAM, 'Implications of package deals in British Collective Bargaining', *ISJ*, 1/5–6, 1964, pp. 520–41.

21. ROBERT DUBIN, 'Industrial workers' worlds: A study of the "central life interests" of industrial workers', *SP*, 3/3 Jan. 1956, pp. 140f.; cf. ROBERT BLAUNER, 'Alienation in work: The diversity of industrial environment', (Berkeley, Cal.), *UC*, 1962 (Diss.), ch. VI.

22. D. BELL, 'Two roads from Marx', in his *End of Ideology*, Free Press, 1960, p. 367. It must be noted that the territory of self-government on the job undergoes a significant change as it is transferred from socialist ideas of the type G. D. H. COLE advocated (cf. his *Introduction to Trade Unionism* (1918), London: Allen & Unwin, 1924 p. 232) to his view: while in both cases, transformation of society is thought to start 'from below', Cole aimed at more efficient utilization of the means of production through workers' control.

23. CLARK KERR, JOHN T. DUNLOP, FREDERICK HARBISON, CHARLES A. MYERS, 'Industrialism and world society', *HBR*, 39/1, Jan.–Feb. 1961, pp. 125f.

24. Cf. R. BENDIX's discussion of the American system, in his *Work and Authority in Industry*, Wiley, 1958, pp. 339f.

25. For the motives, cf., THEODORE J. ST ANTOINE, LANDRUM-GRIFFIN, 1965–66: 'A calculus of democratic values', *Proceedings NYU 19th ACL*, 1967, pp. 35ff.: 'The main push in congress ... came from a conservative coalition ... concerned with blunting the effectiveness of labor organizations.'

26. Cf., JACK STIEBER, WALTER E. OBERER, MICHAEL HARRING-TON, 'Democracy and public reviews', Santa Barbara: Center for the study of democratic institutions, 1960, and 'Drumhead trials or public review?', *Union Democracy in Action*, no. 12, May 1964, pp. 1–7, for the debate on internal vs. external enforcement of members' rights. A vice president of a steel company, in contrast, should be quoted for his ostensible belief in the law at the individual's disposal: 'The individual worker can go to arbitration all on his own, whatever crackpot he is, if he isn't satisfied with the union.' (Interview, Sept. 1968, Pennsylvania.)

27. Cf. BENJAMIN B. NAUMHOFF, 'Landrum-Griffin and the regulation of internal union affairs', *LLJ*, 18/7, July 1967, pp. 394f.; and SEYMOUR MARTIN LIPSET, 'The law and trade union democracy', *Virginia Law Review*, 47/1, Jan. 1961, pp. 47f.

28. HENRY ANDERSON, 'To build a union', quoted in 'Farm workers', *Union Democracy*, no. 6, May 1962, p. 1.

29. Cf. JAMES KUHN, IVAR BERG, 'The trouble with labor is "feather-bedding"', *CUF*, 3/2, Spring 1960, p. 25, and HERBERT R. NORTHRUP, GORDON R. STORHOLM, *Restrictive Practices in the Supermarket Industry*, Philadelphia: University of Pennsylvania Press, 1967, on management's reluctance to 'bargain' over these practices in the same way as over wages and hours, etc.

30. Cf. 'The effect of plant size on industrial relations practices', *MLR*, 78/5, May 1955, pp. 555f.; and PHILIP SELZNICK'S 'Survey of the extent of formalized employee rights in nonunion plants', in his *Foundation of Managerial Self-Restraint*, Berkeley, Cal.: 1968 (mim.), pp. 14–24, for the scale of adjustments to union procedures lowest, unless purely unilaterally administered.

31. For a gallery of fame of such 'common interest' deals in recent years, see BENJAMIN J. TAYLOR, FRED WITNEY, 'Unionism in the American society', *LLJ*, 18/5, May 1967, pp. 307f.

32. See STANLEY WEIR, 'New era', p. 9.

33. Cf. DUNCAN S. GRAY, 'The effect of unemployment upon union policies' Berkeley, Cal.: UC, 1950 (M.A. THESIS), pp. 83–7. For membership statistics, however, the mine workers count 'exonerated' members with those in good standing.

34. This anticipates an objection to the government model of union democracy. Public governments, in contrast to private ones, cannot normally manipulate the boundaries of the constituencies with which they have to achieve consensus.

35. See, for instance, BENJAMIN AARON, 'Unions and civil liberties: Claims vs. performance', *Northwestern University Law Review*, 53/1, March–April, 1958; BENJAMIN AARON, MICHAEL I. KOMAROFF, 'Statutory regulations of internal union affairs I',

Illinois Law Review, 44/4, Sept.–Oct. 1949, p. 464; MARSHALL, *Negro*.

36. The Reuther-led Industrial union department of the AFL–CIO put out a pamphlet, *The Southern Labor Story*, in 1958, on organizing in the South. It never even mentions black workers, nor does a Negro show up in its prolific illustrations. (Washington, DC, Publication No. 25.)

37. It is exclusively for the sake of the unions dealing with management that we discuss union democracy and organizing policies in this chapter, not for the internal life of the union itself (as an occupational community, for instance), or formally described private interests of individual members, as isolated from collective interests.

38. SEYMOUR MARTIN LIPSET, MARTIN A. TROW, JAMES S. COLEMAN, *Union Democracy* (1956), Garden City, NY: Doubleday, 1962, pp. 328 ff.

39. LIPSET *et al.*, *Union Democracy*, p. 1.

40. LIPSET *et al.*, *Union Democracy*, in the leadership profiles, pp. 234–60.

41. ARNOLD S. TANNENBAUM, ROBERT L. KAHN, *Participation in Union Locals*, Evanston, Ill.: Row, Peterson, 1958, p. 98.

42. Rather than being an 'objective' criterion, seniority can be made to reflect the power relationships within the union, for instance, by rigging seniority units. The Civil Rights Act of 1964 has shed light on racial discrimination as exercised through 'appropriate' seniority units.

43. TANNENBAUM, KAHN, *Participation*, p. 104.

44. Cf. STEIBER, *Governing*; MURIEL LEOLA BEACH, 'The problems of the skilled worker in an industrial union: The United Automobile, Aircraft and Agricultural Implement Workers of America (UAW) (AFL–CIO) Case', Ithaca, NY: Graduate School, Cornell University, 1959 (M.A. Thesis), p. 75: 'What's next for labor?' *News*, 2/17, 30 April 1957, pp. 1, 18 on the resentment by production workers. J. STEIBER, *Governing the UAW*, Wiley, 1962.

45. WILLIAM KORNHAUSER, 'The Negro union official: A study of sponsorship and control', *AJS*, 57/5, March 1952.

46. Cf. JOHN R. COLEMAN, 'The compulsive pressures of democracy in unionism' (1956), in GALENSON, LIPSET, eds., *Labor*; L. R. SAYLES and G. STRAUSS, 'Conflicts within the local union', *HBR*, 1952; SIDNEY M. PECK, *The Rank-and-File Leader*, New Haven, Conn.: College & University Press, 1963.

47. ORLEY ASHENFELTER and GEORGE JOHNSON have shown some influence of Landrum-Griffin on strike activity statistically, in their 'Bargaining theory, Trade unions, and industrial strike activity', *AER*, forthcoming.

48. B. AARON, 'Labor-management reporting and disclosure Act

1959', *HLR*, 1960, p. 906.

49. Cf. the doctrine of 'exhaustion of internal remedies' before filing a lawsuit against the union, as espoused by the courts in recent years.

50. *Union Democracy*, p. 465.

51. *Union Democracy*, pp. 339 ff.

52. Cf. TAYLOR, WITNEY, op. cit., *LLJ*, and PAUL JACOBS, 'Union democracy and the public good: Do they necessarily coincide?' (1958), in his *State of the Unions*, Atheneum, 1963, pp. 137, 139, 147.

53. See also LIPSET, 'Political process', in GALENSON, LIPSET, eds., op. cit., p. 217: 'There is a basic conflict between democratic unionism and "responsible" unionism, which many conservatives and business leaders do not recognize, at least in their public pronouncements.'

54. CHARLES A. MYERS, 'Conclusions and implications', in Golden, Parker, *Causes of Industrial Peace under Collective Bargaining*, Harper, 1965, pp. 46–54.

55. Cf. PAUL L. KLEINSORGE, WILLIAM C. KIRBY, 'The pulp and paper rebellion: A new pacific coast union', *IR*, 6/1, Oct. 1966; HAROLD M. LEVINSON, *Determining Forces in Collective Wage Bargaining*. New York, etc.: John Wiley, 1966, ch. 3: *The Northwest Lumber and Pulp and Paper Industries*, especially p. 94; HERBERT R. NORTHRUP, HARVEY A. YOUNG, 'The causes of industrial peace revisited', *ILRR*, 22/1, Oct. 1968, pp. 33–5, 43–6.

56. NORTHRUP, YOUNG, 'Causes', *ILRR*, p. 34.

57. LEVINSON, *Determining*, p. 94.

58. 'Industrial peace', in C. KERR, *Labor and Management in Industrial Society*, 1964, p. 161.

59. KERR, op. cit., pp. 165 f.

60. GALENSON, *Trade Union Democracy in Western Europe*, UCP, 1962, pp. 25, 29.

61. *Trade Union Democracy*, p. 23 – Disastrous for whom?

62. In the late 1950s, for example, the Christian mine workers demanded the 35-hour work week, while the supposedly socialist-dominated industrial miners' union stuck with the 40-hour week.

63. 'The nice kind of union democracy', *CUF*, 5/2, Spring 1962, pp. 18, 20 f.

64. TAYLOR, WITNEY, 'Unionism', *LLJ*.

65. ROSCOE BORN, 'Teamster defections', *WSJ*, 1 Sept. 1961, p. 4.

66. 'Cincinnati Teamsters' revolt gains momentum. More men seek split', *WSJ*, 25 Sept. 1961, p. 4; see also 'Cincinnati locals plan to bolt Teamsters, Join AFL-CIO; No mass revolt predicted', *WSJ*, 17 Aug. 1961, p. 4; 'Four Cincinnati locals leave Teamsters union; Two join AFL-CIO', *WSJ*, 18 Aug. 1961, p. 8; 'Hoffa to debate revolt of Cincinnati Teamsters with dissident leader', *WSJ*, 22 Aug. 1961, p. 5.

67. I. BERG, *Nice Kind of Union Democracy*, p. 18.

68. Of the literature, PAUL JACOBS: 'The world of Jimmy Hoffa' (1957), in his *State*, pp. 17 ff.; also 'The world of Jimmy Hoffa' (2), and 'The respectable Mr Hoffa' (1962)), accepts collusion with employers as an 'extracurricular' rather than intrinsic activity of Hoffa's rule, and so do ROMER (*IBT*) and the JAMESES (RALPH C. and ESTELLE DINERSTEIN JAMES, *Hoffa and the Teamsters*, Princeton, NJ: Nostrand, 1965). On the other side of the argument, we may enlist ROBERT F. KENNEDY (*The Enemy Within*, New York, Evanston, Ill.: Harper & Row, 1960) and STANLEY WEIR ('New era') for the version that Hoffa actually failed to gain the best possible conditions for the membership. ROBERT D. LEITER (*The Teamsters Union*, New York, Bookman, 1957) views both aggressiveness and collusion as spectacular by-products of the process of rationalization and concentration in the trucking industry (p. 267).

69. 'Jammed down the members' throats', in a variety of ways from defiance of convention programmes to rigging elections and breaking pertinent laws were, among others: the American Motors–UAW profit-sharing plan, the Kaiser-Steelworkers long-range sharing plan, the human relations (research) committee in steel, and the Pacific Maritime Association-ILWU mechanization and modernization plan.

70. Cf. the case documentation in LIPSET et al.'s *Union Democracy*, op. cit., and KAHN and TANNENBAUM'S *Participation*, rather than their generalizations.

71. H. W. BENSON's paper, 'Union democracy in action', is a case in point: wherever his reports and comments give the full background or allow a follow-up of violations of democratic principles in unions, complacency of a bureaucratic leadership in its relations to management was almost invariably the issue, but hardly ever spelled out.

72. Aside from the inherent contradictions in some job-control devices such as seniority.

73. For a very pointed statement of this view, see HAROLD L. WILENSKY, 'Class, class consciousness and American workers', in WILLIAM HABER, ed., *Labor in a Changing America*, New York, Basic, 1966, pp. 12–44, especially pp. 34f., 42ff.; also WILENSKY, LEBEAUX, *Industrial Society and Social Welfare*, 1958, pp. 106–14.

74. 'Industrial workers' worlds: A study of the "central life interests" of industrial workers', *SP*, 3/3, Jan. 1956, p. 140.

75. Cf., DAVID RIESMANN's 'Introduction to Chinoy', *Automobile Workers and the American Dream*, Doubleday, 1955, p. xif.

76. Cf. the presentation by HALLOWELL POPE in his 'Economic deprivation and social integration in a group of "middle class" factory workers', Ann Arbor, Mich.: University microfilms (1963), pp. 2–15. See also HARVEY SWADOS, 'Work as a public issue', *Saturday Review*, 12 Dec. 1959 p. 15, for the 'intra-liberal' controversy.

77. Cf. the profile neurosis of 'industrial relations' as an academic discipline; HENRY A. LANDSBERGER, 'The behavioral sciences in industry', *IR*, 7/1, Oct. 1967, p. 9; WILLIAM FOOTE WHYTE, 'A field in search of a focus', *ILRR*, 18/3, April 1965, pp. 306, 316.

78. 'Relative' is meant in comparison to other than wage goals, not to other wage levels: in fact, we have suggested that wage demands in the form of (perhaps even deliberate) inequities rank on a par with working conditions in recent years' revolts.

79. Cf. J. C. LEGGETT, *Class, Race and Labor*, New York, OUP, 1968, p. 149.

80. Interview, NY Ass. Feb. 1969.

81. Cf. A *WSJ* staff reporter, 'Teamsters, UAW join union representation dispute at McDonnell', *WSJ*, 12 Aug. 1968.

82. Cf. ART PREIS, *Labor's Giant Step*, New York: Pioneer, 1964, p. XVI.

83. For both black and students' revolts, however, reflecting the more archaic nature of domination in their realms, means of channelling have been recommended which more or less copy the procedures of collective bargaining: cf. IRVING BERNSTEIN, 'A comparison: Industrial conflict in the thirties and race conflict in the sixties', *Proceedings*, *IRRA*, Spring 1967, p. 20: 'The organizations that dominated the racial conflict of the past decade – CORE, SNCC, SCLC – presently face a crisis of identity. They risk collapse because they have developed no correlative to collective bargaining.' Cf. on students, M. PATRICIA GOLDEN, NED A. ROSEN, 'Student attitudes toward participation in university administration: An empirical study related to managerial prerogatives', *The Journal of College Student Personnel*, Nov. 1966, p. 329: 'Students, like employees in industry, are a force to be reckoned with . . . As Chamberlain said in relation to industry, "organizational procedures must be provided to resolve differences which threaten the integrity of the . . . unit". At the same time, of course, students must acknowledge the proper role of "managerial prerogatives".'

84. The 'translation' of political issues into classical labour grievances, for which strike support can be elicited, has been a frequent phenomenon on the campuses. At one point of the 1967/68 anti-war demonstrations in Berkeley, the campus AFT chapter turned the battle against political suspensions into the established grievances: no on-the-job punishment for off-the-job offences – since one of the student leaders happened to be a unionized teaching assistant. They received the support not only of all campus unions, including blue-collar, but of the County labor council and the building trades as well, who vowed to honour the AFT's picket lines (cf. BARBARA COWAN, 'Labor council sanctions campus AFL-CIO strike', *The Daily Californian*, 197/29, 13 Feb. 1968, p. 1).

85. Cf. *Union Democracy in Action*'s recurring frustrated attempts to obtain press coverage for some of the most savage suppressions of intra-union revolt, such as the murders in the Californian painters' union (nos. 19–24, April 1966–Feb. 1967) and the election frauds in the National Maritime Union (no. 32, Aug. 1968).

86. See for instance, WILENSKY, LEBEAUX, op. cit., p. 107. SLICHTER *et al.*, op. cit., p. 960.

Part Five
Unions and Contemporary Capitalism

The problems caused by advanced capitalism, to which unions have to respond, are world-wide: inflation and unemployment, in particular, beset all capitalist economies. But in Britain unions are also confronted by the specific weaknesses of the British economy due to the low level of industrial investment provided by multi-national companies which prefer to export their capital abroad. These same companies, together with the traditional, domestic and foreign, capitalist financial institutions, create the economic framework within which governments decide their economic policies: in this context, the major aim of government intervention in the British economy has been simple – to suppress working-class militancy and to maintain a cheap labour economy in order to bolster inefficient British capitalism.[1] In this endeavour governments have a wide choice of options as, 'Capitalism contains an armoury of measures to combat labour's attempts to reduce the rate of exploitation: speed up, "productivity deals", intensification of labour, inflation, tax increases, welfare cuts, etc. It is thus not surprising that capitalism can maintain the rate of exploitation even where trade unions are strong.'[2]

In recent years two methods of containing union militancy have proved central: the use of legal restrictions and incomes policies. The attempt to systematically impose legal sanctions on trade union activities and statutory limitations on pay was pioneered by the Labour Governments of 1964–70. The failure of these policies in the face of mass working-class resistance did not deter the following Conservative Government from attempting to impose even more draconian measures in the Industrial Relations Act of 1971, and the incomes policy of 1972–74. But the effort to rigidly curtail strike action and tightly control incomes had the effect of replacing small local stoppages with large national ones in an explosion of militancy in the early 1970s as many groups of workers expressed dissent with government policy for the first time. Finally, the miners' strike of 1974 brought the accession of a Labour Government who rejected legal compulsion – not because it had proved so demonstrably unsuccessful – but because, with inflation *and* unemployment both reaching post-war peaks, the law was superfluous in the short term as a tool of repression of working-class shopfloor or wage militancy. Instead, the government assumed a policy of collaboration with trade union leaders, procuring their voluntary compliance to policies they had rejected when imposed by statute by the previous government. Thus the 'social contract' entailed a significant cut in real wages for most organized workers in 1975 and 1976. Meanwhile threats of redundancy and short-time working were liberally used and frequently implemented by government and employers in a concerted drive to reduce manning levels, increase labour mobility and raise productivity.

Partly as a reward for the voluntary exercise of a stabilizing function by the trade unions, Labour passed a substantial body of legislation supportive of trade unionism, for example the Trade Union and Labour Relations Act of 1974, and the amendments of 1976, encouraged the development of the post-entry closed shop throughout industry. However, the intention of the legislation was in the short-term to defuse industrial relations after the widespread disruption caused by the Industrial Relations Act, and in the long-term the aim was to stimulate the further development of bureaucratic trade union structures, with union officialdom assuming an increasingly collaborative role with government and employers. As Hyman has pointed out: 'The legislation of unions may in itself mute some of the radicalism associated with their former "outlaw" status . . . Conceding terms which consolidated a union's membership and reinforce its organizational security may involve little direct cost to the employer; but such concessions may be traded against more material improvements in workers' conditions, and more crucially they are usually dependent on the adoption of conciliatory and accommodative policies on the part of the union.'[3] The success of this incorporative strategy of the Labour Government was indicated by the union leaders' acceptance in Autumn 1976 of further public expenditure cuts despite the already unprecedented level of unemployment; and, furthermore, the eagerness with which the TUC general council themselves suppressed the seamen's strike declared in September, which threatened to release the floodgates of shopfloor workers' opposition to the social contract which was cutting so savagely into their standard of living.[4]

Given this new context of the interpenetration of the state and monopoly capitalism, and the determined attempt to incorporate trade union leaders into this monolithic control structure, it is important to ask once again, in the readings in the final section, central theoretical questions on the role of modern unionism. What is the relationship between unions and contemporary capitalism: are unions still capable of articulating opposition to the power of capital, or are they now primarily a means of incorporating working-class resistance? Secondly, if unions are still an opposition force, what strategies should unions adopt in pursuit of workers' power; what is the unions' relationship to the socialist political party – and what is the role of the revolutionary party in this struggle? Finally, to what extent in current conditions does trade union activity inspire or deflect socialist consciousness?

In the first reading Mann explores critically the split in the working-class movement between industrial action and political action, and the role of the dominant ideology of capitalism in enforcing this artificial distinction. Within the industrial sphere, the narrowing down of conflict to aggressive economism and defensive job control removes any threat to the existing structure of industry, indeed the economistic orientation of conventional trade unionism actually *weakens* class consciousness Mann contends. However, consideration of the extent to which economism has successfully permeated the labour movement should be qualified by the fact that, 'In Britain it took two hundred years of conflict to subdue the working people to the discipline of direct economic stimuli, and the subjugation has never been more than partial.'[5] Hence, in Mann's analysis of the 'explosion of consciousness' he indicates that at times of intense industrial conflict, a frequently noted phenomenon is how workers reject the blind acceptance of their condition as wage labour usually prevalent, and, in an abrupt transformation of their consciousness may reject individual calculation, and come to accept collectivism as an end in itself. Yet workers rarely grasp fully the alternative socialist ideology necessary to create an alternative society, and Mann identifies this impasse as 'a crucial watershed in contemporary class consciousness'. Furthermore, as experienced in Europe recently, the problem is compounded when, having attained revolutionary consciousness, workers' action is rendered ineffectual by the compromising institutions of the labour movement.

Examining further some of the critical issues Mann has raised, Clements, in the second reading, argues that whereas trade union consciousness manifests the perceptual limitations of the trade union movement, workers do have the ability to transcend the confines of their own experience. He suggests that it is useful to analytically separate trade union consciousness at the macro- and micro-levels of union activity, and that rank-and-file militancy in terms of aggressive wage policy and job control can have immensely disruptive effects upon capitalism. The paper concludes with the paradox that economism, traditionally regarded as the major force binding trade unions to capitalism, can, in certain circumstances, disrupt this relationship. This contradiction may provide a basis for the expansion of workers' consciousness, an essential forerunner to radical social change.

The classic article by Anderson, which examines the place of unions in the socialist movement, is a polemical *tour de force*. Firstly, Anderson demarcates the structural limitations of unionism: trade unions are part of capitalist society, and reflect the division between capitalists and workers, but, 'As institutions, trade unions do not *challenge* the existence of a society based on a division of classes, they merely *express* it.' The corollary of this is that trade unions are shaped and organized in accordance with the contours of capitalist industry: therefore trade union action, consciousness and power all fall short of the positive socialist movement necessary to transform the existing structure. Only a revolutionary party, Anderson asserts, can overthrow capitalism. Paradoxically, however, in some Western countries the traditional parties of the left have become committed to the status quo, leaving trade unions as the sole representative of working-class interests; for in contrast to political parties which are consciously nurtured, trade unions arise spontaneously out of the economic system, and are therefore less easily suppressed. Hence to maintain minimal economic defences against the inroads of capitalism, and as the harbour of working-class consciousness (as distinct from socialist consciousness), trade unions are vital.

Investigating another possible avenue of social change, it is unlikely that acceptance of the need for 'industrial democracy', the most recently proposed panacea for the reform of industrial relations, will prove a path to a socialist society. In a radical critique of the pluralist approach to industrial democracy, Clarke claims that basic misconceptions of the nature and distribution of power and ideology in society have led to the acceptance by the labour movement of proposals likely to have the opposite of their intended effect. That is, most schemes for industrial democracy will involve an absorption of workers into capitalist forms of control, not a transcending of these control structures. The introduction of greater democracy into industry is only possible as part of an independent and sustained campaign against the power of the representatives of capital, not by trade unionists becoming voluntary agents of that power.

In the final reading of the book, Hyman offers a critique of the major socialist analyses of trade unionism. He argues that many critics of trade unionism have assumed a one-sided approach, failing to recognize countervailing tendencies in unionism to the processes of integration, oligarchy and incorporation. Theories of such processes were valid in the specific historical circumstances from which they derive, but there is no inevitability in their application to all historical and structural situations. Thus the present activities of unions, particularly at the shopfloor level, do create instability for capitalism, though workers may not always intend this; moreover the struggle for reforms which are unrealizable within a capitalist context may promote an awareness of the limitations of the existing system. Even Lenin, the severest critic of 'spontaneity' in *What Is To Be Done?* revealed in both his earlier and later writings an appreciation of the role of trade union economic struggles in developing socialist consciousness. The Italian revolutionary, Gramsci, displayed an acute sensitivity to this paradox of unionism: on the one hand recognizing how the union subordinates workers to capitalism, but on the other how the union 'imprints on the industrial apparatus a communistic form'. For Gramsci, the influence of the workers' Factory Councils upon the union was vital – 'a reagent dissolving its bureaucratism'. Hyman concludes that unions are capable of articulating both economic and political conflict given suitable structural conditions: 'the limits of trade union consciousness can vary markedly between different historical contexts and can shift radically with only a brief passage of time.' That is, the future of unions under capitalism can only be decided in the course of the class struggle itself.[6]

NOTES

1. To the extent that competition lies in third world countries – in which multi-national companies are increasingly investing if the regime is repressive enough – rather than the West, wage rates would have to be depressed in Britain to a fraction of their present levels to be competitive.

2. R. BLACKBURN, 'The New Capitalism', in R. BLACKBURN (ed.), *Ideology in Social Science*, Fontana, 1972, pp. 84–5.

3. R. HYMAN, 'Industrial Relations: A Marxist Introduction', op. cit., pp. 89–90.

4. *Financial Times*, 10 September, 1976.

5. E. P. THOMPSON, 'The Peculiarities of the English', *Socialist Register*, 1965, p. 354.

6. The central problem of the position of trade unions in socialist society would consume another lengthy study. Certainly it is crucial to the democratic development of socialism that the working-class maintain independent organizations which may defend their interests and expand their freedom. The existing states of Russia and Eastern Europe do not permit this, and the bureaucratic authoritarianism they uphold conforms to a 'state capitalist' model: therefore much of the analysis contained here on the significance of working-class struggle is directly relevant. The immediate problems encountered in the relationship between the working-class, the Factory Councils, and the Bolshevik Party in Russia during the crucial years of 1917–18 are analysed in C. Goodey, 'Factory Committees and the Dictatorship of the Proletariat (1918)', *Critique* 3, 1974. The development of the great trade union debate in 1921 is presented in I. Deutscher, 'Soviet Trade Unions', 1950. At the present time, the struggle of the rank and file continues, however clandestinely, in the East European countries, directed against similar problems to those faced by the working-class of the West: rising food prices; controlled wages; the reintroduction of unemployment as an instrument of labour discipline; the intensification of work and assembly line production. For example, see M. Holubenko, 'The Soviet Working Class: Discontent and Opposition', *Critique* 4, 1975. Also see R. Blackburn, 'Revolution and Class Struggle', Fontana, 1977.

16 Industrial Relations in Advanced Capitalism and the Explosion of Consciousness

Michael Mann

Reprinted with permission from *Consciousness and Action Among the Western Working Class*, Macmillan, 1973, pp. 19–23, 45–54.

INDUSTRIAL RELATIONS IN ADVANCED CAPITALISM

The values of the countries with which I am dealing remain today identifiably capitalist to the extent that they remain committed to a liberal market view of ethics and society. According to this view, freedom and justice are best secured by 'breaking down' man's needs and activities into separate segments (work, consumption, politics, etc.) and providing each one with a separate market in which individuals can express their preferences and realize their needs. It is therefore anti-totalitarian in the fullest sense, opposed to any attempt to realize total human values in a unified way. As Max Weber observed, capitalist society is relatively unethical and 'disenchanted' – the realization of substantive, ethical aims is a byproduct of individuals and institutions pursuing their separate interests in a formally rational way, and is not actually embodied in social structure itself. What is meant by 'the end of ideology', therefore, is the acceptance by the mass of the people of this instrumental and segmented structure. Industrial or political behaviour is characterized by the separation of each sector, and implicit (though probably non-normative) acceptance of 'the laws of the market' regulating each sector. This is what I shall term the ideology of *hegemonic capitalism*.

Marxists are well aware that the segmentation of life in capitalist society constitutes an obstacle to the realization of class consciousness. For the latter to develop, the worker must make 'connections' between his work and his family life and between his industrial and his political activity. This is assumed to be guaranteed by the centrality of work: alienation and exploitation at work will spill over into non-work spheres and unify the worker's existence. Yet at first sight the reverse might seem true today: that the worker's non-work life *compensates for* work alienation. Indeed, I shall argue that in several ways the worker's experience does not form the totality suggested by either 'end of ideology' theorists or Marxists. Several segmentations – between work and non-work, between industrial and political action, between the economic and social aspects of industrial action itself – give to class relations in contemporary capitalism their peculiarly unstable nature, their paradoxical character of unresolved and unresolvable dialectic. I shall start by examining the nature of industrial action in the West, concentrating for the moment on evidence from Britain and the United States, though, as we shall see, much of my analysis applies to all countries.

If workers possessed full class consciousness they would seek among their other goals worker control of industry and society. Such a form of control would in theory enable them to attain both material and moral fulfilment, economic sufficiency and freedom of self-expression. But very few important working-class movements have pursued this all-embracing goal with any conviction. Instead, industrial action has generally split off from political action, and industrial action itself has split into two subordinate and separate spheres: the economic and the job control spheres. By job control, I mean issues arising out of the worker's attempts to attain a measure of creativity and control within the given work process surrounding him. The type of trade union action which corresponds to this sphere is usually termed job regulation, for it seeks to establish rules which enable the worker to exert control over the work area agreed with management to be 'his'. It is to be distinguished from economism (or instrumentalism) oriented to the pursuit of financial improvements, again within the existing structure of industry. Neither challenges the overall class structure, though both may be militant in pursuit of their goals. Furthermore, job regulation is essentially conservative – it seeks to establish *de jure* what has already occurred *de facto*, namely that workers in their relations with shopfloor management are able, informally and surreptitiously, to increase the scope of their activities by being in physical possession of the shopfloor. It is very rarely that a trade union action is oriented towards an increase in *actual* job control, and this distinguishes job regulation from instrumental demands. Why should the former be a defensive activity while the latter may be aggressive?

The principal reason for the difference is that, whereas economic rewards in the capitalist enterprise can be *collective*, job creativity–control rewards are largely *distributive*. The economic interests of rival parties can in principle be served by increasing the total reward available for share-out by collective co-operation. By contrast, there tends to be a fixed amount of work control available for distribution, and for one party to increase control the other must necessarily lose some of *its* control. It is evidently easier to obtain a working so.ution to conflict on the former than on the latter issue. There will usually be pressures on the rival parties, exerted by their economic exigencies, to make separate settlements of their immediate clash of economic interests independently of the general state of their confrontation. Obviously this process depends on the ability of capitalism to generate increased wealth, but in the past this has been sufficiently demonstrated to render economic compromise an acceptable alternative to prolonged confrontation.

What we call the *institutionalization of industrial conflict* is nothing more nor less than the narrowing down of conflict to aggressive economism and defensive control. This has been taken to its furthest point by contemporary American trade unions, but it is the dominant strategy of all long-surviving unions. For, *provided the employer will play this bargaining game*, it has an inherent advantage for both parties over a wider control confrontation. If the latter were to succeed it would have to eliminate economism beforehand, for its success depends on working-class unity. Yet economism can exist in free competition with more extreme unionism, continually undercutting it by an ability to obtain interim success from compromise bargaining. The employer will yield on economical bargaining more readily than he will on the sacred 'managerial prerogative' of control. Where economism and movements oriented to workers' control have competed, the former have usually won.[1]

As trade unions are organized towards the attainment of economic bargaining gains, they tend in practice to lose sight of control issues, whether these concern the immediate work situation or wider-ranging questions of industrial structure. With the increasing trend towards productivity bargaining, job control is viewed by trade unions as something which can be exchanged periodically for economic rewards; typically workers will gain some shopfloor control informally, and indeed surreptitiously,

and then formally sign it away in union–management negotiations. Where job-control issues are raised positively – and there
may recently have been a slight increase in the proportion of
British strikes concerned with job control – this is likely to be a
shop-steward initiative, relatively independent of the union
leadership.[2] And wider control issues can barely be raised at all if
the framework of a capitalist market is implicitly accepted by the
very activity of compromise economic bargaining. This may be so
even of apparently ideological unions: to anticipate my later
argument, the practical relations with management entered into
by Communist unions may be indistinguishable from those of
reformist unions.

Unions are, of course, conflict organizations, incongruent with
any extreme view of industrial harmony. Nevertheless, their
economistic activities reduce the *class* nature of the conflict.
This is worth stressing, for there is a tendency to view class conflict in industry as grounded in economic disputes. When we
speak loosely of 'classes' in industry we normally mean manual
workers on the one hand and higher management and shareholders on the other. Obviously, difficulties arise in placing intermediate groups and deciding if management and shareholders
are really the same group, but these do not obscure the polariza-
tion in real consciousness on which our distinction is based. Yet
in economic terms the qualitative break is between capital and
all wages and salaries, and there is no quantitative break at the
'class' divide. The break is, in fact, not financial but rather one
of job control.

We can see this from the objective work situation. The manual
worker is normally subjected to a very close form of managerial
control. His pay is geared as closely as possible to his work effort.
He is either paid by the piece he produces or by the smallest practicable unit of the time he spends working. Though most manual
workers are paid by the hour, disciplinary practices generally
distinguish shorter time periods; for example, three minutes late
to work may lose a man fifteen minutes' pay. Where possible,
management will reinforce close monetary control with the
physical presence of a supervisor. From this we can deduce that
the worker regards his effort as a *cost*: he exchanges effort, a
cost, for wages, a benefit. Remove the close control, and he will
not work. It is worth noting that this applies to virtually all
manual workers, skilled as well as unskilled, and generally dis-

tinguishes them from office staff. The latter are usually assumed to have internalized the employer's work norms, while workers need coercing. Why should we doubt the almost unanimous views of Western employers on the nature of classes in industry?

Another way of testing the relative importance of economic and control issues for the development of class consciousness is to look at the situation in which the latter has developed. Evidence is available from Touraine's cross-industry study of France.[3] Class consciousness was at its highest in industries like mining, heavy engineering and foundries, where managerial control was at its tightest, and among its lowest in the building industry, where the cash nexus relationship was comparatively clear and immediate (chs. 1–3). It has long been known, of course, that class consciousness varies directly with size of plant – the largest organizations structure work routines most rigidly, and therefore meet with most worker resistance.

Hence, to the extent that trade unions pursue economic and job-control issues separately and the latter defensively, and to the extent that they do not pursue wider issues of work control, they operate to *weaken* workers' class consciousness. What are the consequences of this for the workers' own attitudes and behaviour? If we were to adopt the 'end of ideology' approach we would expect economistic and defensive control strategies to correspond to workers' own preferences. Wider creativity-control issues would have no, or negligible, salience in workers' consciousness, and workers would not be alienated.

THE EXPLOSION OF CONSCIOUSNESS

The starting-point for the thesis of the explosion of consciousness is a quotation from Marx which has become one of the favourites of twentieth-century Marxists:

> It is not a question of what this or that proletarian or even the whole proletariat momentarily *imagines* to be the aim. It is a question of what the proletariat *is* and what it *consequently* is historically compelled to do.[4]

This has led to a dual conception of consciousness among Marxists from Lukacs onwards: on the one hand, *actual* consciousness (what the worker normally thinks); on the other, *possible* consciousness (what Marxists know will or can occur).[5] This dualism is often expressed in a very idealist way, with the writer merely asserting an 'objective' knowledge of the laws of history which is supra-empirical. Such a position is beyond argument – either one has faith or one has not. Yet it can take a more materialist form, in which possible consciousness normally exists in a latent form and 'explodes' into action during specified revolutionary situations. The transition is thought to occur swiftly and with little prior warning. The 'old-fashioned' view of class consciousness, which sees it as a steady step-by-step progression, is dismissed. Great importance is attached to the unruly strike as the locus of the explosion, and the events of May 1968 in France are seen as its paradigm case in recent years. The need is now for 'a theory of dual consciousness'.[6]

As yet, however, this theory has not been forthcoming, and 'the explosion of consciousness' seems a rather mysterious, and in some ways metaphysical, process. Marxists over-emphasize the split between the two forms of consciousness, and hence the only way that one theory can join the two is with an emphasis on the 'myth' and the violence of strikes, which would have greatly pleased Sorel but horrified Marx. This over-emphasis often results from a desire to attack 'bourgeois' empirical sociology, with its supposed stress on actual consciousness. Robin Blackburn, for example, developed his version of the explosion of consciousness in an attack upon the findings of *The Affluent Worker* sub-sample of Vauxhall car-workers.[7] He claims that the survey, thorough as it was, could not predict the explosion of a subsequent strike because surveys must necessarily reflect mere actual consciousness. If he had read the study thoroughly, however, he would have noticed that the survey *does* reflect dynamic tensions of dual consciousness. Though the workers surveyed had mainly harmonistic views of industry, they were *also* conscious of elements of 'coercion and exploitation' in their employment relationship. If these came to the fore, more conflictual industrial relations could develop. In fact, from surveys we can easily perceive 'latent' consciousness of class, which, in certain situations, can explode. Hence it is not difficult to develop a theory of dual consciousness, and I shall do this below.

A Marxist theory of the explosion of consciousness would run as follows. In 'normal' situations the worker experiences his work as an alien force acting upon him. Though at this stage he is not class-conscious, and may adhere to a conservative ideology, he nevertheless dislikes his situation and seeks ways to avoid it. His compliance is 'pragmatic' and must be explained by an analysis of the balance of power in industry. If this balance is disturbed, as for example in some strike situations, his rejection of his situation will become perfectly evident. It is at this stage that he begins to expand his consciousness. The power of the emergent working class is a collective power, and it is through the experience of solidarity with other workers that a worker experiences in a very concrete way the power that will eventually lead to the collective control by the workers of the means of production. Collective action will normally 'fail', or appear to achieve only limited ends, but its real significance lies in the growth of class consciousness through everyday experiences. Hence two processes occur simultaneously: a steady learning process by the workers, and short-term cycles of conflict emergence and resolution. As the former of these continues, the disjunction between the workers' apparent consciousnesses in normal situations and strike situations will grow wider. While one remains passive, being a realistic appraisal of the balance of power in that period, the other grows more socialistic as the workers learn to make the connection between their own collective action and alternative possible ways of organizing production. 'Explosiveness' will thus increase until it triggers off the proletarian revolution.

Of course, we must cavil at the inevitability of this process, and should add two riders to the argument. Firstly, it appears to give too much emphasis to purely industrial conflict. Once the process is under way, it must become also political if it is to achieve a revolution. The word 'strike' has attained a rather limited meaning in English, and if we read, for example, Rosa Luxemburg's classic analysis of the 1905 strike in Russia,[8] we must remember that she is describing another explosive process: the translation of specific industrial demands into general, political demands. Secondly, the above argument over-emphasizes the steadiness of the growth in latent class consciousness, suggesting that a cumulative process has been under way since the very first strike under capitalism. This would be highly misleading. Many contrary processes are at work, and particularly heavy defeats or, indeed, economistic gains in strikes may set back a development in consciousness. Nevertheless, it must be observed that the 'explosion' theory does depend on some such cumulative process, whether this be short- or long-term.

I would like to emphasize one particular aspect of this theory. Marxists predict not only that there will be a proletarian revolution, but also that this revolution will replace capitalism with a specified alternative system, socialism. This new society conditions the form of the revolution itself: collective experiences herald the new collective organization of production. Hence 'explosions' must be in the direction of collectivism, firstly in the form of sentiments of solidarity with other workers, and secondly in the grasping by workers of an *alternative* socialist ideology. Both must be present for a proletarian revolution to take place. We will see below that the division between the two acts as a crucial watershed in contemporary class consciousness.

There is at least surface plausibility to the 'explosion' thesis. It has often been observed that management–worker conflicts which appear to be conducted in rather confused terms bring to the surface generalized worker discontents which had hitherto escaped notice. This is most evident when the company concerned had previously been stable and paternalist, for in such cases the workers appear to have switched suddenly from deference to class consciousness. However institutionalized industrial relations become, strikes reveal the workers' pent-up feelings, deprivations and hostility to the employer.

One such incident in Britain has been well-documented. This is the 1966 strike at Vauxhall Motors, Luton, Bedfordshire. Only months before the strike, Vauxhall workers had been interviewed in *The Affluent Worker* research project, and 79 per cent of them had chosen the 'same side' answer to the football team analogy of industrial relations. During the strike, however, 'near riot conditions developed . . . Two thousand workers . . . tried to storm the main offices. Dozens of police were brought in . . . "The Red Flag" was sung, and workers shouted that the directors should be "strung up" ' (quoted by Blackburn, 1967).

Dramatic as this appears, however, did it leave any aftermath? The strike subsided days later when specific grievances were settled. Subsequent industrial relations in the firm have been normal, with long periods of calm interspersed with small-scale and short-lived strikes. Where is the evidence for its *cumulative* effect? In fact, there are three great limitations placed upon this kind of explosive strike in the British context.

Firstly, the intentions of the workers must be regarded with some scepticism. How can 'dozens' of policemen hold back 'thousands' of workers? In France or Italy para-military riot police would be needed. Is it not more plausible that this was a *demonstration* to impress management and union negotiators of the seriousness of their grievances? It is always a possibility that such a demonstration will get out of hand, but the workers' representatives will attempt to restrain it; for they view the turbulence *tactically*, as convincing management that they are desperately holding back the workers from excessive violence. Once management has given in to their specific bargaining demands they will see no further point to the agitation.

Secondly, the bargaining mentality is reinforced by the de-centralized structure of negotiations. Employer and shopfloor representatives meet face-to-face in the processing of most British (and American) strikes. Representatives are thus closer to their members than they are in France or Italy, and thus 'exploding consciousness' interacts sooner with, and is more easily restrained by, union bargaining tactics. In Italy, by contrast, one commentator has noticed how the complete absence of regular channels of communication between individual employers and unions leads to strikes taking on an 'insurrectionist and emotional character'. It is not possible to use the workers' attitudes as a 'means of building up in systematic fashion an increasing ground-swell of pressure' towards negotiation and settlement.[9]

The third limitation is the most fundamental, for it casts doubt upon the nature of the 'explosion' itself. It may be doubted whether there is indeed a systematic shift leftwards during British strikes. This is certainly the implication of one close-quarters study of a strike in a Scottish coal mine. The authors were also impressed by the turbulence and the spontaneity of the events. 'Crowd scenes' and shouting matches were normal. However, alongside radical slogans were heard conservative ones: 'It's wrong to strike' competed with 'The only thing they understand is a strike'. Both sets of slogans struck immediate chords of response in most workers, and their overall attitudes continually oscillated.[10]

Even if we concede that the normal shift during strikes is left-ward, we must observe that it is only *certain* leftist slogans that emerge. Hiller, in his classic analysis of strikes in Britain and the US, noted the upsurge in sentiments such as 'the rights of labor', 'brotherhood', and 'solidarity'.[11] These emergent sentiments of collective *identity* are, of course, in line with Marx's own theory, and we find remarkable support for Marx in the clash which occurs during strikes between the emergent collectivism of the workers and the pre-existing individualist values of bourgeois society. It has long been a puzzle to 'economic' theorists of social behaviour why organizations like trade unions can command mass membership; for, if the individual worker calculates his own costs and benefits, the cost of membership (in money, time and employer punishment) will normally outweigh the benefits. During the normal wage claim strike, when the employer has made an offer but seen it rejected, the cost of continuing the strike may often seem too high to the *individual* worker. Yet the sum of individual preferences may not be the only definition of the collective good. This is at the back of unions' characteristic rejection of secret ballots (for mass meetings) during strikes. Employers and mass media normally regard this as intimidation of the silent majority by the militants, but this is too simple (and biased) an explanation, as we can see from the recent study of the Pilkington strike.[12] When they conducted a survey during the strike the authors found that a majority of strikers were in favour of abandoning the strike. Yet this majority actually believed itself to be a minority, and almost all its members were unwilling to incur moral disapproval (and possibly physical violence) from the supposed majority by openly advocating a return to work. And, in fact, the strike was 100 per cent solid, despite majority opinion and the opposition of the official trade union. The workers' spontaneous source of *identity* is collective solidarity with each other: each responds almost automatically to what he perceives as being the group's goals, even if he believes them to be irrational.

Thus strikes are not purely instrumental. During a strike a new form of rationality emerges, one based not on a summation of individual calculations but on collectivism *as an end in itself*. This, however, is its very weakness. For according to Marx there should be two aspects of emergent collectivism: sentiments of solidarity, and socialism. The former should be instrumental to the achievement of the latter. But in Britain, emergent consciousness stops short at the former. As no alternative society is conceived as possible, solidarity cannot be instrumental to long-term ends.

The 'explosion of consciousness' in Britain has two main aspects, therefore. One is its *tactical* use – it helps persuade employers to grant concessions and helps to 'win' strikes (in a short-term sense). The other seems entirely without material use: it is the expansion of a consciousness which is 'free-floating', which does not affect action and which must necessarily subside again. In this setting, 'explosion' is an apt metaphor – it bangs but it cannot build. To see examples of explosions with greater material consequences, we must turn to other countries.

Belgium offers an interesting midway case between Britain and France in the characteristics of its industrial relations, and we have good data available on its most celebrated 'explosion' in recent years, the general strike of 1960–61. This was a violent and turbulent strike, which broke out of purely industrial bounds and involved factory occupation and street barricades. The unions, uneasily poised between revolutionary and reformist stances, were swiftly overtaken by shopfloor militants. Workers interviewed just before the strike were also 'midway' in their ideologies: they were extremely conscious of class conflict in industry but fatalistic about chances of change. They were apathetic trade unionists, hostile to political strikes and completely ignorant of radical reform programmes. But months later, the author of a study of these events was surprised to see these very workers leading the general strike. He concludes:

> The experience of these strikers in the heat of the action, in a climate of social strife, brought forward profound changes in working-class consciousness: political and ideological growth, the spread of a programme of structural reform, active trade union participation, the grasping of sentiments of class solidarity and of the necessity of collective action . . .[13]

Yet such a change did not materialize out of 'thin air'. Another writer notes that the strikers were most active in areas which the trade unions had organized most thoroughly; their consciousness could only have been acquired through the union. He argues: '. . . the explosion is due to the discrepancy perceived by the workers between the ideological themes disseminated by the trade union organization and the latter's own actions.'[14] In this situation the role of the unions was contradictory – promoters of a consciousness which then attacks its own 'betrayal'.

In the even more dramatic events of May–June 1968, in France, the unions and the Communist Party played the same contradictory role. Though many newcomers were brought into working-class politics by the events, the key initiating role in most plants was played by the union militants. In one sample of 182 factories in the north of France, 73 percent of the work-forces followed the call of the union militants, and in only 15 per cent of cases was the strike originated wholly independently of the militants. In another sample, of 45 firms, the role of militants was insignificant in only 8 cases. Even where the workers set up novel forms of strike actions, bypassing the union hierarchy, this was more likely to be in factories that were already highly organized by the CGT.[15] And yet, as all reports indicate, the CGT, the parties of the Left including the Communist Party and (to a lesser extent) the CFDT did not accept the revolutionary reality of the movement, but accepted the Grenelle compromise and eventually betrayed their own militants.

This contradictory role of the organizations creates an unstable yet possibly insoluble situation. This is dialectic without a synthesis: revolutionary consciousness and compromising institutions, each largely ignoring the presence of the other. Some Marxists see the problem only too clearly. Gorz, for example, reflects sombrely that with archaic France absolutely ripe for revolution, the Left had so far failed to steer between the exciting but ineffectual spontaneity of the masses and the efficient organization but gross hypocrisy of the Communist Party (ch. 1).[16] Yet the events of May–June 1968 were not as merely circular as those of the previous strikes I described. Ritual there certainly was, both in the class confrontation of employers and workers and in the compromises they eventually adopted. However, new developments occurred which certainly strengthened the revolutionary prospects of the French proletariat. In the first place, the mass strike itself brought results, not just in terms of material rewards but also in trade union and worker control in matters of job regulation. The study of Dubois et al. (1971) showed that most militants were pleased with these gains, and hopeful that the strike had politically educated the workers to try again in the future.

Secondly, the May events produced an upsurge in worker

interest in the construction of an *alternative* society[17]. I have already noted that the programmes of the working-class organizations contained a crucial area of vagueness where their revolutionary programmes were supposed to be. When, therefore, workers began perceiving the extreme implications of their actions, they received little guidance from their traditional leadership. Unhindered by the responsibilities of compromise politics, their actions were often radical and innovative. This can be seen in the study by Dubois and his colleagues. In their sample 47 per cent of the factories affected by the strike were occupied, itself a relatively unusual event. Furthermore, in 76 per cent of cases the workers formed 'General Assemblies' in which they met in large numbers to discuss both specific and general demands. The Assemblies were part of the democratization of the movement, being subversive of the normal hierarchical system of worker representation (though most were dominated by the trade union activists). Their discussions were wide-ranging, and in 25 per cent of cases concerned workers' control – this became the main goal of the occupation in 19 per cent of the cases. Thus a minority of workers were discussing very concrete aspects of an alternative industrial structure. This was not narrowly conceived, and in 40 per cent of the cases discussions with *cadres* (lower and middle management) were entered into. All of these initiatives, together with the ideals of 'workers' power' and *auto-gestion*, eventually foundered and were seen to be utopian in the France of June–July 1968. Yet they were the first sign of major dialectical progress in the French working-class movement since the war – this is actually the first indication we have observed so far that there may exist cumulative elements in explosions of consciousness. It has not disappeared from view subsequently – Durand (in Dubois *et al.*, 1971, p. 11) notes that in a not-untypical day in November 1969 *Le Monde* reported that no less than seven French factories were occupied by their workers, while in March 1972 around 100,000 French workers, mostly young, took part in the funeral procession of the 'gauchist' shot at Renault, in defiance of the CGT. The occupations, and democratic worker committees, have also been an increasing feature of Italian industrial relations since Italy's 'long hot summer' of 1968.

Why these signs of increasing consciousness at such a late stage in the development of capitalism? Will it increase further? These are the questions we must now consider. Some Marxists answer with very general economic theories of neo-capitalist society. In their view, the proletariat revolution will occur when capitalism has reached its limit of world-wide expansion. Only then will the contradiction between production and consumption and the falling rate of profit produce the kind of economic crisis predicted by Marx. Yet it is difficult to link this to the relative instability of France and Italy, societies characterized by uneven economic development and a relatively weak capitalist sector. Furthermore, this theory neglects two apparently salient features of the May events, the part played in them by technical and scientific workers and that played by students. To analyse these factors we must turn to theories of 'the new working class'.

NOTES

1. D. BELL, *The End of Ideology*, Collier Books, 1961. P. TAFT, *Organised Labour in American History*, Harper and Row, 1964.

2. T. CLIFF and C. BARKER, *Incomes Policy Legislation and Shop Stewards*, London Shop Stewards Defence Committee, 1966.

3. A. TOURRAINE, *La conscience ouvrière*, Paris, Editions du Seuil, 1966.

4. K. MARX, *The Holy Family*, p. 368.

5. e.g. L. GOLDMANN, 'Conscience Réelle et Conscience Possible...', *Transactions of the Fourth World Congress of Sociology*, 1959; G. LUKACS, *History and Class Consciousness*, London, Merlin Books, 1971, p. 51.

6. 'Editorial', *New Left Review*, 1968, no. 52 (see also the articles by Mandel, Glocksmann and Gorz in the same issue); H. LEFEBVRE, *The Explosion*, New York, Monthly Review Press, 1970.

7. R. BLACKBURN, 'The Unequal Society', in R. BLACKBURN and A. COCKBURN, *The Incompatibles: Trade Union Militancy and the Consensus*, Penguin, 1967.

8. *The Mass Strike*, London, Merlin Press.

9. J. A. RAFFAELE, *Labor Leadership in Italy and Denmark*, University of Wisconsin Press, 1962, pp. 283–5, 288–9.

10. T. T. PATERSON and F. J. WILLETT, 'Unofficial strike', *Sociological Review*, XLIII, 1951.

11. E. J. HILLER, *The Strike*, Chicago University Press, 1928.

12. T. LANE and K. ROBERTS, *Strike at Pilkingtons*, Fontana, 1971.

13. M. BOLLE DE BAL, 'Les sociologues, la conscience de classe et la grande grève belge de l'hiver 60–61', *Revue de l'Institut de Sociologie*, no. 3, 1961. Quotation from pp. 577–8 (my translation).

14. M. CHAUMONT, 'Grèves, syndicalisme et attitudes ouvrières les grèves belges de décembre 1960–janvier 1961', *Sociologie d* *Travail*, IV, 1962, p. 156.

15. P. DUBOIS *et al.*, *Grèves Revendicatives ou Grèves Politiques?* Paris, Editions Anthropos, 1971, pp. 273, 345, 392.

16. A. GORZ, *Réforme et Révolution*, Paris, Editions du Seuil, 1969

17. (Thus Mann presents a succinct conception of working-class consciousness: 'Firstly we can separate class *identity* – the definition o oneself as working-class, as playing a distinctive role in common with other workers in the productive process. Secondly comes class *opposition* – the perception that the capitalist and his agents constitute an enduring opponent to oneself. These two elements interact dialectically, that is to say opposition itself serves to reinforce identity, and vice-versa. Thirdly is class *totality* – the acceptance of the two previous elements as the definining characteristics of (a) one's total social situation and (b) the whole society in which one lives. Finally comes the conception of an *alternative* society, a goal towards which one moves through the struggle with the opponent. True revolutionary consciousness is the combination of all four, and an obviously rare occurrence. M. Mann, *Consciousness and Action Among the Western Working Class*, pp. 12–13. – Editors.

17 Reference Groups and Trade Union Consciousness

Laurie Clements

Pluralist analysis of industrial relations is part of a wider analytical approach to the study of contemporary society. The dominant conceptual framework in this analysis has been that of the systems model which originated in the work of Dunlop, and was refined in its application to the British situation by Flanders and Clegg.[1] The major emphasis of pluralist analysis has concentrated upon the institutions which dominate the structure of industrial relations, and the framework of rules by which the system operates. Commentators have, as a result, often underestimated the influence of the social actors involved in the processes of industrial relations and have tended to reify institutional relationships so that 'a definite social relation between men . . . assumes a fantastic form of a relation between things'.[2] Concentration upon institutional forms thus serves to mystify actual power relationships in industry, which are primarily concerned with power over people, whilst simultaneously obfuscating, at both the structural and ideological level, the degree of inequality that dominates not only the economic sphere, but the entire social structure of contemporary British capitalism.[3] The mystification of power relationships in academic industrial relations is perhaps most apparent in the pluralist analysis of industrial conflict which is displayed as a legitimate form of social action between groups of broadly equal power. As such the struggle for control within industry is not treated as a fundamental problem, in the sense that an alternate industrial order is presented, but as a mechanism that allows marginal structural adjustment through the institutional process of collective bargaining. Academic concern is therefore with the process of negotiation over the allocation and distribution of economic rewards within the existing social and industrial structure. Trade unions can thereby be regarded as legitimate pressure groups which provide a limited challenge to managerial control of industry, and collective bargaining provides the 'legal framework' which ensures the long-run stability of the industrial relations system. The essence of pluralism is therefore its implicit support for system integration:

> . . . the discussion may be about marginal adjustments in hierarchical rewards, but not about the principle of hierarchical rewards; about certain practical issues connected with the prevailing extreme sub-division of labour, but not the principle of extreme division of labour . . . about how participant interests can protect and advance themselves within the structure operated by management to pursue its objectives, but not the nature of those objectives.[4]

It is not proposed here to re-analyse the limitations of pluralism which has been adequately done by several commentators.[5] But pluralism, as the dominant orthodoxy in industrial relations literature, has been of considerable ideological importance in that it legitimates the existing distribution of economic power and rewards in capitalist society by largely ignoring the multiple dimensions of inequality. It implicitly accepts the political economy of capitalism and provides both an ideological framework that binds labour to capital, and an in-built justification for the integration of working-class organizations within the prevailing power structure. This ideological function has considerable implications for the development of worker and trade union consciousness. The purpose of this paper is to explore the effect of the dominant ideology upon the frames of reference utilized by workers and trade unions; to suggest that reference group analysis can provide a useful introduction to the study of trade union consciousness; to distinguish different levels of trade union consciousness, and to explore the relationship of reference groups to consciousness under changing economic conditions.

A fuller understanding of the influence of the dominant ideology can be gleaned when it is fitted into a structural context. Marx pointed out,

> Economic conditions had first transformed the mass of the people of the country into workers. The domination of capital has created for this mass a common situation, common

interests. This mass is thus already a class as against capital, but not yet for itself.[6]

The major factor preventing the development of working-class attainment of an objective class identity both in and for itself has been the fragmentation of the class, particularly along industrial lines. The contemporary industrial structure thus provides a framework for the organization of the working class in an institutional form. This segmentation, coupled with the differential autonomy established by work groups, for example craftsmen in relation to the unskilled, has considerably hindered the development of a solidaristic class consciousness that transcends the boundaries of economic institutions which employ wage labour. Marx was confident, however, that such segmentalism could be overcome in the actual process of the struggle whereby the proletariat could achieve a level of consciousness that would provide the basis for wider societal transformation. The *foundation* of struggle was, for Marx, located in the economic arena and he believed that *trade union activity* would encourage *class consciousness* which would develop beyond its initial structural context and inevitably embrace a political dimension. The relationship between activity and consciousness is not a mechanical one, but rather dialectical, being closely related to the Marxian concept of praxis, a creative activity in which consciousness becomes realized in practice. Praxis should therefore be regarded as the content of struggle which enhances the development of consciousness in the process of social action. As such it encapsulates the concepts of productive forces and production relations, that is land, labour, capital and their inter-relationship; the institutional form they take, such as trade unions and political parties; and also the ideologies which dominate these social institutions. Praxis thereby reflects totality; the process of history interpreted through action, and the development of consciousness producing a new *Weltanschauungen* or world view. As such the struggle of subordinate groups is one in which they attempt to impose their own dominance or hegemony upon society which will create the need not only for 'a new form of state [but also] experience the need to construct a new intellectual and moral order'.[7] The essence of the process is therefore its internal dynamism in which the working class attempts to overcome the wage slavery which sublimates it to capital.

The seeking after a new intellectual and moral order, as Gramsci suggests, requires that workers expand the frames of reference which provide the limits of their thought processes and subsequently have considerable effect upon their actions. Much sociological and industrial-relations analysis uses the concepts of reference groups and relative deprivation as implements for understanding the limited frames of reference utilized by work groups. Central to this analysis is the view that individuals and groups become involved in a comparative process in which they evaluate their own position with regard to perceptions, beliefs and attitudes they have towards other individuals, groups or abstract entity.[8] These external stimuli provide, it is argued, the frame of reference with which comparison and evaluation is made. As such this process is also important in developing an understanding of the development of consciousness of one's position in the social structure, yet in the main, reference-group theory stops short of such an implication. Thus conventional analysis of reference-group development tends to be restricted to what reference groups are held rather than the implications of the restructuring of reference groups upon worker consciousness. Such limitations have led Parkin to suggest that whilst reference group analysis has been used to explain the response of subordinate groups to inequality, this begs certain questions of causality; that is, are the reference groups utilized by such groups the cause or consequence of modest expectations in response to inequality?[9] Yet paradoxically, as Runciman noted, the answer is both.[10] However, this paradox is largely ignored by pluralist industrial relations specialists who largely assume the existence of social structures free from internal contradiction. In this way the orthodox use of the concept of reference groups is limited because it assumes an unquestioned subservience of the working class to the ideological domination of capital, and thereby is most conservative in its implications, particularly in its treatment of the comparative processes which permeate collective bargaining. It will be argued, however, that in certain historical circumstances the utilization of sufficiently wide frames of reference can have radical implications for industrial relations and the stability of the wider social structure.

Ross has argued that work groups utilize 'orbits of coercive comparison', that is the force of equitable comparison, as the most potent force in wage negotiation.[11] Analysis of wage rounds at both the national and local level lend substance to this view and the success of Government attempts to regulate wage increases by incomes policy has been largely dependent upon the reaction of wage leaders in the round.[12] The miners are an obvious example in Britain, and the reaction of the miners to incomes policy in the 1970s has provided Governments with a reasonable indicator as to the likely success of such policies. This certainly applied to the Heath administration in 1972 and 1974, and the rejection by the miners of policies that attempted to forcibly impose a reduction in living standards acted as a stimulus to previously industrially placid groups, such as hospital manual workers and teachers. In like manner the reverse has been true in the acceptance of the 'social contract' by the executive of the NUM (together with its narrow success at the pit-head ballot), and this aided the provision of consent on the part of the bulk of the union movement to this 'new form' of incomes policy. In this latter case the executive of the NUM displayed a lack of 'ability to provide a convincing ethical rationale for their aspirations and actions [which] would appear a precondition for the successful pursuit . . . of ambitious pay demands'.[13]

Although this change in reaction to incomes policy can be explained by the links between the trade union movement and the Labour Party, particularly when that party is in the seat of Government, it displays how this link can serve to prevent the radical widening of frames of reference by trade unions at the national level. The importance of this point will be returned to in the discussion of macro-level trade union consciousness.

Failure to *morally* justify aggressive bargaining has led trade unions to concentrate upon the process of negotiations and this has served to direct attention away from the structure of power relations that determine the bargaining framework. As Allen has succinctly argued:

The plain fact is that union action is limited by the system unions have to operate in and is tempered by the values of that system. Because their achievements are at any one time so meagre, unions direct their attention to the means of achievement . . . as if the method can be evaluated independently of what is achieved . . . A result achieved through compromise is seen as fair, just, equitable and decent irrespective of the merits of the initial demand or complaint. Compromise like free collective bargaining prior to it, has virtually become an end in itself.[14]

Allen's pessimism was specifically related to the trade union acceptance of incomes policy in the 1960s, but the example of the miners referred to earlier indicates this is not necessarily inevitable. The question thus arises as to the longer-term effects of the operation of an incomes policy. Goldthorpe has argued that an incomes policy can serve an educative function in that it increases the information available to work groups as to the overall structure of incomes, and this has been highlighted by the media particularly when any group attempts to break the policy. Hyman has also suggested there has been a widening of the 'orbits of coercive comparison' used in wage bargaining in the late 1960s and early 1970s.[15] Thus, whilst Runciman suggested that reference groups would be narrowed in times of economic depression, so that work groups would avoid feelings of relative deprivation, it appears equally plausible to suggest that rising expectations of a period of economic boom can have a spill-over effect in times of recession as work groups have to bargain more militantly to maintain, let alone increase, their standards of living. Rising expectations can serve to broaden reference groups and this has been an important factor in the economic instability of contemporary British capitalism. This has been particularly manifest in the 'wage explosions' that often follow a policy of wage restraint. This led Clegg to suggest:

> Growing workshop power has led to relatively large increases in earnings for certain groups of workers. These have offended against our established standards of fair relationships in pay, and have caused other groups of workers to ask for pay increases. Until recently the process was slow . . . during the last ten years the process has begun to accelerate with more and more industry settlements designed to compensate for industry increases elsewhere.[16]

The development of domestic bargaining facilitating this growth of comparibility claims has been an important force in the growth of factory class consciousness. It has encountered resistance from both management and full-time union officials (whose influence it usurps) and this latter factor has been of considerable importance in the dampening of industrial militancy in the mid-1970s. However, it is reasonable to argue that acceptable comparisons have broadened and aggressive bargaining has led work groups to make inroads into areas of managerial domination on issues of wages and also, with perhaps longer-term consequences, job control. These points will be returned to later.

The extension of reference groups, whilst embodying disruptive potential, has as yet largely occurred within the working class. As such the opacity of the class structure still hinders the process of generalization of comparisons beyond that which can (in the main) be accommodated. It was suggested earlier this was due to the failure of work groups to develop an ideology sufficiently strong to provide a moral justification for large wage increases.[17] Not so the professions which have established the control and definition of the boundaries of the occupation so as to provide a mystique of professionalism to the layman. This leads to a 'social distance' developing between the professions and non-professions which effectively prevents the passage of economic rewards gleaned by professions.[18] Yet when professions *as a group* have made certain demands it is likely, as in the case of the medical profession and the National Health Service, that information of the rewards of doctors will become more readily available and this in itself can produce industrial unrest and militancy among the less skilled and lower paid in the 'medical industry' as the hospital disputes have indicated. However, the ideological strength of professionalism, the close links of professionals with elite groups in society, and the control over entry into the professions have effectively hindered comparison with the professions by working-class groups. As professions largely determine their own remuneration and perhaps more importantly its structure, the stringency of incomes policy is in fact less of a problem for professional groups. Given the current role of the professions in capitalist society and the function they serve therein, it is likely that this elitist position will be maintained and they will remain outside the frames of reference held by working-class groups. Central to the maintenance of this privileged position is the current ideological influence of the professions which is part of a wider dominant ideology. Yet this professional role is problematic, not axiomatic, depending upon the specific stage of capitalist development faced by professional groups. At the level of ideology 'professionalism' is only effective when its claims coincide with the dominant ideology. Also the bureaucratization of professional groups in large corporations and agencies of the State, as in the case of the medical profession, can have disruptive consequences. Bureaucratized professions are subject to more rigid control than 'free' professionals, especially in times of incomes policy, yet attempts to reduce such differentials that may have developed between the two professional groups can lead to other groups in the same employment structure as the bureaucratized professions becoming aware of the considerable differentials that exist between professionals (including in this case managerial executive staff) and non-professionals. The exposure of relative impoverishment can serve therefore to uncover the wide earnings gap between professions and non-professions enhancing the possibility that the bureaucratized professions may become a future source of instability to capitalist employment relations.[19]

The privileged position of the professions has been aided by the fact that as yet they remain outside the major framework of industrial relations which as Eldridge has argued provide 'the arena in which the struggle for the control of labour is carried out'.[20] As such, reference group formation and extension in the economic sphere is ultimately linked to the consciousness of work groups as to the relationship of wage-labour to capital. Collective bargaining is often legitimated by trade union negotiators because it facilitates the deliberate structuring of members' frames of reference in a way that makes negotiators' achievements at the bargaining table appear acceptable. Feelings of deprivation are thereby restricted as workers' expectations are subject to influence by official union representatives. As suggested earlier, the rank-and-file bargaining developments in the 1960s provided a challenge to this influence and this has met with tighter controls from the official union structure. Thus the limits of workers' frames of reference are to a considerable extent structured by the process of collective bargaining. But also crucial to this is the effect of the dominant ideology, which reflects the hegemony of capital and its relationship with the structure of collective bargaining. At this level the frames of reference developed and utilized by work groups form the basis to what we shall designate micro-level trade union consciousness. The above-mentioned factors act as restrictive fetters on the ability of the working class to develop an awareness of the structure of inequality beyond its own existential experience. Micro-level trade union consciousness is in fact limited to the immediate experience of work groups in the economic arena. It is a reaction to the physical facticity of capitalism at the place of work. As Parkin has indicated, such trade union consciousness provides

> . . . a moral framework which promotes *accommodative* responses to the facts of inequality and low status . . . Organized labour directs its main efforts towards winning a greater share of resources for its members – not by challenging the existing framework of rules but by working within this framework.[21]

Micro-level trade union consciousness may be equated with factory class consciousness but the former term is preferred because the existence of trade unions provides the institutional form in which consciousness and action can be joined and also, as will be suggested, some forms of micro-level trade union consciousness transcend the confines of the factory. Rank-and-file understanding of exploitation and wage labour is rooted in the factory system. This system provides the working class with an experience of their place *within* the social structure whilst simultaneously providing them with an experience *of* that social structure but only at a sectional level. At this level trade unions, as the institutional form of the working class in the industrial sector, should be regarded as Hyman and Fryer have suggested as 'secondary organizations, the existence and activity (of which) presuppose the existence of economic institutions employing wage labour'.[22] However, this secondary nature is likely to remain as long as unions fail to develop a consciousness of the wider social framework and the structure of inequality therein.

> Consciousness of capitalism *as a system* is thus remote from normal trade-union perspectives; and the influence of the broader framework *because not consciously appreciated* is all the more powerful.[23]

The dominant ideology thus exerts a powerful influence over trade union consciousness (at this and at higher levels), but before this is dealt with in greater depth it is useful to evaluate briefly Lenin's classic formulation on the difference between revolutionary consciousness and trade union consciousness.

Lenin described trade union consciousness as the bourgeois consciousness of the working class and argued that its central tenets were sectionalism and economism. This had to be compared with the totality of revolutionary class consciousness whereby the revolutionary political party was the embodiment of radical social change. The sectional nature of trade unionism has been alluded to in relation to the institutional forms unions embrace in their dealings with capitalism. By economism Lenin meant not simply issues of money or conditions, but also trade union activity at the political level to win concessions for labour in its relationship with capitalism. This latter aspect of trade union activity will be dealt with under macro-level trade union consciousness, but for *both* levels, Lenin argued, the essence of economism was its reformist tendency in that trade unions' major activity was to seek better terms for the commodity sale of labour power.

In like manner, trade union politics, he suggested, was simply an attempt to reduce the rate of exploitation of the working class but not to abolish the subjugation of labour to capital. His major point was not that the trade union struggle was worthless as such, but that concentration upon economic issues would ensure that unions could be no more than reformist institutions within the capitalist framework. If this point is linked to the sectional nature of trade unions as institutions the *narrow economic* base of trade unions effectively hinders the development of *revolutionary class* consciousness. Differing conditions in each trade and industry provide the impetus for the development of a heterogeneous micro-level class consciousness and consequently increase the pressure upon trade unions to concentrate upon reforms in terms of wages and conditions. Concentration on such reforms, whilst perhaps allowing short-term advantages for the groups of workers concerned, diverted attention, so Lenin argued, away from more fundamental problems of social inequality. To reiterate the essence of economism for Lenin is reformism, and it may be argued, in Lenin's terms, that pluralist advocacy of collective bargaining as a major institution of social reform is implicitly economistic in its approach.

Lenin's initial formulation of 1902 was modified in the light of trade union development and the organization of the Russian working class leading to the revolution in 1917. Trade union struggle served an educative purpose in his later writings but Lenin never abandoned the theory of the need for a revolutionary party to transform the economic into a political struggle. Yet it is difficult to apply the classic Leninist interpretation of trade union consciousness to the micro-level in contemporary industrial relations in Britain. The objective reality facing the Russian working class, and Social Democratic Party, was fundamentally different to that facing the British working class in the 1970s, and to utilize the initial formulation, a polemical political tract, to explain the current exigencies confronting contemporary trade unionists, particularly at the micro-level, would not do justice to either. Central to the contemporary debate are the twin issues of bargaining over the sale of labour power and the attempt by work groups to impose levels of job control in opposition to managerial authority relations in a situation where trade unions are also closely involved in the development of capitalist production relations. It is to the complexities of establishing the link between this role and micro-level trade union consciousness we must now turn.

Micro-level trade union consciousness is highly differentiated between trade unions and within trade unions in different economic establishments. It is thus impossible to forward a specific definition of what one means by such consciousness. The level of union density is an important factor, as is the size of the employing institution. The nature of the work process may also be crucial along with the wage-payment system that is linked to this process.

What can be said, however, is that at the micro-level the vast majority of issues dealt with by union representatives, both full-time and shopfloor, will be specifically related to issues which arise at the place of work. Combine committees have been developed in industries with a strong union movement and a militant rank-and-file, such as the motor industry, but these are an exception rather than a rule and the primary orientation of such committees has been to equalize conditions across factories of the same company. Such activity, in fact, takes one beyond factory class consciousness yet still remains within the confines of micro-level trade union consciousness. The primary concern of unions at the micro-level has been over issues of pay, the importance of comparability claims in 'wage explosions' has already been dealt with, but also important are issues of job control. Goodrich monitored the wide array of shopfloor practices relating to job control earlier this century.[24] The economic conditions of the 1950s and early 1960s led to many work groups establishing degrees of control over such issues as manning, overtime allocation and levels of output (such as prevention of speed-up). This was in fact the major impetus to the establishment of the 'Donovan Commission' to investigate the British system of industrial relations.[25] Issues of job control can be interpreted as attempts by workers to de-alienate their existential experience and which by their very nature involve a political challenge at the point of production. At one level, in terms of Lenin's argument, job-control issues may be interpreted as economistic in as far as these involve an encroachment upon rather than a transcending of managerial control and are thus in the strict sense reformist. Also it is often the case that such developments are sectional rather than universalistic, particularly where the 'restrictive practices' applied are directed at other work groups, for example craft exclusiveness. At this level job-control issues need to be regarded as an element of the employment contract which provide an authority (i.e., control) relationship as well as an instrumental (economic) relationship, and Beynon has indicated the economic nature of job control issues when he suggested that workers' encroachments into areas of job control are, like wage determination, subject to the influence of market forces.[26] Yet whilst the influence of the market is considerable, and given the fact that within capitalism worker control of the market is impossible (in fact in strict terms this also applies to capitalists because of the anarchy of the market), it is still reasonable to argue that issues of job control do transcend economism in as far as work groups do unilaterally seek to *impose* their own definition of key aspects of their own employment situation. Issues of control provide most clearly the rejection of the working class simply to accept capitalism on its own terms, and reflect the attempted imposition of worker rationality over the production process.

Micro-level trade union consciousness as manifest through issues of job control provides a complex interface of economic and political factors in which the plant becomes an arena of class conflict at the point of production. As Beynon has argued in relation to the motor industry,

> There is an inevitable conflict on the shop floor of a car plant. This is one of the facts of life, something the shop steward has to live with. It can push him along the road to militancy or stifle his spirit – because this is the guts of it – the inevitability of struggle day in and day out.[27]

This activity provides the potential for an emergent autonomy among working-class groups that can lead to a challenge to factory authority relations. As Herding has argued:

> . . . shopfloor organization provides fundamental exigencies for militant unionism out of the immediate experience of contradictions in the industrial system.[28]

Issues of shopfloor control and to a certain extent aggressive wage bargaining (where workers attempt to impose a wider structure of reference groups than has previously held to be salient) reflect a political aspect of economism. Thus Gramsci argued that economism is not always opposed to political action but could in fact serve as an educative function in the process of politicization of the working class.[29] He thus widens the Leninist perspective on economism, and whilst Lenin criticized sectionalism because it allowed only a spontaneous development of radicalism (and was therefore of only limited long-term utility), Gramsci argued against the dismissal of spontaneous tendencies on the part of the working class simply as counter-revolutionary. He in fact stressed the importance of the organic link between the mass (and institutionally trade unions) and the revolutionary political party '. . . a unity between spontaneity and conscious direction'.[30] Spontaneity is the prerogative of the masses, and this is most explicitly manifest as an aspect of micro-level union consciousness, because it is at this level that spontaneous reaction to managerial policies are most quickly generated. It may involve many forms of union activity from issues of job control, wage bargaining and strike action each of which can encapsulate the broadening of workers' traditional frames of reference. Implicit in this spectrum of activity is the rejection on the part of labour of the narrow frame of reference that is provided by collective bargaining, and this encapsulates a political development quite different from that which occurs at the macro-level.

Sectionalism is of considerable importance in the development of trade union consciousness at all levels. Collective bargaining, by its very structure, actively supports sectional claims in a way that can be contained, and provides an institutional form for the defusion of industrial militancy. Management are also likely to support sectionalism amongst trade unions because of its divisive implications – the problems of lay-offs in other factories or other parts of the plant provide an excellent example of how such tactics have been used. It thus appears reasonable to argue that the greater the degree of sectionalism within the working class, the more constrained will be the frames of reference used by the working class. Sectional claims can be more easily contained than universalistic claims because the former, unlike the latter, do not challenge the institutional form in which such claims develop. Wider areas of social inequality thus remain unquestioned, and their perpetuation becomes ensured. Whilst sectionalism greatly hinders the development of a radical and coherent macro-level trade union consciousness it can, under certain economic conditions, create problems for the stability of the economic order. For example, in the 1960s capital to a considerable extent legitimated the development of domestic wage bargaining. Economic stagnation in Britain has meant that the economic advances of organized labour in the 1960s are no longer available and sectionalism has been countered by national-level incomes policies, and in the 1974–76 period a virtual imposition of limited national-level bargaining upon the trade union movement. The ultimate sanctions have been deflationary economic policies and drastic cutbacks in social service expenditure that have both increased unemployment and reduced living standards. However, as suggested earlier, Government incomes policies can have the obverse of the intended effect by widening reference groups, but also as Westergaard has indicated:

> . . . industrial disputes formally confined to wages and immediately related questions seem liable to bring wider issues of control, authority and economic policy recurrently into focus.[31]

In this way, even sectional claims can bring into question authority relations of production, a political factor similar to the political implications of economism alluded to earlier. Thus whilst sectionalism tends to limit worker perceptions to a narrow framework rather than expand worker awareness of the objective position of wage labour, the challenge of shopfloor militancy has been sufficiently disruptive to encourage the implementation of new managerial techniques such as productivity bargaining, job evaluation and measured day work and also Government intervention through incomes policy and industrial relations legislation. To counter this therefore, the central problematic, as Gramsci pointed out, is to generalize from this fragmented base thus:

> ... bringing about not only a unison of economic and political aims, but also intellectual and moral unity, posing all the questions around which the struggle rages not on a corporate but on a universal plane, and thus creating a hegemony of a fundamental social group over a series of subordinate groups.[32]

Thus trade union action can never simply be interpreted entirely as economic action, but a coherent ideology is necessary if workers are to perceive the inevitable link between economic and political issues within the context of a capitalist economy. This necessarily brings into focus the concept of macro-level trade union consciousness.

Lenin argued that trade union economism embraced reformist political activity directed at bettering the terms of sale of labour power. This has largely taken place through formal channels with trade union bureaucracies providing the major platform of reform. Such activity serves to bind labour to capital and like pluralist ideology, discussed earlier, aids the integration of working-class institutions into the existing power structure. In fact it is plausible to argue that formal unionism helps to mediate the dominant ideology to the working class in a way that renders it acceptable. This process has also been supported by the political subordination of the trade union movement to a Labour Party, infused within Parliamentarianism, rather than seeking to fundamentally alter the nature of capitalist society. Hindess has in fact argued that without a radical political commitment to reduce inequalities at the societal level the frames of reference utilized by the working class will continue to be restricted.[33] Both industrially and politically therefore the macro-level trade union consciousness reflects the limited sectionalism of the micro-level and in this sense the ideological domination of capital is best understood as 'an ensemble of material practices'.[34] Thus ideology should not be regarded as an abstract set of ideas but as the legitimating process for class subordination to class, and this, in itself, is due to the existing social relations of production. At the macro-level therefore the objective function of trade unions has to be seen in this relational form and would, as Allen has argued, differ between the West and the Soviet bloc because unions would face different social relations of production.[35]

Within capitalism it is necessary to examine why trade unions have levelled their challenge to the limitation but not abolition of exploitation. Anderson has argued that trade unions are an expression of, rather than a challenge to, class society.[36] Union leaders over the last century have largely maintained that position and have rejected the revolutionary platform. Indeed Murphy referred to the period 1850–1900 as the 'heyday of reformism', a time when union leaders 'hated strikes and openly advocated class collaboration'.[37] The establishment of collective bargaining was the major priority of union leaders and this platform was consolidated under the ideological influence of Fabianism in the early years of this century. Trotsky in analysing the British trade union movement in 1925 argued that the Fabians:

> ... are systematically poisoning the labour movement, obscuring the consciousness of the proletariat, paralysing its will ... The Fabians, the Independents, the conservative bureaucracy of the trade unions are now the most counter-revolutionary power in Great Britain.[38]

The role of these parties in the General Strike in the following year was entirely supportive of Trotsky's prognosis. The early radical surge of 'new unionism' offered some qualification to this argument but establishment and consolidation were the forerunners of incorporation. The shop stewards' movement between 1910–20, and later the National Minority Movement were unofficial developments against bureaucratic tendencies within organized labour but the decline of the latter after the

General Strike led to a process of entrenchment on the part of bureaucracies in many unions. The development of the Labour Party reinforced this tendency, particularly as the parliamentary party was hardly likely to support any radical movement that would eventually seek to abolish the capitalist state machine.

Disaffection by the rank-and-file from the official union bureaucracies led to localized unofficial militancy of the 1960s as discussed earlier. This primarily reflected micro-level trade union consciousness but Government intervention through legislation affecting industrial relations was a catalyst that promoted the expansion of militancy and more importantly, the level of activity upon openly political lines. But even when under pressure from the rank-and-file, resistance of the official union movement to the proposed legislation of the Labour Party, and the rendering of the Industrial Relations Act largely impotent, the platform on both occasions was the retention of 'free' collective bargaining. In such a situation the trade union leadership could appear as providing stout resistance to the encroachment of legislation upon their influence, whilst simultaneously directing the militancy of the membership to support a situation in which the position of the leadership was enhanced. This was consolidated by the return of the Labour Government in 1974 and the acceptance of the 'social contract'. Furthermore, concessions made under the Trade Union and Labour Relations Act 1974, with the subsequent amendment in 1976 which was supportive of union organization by encouraging the closed shop were also hailed as a major victory for the trade union leadership. These factors have thereby served to increase the power of the union bureaucracy over the rank-and-file, and the support for a national wages policy between 1974 and 1976 has further reduced the potency of domestic bargaining.

It is reasonable to suggest therefore that union activity at the macro-level has been more explicitly reformist than among the rank-and-file. In granting legal status to trade unions the capitalist state has circumscribed radicalism, promoted the concept of the compromise solution and thereby defused any challenge to the domination of capital. Consciousness and ideology at this level have ensured that workers and unions maintain their subordinate position and provide a barrier to the development by trade unions into radical politically conscious organizations. It is therefore necessary to examine the failure of the British working class to develop a revolutionary consciousness within its principal organizational form. The emergence of class consciousness requires the development of a class ideology strong enough to convince subordinate groups that they would benefit from an alternate social structure. In fact, Anderson has argued that the major failing of the British labour movement has not been due to the limits of trade union consciousness (using the explicitly Leninist approach to this) but to an excess of a class consciousness which was devoid of an ideology. He described this as a

> . . . corporate class consciousness, realized in and through a distinct hermetic culture (which) has blocked the emergence of a universal ideology in the English working class.[39]

Thus, he argued that the lack of a self-generated intellectual tradition has hindered the development of an hegemonic consciousness by the working class and prevented, outside isolated incidents, the politicization of industrial militancy. This has meant the economic and political subordination of the working class. The reformism of 'Fabian socialism' has been dealt with and this anti-radical intellectual tradition continues to dominate the officialdom of the labour movement. Such reformism whilst superficially antagonistic to the dominant ideology is in fact supportive of this ideology; it reinforces the hegemony of dominant social groups economically, politically, culturally and ideologically. An understanding of the ideology which has continued to dominate the labour movement can only be adequately understood in relation to the dominant ideology and is most clearly demonstrated within the higher echelons of the union movement and the Labour Party.

Ideological hegemony may imbue working-class organizations with 'false consciousness' but as Gramsci has suggested, the working class man also has a 'true consciousness':

> '. . . which is implicit in his activity and which truly unites him with all his fellow workers in the practical transformation of reality' as well as a 'false' consciousness which is '. . . superficially explicit or verbal, which he has inherited from the past and uncritically accepted . . . but often powerful enough to produce a situation in which the contradictory character of

consciousness does not permit any action, any decision or any choice, and produces a condition of moral and political passivity.'[40]

Here Gramsci brilliantly summarizes the power of the dominant ideology to defuse conflict, and pre-empts by four decades Goldthorpe's analysis of the resistance of reference groups within the working class which was examined earlier. Institutionalization and internalization of the dominant world view has made it all the more pervasive and has proven a considerable barrier to the development of a coherent working-class ideology and has also proven an effective deterrent to class action. Thus, Lukes, developing this argument asks:

> . . . is it not the most insidious exercise of power to prevent people, to whatever degree, from having grievances by shaping the perceptions, cognitions and preferences in such a way that they accept their role in the existing order of things, either because they can see or imagine no alternative to it, or because they see it as natural and unchangeable, or because they value it as divinely ordained and beneficial?[41]

Consensus can be manipulated to render radical elements within the working class impotent. This occurs in what Gramsci referred to as 'normal times' yet in exceptional circumstances, he believed the working class as an 'organic totality', independent and autonomous, could develop its own conception of the world that could result in revolutionary action.[42] As Westergaard has pointed out, workers have expanded their frames of reference in terms of class action in certain historical periods to provide:

> . . . a widening of horizons, and the displacement (if not total suppression) of localized and sectional loyalties by commitment to a common aim.[43]

He cites the militancy after the First World War which joined the South Wales miners and the Clydeside shipbuilders as an example, but more recent examples can be found between the engineers of Birmingham and the Yorkshire miners to force the closing of Saltley and also in the mass action to free the 'Pentonville Five'. Thus whilst the working-class movement has lacked a consistent and coherent ideology it does possess an awareness of inequality and injustice which can lead to militant non-sectional activity.

Trade union organization at the macro-level has been subject to integrative pressures both structurally and ideologically. This has permeated to the micro-level, but as suggested above, it would be wrong to assume from this that all trade union activity is reformist. Such an assumption would be as incorrect as to accept rank-and-file revolt as a prelude to revolutionary change. What is suggested therefore is that trade union consciousness can be seen at a number of levels. For ease of exposition this paper has sought to distinguish micro- from macro-level, but these provide two basic types of consciousness. In reality what is more likely is that under changing economic and political conditions a spectrum of trade union consciousness will be held by various groups within the union movement. It is necessary, therefore, to insert any analysis of trade union consciousness within specific structural locations and historical periods. Changing socio-economic and political conditions will affect the balance upon which a 'progressive' or 'reformist' consciousness will dominate. The 1960s was the decade of the short, sharp stoppage, usually sectional and often unpredictable; attempted regulation of the industrial relations framework by the State and supported by the introduction of managerial techniques to obliterate such activity led predictably to longer and larger stoppages. It thus appears reasonable to suggest there was a significant broadening of consciousness in the early 1970s. This was not adequately consolidated, however, and was countered by an ideological bombardment by the State, management and leading academics. The solutions to these 'problem areas' which were extolled particularly by pluralist industrial relations specialists, lay in the re-establishment of managerial control, based in the main, upon the restriction of worker frames of reference and activity. Such a strategy has been largely supported by the increase in unemployment in the 1970s. 'Wage drift' (or 'drive') at the local level has been superseded by national-level wage negotiation via 'voluntary' adherence of the trade-union movement to incomes policy, and this development has considerably enhanced the role of the TUC as the seamen's dispute of 1976 bears witness.

The development of the 1960s, such as the widening of reference groups through competitive wage bargaining, and the encroachment of workers into areas of job control, have met with reversals in the 1970s. For the labour movement the central problematic continues to be the process of transition from specific localized activity into a coherent and enduring consciousness. Whether trade unions as institutions can provide the ideology to ensure successful transition is, in the light of historical experience, highly unlikely. However, this does not preclude the potential for working-class radicalism from developing in the process of struggle to assert even the basic trade union rights. The planned development of British capitalism has failed to provide the economic, political and social liberation of the mass of the people and this will endure as long as existing social relations of production survive. But the instability of the current system has been experienced most heavily by the working class. The continued pressure of inflation upon living standards is likely to lead, with or without official union support, to a defensive strategy upon the part of rank-and-file workers. Yet within this, the very act of opposition contains the embryo of positive action within which even traditional trade-union objectives embrace a political countenance. Workers attempting to wrest control from management at the point of production sustain this challenge. Attempts by union officials, management and Government to reduce the power of the rank-and-file leaders has born witness to the disruptive effect such activity has had upon the institutional structures which dominate British industrial relations. The 'system of rules' which govern capitalist production relations are brought more strongly into focus and the contradictions of the economic system more blatantly exposed. However, the relationship between macro-level and micro-level trade union consciousness has to date been a complex dialectic of pressure and counter pressure. The ideology of the macro-level has permeated into the micro-level and has been a fetter upon micro-level action by providing for 'perceptual and conceptual limitations'[44] of what is feasible within the political economy of capitalism. Repression has contained but not destroyed rank-and-file activity and in the last analysis union leaders do have to respond to pressure from the shopfloor. It is upon the unfolding of this dialectic, the outcome of which is problematic, that the levels of aspirations and the future expansion or contraction of trade union consciousness at both the macro- and micro-level will depend.

NOTES

1. J. T. DUNLOP, *Industrial Relations Systems*, Mott, 1958; A. FLANDERS and H. A. CLEGG (eds.), *The System of Industrial Relations in Great Britain*, Blackwell, 1954. This book of readings emphasized the importance of the major formal institutions involved in industrial relations. This has been amended to take into account 'informal' developments by Clegg, see H. A. CLEGG, *The System of Industrial Relations in Great Britain*, Blackwell, 1972. Also A. FLANDERS: *Management and Unions*, Faber, 1970, provides a useful compilation of Flanders' major contributions to pluralist analysis.

2. K. MARX, *Capital*, vol. 1, London, 1970, p. 72.

3. D. WEDDERBURN (ed.), *Poverty, Inequality and Class Structure*, Cambridge University Press, 1974. This provides a useful selection of the literature on inequality in Great Britain.

4. A. FOX, 'Industrial Relations: A Social Critique of Pluralist Ideology' in J. CHILD (ed.), *Man and Organisation*, Allen & Unwin, 1973, p. 219.

5. ibid. Also R. HYMAN, *Industrial Relations: A Marxist Introduction*, Macmillan, 1975; and J. GOLDTHORPE, 'Industrial Relations in Great Britain: A Critique of Reformism'.

6. K. MARX, *The Poverty of Philosophy* in K. Marx and F. Engels, Collected Works, vol. 6, Lawrence & Wishart, 1976, p. 211.

7. A. GRAMSCI, *Selections from Prison Notebooks*, Lawrence & Wishart, 1971, p. 388. Gramsci also provides an incisive analysis of the 'philosophy of praxis' and the role of ideological hegemony in capitalist society.

8. W. RUNCIMAN, *Relative Deprivation and Social Justice*, Routledge & Kegan Paul, 1966. This provides the major analysis of reference group formation in Britain, whilst H. H. HYMAN and E. SINGER, *Readings in Reference Group Theory and Research*, Free Press, 1968, provides an anthology largely of American research into this area.

9. F. PARKIN, *Class Inequality and Political Order*, Paladin, 1975, pp. 61–4.

10. W. RUNCIMAN, op. cit., p. 16.

11. A. M. ROSS, *Trade Union Wage Policy*, University of California Press, 1948. This was part of the famous 'Ross–Dunlop' debate as to the relative importance of 'market' or 'institutional' forces in the process of wage setting. See J. DUNLOP, *Wage Determination Under Trade Unions*, Blackwell, 1950.

12. For an interesting study of the national level in the USA, see O. ECKSTEIN and T. WILSON, 'Money wages in American Industry', reprinted in R. J. BALL and P. DOYLE (eds.), *Inflation*, Penguin, 1969.

Also W. A. BROWN, *Piecework Bargaining*, Heinemann, 1973, provided a detailed account of the process at the domestic level.

13. R. HYMAN and I. BROUGH, *Social Values and Industrial Relations*, Blackwell, 1975, p. 82.

14. V. L. ALLEN, *Militant Trade Unionism*, Merlin Press, 1966, p. 30.

15. See J. GOLDTHORPE, 'Social Inequality and Social Integration' in D. WEDDERBURN (ed.), op. cit., p. 228. Also R. HYMAN, *Marxism and the Sociology of Trade Unions*, Pluto Press, 1971, pp. 27–8.

16. H. A. CLEGG, *How to Run an Incomes Policy and why we made such a mess of the last one*, Heinemann, 1971, p. 66. For example, as Clegg points out that productivity deals in some industries, such as chemicals, has led to a broadening of reference groups, and also that comparability claims have become more important in the Motor Industry.

17. It is interesting in this context, that many rank-and-file miners felt morally justified in the demand for £100 per week for 1976, whereas the National Executive of the NUM has a moral justification for the presentation of this demand at some unspecified future date.

18. T. J. JOHNSON, *Professions and Power*, Macmillan, 1972, pp. 41–7.

19. For a most useful discussion of this, see, T. J. JOHNSON, *Work and Power*, Open University Course Unit No. 16, pp. 33–59. Also G. CARCHEDI, 'On the Economic Identification of the New Middle Class', *Economy and Society*, vol. 4, no. 1, pp. 1–86, and G. CARCHEDI, 'Reproduction of Social Classes on the Level of Relations of Production, *Economy and Society*, vol. 4, no. 4, pp. 365–417. These authors examine, in a sometimes obscurantist manner, the possibility of there occurring a devaluation of the work of the new middle class (particularly the 'managerial professions') through a process of de-qualification due to the simplifying processes of technological advance. This creates the structural conditions necessary for the proletarianization of the professional (although not necessarily the development of proletarian class consciousness), as such work becomes collectivized through the bureaucratization of professional employment.

20. J. E. T. ELDRIDGE, 'Industrial Relations and Industrial Capitalism' in G. ESLAND, G. SALAMAN and M. A. SPEAKMAN (eds.), *People and Work*, Holmes–MacDougal, 1976, pp. 308–9.

21. F. PARKIN, op. cit., pp. 81, 91.

22. R. HYMAN and R. FRYER, 'Trade Unions: Sociology and Political Economy' in J. B. MCKINLAY (ed.), *Processing People*, Holt Rinehart Winston, 1974, p. 158.

23. R. HYMAN, *Industrial Relations*, op. cit., p. 98, Emphasis Original.

24. C. GOODRICH, *The Frontier of Control*, 1920, Pluto Press edn, 1975.

25. Royal Commission Report on Trade Unions and Employers' Associations, HMSO, Cmnd 3623, 1968.

26. H. BEYNON, *Working for Ford*, E.P. Publishing, 1975, pp. 147–50.

27. ibid., p. 103.

28. R. HERDING, *Job Control and Union Structure*, Rotterdam University Press, 1972, p. 12.

29. A. GRAMSCI, op. cit., p. 161.

30. A. GRAMSCI quoted in J. FEMIA, 'Hegemony and Consciousness in the thought of Antonio Gramsci', *Political Studies*, 1975, vol. 1, p. 41.

31. J. WESTERGAARD, 'Sociology: The Myth of Classlessness' in R. BLACKBURN (ed.), *Ideology and Social Science*, Fontana, 1972, p. 162.

32. A. GRAMSCI, op. cit., pp. 181–2.

33. B. HINDESS, *The Decline of Working Class Politics*, MacGibbon & Kee, 1971, p. 40. Also for a discussion of the role of the Labour Party in Parliament and the political subordination of the trade unions to the Labour Party see R. MILIBAND, *Parliamentary Socialism*, Merlin Press, 1975 and D. COATES, *The Labour Party and the Struggle for Socialism*, Cambridge University Press, 1975.

34. N. POULANTZAS, *Classes in Contemporary Capitalism*, New Left Books, 1975, p. 17.

35. V. ALLEN, *Social Analysis*, Longmans, 1975.

36. P. ANDERSON, 'The Limits and Possibilities of Trade Union Action'. Reprinted in this volume, (p. 334).

37. J. T. MURPHY, *Preparing for Power*, Pluto Press edn, 1975, p. 63.

38. L. TROTSKY, 'England, The Fabian Theory of Socialism' in I. DEUTSCHER (ed.), *The Age of Permanent Revolution: A Trotsky Anthology*, Dell Publishing (3rd Printing), 1973, p. 204.

39. P. ANDERSON, 'The Origins of the Present Crisis' in P. ANDERSON and R. BLACKBURN (eds.), *Towards Socialism*, Fontana, 1965, p. 34.

40. A. GRAMSCI, quoted in J. FEMIA, op. cit., p. 33.

41. S. LUKES, *Power: A Radical View*, Macmillan, 1974, p. 24. Lukes provides an insightful analysis of how ideologies are manipulated by dominant power groups in society to forward and protect their own interests.

42. A. GRAMSCI, *Prison Notebooks*, op. cit., p. 327.

43. J. WESTERGAARD, 'Sociology: The Myth of Classlessness' in R. BLACKBURN (ed.), *Ideology and Social Science*, Fontana, 1972, p, 184.

44. J. GOLDTHORPE, 'Social Inequality', op. cit., p. 220.

18 The Limits and Possibilities of Trade Union Action

Perry Anderson

Reprinted with permission from R. Blackburn and A. Cockburn (eds.), *The Incompatibles: Trade Union Militancy and the Consensus*, Penguin in association with *New Left Review*), 1967, pp. 263–80.

What is the role of trade unions in a socialist movement? What is their potential for revolutionary action? What should be the relations between class, unions and political party? These problems have traditionally been at the centre of socialist theory. Today they are in abeyance in Britain; the systematic assault on the trade unions by the Labour government has seemingly relegated them to the realm of speculation. It is obvious that the duty of every socialist now is to defend, unflinchingly and unequivocally, the simple freedom of trade unions to exist as autonomous institutions at all. This does not mean that fundamental discussion of the long-term relationship between trade unionism and socialism should be postponed *sine die* by socialists. On the contrary, only if the Left has a clear conscious vision of the specific place of the unions in a socialist movement will it have much chance of resisting the current bid to deliver British trade unionism its quietus.

LIMITATIONS AND CRITICISMS

All mature socialist theory since Lenin has started by stressing the insurmountable *limitations* of trade union action in a capitalist society. This emphasis emerged in the struggle against the various forms of syndicalism and spontaneism endemic in the European working-class movement in the early years of the century. The belief that trade unions were the chosen instruments for achieving socialism was the main tenet of syndicalism, the revolutionary version of exclusive reliance on trade unions. For this tradition – De Leon, Sorel, Mann – the general strike was the weapon which would abolish capitalist society. The reformist version was simply the belief that trade union wage demands could ultimately lead to a transformation of the conditions of the working class, without any change in the social structure of power. Both of these currents were rejected by the central tradition of European socialism. Marx, Lenin and Gramsci were all emphatic that trade unions could not in themselves be vehicles of advance towards socialism. Trade unionism, in whatever form, was an incomplete and deformed variant of class consciousness, which must at any cost be transcended by a growth of *political* consciousness, created and sustained in a *party*. Before discussing the present role and real potential of trade union action, then, it is worth resuming the key criticisms of trade union limitations. They can be expressed on a number of different levels. All of them concern what can be called the fundamental sociological statute of trade unions in a capitalist society. They are structural limitations, inherent in the nature of trade unions as such.

1. Trade unions are an essential part of a capitalist society because they incarnate the *difference* between Capital and Labour which defines the society. As Gramsci once wrote, trade unions are 'a type of proletarian organization specific to the period when capital dominates history . . . an integral part of capitalist society, whose function is inherent in the regime of private property'.[1]

In this sense, trade unions are dialectically both an opposition to capitalism and a component of it. For they both resist the given unequal distribution of income within the society by their wage demands, and ratify the principle of an unequal distribution by their existence, which implies as its complementary opposite that of management. Hence the power and durability of the notion of 'two sides of industry' as the immutable framework of trade union action. The case with which this ideology of the status quo has established its air of normalcy derives from the fact that trade unions have no built-in socialist horizons as such. Marx saw socialism as the suppression of class society by the proletariat, and therewith its suppression of itself. This dimension of a future 'auto-suppression' is lacking in a trade union. As institutions, trade unions do not *challenge* the existence of society based on a division of classes, they merely *express* it. Thus trade unions can never be viable vehicles of advance towards socialism in themselves; by their nature they are tied to capitalism. They can bargain within the society, but not transform it.

2. Trade unions are essentially a *de facto* representation of the working class at its work place. Formally, they are voluntary associations, but in actual practice they are much more like institutional reflections of their environment. The closed shop, often today supported by employers themselves, has only rendered official what was a spontaneous tendency of trade unionism anyway. Where trade union organization does not follow the natural contours of modern industry, this is not due to a voluntary decision to transcend them for any strategic reason, it is the result of the petrifaction of an earlier 'natural' pattern which has survived into a new industrial age like some geological deposit, such is the force of inertia within trade union organization. British industry today abounds with anachronisms of this kind, with its myriad small craft unions and hybrid general unions. They are signs, not of that purposeful orientation towards the future which is the token of a revolutionary movement, but of the inert domination of the past over the present. Trade unions, then, take on the *natural* hue of the closed, capital-dominated environment of the factory itself. They are a passive reflection of the organization of the work-force. By contrast, a political party is a *rupture* with the natural environment of civil society, a voluntarist *contractual* collectivity, which restructures social contours: the union adheres to them in a one-to-one relationship. A revolutionary party, as Lenin and Gramsci always stressed, embraces more than the working class; it includes intellectual and middle-class elements which are bound by no inevitable ties to the socialist movement at all. Their allegiance is created, *against the grain of the social structure*, by the work of the revolutionary party itself. Thus the political party alone can incarnate a true negation of existing society and a project to overthrow it. It alone is negativity in history.[2]

3. The trade union's inert adhesion to the lay-out of the social system has a crucial practical consequence. Its maximum weapon against the system is a simple *absence* – the strike, which is a *withdrawal* of labour. The efficacy of this form of action is by nature very limited. It can win wage increases, some improvements in working conditions, in rare cases some constitutional rights. But it can never overthrow a social régime. As a political weapon, strikes are nearly always profoundly ineffectual. No general strike has ever been successful. The reason is that socialism requires a conquest of power, which is an *input* of action, an

aggressive *over-participation* in the system, which abolishes it and creates a new social order. The general strike is an abstention, not an assault on capitalism. In some cases, it has actually *demobilized* a working class in a political crisis, when what was needed was to assemble it swiftly against a conservative threat: any paralysis of public transport in a big city, for instance, makes rapid mass demonstrations impossible – while it does not affect the mobility of repressive military action.[3] It can, in other words, be counter-productive. The strike is fundamentally an economic weapon, which easily boomerangs if used on terrain for which it is not designed. Since the nature of the economy as a system is ulti-mately a political question, it follows that strikes have only a relative and not an absolute efficacy in the economic struggle itself. This is another reminder that trade unions cannot put in question the existence of capitalism as a social system.

4. Trade unions by themselves produce only a *sectoral, corpor-ate* consciousness. Lenin's statement of this limitation in *What Is To Be Done?* is so eloquent that it has never since been seriously contested. The corporate character of trade union consciousness does not derive from the nature of trade union action or its aim, 'better terms for the sale of labour power', nor from 'the abolition of the social system that compels the propertyless to sell them-selves to the rich'.[4] It has a cultural-political basis. Trade unions represent only the working class. A revolutionary movement – a party – requires more than this: it must include intellectuals and *petit bourgeois* who can alone provide the essential *theory* of socialism.

> The history of all countries shows that the working class, ex-clusively by its own effort, is able to develop only trade union consciousness, i.e., the conviction that it is necessary to com-bine in unions, fight the employers and strive to compel the government to pass necessary labour legislation, etc. The theory of socialism, however, grew out of the philosophic, historical and economic theories elaborated by educated repre-sentatives of the propertied classes, by intellectuals. By their social status the founders of modern scientific socialism, Marx and Engels, themselves belonged to the bourgeois intel-ligentsia.[5]

Culture in a capitalist society is in this sense a prerogative of a privileged stratum: only if some members of these strata go over to the cause of the working class can a revolutionary movement be born. For without a revolutionary theory, there can be no revolutionary movement. Trade unions represent too limited a sociological base for a socialist movement. By themselves they inevitably produce a corporate consciousness.[6] The introversion which is so striking in the British trade union movement today is the natural sign of its corporatism. It is the antithesis of the universal outlook which defines socialist consciousness.

> Working-class consciousness cannot be genuine political consciousness unless the workers are trained to respond to *all* cases of tyranny, oppression, violence, and abuse, no matter *what class* is affected . . . The consciousness of the working masses cannot be genuine *class* consciousness, unless the workers learn, from concrete, and above all from topical, political facts and events to observe every other social class in all the manifestations of its intellectual, ethical, and political life . . . those who concentrate the attention, observation, and consciousness of the working class exclusively, or even mainly, upon itself alone are not Social-Democrats; for the self-knowledge of the working class is indissolubly bound up, not solely with a fully clear theoretical understanding – or rather, not so much with a theoretical, as with a practical, understanding of the relationships between *all* the various classes of modern society, acquired through the experience of political life.[7]

It is only too evident that the trade union world does not provide this.

5. Trade unions have only a *sectoral* power-potential, not a universal one. There is no parity of power between 'Management' and 'Labour' in a capitalist society, because labour is an untransformable element which can only be withdrawn (or at best used for, say, occupation of factories), whereas capital is *money* – a universally transformable medium of power which can be 'cashed' in any number of different forms. Thus capital can be switched into control of information media, resources for a lockout, support for a propaganda campaign, finance for private education, funds for a political party, budgets for weaponry in a social crisis (the use of goon-squads was common in the USA in the thirties), etc.[8] Trade unions do, of course, amass a certain

amount of capital themselves; if they did not they would never be able to fight any strikes. They can also provide some financial support for political parties, as they do for the Labour Party in England. But this is an auxiliary and it is not comparable with the resources at the disposal of the possessing class. The unions' *basic* sanction is their control of labour power, and this is a singularly rigid and limited weapon. Indeed, a Marxist political party can be seen as precisely an attempt to create, by contrast, a *polyvalent* potential of revolutionary action, which can be crystallized swiftly and interchangeably in a number of different fields – elections, demonstrations, boycotts, agitation, political education, insurrections, etc. A political party is by its nature flexible and versatile where a trade union is fettered and immobile.

Any survey of the historical experience of trade union action beyond the limits of wage bargaining substantiates this. It is striking that no matter whether the trade union movement in question adopts a 'revolutionary' or a 'reformist' stance, it tends to encounter the same *structural limits* to its action. These limits have frequently condemned the most differently inspired ventures to a common failure.

Encroaching Control

This is the strategy of partial advances on the shopfloor, each one wrestling successive local prerogatives from management – over hiring and firing, allocation of bonuses, work tempo, distribution of loads, etc. This, traditionally the most realist of the 'political' trade union strategies, was attempted by Guild Socialism, a reformist movement in England during and just after the First World War. The Guild Socialists were never able to impose their programme on the employers in the engineering industry where they deployed their main efforts. The movement disintegrated without a trace in the early twenties. In the sixties, the Italian trade union movement (CGIL) tried to initiate a revolutionary version of the same strategy. The metallurgical workers' contract of 1962 was perhaps the most famous example of this policy. The results have been disappointing so far. The balance of power in any capitalist enterprise is so unequal that – *without collateral intervention by party or State* – no union can hope to wrest major management prerogatives from the employers. The rare examples where unions do exercise substantial control prerogatives are proof of this: in virtually every case they have been enabled to do this by the political support of the State. Often this has been in nationalized industries such as the Brazilian Railways (up to 1964) and the Bolivian tin mines (up to 1965). 'Encroaching control' is not a myth. But it is only possible where the union receives powerful extra-union reinforcement.

Occupation of Factories

Ostensibly the most aggressive form of work-place action possible, this has occurred both with and without union initiative. A recent reformist attempt to use occupation of factories as a weapon for a combination of economic and constitutional demands (higher wages and pensions, end to restrictions on political activity) was the *Plan de Lucha* of the Peronista unions in Argentina in the summer of 1964. The Plan petered out after more than five hundred thousand workers had invaded their factories, seized hostages, barricaded gates, etc. The same fate essentially overtook the spontaneous, non-union occupations of factories in France during the Popular Front (1936 and again in 1938) and in Italy after the First World War (Turin 1919–29). These were authentically proto-revolutionary movements, but in each case they lost their impetus when it became evident that there was no political horizon towards which they could debouch. For the occupation of a factory is itself a purely *symbolic* act; it is not in any sense a seizure of the factory. In no case could the workers operate the plant, thereby effectively taking it over. This is naturally impossible in modern industry, where circulating capital is necessary to keep any industrial installation going at all. The occupation of factories is in practice no more than a dramatic form of picketing: the massed presence of the workers on the factory floor is a symbolic demonstration that it belongs by right to them, the producers. But it cannot give reality to this claim. The basic law of trade unionism, that strength is only the strength of absence, is in fact underlined by the exception: this intense but impotent presence.

The General Strike

Once again, this too can take a reformist or revolutionary form. The 1926 General Strike in Britain was a defensive movement against wage reductions – the most minimal reformist objective conceivable. It was conducted in a pained, ultra-constitutional spirit and was swiftly and decisively routed. (The limitations of the strike weapon as a simple absence have never been more graphically illustrated: several million men were not reporting for work, and all the General Council could urge them to do was play sports – often with the police who were engaged in repressing the strike.[9]) Nothing could be in greater contrast to this decorous episode than the revolutionary hurricane which swept Russia in 1905, when a spontaneous, unorganized general strike erupted across the length and breadth of the vast Tsarist Empire, from Warsaw to Chita. The historical conditions were exceptionally favourable: the radio and the motor car did not yet exist, the size of the Empire made railways uniquely important, so that a complete paralysis of communications was possible once the printing and railway workers went on strike. The State machine itself started to crumble as government employees enthusiastically joined the movement. 'Not factories only but shops, schools, hospitals, law-courts and local government offices had closed down . . . The police were powerless to intervene – some indeed had gone into hiding . . . amid the sound and fury of this revolt of the masses the mechanism of urban life in Russia had come to a complete halt.[10] If ever a general strike had a chance of revolutionary victory, it was in 1905. But even this elemental explosion finally faded away, as hunger and demoralization eroded popular confidence, and a drift back to work set in when it became evident in October that there was a strategic impasse. The Bolsheviks, at the very end of the strike, saw that it must be superseded by an armed insurrection, its dialectical opposite. A heroic attempt was made to capture Moscow, but military units crushed the uprising. The lesson, however, enabled them to win victory twelve years later.

There have been numerous other attempts to use the general strike as a politico-economic weapon. In combination with complementary forms of action – riots, elections, insurrections, etc. – trade unions can undoubtedly play an important role in a political crisis: the overthrow of the neo-colonial Youlou régime in Congo-Brazzaville in 1963 is a good example. But pure reliance on the General Strike as such has nearly always been doomed to failure. The fundamental reason is evident: a *stoppage*, on however massive a scale, is not the same thing as a *substitution* of one social order for another.

THE REVERSAL OF ROLES: PARTIES AND UNIONS

The limitations of trade unionism, then, are radical. Traditionally, socialist theory has insisted that they must be transcended by the practice of a political party. Lenin expressed this view decisively, when he wrote (in 1900):

> For the socialist, the economic struggle serves as the basis for the organization of workers in a revolutionary party, for the reinforcement and development of the class struggle against the whole capitalist system. But if the economic struggle is regarded as something self-sufficient, then there is nothing socialist in it. In the experience of all European countries we have had many not only socialist but also anti-socialist Trade Unions. To assist in the economic struggle of the proletariat is the job of the bourgeois politician. The job of the socialist is to make the economic struggle of the workers assist the socialist movement and contribute to the success of the revolutionary socialist party.

Only a revolutionary party, not a trade union, can overthrow capitalism. Yet today, a major change has taken place in England and to some extent in Western Europe generally: the relationship between unions and parties, between economic and political struggle, has been empirically reversed. As Tom Nairn has written:

> The trade unions are once again – after a long epoch where the political party occupied the centre of the stage – the avant-garde in the struggle of the working class, the standard-bearers whose position dominates everything else.[11]

How has this come about? What are the reasons for the present eclipse of the political party in any socialist context, and the re-emergence of the trade unions as the main vortex of class conflict? It is obvious that in Britain a special historical situation has determined the present attempt to shatter trade union autonomy: the contemporary crisis of British imperialism, the drive to solve the crisis at the expense of the working class, the assimilation of the Labour government to a straightforward strike-breaking role. This critical conjuncture is discussed elsewhere in this volume.

It is probable, however, that the British case is only the most dramatic example of a general trend in the advanced capitalist countries. A revolutionary political party is an unnatural, con-tractual superstructure – a voluntary organization created against the grain of society. Only because it is not inherent in the political and economic system of capitalism can it decisively abolish it. Its initial structure is oriented to the future: this is why it can revolu-tionize society as a whole. But the converse is equally true. Because it is more 'artificial' and is not produced and reproduced automatically by social conditions it also can be totally assimil-ated into the society, to the point of disappearing as a differential force at all. Where the political struggle in a capitalist society has for a period become the arena of unqualified bourgeois victory, as in Britain and West Germany today – where a monolithic 'con-sensus' excludes the articulation of any socialist options at a national level – the traditional parties of the Left simply become agencies of the status quo. Their degeneration is the obverse of their potential for social transformation.

By contrast, trade unions can never achieve the highest level of action of a political party. Nor, for the very same reason, do they tend to sink to their lowest level either – melting *en bloc* into the system. For their function is rooted in the natural organization of capitalism itself – the labour market. The result is that trade unions are less easily chloroformed and suppressed totally than political parties, because they arise spontaneously out of the ground-work of the economic system. As long as there are classes – and it is no longer in dispute that they exist in the West as much today as ever in the past[12] – there will be class conflict. Where there is no political articulation of this conflict, it will be the most elemental form – economic struggle – that will subsist. This last focus of class struggle is a perpetual anomaly to a society dedi-cated to the myth of classless harmony and social peace. Even today, strikes are a scandal to the ideology of the system. Recently, however, pressing economic exigencies have started to require their practical suppression. The demands of neo-capital-ism – the need to control inflation, to plan long-term capital in-vestments, to increase export markets – have led to a political attack on trade union autonomy in a number of Western nations. This attack has gone much further in Britain than in any other country and the British trade union movement now faces the gravest threat in its history.

The concerted campaign to break the trade unions as an independent force crystallizes quite decisively the value of their creative and irreplaceable role in a socialist movement. Having traced the external limits to their action, it is now necessary to state its specific value and efficacy on its own terrain. How much is at stake in the present contest between unions and government will then be evident.[13]

1. Trade unions are today unable to substantially increase the share of wages in the national income. All the investigations of recent years have shown that the ratio of profits-rents-interest to wages has tended to remain constant for many decades in England and other capitalist countries. This fact is not surprising: it is a necessary consequence of the power structure of a capitalist society, and can only be changed when a political revolution overthrows that structure. It does not mean that trade union action is an illusory labour of Sisyphus. But trade union wage pressure forces productivity up, so that a constant share of the national product creates a higher standard of living for the working class.[14] This is the hard-won *minimal* enclave of working-class resistance in a system of permanent and profound exploitation. It is this enclave which is now threatened. The attempt to manacle the unions is an attempt to enforce a net increase in the share of profits against wages in the national income – and a relative decline in the income of the working class. In England, the inordinate expense of a superannuated imperial system – military, political and financial – makes this the most attractive political option for the dominant class. The English working class will thus suffer a historic defeat and regression if its industrial organizations are confiscated from it.

2. Trade unions are weapons of economic struggle, which are radically maladapted for aggressive political action. This does not mean that they have no political significance. Nothing could be further from the truth. The *socio-political identity* of the European working class is first and foremost incarnate in its trade unions. It experiences itself as a class only through its collective institutions, of which the most elementary is the trade union. Outside these historic institutions, the working class has a purely inert

identity, impenetrable even to itself. It is separated from the rest of society by its characteristic occupations, customs and culture, but it is not a fused group capable of any social action.[15] For this, it must be conscious of itself as a class – and it can only become so in the organizations which it forges against the social system into which it is inserted. Whatever the degree of collaborationism of trade union leaders, the very existence of a trade union *de facto* asserts the unbridgeable *difference* between Capital and Labour in a market society; it embodies the refusal of the working class to become integrated into capitalism on its own terms. Trade unions thus everywhere produce *working-class* consciousness – that is, awareness of the separate identity of the proletariat as a social force, with its own corporate interests in society. This is not the same thing as *socialist* consciousness – the hegemonic vision and will to create a new social order, which only a revolutionary party can create. But the one is a necessary stage towards the other. In even the most unpolitical trade unions, there is ample empirical evidence of this 'preparatory' political role. In Britain the electoral loyalty of two-thirds of the working class to the Labour Party appears to be decided by its membership of trade unions more than by any other single factor. The unions here *visibly confer* its identity on the class; the other third of the working class which votes Conservative is overwhelmingly non-unionized without being significantly different in *any other* sociological respect. The logic of this traditional linkage is now obviously problematic, a fact heavy with potential political consequences. But the linkage itself shows the truth of Marx's account of the reciprocal relationship between industrial and political struggle:

> The political movement of the working class naturally has as its final aim the conquest of political power for it; for this a previous organization of the working class, an organization developed to a certain degree, is naturally necessary, which grows out of economic forces themselves . . . A political movement grows everywhere out of the individual economic movement of the workers, i.e., a movement of the class to gain its ends in a general form, a form which possesses compelling force in a general social sense. If these movements presuppose a certain previous organization, they in their turn are just as much a means of developing the organization.[16]

The identity and memory of the working class as an autonomous force is thus at stake in the freedom of the trade union movement. The threat to subordinate the trade unions to the State ultimately threatens the extinction of working-class consciousness as such. It amounts to an attempt to create a totally co-ordinated and purged social whole – the monolithic integration of Marcuse's 'One-dimensional society'.[17] It must be resisted, if socialism is to retain a future in Britain.

THE FUTURE

From any socialist point of view, the trade union movement today is far from perfect. But it is obvious that it can only be renovated if it has the initial freedom to exist. Given this, what are the main changes which are needed in the current character of British trade unionism?

1. *Industrial Militancy*

The majority of British trade unions today are old and bureaucratic. They do not enjoy the ready confidence of their members. The minimal participation in union elections – the only formal means of control the membership has over its officials – is notorious: the right-wing character and mediocre quality of many trade union leaders is both a cause and consequence of this situation. It is simply not the case that there is a fatal 'iron law of oligarchy' which inevitably produces an authoritarian trade union bureaucracy, unresponsive to the needs of its members. This notion is merely what Alvin Gouldner calls 'the metaphysical pathos of burcaucracy'.[18] There is no inherent reason whatever why trade unions, however large, should not achieve an accountable, participating democracy: that they normally fail to do so is not to be attributed to the blind necessities of large-scale organization, but to the total political environment in which they work. In other words, lack of democracy in trade unions is to be understood in terms of the nature of the system into which they are inserted: that is, *capitalism*.

For it is a rule in a capitalist society that any institution or reform created *for* or *by* the working class can by *that very token* be converted into a weapon *against* it – and it is a further rule that the dominant class exerts a constant pressure towards this end.

There is a permanent social reversibility here. The reason is that any attempt to advance the cause of the working class, to win political power *for* it, must involve a preliminary winning of power *over* it, in the form of collective organization, whether trade unionist co-operative or political party in character. The unionization – or politicization – of the working class requires the creation of institutions which are in one moment a *control* of it, as a necessity of any disciplined action. Of course, in another moment, they are by that fact a *liberation* of the class as well. The working class is only concretely free when it can fight against the system which exploits and oppresses it.[19] It is only in its collective institutions that it can do so: its unity is its strength, and hence its freedom. But precisely because this unity requires disciplined organization, it becomes the natural objective of capitalism to appropriate it for the stabilization of the system. It can then become turned against the very purposes for which it was created. It is this ambiguity – *power-for* as *power-over* – which makes working-class institutions the best of all anti-working-class weapons. Thus many British trade unions today, by their very lack of democracy, serve the objective function of subordinating the working class to capitalism. The union leaders who symbolize this mechanism, with their grotesque knighthoods and earldoms, are too well-known to need discussion here. These leaderships simply act as transmission belts of capitalism within the proletariat. But at the same time, because of the paradoxical nature of trade unionism – a component of capitalism that is also by its nature antagonistic to it – even the worst unions are not normally *just* organizations of adaptation to the status quo. If they were, they would lose their members in the long run, for not achieving any economic gains. It would thus be incorrect to describe rightist trade unions, in the classic phrase, merely as 'fire extinguishers of the revolution'. They perform a dual role, both shackling their members to the system and bringing home limited benefits within it. In Britain, about half the real wage increases in any year are won by national-level union negotiations.

Having said this, it is also true that the other half of annual wage increases is won not by the national trade union apparatuses, but by local shop-steward militancy – normally cross-cutting union lines of demarcation and in forward defiance of union prohibition. Ninety per cent of all strikes in Britain are now unofficial. The enormously enhanced role of shop stewards in class struggle today is an inevitable product of the lack of democracy and accountability in the major unions. For in a capitalist society class conflict *cannot* be suppressed totally: it springs naturally from the operation of the system. To the extent that the trade union function is not performed by trade union leaderships, the contradiction between Capital and Labour is simply *displaced* down the hierarchy to the plant and shopfloor level, and the shop steward 'usurps' it. Bureaucratic repression in the union – a consequence of its capture from above by the environment of capitalism – tends to lead to a revolt from below which acts as a restoration of the *status quo ante* – the *natural* situation of struggle inherent in the capitalist organization of industry. The recent growth and militancy of the shop-steward phenomenon is a sign of this invincible pressure. Every socialist must welcome this growth and defend the shop steward's freedom of action. The numerous witch-hunts against them are merely evidence of the effectiveness of their challenges to the capitalist system and its intermediaries in the trade union movement. But it is wrong to counterpose them to trade unions as such. What they show is that the fight for more militant unions is in the long run also a fight for greater democracy in the unions. In the short run, of course, union members are often even less 'political' than their leaders, and democratization might lead to local losses on the Left. But this low level of political consciousness is itself a consequence of the *type* of trade union leadership that is usual today – mediocre, authoritarian and conformist. Greater freedom of debate inside the union movement must create a more self-reliant working class, and hence could only benefit the militant Left in the long run. For it is obvious that militancy is *industrially* more effective in achieving wage increases than class collaboration. The advantage in fair and open competition for union office therefore must lie with the Left.

The economic struggle which has been the traditional purpose of trade unionism must, then, be complemented today by the struggle to recover the trade unions for their members. One is a condition of the other. The fight for a more democratic and militant union is a fight against capitalist infiltration and domination of the union movement.

2. *The Political Logic*

Trade unions have historically bargained for better terms for the sale of labour power; they have not been able to challenge the existence of the labour market itself. Today, however, the relations between 'political' and 'economic' struggle have changed. The emergence of a state drive to impose a centralized incomes policy is one of the defining characteristics of contemporary capitalism. The effect of this is to make possible an aggregation of local issues and disputes into a *national struggle* over the distribution of the economic surplus. An incomes policy makes capitalism as a system potentially transparent in a sense that it never was previously. The net distribution of the surplus between wages and profits can be seen much more visibly and unmistakeably. In this sense, wage bargaining can in itself become a case for the abolition of 'wage slavery'. Thus a global struggle for the surplus is now possible, rather than a scattering of isolated local demands.[20] This is even more true of England than elsewhere. For our whole historical situation is now dominated by the Labour government's attempt to crush *economic* demands by trade unions in order to pay for a *political* option – the maintenance of the military and financial system of British imperialism: the presence East of Suez, the export of capital, the prestige of the pound. The trade unions can only effectively counter this attack by rejecting the *political* policies of the Government, and by fighting for *socialist policies* which are their diametric opposite. The trade union struggle is now, necessarily, a political struggle. The two can no longer even temporarily be dissociated.

Does this mean that trade unions can or should now, despite everything that has been said earlier, act as political agencies? No. Their efficacy lies elsewhere. The new factor is that their traditional economic demands now have an *immediate* political dimension, whether they like it or not. It is the 'logic' of their industrial struggle. But this logic can only be prosecuted successfully by a political party. The implications of this are of a fundamental kind today. The great majority of British trade unionists are affiliated to the Labour Party – the very party which is now intent on blocking their action and shattering their autonomy. Can this immense contradiction continue indefinitely? How long will the unions go on propping up their executioner? Only the future can tell. But, if the Labour Party persists in its present course, it is plain that a day of reckoning will eventually come. Then the whole question of the political allegiance of the trade union movement will be reopened. Will it opt for a non-party 'business' unionism? Will it transfer its existing allegiance? Will it sponsor new political institutions, as it once sponsored the Labour Party? These questions are waiting, just over the horizon, behind every industrial dispute in wage-frozen Britain.

NOTES

1. *L'Ordine nuovo*, Turin, 1919–20.
2. For a discussion of the concepts of 'proletarian positivity' and 'negativity', see PERRY ANDERSON, 'Origins of the Present Crisis' in *Towards Socialism*, Fontana, 1965.
3. The classic example here is the general strike called in Rio de Janeiro in 1964, to counter the military coup which overthrew the Goulart régime. It merely prevented workers living in suburban districts from moving into the city to mobilize against the putsch.
4. *What Is To Be Done?*
5. ibid.
6. For a discussion of terms 'corporate' and 'hegemonic', see PERRY ANDERSON, op. cit.
7. *What Is To Be Done?*
8. For an heroic account of the struggle against goon squads and industrial warfare by employers, see JOHN STEUBEN's unique volume, *Strike Strategy*, the best manual for the striker ever written.
9. JULIAN SYMONS's *The General Strike*, London, 1957, documents this tragi-comedy very well.
10. R. D. CHARQUES, *The Twilight of Imperial Russia*, London, 1958.
11. In 'The Nature of the Labour Party' in *Towards Socialism*.
12. For a decisive survey of the evidence, see JOHN WESTERGAARD, 'The Withering Away of Class – A Contemporary Myth' in *Towards Socialism*.
13. Trade unions must, of course, also preserve their autonomy under socialism. Lenin emphatically safeguarded their rights in the famous debate with Trotsky and Bukharin on this issue at the Tenth Party Congress in 1921. The trade unions, he insisted, must be free to defend workers, both against specific state policies resulting from political compromises between the interests of the working-class and the peasantry, and against bureaucratic arbitrariness in the implementation of state policies as such. In theoretical terms, it is axio-

matic that socialism is not a monist praxis, but unity in multiplicity, both institutionally and practically. However, the nature of trade unions in a socialist society is so different from that in a capitalist society (Lenin described them as 'educational organizations . . . schools of administration, schools of management, schools of communism') that discussion of this important problem has been omitted here. ISAAC DEUTSCHER'S *Soviet Trade Unions*, London, 1950, contains an admirable discussion of the great trade union debate of the twenties in Russia.

14. This does not preclude historical phases when labour shortages and inter-capitalist competition can have the same effect, even where the trade union movement is shackled. The economy of Nazi Germany is an example. But in the long run, it has been trade union pressure for full employment which has prevented troughs from constantly checking the growth of productivity.

15. For a discussion of the concept of the 'fused group', see ANDRE GORZ, 'Sartre and Marx' in *New Left Review*, 37, May–June 1966.

16. Letter to Bolte, 1870. For a good account of Marx's view on trade unions, see A. LOZOVSKY, *Marx and the Unions*, London, 1935.

17. In *One Dimensional Man*, London, 1964. See also MARCUSE'S essay, 'Industrialization and Capitalism' in *New Left Review*, 30, March–April 1965.

18. ALVIN GOULDNER, 'The Metaphysical Pathos of Bureaucracy' in *Complex Organizations*, edited by AMITAI ETZIONE, USA, 1964.

19. For a discussion of this problem, see J.-P. SARTRE, 'Les Communistes et la Paix' in *Situations*, Paris, 1954.

20. This thesis is developed in ROBIN BLACKBURN, 'The New Capitalism' in *Towards Socialism*.

19 Industrial Democracy: The Institutionalized Suppression of Industrial Conflict?

Tom Clarke

It is exceedingly rare that a concept gains such widespread support from so many diverse organizations as 'industrial democracy' has recently acquired. Political, business and trade union leaders (many of whom are not otherwise distinguished in their commitment to democratic principles and practice) have queued to assert allegiance to the promise of this reform. Of course, it may be argued that a concept which binds together such a range of conflicting interests must be so ethereal that it could be of little practical utility; and this is reflected in the disagreement over the most suitable method by which to arrive at the goal of industrial democracy.[1] Similarly, it is generally agreed that there is a convincing case for industrial democracy, but there is considerable conflict on the nature of that case. A radical view is that whilst workers have achieved political emancipation in civil society, in the operation of parliamentary democracy, they are still disenfranchised in their working lives. Though trade unions have established some defences against the exercise of arbitrary power by employers, due to the limitations of traditional collective bargaining, workers are still in a position of political and economic subjection in industry, with the resulting exploitation and deprivation that this involves, including the restriction of workers' intellectual and social development. The solution to this unacceptable system is the industrial emancipation of workers: that they should have the right to full representation of their economic interests in the factories and companies in which they work; whether by an extension of collective bargaining into areas from which it has been previously excluded, or the establishment of institutional innovations, such as supervisory boards with 50 per cent trade union membership.

Although this argument for industrial democracy has been influential in winning many converts to the cause, it rests on a number of highly dubious assumptions; as Murphy maintained in dismissing the Whitley Report, the first official proposal of worker participation in 1917, 'it is based on false premises . . . it tackles nothing of a fundamental character, and prevents the growth of an independent objective for the working class.'[2] A primary weakness of the contemporary case for industrial democracy is the presupposition that democracy has been attained in the political system with the existence of parliamentary representation, the principles of which may be usefully emulated to provide for the democratic control of industry. Yet, when examined critically, the achievements of parliamentary democracy have been modest to say the least. Though – with great effort in the face of entrenched employer resistance – a measure of governmental co-ordination and provision has been introduced into the operation of the economic and social system, with a certain degree of welfare provision, to a great extent this is no more than is demanded for the efficient functioning of an advanced capitalist economy and the maintenance of a quiescent and reasonably healthy (that is more readily exploitable) working class. The extent of inequality in the distribution of wealth and power, a more accurate index of the efficacy of any pluralist democratic system, has remained remarkably stable despite the advent of parliamentary democracy.

The limitations of parliamentary democracy are scarcely surprising when it is realized that the whole edifice is permeated with what is in essence an elitist theory of democracy 'which is grounded upon a profound distrust of the majority of ordinary men and women, and a reliance upon the established elites'.[3] Indeed, 'modern' theories of democracy have defined out of existence the active and informed involvement of people in political decision-making: no active participation on the part of the governed is expected or encouraged beyond a periodic demonstration of consent or disagreement with the policies of the government.[4] Hence,

the contemporary Western conception of Parliamentary democracy . . . interestingly enough encapsulates as its central feature what was originally an *anti*-democratic position: the view that the populace should be allowed no positive, continuous control over their rulers, and that the legislative body should therefore be composed of representatives, not delegates, fully autonomous in the period between elections.[5]

The inactivity of the mass of the people produced in a political system such as this destroys the potential of elections as an instrument of popular control: on the rare moments when people *are* allowed to participate they cannot do so with the knowledge and skill constant participation would bring.[6] Besides, the 'apathy' ascribed to the majority of people is often only a realistic assessment on their part of their relative powerlessness, even if an attempt were made by them to influence decisions within the system.[7]

The tradition of democracy surrounding Britain's venerable parliamentary institutions has been wildly exaggerated: 'Britain was never called a democracy until war aims had to be found in 1916';[8] universal adult suffrage was not introduced until 1928 (when women between twenty-one and thirty were, at last, enfranchised), permitting most people to vote in national elections perhaps ten times in the course of their whole adult lives. As the policies of the two major parties become increasingly similar when in office, the vote itself is acquiring a purely nominal value, particularly since MPs stoutly defend their independence in parliament and government to interpret their political responsibilities as they themselves view them (which by convention involves reneging any electoral promises at the earliest opportunity). Even if governments *were* orientated towards radical democratic change, the dismal record in office of recent Labour governments is convincing proof of the severe constraints upon possible reform imposed by those who wield determinant economic power. It is not necessary to control governments directly: all that is necessary is so to circumscribe the area of freedom to manoeuvre that no decision implemented could seriously affect the interests of the powerful.[9] Marx and Engels were aware of this duplicity and 'analysed bourgeois-democratic politics as an exercise in convincing a maximum of the people that they were participating in state power, by means of a minimum of concessions to democratic forms'.[10] Why make the effort involved in such pretence? Because, Draper contends, 'Other things being equal, a democratic state form is cheaper to operate than a despotism; as long as it is possible, it is a bargain for a ruling class interested in keeping down overhead costs.'[11] The willing compliance gained by the *appearance* of democratic rule obviates the necessity for the constant deployment of the expensive apparatus of political coercion.

In conclusion, British society, like all other capitalist industrial societies, is profoundly, systematically and pervasively undemocratic and inegalitarian. Only measured against the crudest and most superficial criteria is the British political system democratic, or when compared with other societies in which dictatorship is conspicuous and coercive, rather than subtle, normative and material.

Furthermore, many of the proponents of industrial democracy appear to have not only a fundamental misconception of the extent of democracy in wider society, but also to misconceive the power relations within industry: 'the critical role of power in industrial life has simply been ignored or at best treated cautiously by those who are most active in its cause but whose reasoning at times therefore, has fluctuated between the naïve and the Utopian.'[12]

Typically, both the entrenched power of management and the power of the capitalist system to absorb and overcome change is grossly underestimated, thereby leading to an unjustified confidence in the ameliorative effects of intended reforms. And yet, naked of the camouflage of supposedly democratic machinery, the power relations in industry are starkly apparent to those who care to look: 'The workers show all the characteristics of a subject people when in contact with the employers.'[13] Thus, the oppression of workers is for example tangible in the technology of production, the work organization, the intensity of work and closeness of supervision. Tawney's characterization of 'autocracy checked by insurgence' still has considerable descriptive validity concerning the power relations between management and workers; crucially, so too does Goodrich's rider, 'the present point is that there is a great deal of insurgence.'[14] Paradoxically, the very fact that intense coercion is so evident throughout industry encourages workers to organize and take action in resistance.

Independent trade union organization has enabled workers to impress their interests upon managerial decision-making at the workshop level, achieving what the Donovan Report conceded as 'a very high degree of self-government in industry'.[15] The control exercised by workers is fragmentary and limited, but *does* exist as a viable expression of workers' interests in industry, whereas such interests are largely sublimated in the formal political process by Labour governments' acceptance of the constraints and priorities of capitalist society. Indeed, in some industries, by militant action workers have attained *unilateral* control over work organization at the point of production, maintaining control over manning, output and earnings by short, unpredictable (and therefore more effective) unofficial strikes and other forms of industrial action, which curtails managerial autonomy in operation and planning at the enterprise level. As Hyman has noted: 'The Royal Commission itself asserted the importance "of giving workers the right to representation in decisions affecting their working lives, a right which is or should be the prerogative of every worker in a democratic society". In some circumstances the "spontaneous" strike is perhaps the only effective means of translating this "right" into a reality.'[16] Appreciation of the extent of current workers' controls leads to the conception that: 'Already there is more industrial democracy, more participation in many plants than the senior managers in these plants know of, or would care to admit to':[17] but this 'participation' is largely *independent of*, and *in conflict with*, management. It is in this sense that proposals for worker participation, as if it were a new innovation, are a semantic insult to workers, since they are already heavily engaged in participation in control of their establishments, but *on their own terms*.

Such considerations support the assertion that management 'can only regain control by sharing it' (though when Flanders' well-known comment is contemplated, the question must be asked, 'whether those with whom control is to be shared and those over whom control is to be reimposed are in fact the same people').[18] It may not even be necessary for management to give up any of the power it currently holds, but merely to present the appearance of a formal sharing of control, which may well prove a means to restoring managerial domination. Hence:

> It is clear that in the past management has been less than enthusiastic about any form of participation. Both the philosophy of private enterprise, the high value on formal efficiency and on a structure of hierarchic authority are likely to incline them in this direction. Participation is likely to be considered, therefore, only when there are threats to these and paradoxically in order to maintain them.[19]

The general orientation of managerial proposals on industrial

democracy is to take the initiative away from the labour movement and ensure any developments serve their purposes: as the
CBI explicitly stated, 'Employee participation is a live subject and
likely to remain so. Managements now have the opportunity to
take action themselves according to their own circumstances and
in their own interests.'[20] The motives behind managerially inspired participation schemes, therefore, should be carefully
examined, for example:

> Where management proposes a system of *mutual* agreement,
> we may hazard a shrewd guess that they are faced with an
> existing situation in which workers have already established
> unilateral control over the territory in question. Where man-
> agement proposes vague consultative participatory formulas,
> it is probable that the existing situation is one in which either
> straightforward mutual agreement prevails, or in which there
> is a strong degree of apathy and indifference towards pro-
> duction problems on the part of the workers.[21]

The general aim of management is to restrict conflict by containing it within joint regulatory institutions which blur the divergent
interests of management and workers, erode the basis of independent worker organization, and thereby inhibit the capacity of
workers to take defensive action:

> This means that labour has to accept responsibility for the
> development of property which they do not own, and become
> part of an organization which is pledged to prevent them from
> ever owning it. Further the trade union representatives are
> thus to be used to assist in the development of those forces
> which destroy the foundations of trade unions.[22]

This view is supported by at least one contemporary major trade
union leader:

> there is a fundamental and, in finality, irreconcilable conflict
> between Capital and Labour . . . 'Workers' participation' is,
> in my view, the greatest bulwark for preserving a free enter-
> prise society. It does not seek to change, it seeks to perpetuate.
> It seeks to create the idea that there isn't a fundamental
> difference between us.[23]

So, shallowly concealed behind many conceptions of industrial democracy is a unitary frame of reference which involves an extension of present employer-union collaboration to the virtual integration of the union and management bureaucracies. The result of industrial democracy proposals may be, therefore, to *suppress* democratic expression rather than to extend it, and beneath the rhetoric of reform this is often the implicit intention, as a recent official report concluded: 'Schemes which apparently develop "industrial democracy" have often been less an extension of worker influence than a recognition of its existence and an attempt to channel it.'[24] But proposals to introduce part of a *formal* democratic system may involve institutionalizing in industry some of the undemocratic practices of the political system, in areas where presently democratic practices apply regarding such matters as representation, term of office, rewards, scope of decision-making and information dissemination. Today the industrial-democracy lobby wish to extend the methods of elitist representative democracy into the workplace which will involve undermining the existing participatory democracy entailed in unilateral shopfloor controls. 'Industrial democracy' is not a development of popular power but an attempt to *forestall* it.

In reflection of this, the recent position of the leaders of the labour movement on industrial democracy has proved equivocal. In the post-war period, up to the mid-1960s, the inviolability of the independence of British trade unions from management was asserted. The Donovan Commission, indeed, was cursory in its dismissal of workers' participation in management, advocating an extension of collective bargaining.[25] Yet in 1967, a Labour Party working party, chaired by Jack Jones of the TGWU (who was to become the major publicist of industrial democracy), recommended workers' representation at board level in the public sector, *but not in private companies*.[26] Entry of Britain into the EEC (itself a notoriously bureaucratic body), however, seemed to substantially change the climate within which industrial democracy proposals were discussed: no longer were they an adjunct to workers' control, but, on the contrary, a component of modern technocratic capitalism. Thus the EEC proposals, due ultimately to apply to all member countries, include supervisory boards with one-third of the members elected by shareholders, one-third by employees, and the rest of the board representing outside interests. Secondly, the EEC advocates Works Councils. The TUC were swayed by this influence in particular to accept the principle of worker directors, and itself proposed 50 per cent trade union representatives on supervisory boards *in both* public and private industry. Indeed the TUC had become so much seduced by the idea of worker directors, which it had previously rejected, that it consistently attempted to evade the continued resistance of major trade unions to the idea, even though an amendment passed at the 1975 conference declared 'the only long-term protection for workers' interests is an effective and independent trade union movement. Congress rejects any form of participation in management which would tend to weaken that essential trade union independence.'[27] Despite this conflict, the TUC scheme formed the basis of the terms of reference of the Industrial Democracy Committee of Enquiry appointed in late 1975, which reported with almost unseemly alacrity, considering the complexity of the issues involved, early in 1977.

THE BULLOCK REPORT

Though the committee was weighted in favour of the TUC proposals, the central recommendation of the Bullock majority report was the establishment of management boards with equal representation of worker and shareholder representatives, *plus a third group* of co-opted 'independent' directors; this seems to comply as much with the EEC as the TUC intent, and is a first and significant step in the managerial dilution of any conceivable redistribution of power. In other respects the majority report was diligent in its attempt to overcome the many problems and shortcomings of European schemes, and to integrate worker directors within the existing organization and practice of trade union collective bargaining in this country. Hence, although all workers may participate in the vote on 'triggering' the election of worker directors, the responsibility for the actual election, in contrast to the EEC method, is placed firmly within the trade union machinery (which represents 75 per cent of workers in the establishments of over 2000 to which the scheme applies), and therefore outside the immediate, anti-democratic influence of management. Potential advantages entailed in the report include: the strengthening of joint shop stewards' committees where they are presently weak to perform the work of the Joint Representation Committee of selecting worker directors; the creation of combine committees, where they do not already exist, to perform similar functions of the JRC in groups of companies; the provision of an extra source of information for collective bargaining purposes (though whether information provided to worker representatives at board level will be greater than that which they receive from existing sources, including the shareholders' AGM, remains to be seen); finally, the proposed 'instrument of control' by which worker representatives on the boards of companies that are taken over can insist upon certain 'safeguards' to employment, investment, etc., may help prevent the worst excesses of asset stripping.

But, overshadowing these potential improvements are serious weaknesses entailed in the majority report. In general, its largely uncritical endorsement of worker directors lacks the astringency of the two research reports it commissioned on the European experience of industrial democracy which check any undue optimism on the subject. With regard to board structure, though the report advocated representation on managerial boards, in preference to weak supervisory boards, it recognized that 'the top boards of large companies often play a mainly supervisory role', leaving detailed policy formulation and implementation to individual executives and management committees.[28] This tendency would be greatly accentuated when worker representatives were present on the management board: that is, there would be a *de facto* alteration of management boards into supervisory boards, where this has not already taken place. Moreover, the employers' minority report of Bullock demanded supervisory, not unitary management boards, and when concessions are made to the employers, as undoubtedly they will be, this seems likely to be one of the first. Therefore, criticisms relating to the supervisory board system of the EEC are likely to be largely applicable to the reconstituted boards of the UK, regardless of whether they are unitary or supervisory in formal structure.

A further problem concerns parity of board representation, which was the cornerstone of the original TUC position. However:

Like the TUC, the committee convincingly argues that anything less than numerical parity for worker directors with shareholders would be an unjust and self-defeating allocation of responsibility without power. Then they perpetrate just such an injustice with the incredible '2x+y' formula.[29]

Thus, in suggesting people suitable to act as the third group of co-opted 'independent' directors the majority report reveals a definite preference for outside executives and professionals, who are not renowned for their sympathy towards, or knowledge of, the work, lifestyle and interests of shopfloor workers. Since the additional directors must be an uneven number, even if worker representatives insist upon their 'share', they will have to compromise on at least one director. In relation to the final category of co-opted directors – local and national trade union officials – workers have already learned to their cost that officials will often not reliably represent workers' interests in collective bargaining; once such officials have assumed the cares of directorial management this tendency would be confirmed. Finally, there are the provisions that holding companies, even without a reconstituted board, would have the right to appoint the third group of directors; and that foreign-based multi-nationals would reserve the sanction to replace the third group of directors on a domestic subsidiary board, if that board resisted the policies of the parent board. Both are important explicit erosions of the principle of parity, and permit wide scope for managerial erosion – by the restructuring of groups of companies – of the impact of re-constituted boards.[30]

Therefore, the Bullock majority are not advocating and defending parity – that principle they have already conceded – they are merely defending the *appearance* of parity, which is the prerequisite for the support of the wider labour movement for their proposals, which might otherwise be ignored. Thus, at one point, the report exhibits a paranoia that its scheme could be interpreted as permitting the possibility of worker representatives eventually gaining control of company boards, and declares emphatically that: 'We do not wish our proposals to be open to this criticism, however theoretical it may be. For it is no part of our intention to make recommendations which could possibly produce such a result.'[31] Of course, no similar concern is revealed that shareholders' representatives may remain firmly in control of private companies.

Indeed, the fundamental weakness of Bullock is that it legitimates and sustains capitalist control of industry. The report recognizes the minimal and diminishing role that the issue of new equity plays in the funding of modern companies: in the 1970–74 period, 75 per cent of larger quoted company funds were raised *internally*; 15 per cent came from banks; 8 per cent from preference and long-term loans; and only 2 per cent from ordinary shares issued.[32] Thus, the report is prepared to bestow more than half the board representation of companies upon the shareholders who currently provide a minute amount of industrial funds; whilst workers, who invest their lives and dreams in their enterprises, who *actually* produce the wealth of industry, are restricted to less than half-board representation. Why should shareholders deserve such spectacular privilege? As Table 1[33] reveals, they comprise a tiny, if immensely wealthy and powerful, section of the community.

| Percentage of adult population[34] | Value of Property Yielding Dividends and Interest[35] | |
	Percentage of total amount	Amount in millions
0·1	36·9	£11,874
0·9	71·3	£22,981
4·8	91·3	£29,415

The report, therefore, unabashedly confers control of the major private companies upon less than one per cent of the adult population. In its concluding paragraphs the report compares itself to the Reform Acts of the nineteenth century which extended the political franchise. Though there is some validity in the comparison, there is, however, a crucial difference between Bullock and the first Reform Act: the 1832 Act abolished 'pocket boroughs', Bullock legalizes them.

In this light, the constant references to the 'equal partnership of capital and labour' ('the foundation of industrial democracy as we see it') with which the report is littered may be considered. Firstly there is an inbuilt majority for shareholder representatives or sympathizers. Secondly, the Chairman is to be a shareholder representative. Finally, when the 'partnership of capital and labour' breaks down and workers take industrial action, the ('interested') workers' representatives on the board are formally neutralized, leaving the ('disinterested'?) representatives of capital.[36] The Bullock majority proposals, as they admit, are intended basically to provide a new legitimacy which 'is essential for the long-term efficiency and profitability of the private sector . . .'[37] Thus, as Kinnock has concluded: 'Far from being an assault on either ownership power or on corporatism, Bullock's recommendations provide a democratic face for capitalist hierarchy.'[38]

WORKER DIRECTORS AND CO-DETERMINATION

The incorporative design of industrial democracy is clearly visible in the concept of the supervisory board, whether trade union representation is one third or one half of membership. (The employers' and EEC's suggestion that they should not be trade union based but simply workers' representatives is transparently an attempt to divide the loyalties of workers, and is certain to be rejected by the trade union movement in this country.) This concept is modelled on the German practice of co-determination, though, interestingly, co-determination was adopted in Germany partly because of the lack of viable trade union organization. Also co-determination, along with other aspects of German political life, is based on a confusion between social integration and social harmony: 'The confusion is dangerous because it suggests that creating harmony is the first task of politics; but this can never be accomplished except by repression.'[39] Thus supervisory boards, behind the façade of a redistribution of power, serve a manipulatory function. Important questions are decided in advance between management; supervisory boards are presented with a range of managerially constructed policy alternatives and any information provided to workers' representatives is systematically biased in the direction of managerial interests. Workers' representatives assume responsibility for decisions made but rarely have significant influence in the making of those decisions.[40] Moreover any assumption of a reciprocal influence is naïve, for, 'there is pressure to change the views of the worker directors rather than the policies of management. The worker director is used both directly and indirectly as a lever in the hands of management.'[41] The initial TUC insistence on parity of representation, suggests that tough negotiation would be introduced into the boardroom, and management certainly fear this. However, in practice, negotiation over anything but personnel matters is rare; parity does ensure that workers' representatives 'become integrated into the informal processes of debate and information exchange. But in doing so they tend to become even more integrated into a managerial perspective.'[42]

It is likely that these effects of co-determination have not gone unnoticed in this country, and reinforce the official advocacy of supervisory boards; thus it has been argued that:

The Benn–Foot strategy is essentially a gamble, based on the hope that if the unions are given every conceivable chance to involve themselves in management affairs they will eventually learn to share the responsibility. With the last Labour and Tory Governments both destroyed by the failure of their efforts to discipline the unions from without, it is easy to see why Labour hopes to teach them self-discipline instead.[43]

Even if an attempt were made by trade union board members to resist such pressures and to assume an aggressive and antagonistic stance to the management representatives, by accepting the role of co-managers they would, inevitably, have to relinquish their primary duty of representing workers' interests, since these fall very low on the list of normal managerial priorities: so, under co-determination 'the validity of the principle of profitability as the keynote of entrepreneurial initiative and planning was in no case called into question'.[44] In case there is any doubt as to their obligations as worker directors in Germany, 'Every member of the supervisory board or the managing board is obliged by law to maintain the care of an orderly and conscientious business manager, which means, under the conditions of the present economic system, that they have to go all out for the highest possible profit for the company.'[45] Furthermore, it is expected that worker directors will play no active part in strikes, though ironically worker directors have reported that they are only listened to during crises in the enterprise's industrial relations, that is, when shopfloor workers take, or threaten to take, forms of industrial action which are a more effective safeguard of their interests.[46] Such elements were instrumental in the rather dismal failure of the only major experiment of worker directors in this country, at the British Steel Corporation (though it admittedly was managerially initiated, and supervised, minority representation):

> the worker directors had no effect on the decision-making process because the board was not really the place where it occurred . . . even if it had been things would have changed little; management have a monopoly of knowledge, of language; and of authority; the worker directors were individuals with no sanctions and no power. Nor did the scheme lead to the representation of shopfloor interests at board level or a feeling of involvement in the organization on the part of the work force.[47]

The remoteness of worker directors from their constituents on the shopfloor is not simply a feature of the managerial hierarchy, but is deliberately encouraged since worker directors are formally prevented from effective communication with other workers due to the excessive emphasis on commercial secrecy at board level. In turn, this makes the informed control of worker directors by the electorate impossible, thus: 'Defined as a limited-purpose instrument, co-determination simply waives its claim to involve the workers at the grass roots, which is said to be hard to achieve in a mass organization anyhow.'[48] Consequently improvements achieved at the shopfloor level by this system have proved minimal: 'It is in the democratization and humanization of immediate job conditions that co-determination has probably achieved least. Exhausting physical effort, excessive heat, hazardous safety and health conditions have been far less points of attention (and redress) than in the American steel industry.'[49] This situation prevails because, rather than an attempt at creating more adequate representation of worker interests, 'the attractiveness to the legislature of works councils and minority representation schemes has been as a way of staving off employee discontent which might otherwise have expressed itself in a strong union presence in the plant. In such cases the purpose of the schemes is not to confer effective power upon the employees at board level.'[50] Thus when an official investigatory commission explored the effects of co-determination, 'the Commission was apparently more impressed with the pacifying effects which co-determination had on organized labour than by the sense of participation which it imparted to individual employees.'[51]

Hence becoming a party to the functioning of the existing system is a recipe for class conciliation, not intensified class struggle: 'Conflictual participation contains its own contradictions, and the new working class can be revolutionary only by jettisoning the participation.'[52] This point was appreciated in one contribution to the 1974 TUC debate on worker directors:

> Every victory won by collective bargaining machinery with the backing of a strong trade union shop-steward organization is won in the teeth of opposition from the owners of capital and leads to the strengthening of the power of the workers and the consequential weakening of the power of capital. Any advance that can be made by supervisory boards, even with 50 per cent trade union representatives, can take place only by joint agreement, and the extent of the advance will be limited by these considerations. The Movement can become frustrated and disillusioned as a consequence.[53]

In reasserting control in the new context of a company supervisory board structure, management would have a powerful ally in the influence of the external market which buttresses managerial domination. The capitalist market would immediately overwhelm any formal redistribution of authority at the enterprise level: *reform of the authority relations of the factory is impotent in the absence of structural reform of the production relations of society*. Thus the private sector of capitalist economies is now dominated by multi-national corporations, which have already shown a capacity to fully subvert the formal redistribution of control at the level of their subsidiary national companies.[54] As far as the persistence of the capitalist system is concerned 'it makes little difference whether certain groups of workers see their "rights" increased at any given phase in the production process, as long as Capital retains, consolidates and strengthens its hold on the reproduction process as a whole'.[55] Indeed: 'The experience of West Germany suggests that capitalism can easily thrive on worker directors.'[56] In capitalist society the managerial function is largely to interpret, influence and respond to the dictates of the market: 'Competition makes the immanent laws of capitalist production to be felt by each individual capitalist, as external coercive laws.'[57] *'The market' is a compound of largely unco-ordinated decisions motivated by the self-interested pursuit of profit, reflects the unequal and irrational distribution of power and wealth, and is based on the exchange value of commodities, that is, goods produced for sale – not for social need.* The anarchy of the market is beyond the control of workers' representatives at the individual company level: what is needed is a transformation of the *general* production relations of capitalist society.

However, to the extent that worker directors would reduce workers' resistance to both the demands of management and those of the market, such a development would be contributory to the efficiency of companies in purely capitalist terms. Why then do many managers, the CBI and other establishment organizations in this country oppose such shemes? One explanation is that:

> authoritarian methods are generally preferred to democratic ones by the great majority of managements and that their objections to participation are frequently based on ideological considerations in which concern for industrial efficiency is of a lower order than the maintenance of a particular pattern of domination.[58]

British management would prefer to preserve their privileged status, despite the fact that this rests upon long-since obsolete prerogatives, even if, in the process, the efficiency attainable by more manipulatory methods is impeded.

Thus the capitalist press responded to the Bullock proposals with uniform hostility, and frequently misinformed, well orchestrated hysteria: of course, in damning the Bullock majority report, press commentators were keen to proclaim their democratic zeal, but then they went on to suggest alternative schemes of the most paternalistic and disingenuous nature. The impetus for this came largely from the Bullock minority report, signed by the employers on the committee, which revealed flashes of conceited contempt for the democratic aspirations of workers, only to be matched by the excesses of the *ancien régime* prior to their overdue departure. In a singular bout of hypocrisy the minority report maintains 'It is one of the great strengths of political democracy in the free world that every citizen has equal political rights . . . This basic and fundamental principle of democracy has obvious implications in the industrial field'; but proceeds to suggest a participation scheme which is so weak that it would deprive *all* workers of *any* effective political power in industry if it were ever implemented.[59]

The minority report proposes a system of supervisory boards; devoid of all power; there simply to check 'the quality of management', and to establish a 'climate of public confidence'.[60] The one-third of the board elected by workers would be diluted by a representative of management; and the one-third 'independent' directors would in effect be appointed by the shareholders or their representatives. Furthermore, as a quid pro quo for providing such supervisory boards, the report insists on the establishment of Works Councils, which are clearly intended to undermine trade unionism, and at best would prove a return to the joint-consultation of the 1950s. Finally, subsidiary companies, foreign multi-nationals, banks and insurance companies are exempted from the employers' provisions, thus neatly excluding the majority of enterprises concerned.

When considering the employers' stance, contradictory implications of worker directors emerge: worker directors, as envisaged by the majority report, would probably unsettle the elitism of bourgeois corporate directors, which thrives on their physical and social distance from those whom they control; the presence of worker directors may even restrain their traditional indifference to workers' problems. Moreover, board experience would serve to demystify for participant worker directors the role of executives: workers could see the limitations of management capacities and the self-interest of their motivations. However, whether such awareness was sustained, and made general among the workforce, would depend on the susceptibility of worker directors to the systematic pressures they would encounter.

COLLECTIVE BARGAINING

Collective bargaining, as a method of industrial democracy, formally permits the disjunction, and thus the clearer identification of, the separate interests of management and workers which is precluded by supervisory boards. In a work that was representative of Labour Party and trade union thinking at the time, Clegg argued that in collective bargaining,

The contractual basis of the process tends to emphasize disagreement, for unless there is disagreement there is nothing to-bargain about. One result of this is to emphasize the interests of the parties. The organizations which they develop have their justification in differences of interest.[61]

In a recent report the EEC revealed that it thinks this is still so: 'to some extent collective bargaining will inevitably continue to be associated with industrial confrontation.'[62] Yet, in practice, collective bargaining clearly performs a conjunctive function: conflict is channelled into institutions where it may more effectively be controlled; rules and procedures are arrived at by mutual agreement, and the independent and oppositional quality essential to workers' control is inhibited.[63] Thus bargaining legitimates management authority, and agreements limit the potential scope of autonomous union action. Collective bargaining, therefore, more realistically, is 'a process by which the rank-and-file, inferior in power, status, and treatment, are allowed to press for marginal improvements in their lot on condition that they leave unchallenged those structural features of the system which perpetuate their inferiority.'[64] The enthusiasm of trade union officials for the extension of industrial democracy by the development of collective bargaining, is in large measure, merely an affirmation of their organizational interest in their union, and may involve no real enhancement of the power of shopfloor workers. This can mean, for workers, simply the replacement of one set of masters by another: 'What responsible trade unionism means is that the unions take over certain managerial functions in controlling their members.'[65] Certainly the question of union democracy is crucial to the democratization of industry, but it must be realized that: 'Trade unions, as organizations of the relatively powerless in an environment of power, can achieve any meaningful internal democracy only against external resistance and considerable odds.'[66] That is, trade unions are constantly under pressure to replicate the dominant hierarchical authority pattern of other organizations, with the severe restriction of rank-and-file action. A result of the lack of democracy in unions, and of the conjunctive nature of collective bargaining, is that the formal involvement of trade unions in extended negotiations may serve to *reduce* the power of the shopfloor to assert control over company decisions. As Hyman has pointed out, 'the primary goal is not to open the books but to transcend them.'[67] Thus Beynon found in his study of a car plant:

'The official union-employer contract made no real inroads into management prerogatives. It has allowed speed-up to continue unabated. As a result, the fight against the bosses has given way to a fight against a coalition of union officials and bosses.'[68]

Similar to the effects of supervisory boards, the aim of an extension of collective bargaining to higher levels of decision-making is to bring union representatives closer to the insistent pressure of the market, or, put in rather a different way, 'bringing home to workers the extent to which their claims are dependent upon the firm's ability to surmount and exploit the challenges posed by the external environment.'[69] Hence an expansion of joint regulation through collective bargaining would not prove a great advance since the 'most probable outcome would be not an expansion of industrial democracy but rather, whether intended or not, the consolidation of managerial capitalism'.[70] Intriguingly, therefore, collective bargaining and co-determination, though they have very different forms, have similar consequences; as Herding has maintained, the dichotomy of countervailing power versus co-determination is a false one. Thus, 'beneath the surface of contrary institutionalizations, co-determination and "pure" collective bargaining fulfil many similar functions.'[71] And what is the primary function of such institutionalization? It may be argued that 'the real function of the routinization of industrial conflict is to institutionalize inequalities between manager and managed'.[72]

SHOPFLOOR ACTION

The shopfloor is, in fact, the fulcrum of the ongoing class struggle, where the contradictions of existing class relations are experienced most acutely – at the point of production. Here a genuine redistribution of power has taken place, and workers' advance along the frontier of control is all the surer because of its informality and independence: as Goodrich indicated, 'The shopstewards' control was decidedly *contagious control*; its actual extent may be easily underrated by an outsider. It was recorded in no formal agreements.'[73] Thus, 'long before the movement for "self-government" in industry had become explicit, the line between "management" and "labour" had been, in fact, redrawn.'[74] Shopfloor controls, originally craft-based, though extended and politicized during the first shop stewards' movement, now rest primarily upon contemporary economic and technical developments in industry: increased capital intensity; the integration of the production process under mass production; specialized production in integrated plants, and reliance on constant supplies of components have all served to increase the vulnerability of the modern corporation to the exercise of workers' power at the shopfloor level. (It is ironic to note that the previous government/employer panacea for the 'reform' of industrial relations – productivity bargaining – was intended to undermine the job controls workers had gradually built up in modern industry, which represented the most significant exercise of participation by workers: this again casts doubt on whether the current panacea – participation and industrial democracy – is intended to redistribute control in any way.)

Moreover, shopfloor union organization exhibits a level of democratic organization alien to official union structures, and this represents an achievement in itself: 'Through the shopstewards' movement Britain has developed a unique layer of democratic trade unionism, which should be encouraged by every means, as long as it does not fragment unity.'[75] Although participation in union branches is often almost as negligible as in other forms of political organization, at the workshop level where there is a real opportunity for effective influence on policy, participation is higher, and, for example, in one study over 80 per cent of workers reported regularly voting in shop-steward elections.[76] Further, shop stewards are normally obliged to be responsive to their members' wishes, or they are quickly replaced; there is, therefore, a fairly regular turnover of shop stewards, making experience of the role, and its responsibilities, widespread. Finally, German trade unionists have expressed the desire for a 'shop-steward system similar to that attained in Britain, without becoming enmeshed in the management apparatus, and being surrounded by a rigid legal framework'.[77]

Yet there are serious limitations to present shopfloor action: many of the controls exercised at the shopfloor level are contained within policies determined at a much higher level and represent simply an independent accommodation to these policies; shopfloor controls, as to a great extent workers' control generally in capitalist society, can only be partial and reactive – generally workers' controls are subject to fluctuations in the market; finally, workers' awareness of the source of their problems is limited to their own employer and organization, and they frequently fail to perceive the structural location of their problems in market and government demands: the real enemy is not the capitalist but the capitalist system of production.[78] Thus, Herding contends:

> practice is more advanced than is consciousness. Adherence to job-control aspirations explicitly counteracts the economic rationality of the system but generally does not conspicuously reject it as a whole; the vast majority of rank-and-file articulations tend to include the problem of domination at the job level, rather than view it, other than vaguely, as a necessary symptom of the overall social system of production.[79]

This failure to comprehend the societal basis of capitalism imbues in workers' action a predominantly negative quality and restrains workers' potential to build an alternative society:

> The crisis of industrial relations in Britain today surely reflects this hiatus between the exercise of negative control and the will for positive control: organized employees are increasingly able to obstruct the economic objectives of management and governments when these conflict with their own desires, yet show little aspiration to transcend the resulting impasse.[80]

WORKERS' CO-OPERATIVES AND WORKERS' CONTROL

The hiatus between the entrenched oppositional character of contemporary shopfloor unionism and the organization and will necessary to begin to construct a different economic system, places in a particularly acute dilemma those workers who, whether by accident or design, find themselves at the brink of capitalism but unable, in isolation, to initiate an alternative system. Such a problem confronted three separate groups of workers at Kirkby, Meriden and Glasgow in the mid-1970s: working in subsidiaries of larger concerns they were declared redundant by 'rationalization' programmes that made centralization, automation, and the lowest possible labour costs the vital criteria, and treated craftsmanship and men's livelihoods with a careless contempt. In contrast to the languor with which British workers generally have come to accept redundancy, the ultimate confirmation of their commodity status, these workers, following the example of UCS, determined to fight by engaging in protracted factory occupations. However, in the absence of a general working-class mobilization against capitalism, and with a Labour government fastidious in its concern not to be associated with random nationalization (and to be associated with supposedly hard-headed corporate reorganization, i.e., asset stripping), the workers were faced with a dilemma as to what to do next, which was fatefully resolved in the compromise of establishing workers' co-operatives on an experimental basis.[81]

Traditionally, workers' co-operatives have endured a chequered existence. Marx appreciated the demonstrative impact of nineteenth-century producer co-operation, for example, referring to a 'Spectator' report on this of 1866, he commented with glee, 'The same paper finds that the main defect in the Rochdale co-operative experiments is this: "They showed that associations of workmen could manage shops, mills, and almost all forms of industry with success, and they immediately improved the condition of the men, but then they did not leave a clear place for masters." What a dreadful thing!'[82] However, Marx was also aware of the shortcomings of producer co-operation:

> Its great merit is to practically show that the present pauperizing and despotic system of the subordination of labour to capital can be superseded by the republican and beneficent system of the association of free and equal producers . . . Restricted, however, to the dwarfish form into which individual wage slaves can elaborate it by their private efforts, the co-operative system will never transform capitalist society. To convert social production into one large and harmonious system of free and co-operative labour, general social changes are wanted, changes of the general conditions of society, never to be realized save by the transfer of the organized forces of society, viz., the state power, from capitalists and landlords to the producers themselves.[83]

Hence, in the absence of a general transformation of production relations, workers in isolated co-operatives remain at the mercy of market forces and government controls which destroy the possibility of substantial internal reform. This has been particularly true for the three new co-operatives. Dependent on government finance, they have been tightly controlled by the Department of Industry; the control has been particularly severe since there are grounds to believe each of the co-operatives was seriously under-capitalized at launch, and in the case of the *Scottish Daily News* this proved fatal: again Marx argued, 'as far as the present co-operative societies are concerned, they are of value *only* in so far as they are the independent creations of the workers and not the protegés either of the governments or of the bourgeois.'[84]

Although at each of the three new co-operatives the venture was approached with a fair degree of idealism, much of this was destroyed as the co-operatives were impelled to conform to many of the practices of private industry on matters of pay, hours, intensity of work, management control and so on. Efforts were made in two of the co-operatives to significantly reduce differentials of pay and status with some success. Nevertheless, pay was generally lower than in outside industry and, for various reasons, the co-operatives provided few intrinsic benefits to compensate for this. The market influence upon the *Scottish Daily News* in Glasgow was particularly intense, because it directly determined not only how the product should be produced, but also the nature of the product. The newspaper public had been saturated and shaped for decades by reactionary proprietorial newspapers, including the forerunner to the *Daily News*, and the attempt to present a left-wing newspaper, yet attain a mass readership, in this context proved impossible, when combined with the other difficulties of the *Daily News*. Survival for the other workers' co-operatives is only assured by competing with other producers, which, if successful, necessarily involves undermining the job security of those workers.

A central problem of the co-operatives was the role of worker directors: though in each factory workers quickly proved they were competent to assume the position of director with a minimum of guidance, having accomplished this, they found that there was little freedom of manœuvre to innovate. Moreover at Kirkby where the two convenors became also the sole directors, ostensibly to prevent conventional managerial directors reasserting control, their business concerns predominated with a consequential weakening of trade union representation. In contrast, at the *Daily News* the crucial problem was that the constitution allowed election of the Executive Council *by* the employees, but not necessarily *from* the employees. This permitted Maxwell, with all his financial muscle, to convince a sufficient number of workers that he should be elected, however incongruous it should be, and although, as the assistant editor wryly maintained, 'it's obviously against the principle of a workers' co-operative to have a millionaire in Oxford who's a shopfloor representative'. Maxwell's arrival as the self-styled 'overlord' of the *Scottish Daily News*, was, of course, the negation of workers' control.[85]

At a lower level problems were also experienced in the new co-operatives: the retention of foremen at two of the co-operatives was thought unnecessary by many workers; indeed where managerial control survived in the co-operatives, its command was strengthened by the novel tool of the claim 'it's for the co-operative'. As Warner has indicated, 'Comparative studies . . . suggest that in spite of (although one could as well argue because of) the structure of self-management, Yugoslav managers have more power than in any of the other countries studied . . .'[86] Furthermore, in the new organizations shop stewards were confused as to whether their primary loyalty was to the co-operative, for which can be read 'company', or to their members; moreover at Kirkby the Works Council assumed a purely nominal role, similar to Benson's analysis of the Yugoslavian system: 'the workers' self-management body tends to become an ancillary committee for deciding questions of relatively small importance.'[87] Finally, the merger of union officials into management did not guarantee the more effective settlement of workers' grievances, whilst inhibiting the capacity of workers to make the traditional union response to unresolved grievances. Whereas in Yugoslavia:

workers have learned that management has the whip hand, and the classic weapon of the strike is more effective in combatting managerial power than is the workers' council. It has, in fact, been suggested that the workers increasingly see the self-management structure as a sort of talking shop, ideally suited to the tendency of managements to compromise and procrastinate in their own favour, which actually detracts from the power of the working class to take direct action.[88]

In conclusion, the constraints upon reform in the co-operatives provided by the market and government were compounded by the limitations of the consciousness and organization of the workers themselves: indeed, at Meriden little explicit political consciousness was exhibited whatsoever; an abundance of motorcycle and craft consciousness was displayed, but that is a different matter. During the factory occupations, which could have been periods of immense educational value for all the workers, many were not involved at all, and most of the organizational effort was provided by the workers normally active in union matters; given the external pressures, this allowed the co-operatives, once operative, to slip back into traditional practices without significant thought or resistance.

CONCLUSIONS

From the foregoing analysis it may be argued that industrial democracy proposals are likely to have the opposite of their supposed effect. That is, most schemes for industrial democracy will involve an absorption of workers' representatives into capitalist forms of control, not a transcending of these: they will bring about the more effective integration of workers into existing economic and social relations rather than produce any basic alteration in the capitalist system.

> The chasm between their respective economic positions has not been bridged, and therefore the joint councils and committees can turn out to be nothing other than an extension of organization on the part of the capitalist class, drawing within itself the trade union organization for the purpose of safe-guarding its own interests by the policy of peaceful persuasion and permeation of the forces of the opposition.[89]

Most employers resent trade unions, and similarly resent participation: they would prefer complete, unilateral, unquestioned control. But this is now unrealistic, and collective bargaining and worker participation are means by which employers may preserve and consolidate their existing partial degree of control. This is not ideal in the employer's view, but at present the most likely alternative in many industries is not the complete control of management, but *the entrenched control of workers*. Some workers are alert to these implications of workers' participation and worker directors. For example, the Lucas Aerospace shop stewards have argued: 'This Combine Committee is opposed to such concepts and is not prepared to share in the management of means of production and the production of products which they find abhorrent . . . There cannot be "industrial democracy" until there is a real shift in power to the workers themselves.'[90] The Bullock proposals, regrettably, do not encompass such a shift in class power: though they are not a magical defusion of capitalist contradictions, by extending the 'unarbitrary' power of management, they may be one more means to, at least temporarily, contain them. Furthermore, it is unlikely that the majority proposals will be introduced, except in a weakened form: thus the cynical attitude of the Labour government was illustrated by its eagerness to comply with CBI objections, and its attempt to use Bullock as part of an incomes policy package. And yet, the struggle for worker directors could divert the labour movement for years to come.

The tone of this discussion has been deliberately polemical: in some circumstances, given an independent, militant, and politically conscious union organization it is conceivable that industrial democracy schemes could provide the opportunity to extend workers' influence. Yet if unions were independent, militant and politically conscious, they would not settle for the cosmetic embellishment of the hierarchical and authoritarian structure of management currently proposed – they would insist on a transformation of the whole economic system, attainable because of the present weakness of British capitalism. Moreover there is a danger in treating worker directors on supervisory boards as an interim advance, for, as Murphy recognized:

Once the organization has become established it will, like all other organizations, have a prejudice in favour of the continuance of its existence, and fight against anything which seeks its overthrow. This means that the organized labour movement is to be used as a means to prevent the transition from wagedom to socialism.[91]

Not only would worker directors become committed to the stability of the existing system, but they would also have an impossibly difficult task in striving for reforms within that system: thus Allen has persuasively argued,

An institution . . . has a perspective built into it and which belongs to its structure. A hierarchical, monolithic business organization embodies inequalities no matter what its stated purpose is, and these cannot be removed by adaption such as drawing wage-earners into managerial positions or putting trade unionists on boards of directors. They can be eliminated only by its destruction and recreation from a structure based on equality.[92]

To accomplish such a reconstruction social ownership is indispensable, if, in itself, not sufficient.[93]

Nor will implementation of a democratically planned and controlled economy be attained by the piecemeal nationalization of previous Labour governments: for although some important industries were nationalized, invariably they were in bad condition due to neglect, their private owners were massively compensated, and they required vast investment programmes to renovate them. Profitable and growth industries were left in private hands, and so ironically nationalization *strengthened* the private sector and capitalist class:

It did this by relieving them of the responsibility for derelict industries, by removing from them the economic consequences of their inter-war policies of low investment and inefficient management, and by providing them instead with an infrastructure of publicly owned basic industries whose pricing policies could be designed so as to subsidize the private sector on which economic growth and export earnings so critically depended.[94]

No attempt was made to shift power towards the workers in the nationalized industries; rather, executive hierarchies were consciously created to rival the splendour of the private sector, with chairmen so powerful and remote that one leading figure was described as 'bossman personified: omniscient, intolerant, domineering and responsive to only the crudest flattery'.[95]

Future nationalization could only be successful as part of a democratic socialist society if the workers themselves take control of their industries.

In the meantime, capitalist economic relations remain essentially exploitative and hierarchical. There is, therefore, no question of employers voluntarily introducing an element of industrial democracy except as a manipulatory device. Democracy may be introduced in industry only *in opposition* to capitalist control, not as part of it, which entails a heightening, not diminution of industrial militancy. To achieve this, the maintenance of independent workers' organizations is necessary.

NOTES

1. TUC, *Industrial Democracy*, 1974. The Labour Party, *The Community and the Company*, Green Paper, 1974. CBI, *Employee Participation*, 1974.

2. J. T. MURPHY, 'Compromise or Independence: An Examination of the Whitley Report', Sheffield Workers Committee, 1918, p. 11. Lenin was equally scathing: 'The closer I look at this "industrial democracy", the more clearly I see that it is half-baked and theoretically false. It is nothing but a hodgepodge.' V. I. LENIN, *Lenin on Trade Unions*, Moscow Publishers, 1970.

3. P. BACHRACH, *The Theory of Democratic Elitism*, University of London Press, 1970, p. 93. C. B. MACPHERSON, *The Real World of Democracy*, Oxford University Press, 1972. J. LIVELY, *Democracy*, Blackwell, 1975.

4. C. PATEMAN, *Participation and Democratic Theory*, Cambridge University Press, 1970.

5. R. HYMAN, *The Workers' Union*, Clarendon Press, 1971, p. 207.

6. R. HYMAN, *Industrial Relations – A Marxist Analysis*, Macmillan, 1975, p. 124.

7. C. H. ANDERSON, *The Political Economy of Social Class*, Prentice-Hall, 1974, p. 197.

8. *Political Studies*, 1967, vol. 15, p. 55.

9. S. LUKES, *Power: A Radical View*, Macmillan, 1974.

10. H. DRAPER, 'Marx on Democratic Forms of Government', *Socialist Register*, 1974, p. 119.

11. ibid.

12. M. POOLE, *Workers' Participation in Industry*, Routledge & Kegan Paul, 1975, pp. 8–9.

13. MURPHY, op. cit., p. 7.

14. C. GOODRICH, *The Frontier of Control*, p. 229 of this book.

15. Royal Commission on Trade Unions and Employers' Associations 1965–8, *Report*, HMSO, paragraph 129.

16. R. HYMAN, *Strikes*, Fontana/Collins, 1972, p. 42; The Royal Commission on Trade Unions, p. 54.

17. K. ALEXANDER, *Worker Participation Symposium*, Keele University, 1975.

18. J. H. GOLDTHORPE, 'Industrial Relations in Great Britain: A Critique of Reformism,' pp. 203-4 of this book.

19. P. BRANNEN, *et al.*, *The Worker Directors*, Hutchinson, 1976, p. 257.

20. CBI, *Employee Participation*, p. 12.

21. K. COATES and T. TOPHAM, *The New Unionism*, Penguin, 1974, p. 81.

22. MURPHY, op. cit., p. 10.

23. HUGH SCANLON, *Worker Participation Symposium*, Keele University, 1975.

24. E. BATSTONE and P. L. DAVIES, *Industrial Democracy: European Experience*, HMSO, p. 39.

25. The Royal Commission on Trade Unions, pp. 257–60.

26. Labour Research Department, *Industrial Democracy: A Trade Unionist's Guide*, 1976, p. 12. This is an extremely useful summary of the proposals and problems involved in industrial democracy.

27. TUC, *Conference Report*, 1975.

28. *Report of the Committee of Inquiry on Industrial Democracy*, HMSO, 1977, pp. 68 and 74.

29. N. KINNOCK, 'Bullock and the Left', *New Statesman*, 11 February 1977, pp. 175–6.

30. *Report of the Committee*, pp. 134–7 and 149.

31. ibid., pp. 138–9.

32. ibid., p. 9.

33. Royal Commission on the Distribution of Income and Wealth, HMSO, 1975, *Report No. 2, Income From Companies and Its Distribution*, pp. 36–7, derived from Table 17.

34. This assumes, as t commission does elsewhere (*Report No. 1*, p. 139), that wealth holders constitute one half of the adult population.

35. Includes British government securities (excluding those held through the National Savings register); municipal and other government securities; shares and debentures in companies (including investment trusts); unit trusts; money on municipal bonds; money on loan to companies.

36. 'Report of the Committee of Inquiry on Industrial Democracy', op. cit., pp. 105, 121, 148.

37. ibid., p. 95.

38. KINNOCK, op. cit., p. 176.

39. R. DAHRENDORF, *Society and Democracy in Germany*, Weidenfeld and Nicolson, 1968, p. 195. Also, I. L. HOROWITZ, 'Consensus, Conflict and Co-operation: A Sociological Inventory', *Social Forces*, 1963.

40. G. STRAUSS and E. ROSSENSTEIN, 'Workers' Participation: A Critical View', *Industrial Relations*, vol. 9, no. 2, 1970. B. WILPERT, 'Research on Industrial Democracy: the German Case', *Industrial Relations*, Spring, 1975.

41. E. BATSTONE and P. L. DAVIES, *Industrial Democracy: European Experience*, p. 25.

42. ibid., p. 40 and pp. 64–9.

43. E. JACOBS, 'Boardroom Jobs for the Boys', *Sunday Times*, 30 March, 1975.

44. E. BATSTONE and P. L. DAVIES, op. cit., p. 65.

45. W. DAUBLER, 'Co-determination: The German Experience', *Industrial Law Journal*, vol. 4, p. 225.

46. E. BATSTONE and P. L. DAVIES, op. cit., pp. 33 and 59.

47. P. BRANNEN *et al.*, *The Worker Directors*, p. 236.

48. R. HERDING, *Job Control and Union Structure*, Rotterdam University Press, 1972, p. 320.

49. ibid., pp. 329–30.

50. E. BATSTONE and P. L. DAVIES, op. cit., p. 83.

51. H. HARTMANN, 'Co-determination Today and Tomorrow', *British Journal of Industrial Relations*, 1975, p. 56.

52. M. MANN, *Consciousness and Action Among the Western Working Class*, Macmillan, 1973, p. 65.

53. TUC, *1974 Conference Report*, p. 524.

54. E. BATSTONE and P. L. DAVIES, op. cit., pp. 72–4.

55. E. MANDEL, *Workers' Control and Workers' Councils*.

56. Labour Research Department, op. cit., p. 10.

57. K. MARX, *Capital*, vol. 1, Lawrence & Wishart, 1959, p. 592. For a contemporary discussion see R. BLACKBURN, 'The New Capitalism' in *Ideology and Social Science*, Fontana, 1972.

58. M. POOLE, op. cit., p. 59.

59. *Report of the Committee*, p. 175.

60. ibid., p. 178.

61. H. A. CLEGG, *A New Approach to Industrial Democracy*, Blackwell, 1960, p. 109. In this work Clegg disavowed his earlier commitment to nationalization as a prerequisite of industrial democracy, and maintained that industrial democracy was synonymous with collective bargaining. A rather histrionic, though in places telling, critique of Clegg's 'new' theory is provided by P. BLUMBERG, *Industrial Democracy*, Constable, 1968.

62. EEC, *Employer Participation and Company Structure*, 1975.

63. R. HYMAN, introduction to GOODRICH, *The Frontier of Control*, Pluto Press, 1975, p. xxv.

64. A. FOX, *Man Mismanagement*, Hutchinson, 1974, p. 143.

65. P. BRANNEN *et al.*, op. cit., p. 242.

66. R. HYMAN, *Industrial Relations: A Marxist Introduction*, p. 168.

67. R. HYMAN, 'Workers' Control and Revolutionary Theory', *Socialist Register*, 1974, p. 247.

68. H. BEYNON, *Working for Ford*, Penguin, 1973, p. 40.

69. W. E. J. MCCARTHY and N. D. ELLIS, *Management by Agreement*, Hutchinson, 1973, p. 101.

70. J. H. GOLDTHORPE, op. cit.

71. R. HERDING, op, cit., p. 333. This view is implicit in the Bullock Report, p. 124.

72. J. E. T. ELDRIDGE, 'Industrial Conflict', in J. CHILD, *Man and Organization*, Allen & Unwin, 1973, p. 161.

73. C. GOODRICH, *Frontier of Control*, Pluto, 1975, p. 11.

74. TAWNEY, Foreword to GOODRICH, op. cit.

75. R. TAYLOR, 'How Democratic Are The Trade Unions?', *Political Quarterly*, vol. 47, no. 1, 1976, p. 37.

76. J. H. GOLDTHORPE et al., *The Affluent Worker: Industrial Attitudes and Behaviour*, Cambridge University Press, 1968, p. 103.

77. B. BYE, *The Struggle for Workers' Participation in Germany*, LPSC/Quartet Books, 1974, p. 34.

78. R. HYMAN, *Workers' Control and Revolutionary Theory*.

79. R. HERDING, op. cit., p. 349.

80. R. HYMAN, 'G. D. H. Cole and Industrial Democracy: A Review', *Industrial Relations*, vol. 5, no. 3, 1974.

81. For a more detailed analysis, see T. CLARKE, *The Workers' Cooperatives: A Social Experiment* (forthcoming).

82. K. MARX, *Capital*, ch. 13, 'Co-operation', Penguin, 1976, p. 449.

83. K. MARX, *First International and After*, Penguin, 1974, p. 90.

84. K. MARX, *Critique of the Gotha Programme*, Selected Works, Lawrence and Wishart, 1970, p. 326.

85. See the account of the downfall of the paper by the ex-chairman: A. MACKIE, *The Scottish Daily News*, in *The New Workers' Cooperatives*, Spokesman, 1976. The story from the journalists' side is presented in R. MCKAY and B. BARR, *The Scottish Daily News*, Canongate, 1976.

86. M. WARNER, 'Whither Yugoslav Self-Management?', *Industrial Relations Journal*, 1975.

87. L. BENSON, 'Market Socialism and Class Structure: Manual Workers and Managerial Power in the Yugoslav Enterprise' in F. PARKIN, *The Social Analysis of Class Structure*, Tavistock, 1974, p. 260.

88. ibid., p. 264.

89. J. T. MURPHY, op. cit., p. 8.

90. Lucas Aerospace Shop Stewards' Combine Committee, *Corporate Plan: a contingency strategy as a positive alternative to recession and redundancies.*

91. J. T. MURPHY, op. cit., p. 7.

92. V. L. ALLEN, *Ideology, Consciousness and Experience: The Case of the British Miners*, British Sociological Association, 1975.

93. R. HARRISON, 'Retreat from Industrial Democracy', *New Left Review*, no. 4, 1960, p. 37, and BLUMBERG, op. cit.

94. DAVID COATES, *The Labour Party and the Struggle for Socialism*, Cambridge University Press, 1975, p. 42.

95. 'The Defectors – Poor Old King Coal', *New Statesman*, 24 January 1975, p. 103.

20 Marxism and the Sociology of Trade Unionism

Richard Hyman

Reprinted with permission from R. Hyman, *Marxism and the Sociology of Trade Unionism*, Pluto Press, 1971, pp. 37–53.

THE LIMITS OF TRADE UNION CONSCIOUSNESS

The argument of the previous section was that recent British experience reveals countervailing tendencies to those discerned by Lenin, Michels and Trotsky. Pure-and-simple trade union activity *does* pose a substantial threat to the stability of the capitalist economy in certain circumstances. The 'iron law of oligarchy' *is* subject to important constraints. Attempts to extend the process of incorporation *do* meet significant obstacles to success. To this extent, the 'optimistic' interpretation of trade unionism cannot be rejected *outright*.

The essential insight of Marx and Engels, the significance of which subsequent writers have tended to minimize, is that trade unionism necessarily articulates the conflicts generated by capitalist industry. More specifically, unionism can be seen as embodying workers' revolt (however tentative) against the deprivations inherent in their role: a revolt which can challenge the fundamental basis of capitalism on two fronts.

Firstly, unionism represents a reaction against economic exploitation: the extraction of surplus value from workers' labour. Unions have always conducted a struggle, within this economic context, to regulate and improve the terms on which workers are obliged to dispose of their labour power. Lenin's arguments on this score have already been critically evaluated: while it is true that workers' economic demands can normally be accommodated within the framework of capitalism, this is not universally the case.

Secondly, and less coherently, unionism also raises issues of power and control. At the very least, as Goodrich argued in a sadly neglected study, 'the demand not to be controlled disagreeably' – which can form the basis for far more explicitly 'political' demands – 'runs through all trade union activity'.[1] More generally, the recurrence in British industrial relations of disputes concerning 'managerial functions' indicates the extent to which union concern with issues of wages and conditions necessitates an interest in the question of managerial control.[2] In a pure form, it might be argued, business unionism is inconceivable; not merely because it seems improbable that workers' deprivations are ever experienced as exclusively economic, but also because the 'effort bargain' implicit in every employment relationship is a persistent source of 'political' conflict.[3]

This is not of course to argue that the 'optimistic' analysis can be accepted without substantial qualification. Relevant here is a further aspect of the current British situation: the manifest gap between the activity and the consciousness of organized workers. While the day-to-day activities of trade unionism, particularly at shopfloor level, create a situation of dangerous instability for British capitalism, this consequence is wholly unintended.

> Large numbers of workers are recognizing for the first time the need for collective self-activity to protect their living standards and working conditions; but this activity does not reflect any *general* questioning of the relations of production in capitalist society. The hegemony of bourgeois ideology is evident in the findings of 'public opinion' surveys: the majority of trade unionists are willing to criticize the unions for economic difficulties, blame workers for most disputes, and support legal restrictions on the right to strike. Such findings follow naturally from the purely sectional consciousness of most organized workers: they are ready to accept the condemnation, by press and politicians, of *other* workers' strikes. Though they are unable to accept the dominant ideology in relation to their *own* activity, this activity is itself – whether or not it results in concrete gains – often transient; rarely does it result in any enduring revision of consciousness.[4]

Another example of the uncritical acceptance of bourgeois ideology is the British labour movement's traditional reverence for parliamentarism, its fervent refusal – despite the virtual fusion of 'politics' and 'economics' in contemporary capitalism – to contemplate the use of workers' industrial strength in pursuit of 'political' goals.[5] In the current situation, such ideological blinkers allow a very real possibility that organized workers, meeting an increasingly concerted assault in a fragmented manner, may sustain a series of sectional defeats which could rapidly transform self-confidence into demoralization. Through such a process, workers' shopfloor power could indeed be neutralized – with or without the collaboration of union official-dom.

Thus the question naturally arises whether the handicap of a partial and sectional consciousness is inevitable – whether all challenges which union activity may pose to the stability of the system (unless conducted under the direct leadership of a revolutionary party) are necessarily unintentional. Evidently the Leninist theory of trade union consciousness must be examined in detail.

Lenin's formulation in *What Is To Be Done?* has already been cited. Discussion of his arguments may however be facilitated by consideration of a recent presentation, ostensibly of the same thesis, by Hobsbawm:

The 'spontaneous' experience of the working class leads it to develop two things: on the one hand a set of immediate demands (e.g., for higher wages) and of institutions, modes of behaviour, etc., designed to achieve them; on the other – but in a much vaguer form and not invariably – a general discontent with the existing system, a general aspiration after a more satisfactory one, and a general outline (co-operative against competitive, socialist against individualist) of alternative social arrangements. The first group of ideas is in the nature of things far more precise and specific than the second. Moreover they operate all the time whereas the second are of little practical importance – though of immense moral importance – except at the comparatively rare moments when the complete overthrow of the existing system appears likely or immediately practicable. Under conditions of stable capitalism 'trade union consciousness' is quite compatible with the *de facto* (or even the formal) acceptance of capitalism, unless that system fails to allow for the *minimum* trade unionist demand of 'a fair day's work for a fair day's pay'. (When it does not, trade union consciousness appears automatically to imply changes of the second order.)[6]

In the light of the previous appraisal of Lenin's arguments, one question immediately suggests itself: what sets the parameters of workers' conception of 'the minimum trade unionist demand of "a fair day's work for a fair day's pay"'? If workers were to define 'fairness' in terms of 'the full fruits of their labours', a demand which is superficially purely economic would have obvious revolutionary implications. As argued earlier, the level of demands which can be accommodated varies according to the economic context. In some contexts, *any* demands for improvements are unrealizable; and in *any* situation, there will be some point in excess of which demands are intolerable. The essence of the Trotskyist conception of the 'transitional demand' is precisely the assumption that a struggle for objectively unattainable reforms will generate consciousness of the structural limitations of the capitalist system. History permits this thesis at least a certain plausibility.

This leads to a more specific criticism of Lenin's analysis: his rigid dichotomy between trade union and Social-Democratic (i.e., revolutionary socialist) consciousness, together with his insistence that there could be 'no middle ideology'. The bizarre implications of this position are revealed – presumably unintentionally – in Hobsbawm's formulation: for he accepts that 'trade union consciousness' can extend to a generalized discontent with capitalism and the conception of and aspiration for a form of socialist society. Indeed, he asserts that 'a vague – and consequently entirely ineffective – utopianism can be as "spontaneous" a product of proletarian experience as reformism. British craft unions are in this respect no more spontaneous than Spanish anarchism'.[7] Yet in Lenin's own terms, such 'utopianism' would of necessity be classified as the ideological enslavement of the workers to the bourgeoisie: a position which, it might be thought, even the most hostile critic of anarcho-syndicalism would hesitate to embrace explicitly. It seems reasonable, therefore, to question whether the assertion of 'no middle ideology' is in fact valid: whether, indeed, the dichotomy between trade union and revolutionary socialist consciousness may mask a continuum along which escalation is in certain circumstances possible.[8]

It might be noted that the inflexible position adopted by Lenin in *What Is To Be Done?* accords ill with certain of his earlier and later writings, where the potential of the trade union struggle in raising workers' consciousness received considerable emphasis. His draft Programme for the Russian Social-Democratic Party, written in 1895–96, presented the straightforward 'optimistic' thesis of traditional Marxism;[9] while in his article 'On Strikes' in 1899 he went considerably further:

> Every strike brings thoughts of socialism very forcibly to the worker's mind, thoughts of the struggle of the entire working class for emancipation from the oppression of capital . . . A strike teaches workers to understand what the strength of the employers and what the strength of the workers consists in; it teaches them not to think of their own employer alone and not of their own immediate workmates alone but of all the employers, the whole class of capitalists and the whole class of workers . . .
>
> A strike, moreover, opens the eyes of the workers to the nature, not only of the capitalists, but of government and the laws as well . . . Strikes, therefore, teach the workers to unite; they show them that they can struggle against the capitalist only when they are united; strikes teach the workers to think of the struggle of the whole working class against the whole class of factory owners and against the arbitrary, police government. This is the reason that socialists call strikes 'a school of war', a school in which the workers learn to make war on their enemies for the liberation of the whole people, of all who labour, from the yoke of government officials and from the yoke of capital.[10]

What Is To Be Done? of course denied absolutely that through experience in trade union struggles, workers' consciousness could develop spontaneously to such a degree; but Lenin's experience of the revolutionary events of 1905 turned him again towards his earlier 'optimistic' assessment. Workers' experience in a spontaneous strike movement at the Putilov Works he saw as generating a 'revolutionary instinct':

> One is struck by the amazingly rapid shift of the movement from purely economic to the political ground, by the tremendous solidarity and energy displayed by hundreds of thousands of proletarians – and all this, notwithstanding the fact that conscious Social-Democratic influence is lacking or is but slightly evident.[11]

As the events of 1905 developed, Lenin went on to suggest that 'the working class is instinctively, spontaneously Social-Democratic'.[12] And reviewing this same period in retrospect, he returned effectively to the classic Marxian position:

> Capital collects the workers in great masses in big cities, uniting them, teaching them to act in unison. At every step the workers come face to face with their main enemy – the capitalist class. In combat with this enemy the worker becomes a *socialist*, comes to realize the necessity of a complete reconstruction of the whole of society, the complete abolition of all poverty and all oppression.[13]

This interpretation was repeated on the eve of the 1917 revolution:

> A specifically proletarian weapon of struggle – the strike – was the principal means of bringing the masses into motion . . . Only struggle educates the exploited class. Only struggle discloses to it the magnitude of its own power, widens its horizons, enhances its abilities, clarifies its mind, forges its will. . . . The economic struggle, the struggle for immediate and direct improvement of conditions, is alone capable of rousing the most backward strata of the exploited masses, gives them a real education and transforms them – during a revolutionary period – into an army of political fighters within the space of a few months.[14]

Ironically, these views represent a close parallel to Rosa Luxemburg's theory of spontaneity – which is commonly presented as a total contradiction of Leninism. It is of interest that her own views owed much to Russian experience:

> What do we see, however, in the phases through which the Russian movement has already passed? Its most important and most fruitful tactical turns of the last decade were not by any means 'invented' by determinate leaders of the movement, and much less by leading organizations, but were in each case the spontaneous product of the unfettered movement itself . . . Of all these cases, we may say that, in the beginning was 'the deed'. The initiative and conscious leadership of the social-demo-

cratic organizations played an exceedingly small role . . . Social-democratic action . . . grows historically out of the elemental class struggle. In so doing, it works and moves in the dialectical contradiction that the proletarian army is first recruited in the struggle itself, where it also becomes clear regarding the tasks of the struggle. Organization, enlightenment and struggle are not separate, mechanical and also temporarily disconnected factors . . . but are only different sides of the same process.[15]

Unlike the syndicalists, Luxemburg did not suggest that trade union struggles would in all circumstances lead naturally to revolutionary action: 'only in the strong atmosphere of a revolutionary period can every partial little clash between labour and capital build up into a general explosion.'[16] But her central argument remained clear: 'activity itself educates the masses'.[17] As she insisted in her last major speech:

The battle for Socialism can only be carried on by the masses, directly against capitalism, in every factory, by every proletarian against his particular employer . . . Socialism cannot be made and will not be made by order, not even by the best and most capable Socialist government. It must be made by the masses, through every proletarian individual.[18]

The 'optimistic' alternative to the one-sided pessimism of *What Is To Be Done?* need not of course imply an acceptance of anarcho-syndicalism: the thesis that economic struggles can directly and exclusively generate revolution. The issue between Lenin and Luxemburg, or between the Lenin of 1902 and the Lenin of 1905, was essentially the question of the *limits* of trade union consciousness. The need for a revolutionary party to articulate workers' opposition to capitalism, to spearhead its overthrow, and to guide the construction of a new society was not in dispute. The difference was more subtle: a question of the *degree* to which trade union struggles rendered workers susceptible to a revolutionary broadening of consciousness; a question of the *type* of relationship to be established between the revolutionary party and spontaneous trade union activity.

This issue was central to the articles in which Gramsci, in 1919 and 1920, explored the ambivalence inherent in trade unionism.[19] On the one hand, he characterized unions as types of proletarian organization specific to the historical period dominated by capital. It can be maintained that they are in a certain sense an integral part of capitalist society, and have a function which is inherent in the régime of private property.[20]

To the thesis of integration he added that of bureaucratization:

The workers feel that the complex of 'their' organization, the trade union, has become such an enormous apparatus that it now obeys laws internal to its structure and its complicated functions, but foreign to the masses . . . They feel that their will for power is not adequately expressed, in a clear and precise sense, in the present institutional hierarchy . . .

These *de facto* conditions irritate the workers, but as individuals they are powerless to change them: the worlds and desires of each single man are too small in comparison to the iron laws inherent in the bureaucratic structure of the trade union apparatus.[21]

Gramsci appreciated that such internal developments followed naturally from the external activities of unions in collective bargaining.

The union concentrates and generalizes its scope so that the power and discipline of the movement are focused in a central office. This office detaches itself from the masses it regiments, removing itself from the fickle eddy of moods and currents that are typical of the great tumultuous masses. The union thus acquires the ability to sign agreements and take on responsibilities, obliging the entrepreneur to accept a certain legality in his relations with the workers. This legality is conditional on the trust the entrepreneur has in the *solvency* of the union, and in its ability to ensure that the working masses respect their contractual obligations.[22]

Necessary as this was to the unions' task of achieving concrete gains for their members, the order established by collective agreement came naturally to be regarded as good in itself.

The union bureaucrat conceives industrial legality as a permanent state of affairs. He too often defends it from the same viewpoint as the proprietor. He sees only chaos and wilfulness in everything that emerges from the working masses. He does not understand the worker's act of rebellion against capitalist discipline as a rebellion; he perceives only the physical act, which may in itself and for itself be trivial . . . In these conditions union discipline can only be a service to capital.[23]

Yet at the same time as Gramsci developed these arguments, he insisted that the same characteristics of trade unionism were of great positive value in their contribution to working-class cohesion and self-confidence: 'the union co-ordinates the productive forces and imprints on the industrial apparatus a communistic form'.[24] What was essential, from the socialist viewpoint, was that the *transitional* nature of trade union 'legality' should be recognized.

The emergence of an industrial legality is a great victory for the working class, but it is not the ultimate and definitive victory. Industrial legality has improved the working class's material living conditions, but it is no more than a compromise – a compromise which had to be made and which must be supported until the balance of forces favours the working class.[25]

Central to his analysis was the dialectical opposition between the institutionalization inherent in the functions of official unionism, and the activities of the Factory Councils which had emerged in Italian industry. The latter, he argued, were 'proletarian institutions of a new type: representative in basis and industrial in arena'.[26]

In so far as it builds this representative apparatus, the working class effectively completes the expropriation of the primary machine, of the most important instrument of production: the working class itself. It thereby rediscovers itself, acquiring consciousness of its organic unity and counterposing itself as a whole to capitalism. The working class thus asserts that industrial power and its source ought to return to the factory. It presents the factory in a new light, from the workers' point of view, as a form in which the working class constitutes itself into a specific organic body, as the cell of a new State, the workers' State – and as the basis of a new representative system, a system of Councils . . .

The Factory Council is the negation of industrial legality. It tends at every moment to destroy it, for it necessarily leads the working class towards the conquest of industrial power, and indeed makes the working class the source of industrial power . . . By its revolutionary spontaneity, the Factory Council tends to unleash the class war at any moment; by its bureaucratic form, the trade union tends to prevent the class war ever being unleashed. The relations between the two institutions should be such that a capricious impulse on the part of the Councils could not cause a step backwards by the working class, a working-class defeat; in other words, the Council should accept and assimilate the discipline of the union, while the revolutionary character of the Council exercises influence on the union, as a reagent dissolving its bureaucratism.

The Council tends to move beyond industrial legality at any moment. The Council is the exploited, tyrannized mass, forced to perform servile labour; hence it tends to universalize every rebellion, to give a revolutionary scope and value to each of its acts of power.[27]

Gramsci's analysis of the Factory Councils possessed certain close affinities with the theories developed contemporaneously by the ideologists of the British shop stewards' movement.[28] Murphy, for example, insisted that 'with the workshops . . . as the new units of organization . . . we can erect the structure of the Great Industrial Union, invigorate the labour movement with the real democratic spirit, and in the process lose none of the real values won in the historic struggle of the Trade Union movement'.[29] With hindsight, the romanticism underlying many of the characterizations of workshop organization then prevalent is undeniable;[30] given the turbulent social context, and the revolutionary leadership of the most prominent rank-and-file movements, a certain one-sided optimism was understandable. This was particularly evident in the case of Gramsci: his assertion of the immunity of the Factory Councils from the integrative and bureaucratic tendencies inherent in official unionism owed far more to aspiration than to reality.

Nevertheless, such theories possess continuing significance, and for two main reasons. In the first place, their assertion of a natural tendency for rank-and-file organization to constrain

leadership autocracy constitutes the first coherent statement of
the 'iron law of democracy' which Gouldner counterposed to
Michels' more familiar analysis.[31] But in some ways even more
important is the challenge to the thesis of trade union integration contained in their discussion of the revolutionary potential
of the power and control exercised by workshop union organization.

This potential was explicitly asserted by Gramsci in his analysis
of the Italian 'internal commissions' (which paralleled the British
shop stewards' committees): 'today, the internal commissions
limit the power of the capitalist in the factory and perform
functions of arbitration and discipline. Tomorrow, developed
and enriched, they must be the organs of proletarian power, replacing the capitalist in all his useful functions of management
and administration'.[32] This tendency for 'orthodox' trade union
activity within the factory to extend to the imposition of forms of
workers' control[33] was noted even before the outbreak of war by
Cole:

> It is being realized that the method of collective bargaining can
> be applied, not only to wages and hours, but to every point of
> difference that can arise in the workshop between employers
> and employed. Not only can it safeguard the standard of living
> for the workers collectively; it can also be used for the redress
> of individual grievances. Moreover, it can be used as a means
> of getting a share in the actual control of management. Discus-
> sion of wages inevitably leads on to discussion of management,
> and the right to discuss can be turned into the right to interfere.
> In the recent unrest the workers are demanding the extension
> of their industrial jurisdiction to cover new fields. Autocracy in
> the workshop is already breaking down . . .[34]

Subsequently the potentialities of such a process were explored in
detail by a range of British theorists of workers' control, and in
particular by the Guild Socialists with their concept of 'encroaching control'.[35]

Integral to any theory of encroaching control is the conception
of social revolution as a process rather than as an act. Or more
accurately, while such theories need not exclude the perspective
of a 'classic' revolutionary climax, they emphasize the possibility
and even the necessity of inroads *within* capitalism as a basis for

eventual transition to socialism. In this respect, a parallel may be noted with Marx's concept of the 'political economy of labour'. The novelty of the *Inaugural Address*, as Harrison has indicated, was that for the first time

> Marx accepted that the proletariat might establish its own forms of property and principles of productive organization within the capitalist mode of production . . . Consequently, the working class might precisely seek to secure, extend, fortify and generalize these achievements. Its advance is now measured not merely by *the perfection of its party organization*, but by the *inroads* which it can make on the existing mode of production.[36]

This perspective, contrasting sharply with more cataclysmic theories or socialist revolution, has been termed by one writer 'the pattern of competing systems'.[37] The implication is presumably that every inroad made within the capitalist mode of production increases the strength of the proletariat and reduces that of the capitalist class, leading in the direction of a situation of 'dual power' – such as existed in Russia in 1917, between the February and October revolutions.[38] These are echoes of the *Inaugural Address* in Trotsky's account of this period:

> This double sovereignty does not presuppose – generally speaking, indeed, it excludes – the possibility of a division of the power into two equal halves, or indeed any formal equilibrium of forces whatever. It is not a constitutional, but a revolutionary fact. It implies that a destruction of the social equilibrium has already split the state superstructure. It arises where the hostile classes are already each relying upon essentially incompatible governmental organizations – the one outlived, the other in process of formation – which jostle against each other at every step in the sphere of government.[39]

Such a situation, in which 'the political economy of the working class' poses a comprehensive challenge to the hegemony of 'the political economy of the middle class', is necessarily unstable.

> Society needs a concentration of power, and in the person of the ruling class . . . irresistibly strives to get it. The splitting of

sovereignty foretells nothing less than a civil war. But before
the competing classes and parties will go to that extreme . . .
they may feel compelled for quite a long time to endure, and
even to sanction, a two-power system. This system will nevertheless inevitably explode.[40]

While the concept of dual power is customarily used in analysis
of the control of the state, it is of relevance also in the context of
the control of production within the factory. Trotsky himself
appreciated this in his discussion of the situation in Russia in the
summer of 1917, arguing that the factory committees had established a form of dual power within industry: 'it was impossible
. . . to do anything against the will of the workers'.[41] Elsewhere
he considered in detail the relationship between 'dual power in
the factory and dual power in the state'.[42] Here, Marx's own
qualifications to his argument in the *Inaugural Address* are of
relevance: 'the lords of land and the lords of capital will always
use their political privileges for the defence and perpetuation of
their economical monopolies. So far from promoting, they will
continue to lay every possible impediment in the way of the
emancipation of labour . . . To conquer political power has
therefore become the great duty of the working class.'[43] Similarly, Trotsky insisted that

A bourgeoisie which feels itself firm in the saddle will never
tolerate dual power in its factories . . . Thus the régime of
workers' control is by its very essence provisional, a transitional régime, and can correspond only to the period of the
shaking of the bourgeois state, of the proletarian offensive,
and of the retreat of the bourgeoisie . . . This means – the régime
of dual power in the factories corresponds to the régime of dual
power in the state. This relationship, however, should not be
understood mechanically, that is, in the sense that dual power
in the factory and dual power in the state see the light of day on
one and the same day . . . Under certain circumstances . . .
workers' control of production can considerably precede
political dual power in a given country.[44]

This analysis provides a further link with Gramsci's writings.
Noting the determined (and ultimately successful) efforts of
Italian government and employers to destroy the growing power

of the Factory Councils, he insisted that the autonomous operation of two systems of control could not long persist.

> The present phase of the class struggle in Italy is the phase that
> precedes: either the conquest of political power by the revolu-
> tionary proletariat and the transition to new modes of pro-
> duction and distribution that will make possible a rise in
> productivity – or a tremendous reaction by the propertied
> classes and the governmental caste. No violence will be spared
> in this subjection of the industrial and agricultural proletariat
> to servile labour: a bid will be made to smash inexorably the
> working class's institutions of political struggle (the Socialist
> Party) and to incorporate its institutions of economic resistance
> (unions and co-operatives) into the machinery of the bourgeois
> State.[45]

The current British situation cannot, of course, be readily interpreted in the terms of Trotsky and Gramsci; contemporary conflicts derive less from the fact of workers' encroaching control
within the place of work as from the fact of *traditional* controls
being rendered intolerable in a changing economic and technological context. Yet if the present stance of organized labour in
Britain is defensive rather than offensive, the logic of the arguments cited still applies: in the last resort, workers' customary
controls at the point of production can be sustained only by an
aggressive strategy which extends to the broader structures of
political and economic power.

SOME IMPLICATIONS

Marx's most familiar conception of revolution identified the
immiseration of workers with their radicalization; his early
theory of trade unions diagnosed their political significance
precisely in their presumed inability to prevent deterioration in
workers' economic conditions. The same equation of misery and
revolutionary ardour has led 'orthodox' Marxists (as well as contemporary exponents of 'the end of ideology') to interpret the
reality of trade union economic achievements as a fatal obstacle
to the growth of revolutionary consciousness within the working
class.

Yet Marx's own formulation of the 'political economy of

labour', and the related theories developed by a subsequent generation of socialists, permit the alternative perspective of the concrete achievements of the working class as the basis for increasingly ambitious and importunate demands, culminating in the overt confrontation of two irreconcilable foci of class power. The question thus arises: in what contexts do material improvements serve as palliatives, and in what contexts do they act as stimulants? What gains represent inroads into capitalist control of production, and what gains lead rather to the incorporation of workers and their organizations within capitalist hegemony?

A factor of critical importance is the manner in which such reforms are achieved. Trotsky expressed this point succinctly when he distinguished participation in decision-making based on class struggle from that based on class collaboration. The latter posed no threat to the stability of the economic and political system: 'it was not a case of workers' control *over* capital but of the subserviency of the labour bureaucracy *to* capital. Such subserviency, as experience shows, can last for a long time – as long as the patience of the proletariat.'[46] A similar distinction was basic to the theories of the British shop stewards' movement: 'invasion, not admission, should be the trade unionist's watchword'.[47] What essentially distinguishes invasion from incorporation is the continuing existence of an independent power base, the mobilization of which remains permanently on the agenda. In current industrial relations theory, the contrast between unilateral and joint regulation provides an important parallel. What so alarms employers, politicians and their academic advisers is the *autonomous* nature of the control exercised by workers' shop-floor organization. That managements should 'regain control by (nominally) sharing it' is, as has been seen, the natural incorporationist prescription. Hence the need to insist that

a share in control does not imply that the workers should enter into any sort of alliance with the employer, or incur joint responsibility with him, or be identified with him in any way ... We shall be obliged, indeed, to negotiate with him through his representatives in the daily routine of the workshop, but not to espouse his interests, or to advance them in any way when it lies in our power to do otherwise. Our policy is that of invaders of our native province of industry, now in the hands of an arrogant and tyrannical usurper, and what we win in our advance we control *exclusively and independently*.[48]

Also of great significance is a related but not identical factor which has received little systematic attention: workers' *perception* of the mechanics of material improvement. One illuminating insight into this dimension is provided by Lenin's discussion of the workers' bread:

> In a small working-class house in a remote working-class suburb of Petrograd, dinner is being served. The hostess puts bread on the table. The host says: 'Look what fine bread. "They" dare not give us bad bread now. And we had almost given up even thinking that we'd ever get good bread in Petrograd again.'
>
> I was amazed at this class appraisal of the July days ... As for bread, I, who had not known want, did not give it a thought. I took bread for granted, as a by-product of the writer's work, as it were ...
>
> This member of the oppressed class, however, even though one of the well-paid and quite intelligent workers, takes the bull by the horns with that astonishing simplicity and straightforwardness, with that firm determination and amazing clarity of outlook from which we intellectuals are as remote as the stars in the sky ...
>
> 'We squeezed "them" a bit; "they" won't dare to lord it over us as they did before. We'll squeeze again – and chuck them out altogether,' that's how the worker thinks and feels.[49]

While the actual disposition of power relationships is obviously of major salience in determining workers' perceptions, it is not the only factor: hence the gap between activity and consciousness which was considered earlier. In seeking to interpret this gap, it seems of particular relevance that the typical functions of trade unionism centre around routinization and accommodation; an ongoing consciousness of 'invasion', it might be argued, will prove self-sustaining only in abnormal circumstances. It is not altogether irrelevant that 'defence, not defiance' stood as one of the most persistent slogans of British trade union history.[50]

Thus the problem recurs: what type of relationship between trade union activity and revolutionary party is most likely to neutralize the tendencies towards 'normalization'? For Gramsci in the period of the Factory Councils, the prescription was clear: 'the Party is identified with the historical consciousness of the popular masses and governs their irresistible spontaneous movement'.[51] Its task was to 'transform the rebellious impulses produced by the situation capitalism has imposed on the working class into consciousness and revolutionary creativity'.[52] This function was conceived as ideological rather than organizational; like Luxemburg, Gramsci insisted that the party must not seek to *dominate* the spontaneous struggle. 'It would be disastrous if a sectarian conception of the Party role were to fix in mechanical forms of immediate power an apparatus governing the masses in movement, forcing the revolutionary process into the forms of the Party.'[53] Rather, the party was to interact with the spontaneous movements 'in a single dialectical process of development during which relations of cause and effect interlace, reverse, and interweave with one another'.[54]

> It is essential that the Party live permanently immersed in the reality of the class struggle fought by the industrial and agricultural proletariat, that it be able to understand its various phases and episodes, its manifold manifestations, drawing unity from this manifold diversity. It should be in a position to give a real leadership to the movement as a whole and impress on the masses the conviction that there is an order immanent in the present terrible disorder . . .[55]

Experience was soon to prove that Gramsci's assessment of the spontaneous movement was over-optimistic.[56] Events in Italy – and in Europe generally – in the 1920s clearly demonstrated the volatility of working-class consciousness and the transient nature of overtly revolutionary trade unionism. The conclusion to be drawn – as from the earlier consideration of the arguments of Lenin and Luxemburg – is surely that the limits of trade union consciousness can vary markedly between different historical contexts and can shift radically with only a brief passage of time. Under specific objective conditions the educative potential of collective industrial action may be immense; in other, perhaps more typical circumstances the spontaneous development of workers' consciousness may fail absolutely to transcend the confines of bourgeois ideology. And involvement in a specific victory or defeat, in itself of little obvious world-historical significance, may have critical consequences in terms of workers' subjective confidence and aspirations.

Hence no *general* theory is available to relate the struggle for material reforms to the development of consciousness. The current British situation, for the reasons discussed previously, can only in the most tenuous sense be regarded as a state of 'dual power'. But whether the circumstances are such as to permit a spontaneous bridging of the gap between activity and consciousness; whether exposure to co-ordinated attacks on long-established rights of trade union organization may precipitate a natural heightening of critical social awareness; or whether the limited horizons which now prevail will persist to make inevitable an interaction of defeat and demoralization – must remain as yet an open question, which in the last resort can be answered not by theoretical speculation but only through practical activity and practical experience. The theoretical issue, in other words, can be resolved only through the *praxis* of the struggle itself.

NOTES

1. C. L. GOODRICH, *The Frontier of Control*, 1920, p. 37. New edition, Pluto Press, 1975.

2. See B. PRIBICEVIC, *The Shop Stewards' Movement and Workers' Control*, 1959, pp. 53–64. For a more recent argument that the essence of union activity is as much 'political' as 'economic' see FLANDERS, 'Collective Bargaining: a Theoretical Analysis', *British Journal of Industrial Relations*, 1968.

3. H. A. TURNER (*The Trend of Strikes*, 1963, p. 18) has argued that disputes overtly involving issues of control have become increasingly prominent in British industrial relations. Other writers have insisted that such issues typically underlie wage disputes also; see for example, K. G. J. C. KNOWLES, *Strikes*, 1952, pp. 219–21; A. W. GOULDNER, *Wildcat Strike* 1954, pp. 25–6; A. GORZ, 'Work and Consumption', in P. ANDERSON and R. BLACKBURN (eds.), *Towards Socialism*, 1965, p. 319. This issue is examined in detail in R. HYMAN, *Strikes*.

4. HYMAN, 'Strikes in Britain', Centro di Documentazione de Torino, 1971.

5. See R. MILIBAND, *Parliamentary Socialism*, 1961, p. 13. Conceivably the strikes against the Industrial Relations Bill represented an incipient freeing of this ideological blockage.

6. E. J. HOBSBAWM, 'Trends in the British Labour Movement Since 1850', in *Labouring Men*, Weidenfield & Nicolson, 1964, pp. 334–5.

7. ibid.
8. It could indeed be argued that such a continuum is implicit in Lenin's own discussion in *What Is To Be Done?*. In his first references to trade union consciousness he stressed its sectional nature, its inability to transcend individual trade interests. In his subsequent, and more detailed, consideration of socialist consciousness he emphasized the ability to 'respond to all cases of tyranny, oppression, violence, and abuse, no matter *what class* is affected'. (*Collected Works*, vol. V, p. 375); this emphasis might be considered particularly appropriate in the semi-feudal conditions of Czarist Russia. What Lenin failed to confront explicitly was the existence of an intermediate stage of consciousness: the recognition of the common interests of *workers* as a class and the opposition of these interests to the existing structure of society.
9. *Collected Works*, vol. II, 1960.
10. ibid., vol. IV, 1960, pp. 315–17.
11. 'The St Petersburg Strike', ibid., vol. VIII, 1962, pp. 92–3.
12. 'The Reorganisation of the Party', ibid., vol. X, 1962, p. 32.
13. 'The Lessons of the Revolution' (1910), ibid., vol. XVI, 1963, pp 301–2.
14. 'Lecture on the 1905 Revolution' (1917), ibid., vol. XXIII, 1964, pp. 239–42.
15. 'Organisational Questions of Russian Social Democracy' (1904), published as *Leninism or Marxism?*, 1935. Luxemburg's views, and the extent of her 'latent agreement' with Lenin, are discussed by J. P. NETTL, *Rosa Luxemburg*, Oxford University Press, 1966; see in particular pp. 286–93, 334, 496–503.
16. 'Massenstreik, Partei und Gewerkschaften' (1906), quoted in Nettl, p. 501.
17. Speech to Foundation Congress of the German Communist Party (1918), quoted in CLIFF, *Rosa Luxemburg*, p. 41.
18. ibid., quoted in Nettl, p. 756.
19. *L'Ordine Nuovo*. A selection of these articles were published as 'Soviets in Italy', *New Left Review*, 1968 (and republished in pamphlet form under the same title by the Institute for Workers' Control, 1969). For a discussion of Gramsci's views, see J. M. CAMMETT, *Antonio Gramsci and the Origins of Italian Communism*, 1967 and A. POZZOLINI, *Antonio Gramsci: an Introduction to his Thought*, 1971.
20. 'Soviets in Italy', *New Left Review*, no. 51, 1968, p. 36.
21. ibid., p. 35.
22. ibid., p. 39.
23. ibid., p. 41.
24. ibid., p. 45.
25. ibid., p. 39.
26. ibid., p. 33.

27. ibid., pp. 34, 39–40.

28. The parallels are considered by JAMES HINTON in his study *The First Shop Stewards' Movement*, George Allen & Unwin, 1973.

29. J. T. MURPHY, *The Workers' Committee*, 1918, p. 8.

30. G. D. H. COLE, the main academic theorist of the British movement, later dismissed as 'a good deal of nonsense' the argument he had expounded 'that trade unions, with all their shortcomings and limitations, could be converted into guilds animated by the highest social purposes and could take over the full control of industry by a process of "encroaching control" that would presumably render the employing class functionless and ready for supersession'. (Foreword to PRIBICEVIC, *The Shop Stewards' Movement*, p. VII).

31. A. W. GOULDNER, 'Metaphysical Pathos and the Theory of Bureaucracy', in L. A. COSER and B. ROSENBERG (eds.), *Sociological Theory*, Collier Macmillan, 1964.

32. 'Soviets in Italy', *New Left Review*, p. 29.

33. The term 'workers' control' is here used in its traditionally precise sense of the *limitation* by workers of managerial autonomy: the surveillance and even the obstruction by workers as *subordinates* of the decisions taken by a management which retains ultimate sovereignty. The situation in which workers themselves possess sovereignty and collectively *initiate* all decisions in respect of production – in looser usage referred to as 'workers' control' – is more precisely classified as 'workers' management'.

34. *The World of Labour*, 1913, pp. 8–9.

35. For a selection of such theories see K. COATES and A. TOPHAM (eds.), *Industrial Democracy in Great Britain*, MacGibbon & Kee, 1968. (Republished 1970 as *Workers' Control*.)

36. R. HARRISON, 'The British Labour Movement and the International in 1864', *Socialist Register*, 1964, p. 305.

37. S. MOORE, *Three Tactics*, (1943), p. 58.

38. This was discussed in some detail by Lenin, 'The Tasks of the Proletariat in Our Revolution', *Collected Works*, vol. XIV, 1964.

39. *The History of the Russian Revolution*, 1932, vol. I, p. 222.

40. ibid., pp. 222–3.

41. ibid., vol. II, p. 325.

42. 'Letter to Correspondents in Germany', *The Militant*, October 1931. See also *What Next ?: Vital Questions for the German Proletariat*, 1932.

43. *Selected Works*, vol. I, p. 384.

44. 'Letter to Correspondents in Germany' (see note 42 above).

45. 'Soviets in Italy', *New Left Review*, pp. 51–2.

46. 'Letter to Correspondents in Germany'.

47. GOODRICH, *Frontier of Control*, p. 253.

48. W. GALLACHER and J. PATON, *Towards Industrial Democracy*, 1917.

49. 'Can the Bolsheviks Retain State Power?' (1917), *Collected Works*, vol, XIV, p. 120.

50. Of obvious relevance here is Anderson's distinction between corporate and hegemonic class consciousness; see 'Origins of the Present Crisis', in *Towards Socialism*, pp. 33–9.

51. 'Soviets in Italy', *New Left Review*, p. 43.

52. ibid., p. 41.

53. ibid., p. 44.

54. ibid., p. 47.

55. ibid., p. 52.

56. The collapse of the Factory Councils led Gramsci to a radical revision of his analysis of the role of the party, and the adoption of a position virtually identical to that of Lenin in *What Is To Be Done?*

Index of Names

Subject Index

Fontana Modern Masters

General Editor: Frank Kermode

ARTAUD	*Martin Esslin*
BECKETT	*A. Alvarez*
CAMUS	*Conor Cruise O'Brien*
CHOMSKY	*John Lyons*
EINSTEIN	*Jeremy Bernstein*
ELIOT	*Stephen Spender*
ENGELS	*David McLellan*
FANON	*David Caute*
FREUD	*Richard Wollheim*
GANDHI	*George Woodcock*
GRAMSCI	*James Joll*
JOYCE	*John Gross*
JUNG	*Anthony Storr*
KAFKA	*Erich Heller*
KEYNES	*D. E. Moggridge*
LAWRENCE	*Frank Kermode*
LAING	*E. Z. Friedenberg*
LE CORBUSIER	*Stephen Gardiner*
LENIN	*Robert Conquest*
LEVI-STRAUSS	*Edmund Leach*
MARCUSE	*Alasdair MacIntyre*
MARX	*David McLellan*
ORWELL	*Raymond Williams*
POPPER	*Brian Magee*
POUND	*Donald Davie*
PROUST	*Roger Shattuck*
REICH	*Charles Rycroft*
RUSSELL	*A. J. Ayer*
SARTRE	*Arthur C. Danto*
SAUSSURE	*Jonathan Culler*
SCHOENBERG	*Charles Rosen*
WEBER	*Donald MacRae*
WITTGENSTEIN	*David Pears*
YEATS	*Denis Donoghue*

The Fontana Economic History of Europe

General Editor: Carlo M. Cipolla, Professor of Economic History at the Universities of Pavia and California, Berkeley.

'There can be no doubt that these volumes make an extremely significant addition to the literature of European economic history, where the need for new large comparative works has long been felt . . . It is overall a project of vision and enormous value.'

Times Literary Supplement

1. The Middle Ages

Contributors: Cipolla: J. C. Russell: Jacques Le Goff: Richard Roehl: Lynn White Jr.: Georges Duby: Sylvia Thrupp: Jacques Bernard: Edward Miller.

2. The Sixteenth and Seventeenth Centuries

Contributors: Cipolla: Roger Mols: Walter Minchinton: Hermann Kellenbenz: Aldo de Maddalena: Domenico Sella: Kristof Glamann: Geoffrey Parker.

3. The Industrial Revolution

Contributors: André Armengaud: Walter Minchinton: Samuel Lilley: Gertrand Gille: Barry Supple: R. M. Hartwell: J. F. Bergier: Paul Bairoch: Donald Winch: M. J. T. Lewis.

4. The Emergence of Industrial Societies

Part 1: Contributors: Claude Fohlen: Knut Borchardt: Phyllis Deane: N. T. Gross: Luciano Cafagna: Jan Dhondt & Marinette Bruwier.
Part 2: Contributors: Lennart Jörberg: Gregory Crossman: Jordi Nadal: B. M. Biucchi: William Woodruff: B. R. Mitchell.

5. The Twentieth Century

Part 1: Contributors: Milos Macura: A. S. Deaton: Walter Galenson: Giorgio Pellicelli: Roy and Kay MacLeod: Georges Brondel: Robert Campbell.
Part 2: Contributors: Hermann Priebe: Angus Maddison: Carlo Zacchia: Fred Hirsch and Peter Oppenheimer: Benjamin Ward: Max Nicholson.

6. Contemporary Economics

Part 1: Contributors: Johan de Vries: Claude Fohlen: A. J. Youngson: Karl Hardach: Sergio Ricossa: John Pinder.
Part 2: Contributors: Lennart Jörberg: and Olle Krantz: Josep Fontana and Jordi Nadal: Hansjörg Siegenthaler: Alfred Zauberman: B. R. Mitchell.

Fontana Politics

The English Constitution Walter Bagehot
edited by R. H. S. Crossman

Problems of Knowledge and Freedom Noam Chomsky

Understanding American Politics R. V. Denenberg

Marx and Engels: Basic Writings
edited by Lewis S. Feuer

Governing Britain A. H. Hanson and Malcolm Walles

Edmund Burke on Government, Politics and Society
edited by Brian Hill

Machiavelli: Selections
edited by John Plamenatz

Mao Ninian Smart

Lenin and the Bolsheviks Adam B. Ulam

The National Front Martin Walker

The Commons in the Seventies
edited by S. A. Walkland and Michael Ryle

John Stuart Mill on Politics and Society
Geraint Williams

To the Finland Station Edmund Wilson

The Anarchist Reader
edited by George Woodcock